Murder on Several Occasions

TRUE CRIME HISTORY SERIES
Albert Borowitz, editor

Murder
on Several Occasions

JONATHAN GOODMAN

ILLUSTRATIONS BY NINA LEWIS SMART

THE KENT STATE UNIVERSITY PRESS
Kent, Ohio

© 2007 by The Kent State University Press, Kent, Ohio 44242
ALL RIGHTS RESERVED
Library of Congress Catalog Card Number 2006037737
ISBN: 978-0-87338-898-6
Manufactured in the United States of America

11 10 09 08 07   5 4 3 2 1

"The Passing on the Fourth Floor Back" and "Slaughter at the Governor's Lodge" first appeared in *Murder in High Places* (London, Piatkus Books, 1986).

"The Death of the Devil's Disciple" first appeared in *Acts of Murder* (London: Futura, 1986).

"A Wolf in Tan Clothing" and "An Anatomy of Murders" first appeared in *Murder in Low Places* (London: Piatkus Books, 1988).

"A Coincidence of Corpses" first appeared in *The Railway Murders* (1984). "The First Trunk Murder" and "Also Known as Love" first appeared in *The Seaside Murders* (1985) (London: Alison & Busby).

"Yours—Truly?" first appeared in the *New Law Journal* (London: Butterworth; serial publication).

"Doubts about Hauptmann" first appeared in *The Modern Murder Yearbook* and is reprinted with the permission of Constable & Robinson.

LIBRARY OF CONGRESS CATALOGING-IN-PUBLICATION DATA

Goodman, Jonathan.
Murder on several occasions / Jonathan Goodman.
      p.   cm. — (True crime series)
ISBN-13: 978-0-87338-898-6 (pbk. : alk. paper) ∞
ISBN-10: 0-87338-898-4 (pbk. : alk. paper) ∞
      1. Murder—Case studies.   I. Title.
HV6513.G664 2007
364.152'3—dc22   2006037737

British Library Cataloging-in-Publication data are available.

Contents

Some Slight Explanations

Sparked by two of my collections of essays, *Murder in High Places* and *Murder in Low Places,* Jacques Barzun suggested that "every geographical level has been scanned by our tireless crime chronicler except perhaps the middle distance," and went on to grumble: "It seems no longer possible to publish studies of crime without attaching them to some extraneous feature that provides a link."

Apropos of the latter comment, I was, of course, surprised, also delighted, to be asked by the enterprising Kent State University Press to put together an assortment of essays, diverse apart from being about murder.

Jacques Barzun calls me a crime chronicler—and (I had forgotten) I notice that in one of the pieces I have included here, written a long, long time ago, I used the same term. Better—oh, so much better—than "criminologist," which was the invariable job title when I turned to crime. I am advised to say that I am sure that criminologists are worthy people; but, even so, neither I nor any of the colleagues I respect has the least interest in, or slightest use for, their statistics, extrapolations, and psychiatric guesses. No; for many years now I have quietly campaigned (eventually, I believe, successfully) for acceptance of "crime *historian*"—"historian" being preferable to "chronicler" because a chronicle is a bare-bones retelling, without analysis or interpretation, and an account of a case should surely be subjective—should permit the expression of personal likes and dislikes, the inclusion of associated peculiarities.

For me, the peculiarities are usually of a theatrical kind (and I have just been amazed, looking at my account of the Brighton Trunk Crimes, that I somehow resisted the temptation to attach a footnote to the first of its several references to the adjacent town of Hove, noting that in the programme for a Brighton light-operatic society's production of

Oklahoma! a misprint appeared in the list of musical numbers, giving local significance to one of them by entitling it "People Will Say We're in Hove."

Grimness is sufficiently in the tales; there is no need for it in the telling of them. Remembering that if the "s" is detached from "slaughter," one is left with "laughter," I hope that my sense of (often gallows) humour, my delight in unintended oddities, chimes with yours.

The Passing on the Fourth Floor Back

Were you born of some queer magic,
In your shimmering gown?
Is there something strange and tragic,
Deep, deep down?

—*Noël Coward*

The Passing on the Fourth Floor Back

I start uncertainly. I believe that the slaying of Prince Ali Kamel Fahmy Bey was the first murder case I heard of, but I may be wrong. Perhaps earlier tellings of other murders had gone in one twice-daily-washed ear and out the other.

My parents were unconventional bedtime tale-tellers: they referred to, but never actually told me, fairy stories, assuming that I would prefer to hear how Dorothy Ward, boyish as Jack, had scaled a giant beanstalk and, vanishing from the audience's view, received rapturous applause for her vertical exit; of the Australian Oscar Asche, sort of Chinese as Chu-Chin-Chow; of Jose Collins, the exalted Maid of the Mountains; of Phyllis Neilson-Terry, masculinized as Oberon at the Open Air Theatre in Regent's Park; of young Meggie Albanesi, a bright flame that suddenly died. My parents, as you will have gathered, were great ones for the theatre. And, for them, "theatre" was not confined to the stage. They were what would now be called, I suppose, lateral thinkers: memories were corroborated by other memories, or were jogged into being mentioned by recollection of things that had happened at the time, or in the locality, of things that had stayed, higgledy-piggledy, in their minds.

I know the day of the month when I first heard of the Fahmy case: the seventeenth day of a January between King Edward VIII's announcement on the wireless that he had abdicated (I was too young to be awake for it) and Prime Minister Neville Chamberlain's announcement on what people were starting to call the radio that Great Britain was at war with Germany. (I heard that in the cottage at Castle Combe to which, presciently, I had been evacuated—and from which, later that day, I, hopelessly homesick, would be driven back to dangerous London. Certainly selfishly, perhaps irrationally, I hated the Germans, not long enough ago calling themselves "the master race," for having taken away part of my childhood.)

On that 17 January, a birthday for me, my Aunts Amy, Henrietta, and Rachel were supposed to call; for days before, my mother had unsubtly hinted that if I behaved myself, the aunts would bear gifts. But—and this could probably fix the year—by the time the table was laid, cake and all, it had started to rain, to pour. The hour arranged for the aunts' arrival passed; my father returned, dripping wet, from work; we were not on the phone, and so the aunts—who had told my mother that they would gather together in Putney and travel en masse to Wimbledon—could not explain to us the reason for their absence. I was told, first, to stop making naughty faces, and then to sit at the table, to sit up straight, to eat my allotment of the birthday feast, sticking to the established order of fishpaste sandwich, buttered scone with raspberry preserve, a helping of pink junket, and, if I really wanted it, a slice of the centrepiece cake (which, my memory says, had not been decked with candles for me to blow out).

When for the umpteenth time I swallowed (my parents were stern against my speaking with my mouth full) and asked about the absent aunts, my mother at last spoke critically of them, saying: "They're frightened of a spot of rain—think they're made of sugar."

However, my father stuck up for them. If what was teeming down outside was a spot, he said, then the Sahara was a sand castle (a comparison that made me, just starting to learn geography, smirk pretentiously). Continuing, he said that he couldn't remember a worse deluge than this—always excepting, of course, that dreadful storm during a summer night in 1923. Very young then, he had been told by much older people that they couldn't remember a worse storm: thunder and lightning as well as the pelting rain. It was the night, he went on, of that shooting at the Savoy Hotel. . . . Madame Fahmy, she killed her husband, he as rich as Croesus: a blackguard, peculiar in his appetite for—

Then my mother interrupted, pointing out that such tales were not nice at any time, least of all at the tea table.

I was grown up before I read about Prince and Madame Fahmy: not so grown up that I did not worry that my mother, by then dead, might have disapproved of my reading about them. Ever since I had worked out that my father had made up a legend on the spur of the moment when, walking me on Wimbledon Common, he had declared that particular hoofprints on the bridle path near the Leg-o'-Mutton Pond were those of Black Bess, implanted during the highwayman Dick Turpin's ride to York, I had tended to suspect fabrication of or exaggeration in his tales. But it turned out that he had not overstated the natural violence of the night of the shooting at the Savoy. On 10 July 1923, late editions of the *Daily Telegraph* reported that, from round about midnight, London had experienced its worst storm for many years:

> The outbreak appeared to travel [northeast] from the direction of Kingston and Richmond. Soon afterwards the storm reached London itself, and broke with all its fury at a time when, luckily, most of the theatre-goers had been able to reach their homes in safety. The lightning was vivid to a degree. For over two hours the sky was illuminated by brilliant, continuous flashes that gave the buildings an eerie appearance, and at least once what seemed to be a gigantic fireball broke into a million fragments of dazzling fiery sparks. Equally dramatic were the heavy crashes of thunder which grew in a mighty *crescendo,* intense and majestic, and then into a *diminuendo* as the storm swept irresistibly over the city. The storm followed a day of almost tropical heat.

In the early 1970s I was, between times, general editor of a series of volumes called *Celebrated Trials.* Because of its outcome, the trial of Madame Fahmy had not been reported as a Hodge *Notable British Trial*—nor, inexplicably, had it figured among Geoffrey Bles's inferior *Famous Trials.* Since it could scarcely have been more celebrated, I determined to include it in my series; and as Rayner Heppenstall, among too many avocations a crime historian and a studier of the French people and their language, seemed cut out to edit and introduce the transcript, I invited him to do so. His explanation of why, having accepted the invitation, he, like my aunts, disappointed me is given in the journals he wrote between 1969 and 1981, when he died, and which I edited into a book called *The Master Eccentric.* I have once or twice wondered how he would have told the story of Madame Fahmy. Much as his account of why he didn't differs from the one in my mind, it would have come out merely saliently similar to my version of the events.

I have quoted a description of the storm that was raging as Madame Fahmy fired three bullets into her husband. Now let me quote from *Bella Donna,* a novel by Robert Hichens, published in 1909, and so widely read thereafter that Madame Fahmy's defender at her trial was confident that, in speaking of it, he was striking a chord in the minds of the two women on the jury; of most of the men as well:

"Al-làh!" he murmured, saying the word like an Egyptian man. He looked into her eyes. "The first word you hear in the night from Egypt, Ruby; Egypt's night greeting to you. I have heard that song up the river in Nubia often, but—oh, it's so different now!"

During her long experience in a life that had been complex and full of changes, she had heard the sound of love many times in the voices of men, but she had never heard until this moment Nigel's full sound of love. There was something in it that she did not know how to reply to, though she had the instinct of the great courtezan to make the full and perfect reply to the desires of the man with whom she had schemed to ally herself. . . .

He drew a little nearer to her, and she understood, and could reply to the demand which prompted that movement.

"We must drink Nile water together, Ruby—Nile water—in all the different ways. I'll take you to the tombs of the Kings, and to the Colossi when the sun is setting. And when the moon comes, we'll go to Karnak. I believe you'll love it all as I do. One can never tell, of course, for another. But—but do you think you'll love it all with me?"

Mingled with the ardour and the desire, there was a hint in his voice of anxiety, of the self-doubt which in certain types of nature is the accompaniment of love.

"I know I shall love it all—with you," she said. . . .

"Ruby!" he exclaimed.

He tried to seize her hand, but she would not let him.

"No, Nigel! Don't touch me now. I—I shall hate you if you touch me now. . . ." She turned hurriedly away.

"Ruby!" he said, with a passion of tenderness.

"No, no! Leave me alone for a little. I tell you I must be alone!" she exclaimed as he followed her.

He stopped on the garden path and watched her go into the house.

"Beast, brute that I am!" he said to himself.

Steamy stuff. But only literarily more so than Madame Fahmy's life under that name. Her descriptions of that life—or descriptions of it given by others on her behalf, to the jury by her counsel, to readers of newspapers by reporters, ghostwriters, and sob sisters—erred from reality in particulars but were as accurate as most general truths ever are. Speaking both geographically and culturally, it was a far cry, that Muslim married life of hers, from her earlier existences: farthest of all from the earliest.

She was born to a couple called Alibert, living in a sombre suburb of Paris, on 9 December 1890. Then, perhaps, or earlier or later, her father was a cabdriver. She was given the names of Marie and Marguerite; when she considered herself mature, she sometimes hyphenated the names, sometimes used the second of them only, and was known to friends as Maggie. The names, presumably chosen on an alliterative ground, happened to be the respective true and posthumously fictive names of the Lady of the Camellias. That comment will become relevant. To save confusion until she can be called Madame Fahmy, I shall refer to her as Marguerite.

Her parents being devout Roman Catholics, she was sent to a convent school: run by Sisters of St. Mary, it was in the Avenue des Ternes, within walking distance of her home. More than a quarter of a century later, she would explain, or agree with the explanation, that "I was very devout myself, in a mystic way, as young, sensitive girls often are."

None of her kin was well off, but she had a godmother who was very rich indeed. This was Madame Langlois, the wife of one of the several lawyers who, when Marguerite was twelve, assisted Therese Humbert, perhaps the most excessive and successful swindler of all time, in squeezing away from a just punishment.[1] "My godmother had very refined tastes, and loved the arts and music. As I lived with her a great deal, my natural leaning towards art was accentuated. I love singing, my voice having been cultivated at the convent, where I sang sacred solos. My voice is mezzo-soprano, and among my favourite pieces is 'Butterfly.' I was an admirer of Mlle. Chenal, an opera star in Paris, and amused myself learning all her parts. In this people said that I succeeded very well."

Her vocal precocity was—in those days—less remarkable than her sexual forwardness. Soon after her sixteenth birthday, she gave birth to a child, a girl she called Raymonde. The surmise of earlier writers that the father of Raymonde was a Raymond gives Marguerite the benefit of the doubt that she became fecund from her inaugural liaison. So far as I can tell, if the name she gave the child was a clue to

---

1. The best account of the case for nonaccountants is by Rayner Heppenstall, in *A Little Pattern of French Crime* (London, 1969), 7.

the father's identity, she let slip no others. Having suckled Raymonde, Marguerite gave her into the care of an aunt. Within a short time—no more than a couple of months—she became engaged to Andre Meller, a man of twenty-eight who was better known for being a brother of an owner of racing stables and some horses therein than for any attribute or achievement. "Unfortunately I had not a sufficient dowry, and that first beautiful dream collapsed. We were separated."

"I was as tall as I am today, rather stronger, and I had chestnut-red hair falling to my knees. My nature was mercurial, and under my love-sorrow my life quite changed. I left my dear godmother and my family in order to go to friends at Bordeaux with my young sister, who was eight years old at the time." (She gives no hint of how her parents reacted to her sister's departure, let alone her own. It seems sensible to sacrifice chronology to tidiness and mention here that one of her brothers was killed in an accident, the other while serving on the front near Rheims during the Great War. There must have been times when the Aliberts wished they had stayed childless.) "At Bordeaux, I made the acquaintance of a charming man who loved me deeply. Twice he told me I must be his wife. But always my first deception in love prevented realisation of a definite arrangement of life." (Is she speaking of the affair that begot Raymonde or of the engagement that was broken for want of a sufficient dowry? One cannot tell.)

The years [about six] passed. I came back to live in Paris in 1913. I took a flat alone in the rue Pergolese. I led a very quiet and wise life, scarcely going out at all. My daughter was in the country. I expected to be able to smooth away the difficulties which prevented my wedding, and in April, 1913, my marriage was publicly announced. However, Monsieur X [Paul Channon], of Bordeaux, was waiting for the annulment of his first marriage, which was pending at Rome. At the last moment he was not able to obtain satisfaction, and all intention of marriage between us was given up in August, 1913, at Deauville, where I had a villa, and entertained a great many acquaintances. With a view to my marriage we had acquired a magnificent flat in Paris, which I retained on my return from Deauville.

While in Paris I entertained a great deal. There came to my house a number of actresses, a few celebrities—a very Parisian circle. During the war I served with the Red Cross, driving my own Renault, and sang at charity concerts.

I fell ill and had to enter a nursing home for an operation. A strange romance followed. In the same building, I learned, was an old friend [Charles Laurent], who had come in for the same purpose. During our convalescence we fell in love and were married in 1919.

Laurent's love for her, and hers for him, soon proved susceptible to impediment. He was a rare sort of Frenchman in that he was a fluent speaker and artistic writer of Japanese. His facility with that language seems to have caused a longing in him to live where it was native, and when the chance to do so arose, he told Marguerite that he intended to take it, giving up his job as an interpreter at the Japanese consulate in Paris, and, of course, expected her to migrate with him. The expectation was forlorn. Citing her patriotic deeds during the war—as a transporter of the lame, as a stage entertainer of the fit (her busyness at each of which she preferred not to boast about)—she told her husband that she would need a far, far better reason for leaving France than going to Japan: unlike him, she was linguistically inept, and the very thought of living in a country so inscrutably foreign appalled her. And so Laurent shrugged Gallicly or bobbed Orientally, said that he would help her to effect a divorce (an action which she, despite her Catholicism, was prepared to take), gave her the deeds of his house (which meant that, what with the villa at Deauville and the Paris property conceded to her by the matrimonially encumbered Paul Channon, she was pretty well off for real estate), promised a handsome allowance until such time as she remarried, threw in his motorcar (no common Renault, that), and, saying sayonara, walked out of her life.

Marguerite went on the town; became a talk of it. She gave lavish parties, and—usually with a male escort, rarely the same one twice—attended parties given by others of the Smart Set. On most partyless nights, she whiled the time away in exclusive restaurants and expensive nightclubs, often dancing until the small hours at the latter: "I love dancing, but I do not care for such eccentric dances as the Shimmy. Indeed, I prefer to dance in the English fashion, which I find very correct." Not all of the daylight hours were spent in bed or preparing for nocturnal fun—buying clothes, having things done to her hair, getting her fingernails trimmed and lacquered, her face and neck smoothed: sometimes when the weather was fine, she rode or played lawn tennis or golf, and sometimes when it wasn't, she drove—not to get somewhere but because she enjoyed driving. Once or twice she visited or was visited by her daughter Raymonde, who was at boarding school—and who, she believed (perhaps rightly; I have not enquired into French law on the subject), had been legitimised by her marriage to Charles Laurent.

In January 1922, she and some friends, seeking the sun in an exotic setting, visited Egypt, and—she usually driving the hired limousine, her face shaded by a Paris milliner's version of the sola topi—toured northern parts of that land, using as their base Shepheard's in Cairo, which was said by English guests wishing to be complimentary to it to be more English than any English hotel.

On an evening toward the end of their visit, they attended a reception given by an Egyptian acquaintance of one of them. The host was approached by a native guest, who, indicating Marguerite, said: "Tell her that I will arrange a *fête Vénitienne* on my yacht in her honour." The host did as he was told, explaining to Marguerite that the offer came from Prince Ali Kamel Fahmy Bey. Before saying yes or no, or murmuring an option-retaining *peut-être,* she asked for information about him.

Fahmy was a playboy of the eastern world. Though only midway through his twenty-first year (which meant that he was almost ten years younger than Marguerite), he was among the wealthiest of Egyptians; and, despite his excesses, there seemed no reason why he should not grow richer still—become a millionaire, not just of his own country's pound but in terms of the Bank of England's, too. Keeping to the latter currency, estimates of his annual income ranged from £40,000 to five times that amount. (Multiplying by twenty gives an idea of the purchasing power of such sums today.) He owed his wealth to the death of his father, an engineer by training but a tycoon by vocation, who had bequeathed him the lion's share of his estate: vast cotton plantations throughout northern Egypt, commercial and residential property in and around Cairo, interests in financial institutions, shares in mighty trading companies.

Young Fahmy's education had not been entrusted to Egyptian teachers but to French and English ones, each in their own land—at a well-regarded academy near Paris and at a public school other than Eton or Harrow. At those places he had picked up the respective native languages; had received the tuition in the "arts of cosmopolitan-ism" that was stressed in the brochures of those places, setting them apart from less expensive educational establishments. Perhaps partly because in the English school, fellow students, pink-complexioned whereas he was olive-skinned, had looked down on him on account of his nationality, he had grown toward manhood cosmopolitan in one sense, determinedly Egyptian in another. Perhaps partly because of his acceptance that he could not disguise his nationality, as soon as he was enriched by his father's will he became intensely nationalistic and, while often behaving irreligiously, boasted of entire adherence to Mohammedanism. His good works in aid of his country, his country-men—grants to clever young Egyptians so that they could study else-where; contributions toward the building of hospitals—seemed mu-nificent to people of modest means and caused the many who were poor to revere him. When he was already entitled Bey, the head of the government, keen to encourage his charity, said that before long he would receive a higher honour, and that, meanwhile, it was perfectly all right for him to call himself a prince; thus he became—oddly, it seems to an Englishman, used to one title supplanting a lesser one—*Prince* Ali Kamel Fahmy *Bey*.

Most of his friends called him Ali; some of the others, few of them Egyptian, referred to him, even to his face, as Baba—a nickname less likely to have been derived directly from the tale of the Forty Thieves, told in one of the *Thousand and One Nights,* than from the Chu-Chin-Chowing of it that had been performed on 2,238 nights or afternoons at His Majesty's Theatre in London's Haymarket, for the last time only months before. Ali, a frequent visitor to London, had seen the show several times, always from the same stage-side box, and may have been provoked by it into presenting, for one night only in a grand Mayfair house, a truly Arabian spectacular—that being (if the sole critic to write of it got things straight) "a Terpsichorean celebration, carried out with many mystic accompaniments, of the Goddess of the Sun, Ta Aha." Ali took no performing part in the presentation; but it seems that he might, undisgracingly, have done, had he felt like exchanging his Saville Row suit for raiment resembling that worn by Egyptians of thirty-five centuries before. Ballroom dancing was one of Ali's fa-vourite public pastimes: gossip columnists of Cairo's papers, ordered by their editors to publicise the Prince (but not to speak of certain of his unmusical amusements), spun yards of admiring print, all of it devoted to his excellence and endurance as two-stepper and tangoist, repeating—over and over again but ever with a tone of wonder—words like "twinkling," "lithe," and "sinuous" with regard to his mastery of motion in time with the new music from America and Europe.

Having been told at least some of all of this, and maybe other things, by her host, relayer of Ali's offer of a fête, Marguerite repaired to a powder room, where she smoked a Regie as an aid to deciding how to respond. Her mind made up, she emerged, and when her host enquired what message he should take to the Prince, told him: "'Non, merci.' (Naturally I felt intrigued at the thought of such a personality, but somehow or other I felt that it was better to refuse.)"

It seems unlikely that she was being subtle, playing hard-to-get. The fact that she was returning to Paris in a day or so would surely have erased the thought, if the thought had entered her head, of playing that game in which a man chases a woman to where she means to catch him. Absence, so long as it is not prolonged, may, just may, make the heart of an established lover grow fonder; but the absence of someone who has simply aroused interest at first sight is almost bound to diminish the interest until, soon, the interesting party is barely recollectable, never intentionally thought of.

Therefore, however conceited she was, Marguerite must have been surprised when, a few months later, toward the end of springtime in Paris, she saw a now-fezless Ali peering at her across a crowded room. He did not approach her; she pretended that she had not noticed him. At subsequent swell-elegant gatherings, he peered at her from the outskirts, and she, centre-stage, feigned unawareness of his gaze. Now she *was* playing hard-to-get. And she played at that harder still when, following more nonencounters, Ali sought an introduction. She declined to meet him.

By now, it was July. She spent part of that month at Deauville, and there got to know a woman from Morocco. Or rather (and the reason for saying this will soon be apparent), was befriended by the woman. When she mentioned that she was returning to Paris, the woman said that she was going there too, and begged a lift. During the drive, the woman chattered about her past with such indiscretion that Marguerite felt that it would be impolite not to return the compliment.

A day or so later, the woman telephoned Marguerite, saying, "I have a friend who absolutely must make your acquaintance. He says that it is his sole ambition while he is in Paris."

"Mystified, I agreed to a rendezvous for tea in the lounge of the Majestic Hotel on the 30th. When I walked into the lounge and again found fixed upon me the large, dark eyes of the man whom I knew to be Ali Fahmy, I experienced a curious *tressaillement*. The thought had never occurred to me that the individual who so longed to meet me was this Egyptian 'prince.'"

Only the middle one of those sentences can be accepted as almost-whole truth. Were it not for the inclusion of the word "curious," it would be a model of veracity. There was nothing at all curious about her *tressaillement*. Though she was a practised siren, she would have had to be made of stone not to be thrilled.

Once the introduction had been effected, and the introducer had departed (and was now, presumably, in no bibliographic sense, Morocco-bound, having completed her assignment), Ali set about sweeping Marguerite off her dainty feet.

> He suggested going to the Chateau de Madrid, and I agreed. As we walked to the door there came the first incident revealing how he sought always to carry out an affair en prince. Pointing to two superb cars, one a Rolls-Royce coupé limousine and the other a dazzling "torpedo," he said: "Which do you prefer?" With, I am afraid, rather an amused smile, I said I would prefer the closed car.
>
> Let me describe, if I can, Ali's appearance. He was a man of exceptional powers of fascination. He would be about five feet nine inches in height, and though he did not go in for athletics, he was of singularly muscular and powerful build. Never have I met a man who possessed to such a degree that kind of charm which we are accustomed to call Oriental. About his black hair there was just a reddish tint—most unusual in one of his race. His eyes were remarkably expressive, striking one with the exceptionally caressing quality of their glance, but suddenly hardening on occasions into a ferocity which was positively terrifying.
>
> Most of the conversation during our first meeting consisted of gentle raillery concerning my having avoided him for so long.

Both made up for the lost time. Toward the end of the return journey from the Chateau de Madrid, Marguerite agreed to be driven somewhere almost as splendid the next day; this despite the fact that Ali's vanity was exemplified by his driving, which brooked no interference from lesser road-users; he was, she decided, straightway telling him so, a "velocimaniac." During the following fortnight, there were more car trips; together, they joined in galas; near the end of the period, they enjoyed each other's company tête-à-tête, both at her residence and in his suite at the Majestic; she introduced him to her friends, and he displayed her to his. And she got to know, or had pointed out to her, the members of his entourage: foremost, Said Enani, whose responsibilities were greater and more varied than those of most private secretaries; also a lawyer, a second secretary, a black valet, and a body-guard-cum-chauffeur—later referred to by Marguerite as a "chocolate-coloured Colossus."

In mid-August, she returned to Deauville, accompanied by a girl-friend. And Ali went there, too.

At Deauville a more serious note began to creep into his expressions of affection. Then rapidly he made *des avances furieuses.* But I would not yield, and after three days of vain supplication he decided to leave and go to Italy. Fervently he tried to persuade my friend and myself to travel with him. He besought, implored, entreated; but I would not listen. At last, with a great show of temper, he flung himself off. Whether by his instructions or not, I do not know, but before the departure Said Enani began to boast to me of Ali's great fortune and the wonderfully luxurious life he led in his palace at Cairo. At this stage there were only thrown open gates through which with the eyes of imagination I could dimly perceive some of the splendours which awaited his wife.

Of the following sentence a cynic might remark: "If you believe this, you'll believe anything."

What, however, appealed to me most about Ali was his smile, which was like that of a child.

Yet behind it was that well-developed jaw, which, as I experienced before long, could set any moment into cruel outline.

But at present all was charm and sweetness. As I was going to Biarritz on the first of September, I promised to allow him to accompany me. For eight days in that wonderful resort he was so affectionate that I felt my whole being suffused with a sort of radiant sympathy toward him. These were perhaps the happiest days of my life. We made excursions to San Sebastian in Spain, St. Jean de Luz, where we dined in "La Réservée," decorated like a miniature fairyland. He was always accompanied by the same train of attendants. Money was poured out lavishly. Nothing was too good, too beautiful, or too dear for me. Cartier's was ransacked for the latest creation in jewellery, and Ali chose and gave me a really beautiful bracelet of coral and emeralds.

Still Ali wanted to take her to Italy; still she refused. Even when he said, "I will marry you. Come," she said no. And so he went to Milan alone—except, of course, for his half-dozen minions. "From there commenced a series of wonderful letters couched in the extravagant phraseology of the Orient. When, at the end of September, he went to Egypt, he wrote that he was sick with despair, and that I must come. He sent me tickets for the journey, but I replied that I would not go until later. Then he started to bombard me with telegrams, using every artifice to get me to go to Egypt immediately. 'I am dying,' he said. 'Your name alone is on my lips.' I could resist no longer and said I would travel on 17 November."

Concerned that she might change her mind—perhaps because of hearing tittle-tattle about him—Ali wrote more letters. One began, "My dear little Bella," and read, in part:

Your presence everywhere pursues me incessantly. These are not memories I am invoking, they are realities. Sincerity—it is so difficult to find. Confidence and sincerity, cause and effect. I believe I have obtained it and I believe I have merited it. I believe I have proved sufficiently that I am worthy of it. How can one fail to recognise qualities which stand out so blindingly clear?

Torch of my life—you appear to me surrounded by a halo. I see your head encircled by a crown which I reserve for it here. It is a crown I have reserved for you on your arrival in this beautiful country of my ancestors. If you abandon your journey scheme, you will have made my life aimless. Envy and jealousy should never have any weight with any of us. Come, come quickly, and appreciate the beautiful sun of Egypt. My only consolation is you. Believe me, I love you very much. From your faithful Little Baba.

Marguerite's contribution to the correspondence was comparatively slight; and her notes tended to deal with practical matters. For
instance, she asked about the arrangements for her accommodation
in Cairo.

"His reply was a magnificent gesture. 'You shall have my palace,' he
declared splendidly. 'As for me, I will live in my Daira [a word meaning, in effect, his offices].'"

(Actually, the gesture was not all that magnificent. Ali's offices, in
the centre of Cairo, were sumptuous: part of a mansion set in acres of
garden, and with stables and garages at the rear.)

She reached Alexandria on 22 November.

There was Ali, armed with special permission, coming on board
to seek me out. A powerful motor-car was waiting, and in this
we swiftly travelled to his villa, a few miles from Alexandria on
the sea-coast—the Biarritz of Egypt. The journey to Cairo was
made by train, where we arrived three hours later. Making our
way through a crowd of Arabs, we stepped into a powerful car,
drove through the town, and reached the palace of Zamalik on
the other side of the Nile. Two other cars followed with the luggage and the servants.

I was installed like a princess. Twelve black servants in uni-
forms laced with gold awaited us at intervals on the steps. The
interior of the palace is a copy of Fontainebleau—wonderful
marble, splendid tapestries, furniture of Aubusson Louis XVI,
old Persian carpets, and there is Empire plate, delicately chased,
worth 550,000 francs.

My own room had been designed for the King of Serbia and
on his instructions before that dreadful year 1914. On the wall are
marvellous blue and gold silk hangings. The bed rests on a huge
dais in the shape of a boat. Around it are carven bronze figures. A
canopy in the same silk as that which covers the walls, draped with
real lace and surmounted by immense white ostrich plumes, rises
dome-like above the bed. There are two secretaires, a Psyche glass
with huge columns, a white and gold couch with a little white
and gold table, all in the Empire style. On the dressing-table is a
complete toilet set in gold and tortoiseshell. The bathroom is like
a Greek temple, in white marble. An arch in the same rich stone
rises canopy-like over the centre, enshrining, as it were, a massive

solid silver bath. Between the marble columns on either side are draperies of real lace. Between them stand toilette tables of carved onyx and a divan covered with gold lace.

On the smaller household requisites for personal use Ali had spent a small fortune. There were, for example, so many solid gold cigarette boxes that they got in the way.

Ali had had my monogram in diamonds worked on all my *objets de toilette*. It was almost impossible to find any convenient article in the living rooms on to which he had not somehow or other contrived to introduce what he called his family crest; this, of course, he had designed himself. It was composed of a fantastic reproduction in Arabic of his own name. This strange-looking device was on the uniform of all the servants in appropriate material or gold lace. Where possible, it was picked out in precious stones.

While my eyes were still dazzled, Ali told me that he had prepared all this for me.

(It was natural, his saying that he had made the preparations; but, in fact, he had simply paid for what Said Enani had decided to lay on. Ali had given his so-called secretary an incentive to be excessive, this being the perk of a payment of five percent of the entire bill; since, it is reasonable to assume, Said Enani received commission from most of the dealers and decorators, he was considerably enriched through his master's desire to impress Marguerite into marriage.)

"You are to become my wife," Ali went on. "You are my only happiness." I refused, saying, "Later, later. Let me become accustomed to the idea."

I had, indeed, reason to reflect. Already I was realising the difference between the modes of life of East and West.

Having reflected, Marguerite succumbed.

Ali hired a banqueting room at Shepheard's for a celebratory feast, an engagement party writ large, at which the guests—potentates, captains of industry, members of the diplomatic corps, the wives or concubines of some or all of these, playboy friends of Ali, his relatives (most of whom were on his payroll, one aunt for the unprincely sum

of a pound a week)—were stupefied by countless courses, as geographically diverse as red caviare, soufflé Suissesse, and skewered chunks of
Scotch beef and Jerusalem artichoke.

Thankfully, it seems to me, the marriage ceremonies were, if not
simple, unblatant; the only people to profit from them were civil servants, priests, and attorneys. There was not even musical accompaniment. The civil contract was made on 26 December. Ignoring the pro-
tests of a representative of her inherited religion, Marguerite agreed to
declare, *"La ilah illa Lah wa Mohamad Rassoul Allah"* (which means, so I
have been told, "There is one God, and Mohammed is His Prophet"),
thus becoming a Muslim, like Ali; and, again acceding to a wish of his,
honoured his mother by signing the documents in that woman's name
of Munira, which means "shining." Then, with Marguerite dressed in
black and having to be led because of the near-opaqueness of a heavy
black veil, a religious ceremony got under way at Ali's Daira. All went
well until, coming as a complete surprise to her, she was asked to waive
the right of divorce. It seems that she had attended a Muslim version of
a confirmation class, for she knew, at least, that Muslim husbands had
plenty of licence: their wives—unless they had premaritally been wary,
and stubborn in sticking up for their rights—virtually none. Salient
now was her knowledge that Ali could cast her aside simply by getting
a couple of witnesses to say that he had remarked, "I put away this
woman"; or, wanting variety while wishing to retain her, could take
on as many as three more wives and yet be matrimonially lawful. And
so she jibbed at the thought of being bound to Ali, like it or not, until
death did them part. There was an adjournment to a proximate salon
of the principals, their respective advisers, and the priests, leaving the
guests, uncomfortable on antique upright chairs and not permitted to
chat, not even to make expeditions to toilettes, to gaze at the deserted
stage, pretending continued pleasure in the occasion. For four solid
hours. Though Marguerite never subsequently said so, the deadlock
was broken at last by Ali's offering of a gift, in return for guaranteed
constancy, of such prodigiousness that she just couldn't refuse. All
formalities over, the wedding party, each person of it by now fatigued,
repaired to Shepheard's, where a banquet made ready hours before was
revitalised, served, and devoured with a hunger uncharacteristic of the
hotel's clientele.

During the honeymoon—a cruise on Ali's largest yacht along the
Nile, to and from Luxor—Marguerite was, so she afterward said, given

cause to regret having agreed to the until-death clause. If one believes her assertion that she had not permitted the bachelor Ali to use her body, she was presumably surprised, perhaps even shocked, by the way in which he used it; he had spoken of his responsibility to extend the Fahmy dynasty, but his sexual modus operandi, done behind her back, so to speak, was neither purposely nor incidentally toward that end. Being petite of rump, she was physically pained as well as mentally disturbed by his unconventional approach. Anticipation of what was to come gloomed her days; was, chronically, quite as misery-making as the nightly coming. Protest made Ali pout but also roughened his vigour; excuses or, soon, visible causes for denying him entry were ignored. Marguerite put two and two together—her subjection with recollections of Ali's fondling friendliness toward pretty youths, some of whom augmented their prettiness cosmetically—and came up with the inexact answer that Ali was either quite homosexual or transsexual, and that, whichever he was, the bedtime pleasure he derived from her was wholly or intermittently due to a fantasising that her body was male. The fuzzy understanding upset her: if for no other reason than that, having grown used to being adored, her self-esteem, fragile because she had had no need to bolster it, collapsed when pricked by the realisation that a man—now, officially, the only man in the rest of her life—looked upon her as a sexual surrogate.

As if it were not bad enough that she was demeaned in private, Ali—until the one-sided marriage contract was signed and sealed, obsequious in his ostensible reverence of her—was pleased to degrade her in the eyes of his henchmen and of the crew of and helpers aboard the yacht (well-attended degrading, then, for the vessel had a crew of twenty-five and carried a chef de cuisine and his half-dozen assistants, two stewards, and a maid). On an occasion when she remonstrated with him for abusing a seaman, he shouted at her to the effect that as she so enjoyed the company of sailors, she would no doubt appreciate being left alone with an entire crew; then, calling his entourage to heel, he went ashore, and remained there for some hours. Another time, having decided to go ashore, he forbade Marguerite to leave the yacht. "Surely," she said, unwittingly mimicking an ingenue in an Adelphi melodrama, "you will not imprison me on my own honeymoon?" "The yacht is beautiful," he replied, "and you have many servants. Stay here." Thinking to ensure her obedience, he made up a guard from four of his employees ("veritable giants . . . black colossi," they seemed to her;

whether they were of the crew or temporary, duration-of-honeymoon members of his entourage, one cannot make out) and, still not satisfied with the security, ordered the gangplank lifted behind him. After a sensible wait, she demanded of the quartet that they stop surrounding her and told one of them to drop the gangplank. Severally and singularly, they obeyed. But she had been lulled into a false sense of achievement. Moving to the opening in the rail, she looked across to the embankment and saw that four more black colossi were stationed there. (Where they had been mustered from is anyone's guess.)

The town of Luxor had been much in the news since 4 November, when British archeologists had found, not far away, the tomb of King Tutankhamen. Arriving there, the Fahmys jaunted to the Valley of the Kings. While subterranean, Ali, a keen snapper, got Marguerite to lie, eyes closed, fingers laced on her breast, in a sarcophagus that until recently had held the dust of a long-dead king, and, as Said Enani made a flash, captured a likeness of her that must, surely, have been deemed eccentric enough to occupy the centre spread of the honeymoon album.

The setting for the snap may have put an idea into Ali's mind—or into Marguerite's. A day or so after the honeymoon, while closeted in her bedroom, she wrote a statement; the following September, it would be made an exhibit, translation attached, in an English courtroom; it would be headlined as "The Secret Document" in newspapers throughout the world.

> I, Marie Marguerite Alibert, of full age, of sound mind and body, formally accuse, in the case of my death, violent or otherwise, Ali Fahmy Bey, of having contributed in my disappearance.
>
> Yesterday, 21 January 1923, at three o'clock in the afternoon, he took his Bible or Koran—I do not know how it is called—kissed it, put his hand on it, and swore to avenge himself upon me tomorrow, in eight days, a month, or three months, but I must disappear by his hand. This oath was taken without any reason, neither jealousy, bad conduct, nor a scene on my part.
>
> I desire and demand justice for my daughter and for my family.
>
> Done at Zamalik, at about eleven o'clock in the morning, 22 January 1923.
>
> M. MARGUERITE ALIBERT
>
> P.S. Today he wanted to take my jewellery from me. I refused; hence a fresh scene.

The statement, folded within a plain envelope (not a crested one, because Ali kept a tally of those), went to her lawyer in Paris.

Soon afterward, apparently (dates of incidents are scarce in this period of the tale), Ali likewise sent a letter to Paris. Addressed to Marguerite's sister, it read, in part:

> The question of my marriage, unfortunately, with Munira: Ha, ha, ha, just now I am engaged in training her. Yesterday, to begin, I did not come in to lunch or to dinner, and I also left her at the theatre. This will teach her, I hope, to respect my wishes. With women one must act with energy to be severe.

It is a small pity that one doesn't know which theatre, or what sort of theatre, figured in Ali's training programme. A place in wherever Cairo's Soho was would have been the ideal choice, for just as Marguerite was fastidious as to how she danced, never venturing to shimmy, her taste in stage entertainment was prim. Unlike Ali's: "He frequented those Arab theatres which are a kind of music-hall and which no self-respecting woman can visit."

During March and April, Ali the trainer teased his trainee with unmeant promises that if she were good, he would take her to Europe. But early in May, a friend, highly placed in the Egyptian government, advised him to accept a sinecure diplomatic position in Paris, saying that a brief spell as a seeming servant of his country would be noted by its title-bestowers and contract-givers, doing him no harm at all. And so he, with his entourage and Marguerite, set sail from Alexandria. Perhaps because he wanted to give Marguerite a nice surprise, or perhaps not, he kept her guessing about the destination until disembarkation at Marseilles.

A suite for them, rooms for his followers, had been reserved at the Majestic. Fresh among the followers, and looming over those longer employed, was an Algerian; called Le Costaud on account of his looming, and thought of by Marguerite as the "Black Hercules," he took turns with the chauffeur at guarding Ali (who, having taken to wearing an extravagance of jewellery, was as much at risk of being stolen as of being kidnapped) and the rest of the time kept tabs on Marguerite. Ali, liking the idea of being called a diplomat, spent a lot of time pretending to be one, and this meant that Marguerite was almost as free in Paris—though often dogged by Le Costaud—as when it had been her home. She visited friends, went riding (a fact that may seem surprising shortly), attended the opera, listened to concerts. And she consulted a doctor; and then, at the latter's instigation, was examined by a specialist surgeon.

At the start of July, Ali, fagged from more than a month of diplomacy, announced that he was taking a holiday. In London. Marguerite pleaded to be left behind, but he would not hear of it.

She was of the Prince's party that arrived at the Savoy Hotel on Sunday, 1 July. He and she were installed in a suite on the fourth floor—at the rear of the building, away from the noisy Strand (where, said the legend, if one lingered long enough and took not a wink of sleep, one would see, passing by, the entire rest of the white population of the world), and so with a fine view of the Thames, Waterloo Bridge on the left, to the northeast, and Hungerford Bridge farther away (and just as well, for it was rather an eyesore) on the right. The others at once or eventually went to rooms either two storeys below or three above; last of all, Ali's valet and Marguerite's pair of maids.

The longer the party stayed in town, the harder the valet and the maids had to work, for on each succeeding day the sweatiness of the master and his wife required more frequent bathing or dabbing of their bodies, more frequent exchanging of moist garments for dry ones. The increasing workload was chiefly caused by the ever more uncomfortable sultriness of a heat wave that Londoners, lobster-faced, sopping wet, odoriferous, in danger, some of them, from apoplexy, told one another, alluding to the usual miserable weather, that they couldn't complain about—but Ali and Marguerite would not have needed so much renovation had their joint and individual appointment cards been left with a few gaps, breaks from the gay social whirl of the capital.

Sometimes together, sometimes separately, the Fahmys worked hard at being smart; and Marguerite managed to fit in daily visits from Dr. Edward Gordon, whose surgery, also his residence, was just across the Strand, in Southampton Street. (One gathers that general practitioner Gordon had come to a mutually rewarding arrangement with the person in charge of the information desk at the Savoy; that when Marguerite, on the day of her arrival, had asked to be put in touch with a doctor, a phone call from an informer had caused Gordon to change from Sabbath casualwear into his uniform of black jacket, striped trousers, spats, cravat and things, grab his Gladstone, and has-

ten to the hotel.) Marguerite's ailment was that for which she had obtained advice and medication in Paris. Gordon probed and prescribed,
and then, after eight daily visits (during some of which the patient's
husband was present in the suite, but did not say a word), came on
the morning of the following day, Monday the ninth, with a specialist
colleague—who, having peered at the problem, advised Marguerite to
enter a nursing home, *his* nursing home, without delay, there to receive
the benefit of his surgical skills. She accepted a modicum of the advice,
saying that she would cancel engagements after that night's.

Shortly before or soon after the doctors' visit, a bellboy, offered an
encouraging tip by someone in the foyer for delivering to Marguerite
a tightly sealed envelope when she was alone, carried out the mysterious errand, and scampered back to bag the reward. Inside the envelope was a note in French, unsigned:

> Please permit a friend who has travelled widely among Orien-
> tals, and who knows the craftiness of their acts, to give you some
> advice.
>
> Do not agree to return to Egypt, or even Japan, for any object.
> Rather abandon fortune than risk your life. Money can always
> be recovered by a good lawyer; but think of your life. A journey
> means a possible accident, a poison in the flower, a subtle weap-
> on that is neither seen nor heard. Remain in Paris with those
> who love you and will protect you.

The coupling of Japan with Egypt may have made Marguerite wonder whether the writer, whoever he or she was, knew of the Orient-
obsessed Charles Laurent. And certainly, so she was to say to a lawyer
a few days later, the reference to "a poison in the flower, a subtle weapon that is neither seen nor heard" jogged her memory of how on more
than one occasion she, with others, had drunk coffee in the palace at
Zamalik—and straightway afterward, singularly in the gathering, been
taken ill.

But the latter thought did not put her off lunch, taken with Ali and
Said Enani in one of the Savoy's eating-places. Toward the end of the
meal—irritatingly to ruminative neighbours, entertainingly to others,
enjoying scenes or liking reasons to growl "bloody foreigners"—Ali and
Marguerite loudly argued. The subject was her proposed operation.
Said Enani, taking no part in the squabble, not even as mediator or

shusher, afterward swore that it was sparked by a fait accompli remark by Marguerite to the effect that she was returning to Paris to have the operation there; that it was exacerbated by her refusal to consider Ali's suggestion that she should enter an English nursing home.

The secretary's version is corroborated by the fact that, some time between the doctors' departure and the lunch, Marguerite had told an hotel employee to make Paris-bound travel arrangements for her. And yet, at some time after the lunch—and before about half past two the next morning—she wrote a note to Dr. Gordon:

> Doctor: Affairs have come to a crisis. My husband refuses to take the responsibility for my operation. I am therefore return-ing to my family—that is to say, tomorrow I leave for Paris. Will you excuse me to the doctor who was kind enough to look at me? Believe me, yours gratefully, M. FAHMY
>
> Will you please pay the doctor for his trouble? This account is a personal one.

Perhaps the sequence of events was this: she told Gordon's special-ist colleague that she would enter his nursing home; (having mulled over the anonymous note?) she decided to have the operation done in Paris, and spoke to the Savoy's travel arranger; lunch; she wrote the change-of-mind note to Gordon—but neglected to send it.

There seems to be no credible testimony as to how the Fahmys spent the afternoon and early evening of that Monday. However, it is reasonable to surmise that if at times they were together, there were addenda to the lunchtime contretemps—that though both of them, Ali especially, were used to extreme humidity, they were made more snappy by the fact that, as the *Daily Telegraph* put it next morning, Monday was "a day of almost tropical heat."

Excepting the lessee of the Open Air Theatre in Regent's Park, London's impresarios hated the heat wave, which was vastly dimin-ishing passing trade at their box offices. Productions that had not attracted much advance booking were in peril from the weather. The show at Daly's, in Leicester Square, was not one of those. Sixteen years before, Daly's had housed the first West End production of a play with music by Franz Lehar; now the play had returned to that theatre, was again successful. *The Merry Widow,* it was called. Soon after the Fahmy party's arrival in town, Ali, keen on Viennese music because he was so adept at dancing to it, had insisted on seeing the show, had insisted that Marguerite and Said Enani accompany him. A further insistence on getting a stage-side box had meant that the night for *The Merry Widow* had to be that of Monday, 9 July.

It is, I think, apposite to recall the joke in the form of a question to the just-widowed Mrs. Lincoln: "Apart from that, how did you enjoy the show?" How Ali or Marguerite or Said Enani enjoyed the show at Daly's doesn't seem to have been revealed—perhaps because, when, shortly thereafter, two of them were plied with questions owing to the absence of the third, theatrical enjoyment was a topic that seemed not merely irrelevant but in doubtful taste to broach (particularly so, considering the title of the entertainment, *The Merry Widow*).

Even more shortly afterward, when all three were seated at a table in the Savoy Grill, eating and, as will be proved, drinking wine, one of them, Marguerite, turned down a perfect opportunity to indicate that she had enjoyed the night at the theatre and desired a recollection of it. The leader of the band asked her if she would like a particular tune to be played, and was told (in French, you may need to be reminded): "I don't want any music—my husband has threatened to kill me tonight." Already backing away, the musician, who must have been bilingual, murmured, "I hope you will be here tomorrow, madam." Before or after that exchange, she shouted at Ali: "Shut up! or I'll smash this" (indicating a bottle of Chateau Mouton Rothschild) "over your head." From those two incidents one can draw the conclusion that the after-theatre supper was not a gay occasion.

It broke up after midnight. Despite the pelting rain, the thunder and lightning, Ali stalked out to the forecourt and took a cab to somewhere off Piccadilly. (Although the driver was subsequently interviewed by the police, Ali's dropping-off place was never revealed, which raises the suspicion that it was a den of such vice that the authorities fuzzed its exact whereabouts, and said nothing of its amenities, for fear of being accused of drumming up business on behalf of the proprietor—or of raising awkward questions as to why no attempt had been made, or was being made, to close the place.) Said Enani may have accompanied his master; if not, he went to his bedroom on the second floor. Certainly, Marguerite took an elevator to the suite at the back of the fourth floor.

Wherever it was that Ali went, he did not stay there long. He was back at the Savoy, and in the suite, before two o'clock . . .

. . . and out of the suite, loitering in the oyster-grey-carpeted, silvery-grey-walled corridor, by about thirty minutes past that hour.

John Beattie, a night porter who happened to be wheeling a trolley-load of luggage along the corridor, feigned unobservance of the guest, who was—so far as Beattie had made out from one subtle glance—wearing only admittedly buttoned-up and tightly tied pyjamas of mauve silk and backless slippers of green velvet. Beattie continued his wheeling, eyes downcast, swerving to the left a little so that there was no fear of the trolley's well-lubricated castors running over the guest's toes. As he was about to pass, the guest issued an order:

"Look at my face! Look what she has done!"

Beattie paused in his wheeling and, since he had been told to, looked—and saw, but only just, a slight pink mark on the guest's left cheek. The door to one of the rooms of the suite was ajar; the room was lit merely by a table lamp, and while Beattie was doing as he had been told, lightning blazed through the windows and across the room and into the corridor, silhouetting the guest and rimming his pyjamas to a sort of purple.

As if cued by the subsequent rattle of thunder, the other door of the suite was flung open, and a woman—beautiful, Beattie couldn't help but notice—stepped into the corridor. Beattie's first impression—a reasonable one considering the male guest's attire, the wee small hour—was that she was wearing a knobby nightgown. But even before she started shrieking words of French at the man, Beattie understood that the garment was a low-cut, sleeveless evening-dress, fashioned almost entirely from shimmering white beads. Flustered away from subservience, he requested the couple to return to the suite, to stop making a disturbance in the corridor—and then instantly showed that he knew his place by bowing neutrally at the wall between the dispu-tants before going on his way, faster than before.

He had wheeled for ten yards or so when, hearing a whistle and as-suming that he was being commanded to take notice, he looked over his shoulder—only to see that the male guest, now solitary, was snap-ping his fingers at an oblivious small dog, perhaps a puppy, that must have ambled out of the suite. (Had one or both of the Fahmys bought or been given the dog? Seemingly so. I have found no reference to the animal's antecedents, no mention of what became of it—and so I am reminded of the black cat that slipped into the Wallace murder case, supped evidential milk, then disappeared for good.)

A moment after Beattie had turned the corner toward the front of the hotel, there was a loud bang—and almost at once another—and almost at once a third. None to do with the storm.

Deserting the trolley, Beattie hastened back to the corner and looked along the corridor to where his journey had first been interrupted.

A tableau.

The lovely woman was standing stock-still. Her right arm was stretched diagonally down, and, like an obscene mechanical extension of it, a pistol was clutched in her hand. The hem of her shimmering white dress was polka-dotted—not in a blemishing way but quite prettily: much as an impressionist artist of her country might have expressed *Poppies in the Snow*.

The tidiness of the woman contrasted with the mess her pistol pointed at. A spilled bundle of mauve and green materials, dusky skin, black hair; all splashed, and splashed round about on the oyster-grey carpet, with blood. (Hours later, when the body, straightened and bare, was explored by a pathologist, it was found that, ancillary to the salient fact that death was due to severe laceration of brain tissues, one of the bullets had caused four wounds, another two—suggesting that the victim, just before he fell, had contorted his arms to make an inefficient shield for his torso, his face, and that after he had fallen, even when he was dead, his arms had stayed in the peculiar angles of forlorn protectiveness.)

Beattie ran toward the scene—bravely until, when he was a few steps away, the woman threw the pistol beside the body. He knelt, pocketed the pistol, looked at the man's glistening face and saw that he was not yet dead but soon would be. Meanwhile—and we are dealing only in seconds—the woman was saying, over and over again, "What have I done?" At least, that is what Beattie thought she said. Did he, knowing some French, translate the question the moment it was asked, or did he afterward speak his remembrance of the sounds so that someone knowing French could turn them into words? The former possibility is not unlikely. True, he was English and menial, but if he had soldiered in France during the Great War, he must have picked up and may have retained some knowledge of the language. (My father, illicitly youthful when he volunteered for the Royal Flying Corps, was, within weeks of being enlisted, posted to Mesopotamia; and long after surviving the expedition, he sought to impress me by saying things in what he said was Arabic.)

Accounts of what happened during the next several minutes are confused, confusing; there are gaps, and it is sometimes hard to make out the chronology of events. Beattie must have gone into the suite and used the house phone to summon other employees; before he did so or by the time he had made the call, the corridor was littered with awakened guests; assisted, forced, or of her own volition, Madame Fahmy, weeping and trembling by now, returned to the suite.

Foremost among the employees who hastened to the fourth floor back were Thomas De Bich, the assistant manager of the Savoy, and Arthur Mariani, a night manager. Both claimed fluency in French. Mariani, who was as brilliantined and mustachioed as his name suggests, had been ready clothed, and so was the more prompt. Having noted the untidiness in the corridor, he clapped his hands at Beattie and told him to squeeze a pillow under the head and to lay a sheet over the remainder—taking care, he added (for, trained to observe minutiae, he had seen tiny bubbles of reddened spittle drooling from the mouth, perhaps a sign of life), not to cover the face. He may also have issued other orders to other employees: for instance, to persuade guests back to their rooms, to accelerate the progress of medical men, to alert the Savoy's public relations staff and press officers to a need for diminishment of harmful publicity, and, once such vital tasks had been accomplished, to telephone a high-ranking Metropolitan policeman, outlining what had occurred and requesting that the detectives assigned to look into it be reasonably spruce and nicely spoken.

Mariani's recollection of his interview with Madame Fahmy was, so he said, uncertain—"because it took place in the awful storm, during the flash of the lightning and the crash of the thunder." She was "agitated and excited. She said in French, 'What have I done? What will happen?' I asked why she had done this, and she replied, 'I have been married six months, and I have suffered terribly.' I also understood her to say that she and her husband had quarrelled about divorce."

Thomas De Bich (whose surname, I have been told, was amended to a behind-his-back sobriquet by his British subordinates) found Madame Fahmy "very frightened and distressed. She caught hold of my arm and then all of a sudden dropped down dazed." When recovered, she asked the same question of De Bich as she had asked of Mariani (or maybe they both heard a once-asked question): "What have I done?" She also said something that De Bich at the time translated as "I have lost my head" but which afterward, helpfully to her, he admitted might have been "I was frightened out of my wits."

Did Mariani and De Bich leave her alone in the suite? It seems that they did, since neither of them subsequently said anything about a call that she made on the house phone to Said Enani. The ringing woke him at about 2:40, he reckoned. Her voice was crackling through the receiver before he had it to his ear. He muttered a sleepy something, then was instantly made wide awake by *"Venez vite, venez vite! J'ai tire sur Ali"*—which was one of the few of her utterances shortly after the shooting which would be translated for her prosecutors uncontroversially so far as her protectors were concerned: there would be no attempt to tamper with "Come quickly, come quickly! I have shot at Ali!"

Said Enani—"in a very bad state of nerves"—went quickly to the fourth floor back, but arrived only just in time to see his master being carried on a stretcher into a luggage lift; to be told by a chatty porter—Beattie, it may have been—that though the gentleman was dead, the destination was Charing Cross Hospital, at the Trafalgar Square end of the Strand. Said Enani went straight back to his room. Either he didn't feel like talking to his mistress—ex-mistress now—or she, despite her peremptory telephone command, didn't want to see him. Not at the moment, at any rate, while she was talking to someone else. She had, you see, made an outside call to the available-at-all-hours Dr. Gordon, and (one wonders whether he slept in his black jacket and striped trousers) he had got to the suite in his usual double-quick time.

According to Gordon,

> Madame Fahmy, in an excited state, explained to me in French that her husband had been ill-treating her that evening and that he had forced his attentions upon her; she also said that at supper he had threatened to smash her head in.[2] She alleged that, when they were together in the suite, he had approached her and threatened her, and that she had fired her automatic pistol out of the window. She then thought the pistol was unloaded. When, later, her husband advanced, she fired the pistol and was

2. Which way round was it? Did she (see page 25) threaten to bean Ali with a champagne bottle—or did *he* threaten her similarly?

surprised to hear a report. She lost her head when her husband fell, although she thought he was shamming. It was not until she saw blood that she realised what she had done. She said that when she fired one shot she did not know that another would come up into the magazine.

She gave Gordon the note cancelling whatever arrangements she had made with his specialist colleague; and she reminded him of comments she had made during his earlier visits, apropos of the cause and aggravation of her medical complaint—comments that I shall refer to later.

Gordon was still with her, and insisted on staying with her, when Detective Inspector Edward Grosse, with one or two officers of lower rank, arrived to investigate the shooting occurrence. Grosse was just the sort of detective that the Savoy might have ordered: smart but not dandy, taciturn, and quiet when he did speak; clearly not a paying guest of the hotel but possibly a paying guest's valet. Nice and unobtrusive.

Not nice to John Beattie, though. The porter—perhaps because he felt rather proprietorial about what had happened (over the next few days he would, strictly on the quiet, make more in tips—all from reporters—than he usually made in a year) or because he had been deputed to tidy up—had found three cartridge cases and a spent bullet, and stowed them in the hidey-hole in which he had already placed the gun that had discharged them. When he handed the collection to Grosse, far from being thanked, he was scolded for disarranging material evidence and getting his fingerprints all over it.

Grosse doesn't seem to have said anything to Madame Fahmy other than to ask her to accompany him to Bow Street Police Station. She went quietly. The only delay was sparked by Dr. Gordon, who after insisting to Grosse that he was coming too, advised his patient to exchange her evening garb for daytime wear. Grosse waited in the corridor while she—unaided, for neither of her maids had been stirred—slipped out of her shimmering dress and put on (I quote from the *Daily Express*'s report of her appearance when she appeared, to be remanded in custody, in the police court next day) "a black mushroom-shaped hat and a jade blouse beneath a black charmeuse coat" . . . or (going by the *Daily Graphic*'s account) attired herself in "a long, dark satin coat, trimmed with brown fur at the neck, sleeves and round the bottom, a rope of tiny pearls round her neck, long dropped earrings, and glistening rings on each hand."

Now comes an if not inexplicable, then distinctly odd hiatus of about two hours in Edward Grosse's night shift. One must presume that he left one or more of his helpmates in the corridor; but that presumption does not extend to a belief that any investigating was done while he was away. Apart from arranging for two wardresses to be closeted with Madame Fahmy in a room at the police station, ensuring that Dr. Gordon was comfortable adjacently, and telling a constable to rustle up tea and biscuits for the lady and her leech, he seems to have been inactive until shortly before five o'clock, when he made his way down the Strand, passing the Savoy on his left, and turned right at Agar Street, making for the Charing Cross Hospital. There, he obtained written confirmation that Madame Fahmy was a widow. Then he went back to the Savoy:

> I examined the corridor of the fourth floor. I found a hole in the wall. It was the size of a bullet, and approximately three feet from the floor. Some yards farther on I found that the beading of a glass door had apparently recently been shot away, and I found a hole in the beading through which a bullet had passed. A dent somewhat similar to the other marks was found on the banisters at the top of the stairway.
>
> I then entered the suite of rooms where the victim and his wife were living, and found in the wife's room a white evening-dress adorned with white beads. The lower part of the garment was bloodstained. I then entered the victim's room, and found on the ground broken beads like those I saw on the wife's dress.

It was six o'clock when he finished his foraging. By that time, too, a photographer having taken shots of the scene of the crime, Grosse had given Arthur Mariani the go-ahead for the eradication of signs of the crime that might upset passing guests, and a number of cleaning women, warned to work silently, were sponging and wiping outside the suite. After six, a statement was taken from Mariani; also from Thomas De Bich, John Beattie, and Said Enani.

Returning to the police station, Grosse asked after Madame Fahmy, and was told that she was sleeping. He arranged for a statement to be taken from Dr. Gordon. Perhaps because of delay in getting an interpreter, or perhaps because Grosse's mother had told him, as mine told me, that a lady's day should not begin before that of an office worker, he waited until nine o'clock before asking for Madame Fahmy to be roused so that he might charge her with the murder of her husband.

According to the interpreter, she replied, "I have told the police I did it. I told the truth. It does not matter. My husband has assaulted me in front of many people since we have been married. He has told me many times to kill him. I lost my head."

On the dot of nine o'clock, Dr. Gordon made a phone call to the offices of Freke Palmer, who, for close to a decade, ever since the naughty Arthur Newton had been struck off the roll of solicitors of the Supreme Court, had had the busiest criminal practice in the country. Palmer, as fast in responding to a call for assistance of the wealthy as was the good doctor, got to Bow Street, without looking as if he had hurried, shortly after Inspector Grosse had finished interviewing Madame Fahmy. Gordon effected an introduction between her and the solicitor, advised her that Palmer was the best of his kind that money could buy (calumnious to say this, I suppose, but I shouldn't be surprised if Gordon had fixed a cut from Palmer's fee), and withdrew.

Freke Palmer, having got the gist of his client's version of what had happened at the Savoy earlier that morning, and—as important—having taken in every mite of her black reminiscences of life with Ali, sat fairly quietly by her during the brief magisterial proceedings. He asked only two questions, both of Inspector Grosse—who replied, unpleasingly, to the first that the prisoner, when and after being charged, had "seemed calm and collected, not at all hysterical," and to the second that, yes, he *had* been told by Dr. Gordon that she had arranged to enter a nursing home for an operation that day. After saying that his client would reserve her defence, Palmer was granted the request that she be driven to Holloway Gaol, not in a black Maria, but in a hired limousine.

It would be interesting to know whether or not she received similarly special treatment—privacy from poorer remandees in the hospital block, for instance—after her admission to Holloway.

Expense was no object to Freke Palmer's briefing, hiring, tipping, and buying in aid of saving Madame Fahmy from either the sudden punishment of dislocation of her neck or a long term of imprisonment. As he had done many times before, he briefed the roly-poly, seemingly genial Sir Henry Curtis-Bennett, whose fame as a defender in criminal cases was surpassed by only one other King's Counsel; also, he briefed the eminent junior counsel, the slim, saturnine Roland Oliver. In the previous December, those two barristers had been on opposing sides at the Old Bailey, the former leading the defence of Edith Thompson, the latter assisting the Crown to prove, so the jury decided, that Mrs. Thompson and her young lover Frederick Bywaters were both guilty of her husband's murder. Palmer's pairing of Curtis-Bennett with Oliver was still red-hot news within the Inns of Court when he announced, astonishingly, that there was to be a third member of the defence team, a coleader of it—none other than Sir Edward Marshall Hall, the most famed defender of all time.

Never before had such a trio of forensic talents been assembled. A trio a trifle too starry, it seemed to some. Curtis-Bennett was an "actor-barrister" (he once remarked that it might be a good thing if he had an orchestra to play soft music while he made a speech for the defence)—but his courtroom histrionics were delicate compared with those of Marshall Hall: if "Curtis" was the Gerald Du Maurier of Theatre Royal, Old Bailey, then "the Marshall" was its Henry Irving. Were they to share top billing for the defence at the Fahmy trial, the audience of jurors might, while being entranced by the double act, feel that the defence case was all show and no substance.

That thought may have occurred, post-briefing, to Freke Palmer, causing him to request Curtis-Bennett to become, as it were, the director and prompter of a Marshall Hall solo performance; or perhaps Curtis-Bennett, assured of his fee whether he shared the advocacy or took a figurative backseat, alongside Roland Oliver, decided not to risk being outshone. Either way, it was agreed that Marshall Hall should do all the acting at the trial; that Curtis-Bennett and Oliver should prepare his material—and learn their own lines based on it, so that in the event of his going so far over the top that he required out-of-court medical aid, one or both of them, expensive understudies, could take over.

Early in the discussions between the solicitor and the barristers, a two-tier strategy was worked out. The jury would be asked to believe Madame Fahmy's statement that the shooting was a nasty accident—that, believing that her automatic pistol was empty, she had used it merely as a "frightener," pointing it at the threateningly advancing Ali in the hope of halting his progress . . . and that when it had no such effect, she had instinctively clenched the trigger—and only released it after three completely unexpected shots had been fired. Even if the jury found that explanation not entirely implausible, they might return a verdict of manslaughter. And so they had to be persuaded—probably contra to a warning by the judge that the concept of *crime passionnel* was not accepted excusingly under English law—that the defendant, tormented and sexually abused for months on end, eventually fearing that further outrage would endanger her life, had no choice but to kill her husband, a perverted Arab, lest he kill her.

The no-intention component of the defence case could be left to Marshall Hall, who was a dab hand at firearms, and yet more expert at making juries accept his science of ballistics in preference to that of firearms experts called by the Crown: he would get his friend George Stopp, manager of Whistler's gun shop in the Strand, to cram him with the ins and outs of the Browning .25 automatic pistol, which was the type of weapon used by Madame Fahmy (one of a matching pair, His and Hers, that the Fahmys always kept by their bedsides)—and then, if he couldn't make the firing of one—two—three bullets seem unintended, no advocate could.

As for the no-choice component, every effort would be made, many back-handers paid, to create a warts-and-all (the "and-all" redundant to the purpose) picture of Prince Ali Kamel Fahmy Bey. Ex-employees of his would be traced, tempted, quizzed; a firm of private investigators in Cairo, and another in Paris, would be engaged to ferret for uncomplimentary information about him.

Madame Fahmy's defenders had one large dilemma. It concerned her ailment—that which, as you will recall, she had planned to have surgical treatment for. The ailment, so she had told Dr. Gordon before the shooting and Freke Palmer afterward, had been caused by her husband, and made worse, until the discomfort was fierce, by his continuance of the pastime that had caused it. The knotty problem for her defenders was composed of the following strands:

They wanted her to be seen as a Romantic Figure—but if the name of her complaint were revealed, it would, like a spot of ink on blotting paper, spread pretentiously, obsessing observers of her and casting all thoughts of Romance from their minds. On the other hand, her terror that Ali, creator and exciter of the complaint, intended imminently to pleasure himself, no matter how she was thereby pained, gave her a motive for killing him—or at least incapacitating him—that no one, not even a dedicated masochist, could possibly look down upon; but the trouble there was that Ali's pleasurable pursuit was even more unmentionable than the complaint that Madame Fahmy blamed upon it; and suppose that if the defence hired the leading euphemist and, having accepted his discreet advice, spoke of the unspeakable at the trial, there was the fearful danger that the jury, not quite cottoning on, would think that, just as it took two to tango, Ali and his wife had been consenting partners in the pursuit, she deriving nearly as much pleasure from it as did he, prior to the onset of the resultant ailment.

Having weighed the pros and cons, the defenders agreed that both the pursuit and the complaint had to be skirted.

I think that now, in an age when outspokenness is expected by most people and practised like a profession by those who have little to speak of that is worth hearing about, it is all right to say that the pursuit was sodomy, the ailment hemorrhoids, otherwise called piles. As one or two specially gentle readers may appreciate a moment to recover from those disclosures, I shall leave a space.

The trial of Madame Fahmy occupied Number One Court in the Old Bailey for six days, from ten o'clock on the morning of Monday, 10 September—exactly two months since she had been charged and cautioned by, and had made a statement to, Detective Inspector Grosse. Her judge was Mr. Justice Rigby Swift, who is recalled by Edward Spencer Shew, for years a court reporter, in his good reference book, *A Companion to Murder* (London, 1960):

> One [hears] in one's fancy the drawling voice, with its flattened vowel sounds, the short "a," the tones which suggested, rather than reproduced, the speech of his native Lancashire, above all the peculiar habit he had of elongating the final syllable of certain words and then snapping if off, explosively. (The very word "remember" recalls this trick. On the lips of Mr. Justice Swift it would be certain to come out as "remem-*bah.*" This mannerism was so well known in the Temple that lawyers used to refer to him—and still do—as "Rig-*bah.*") One needs to remember, also, how he looked as he sat on the Bench; the round, rubicund face under the bob wig, the glowing cheeks, the nose like a button, the amiable lift of the mouth, the bright, observant eyes, the endearing air of bonhomie. And all the various tricks and mannerisms which were so much a part of the man need to be remembered, too—such as the habit of slowly tapping his pencil three times upon the desk before him as a warning that he was about

to say something apt and shrewd, and frequently devastating. (At those premonitory taps, much to his delight, an awful silence would descend upon the court.)

The leading Crown counsel was Percival Clarke, the eldest son of a greater advocate.

There were two women on the jury.

And, every day, as many women as men contributed to the crowding of the public spaces—shamefully, in the view of "A Psychologist," paid by the *Daily Express* to sit in the no less crowded Press pen:

> The woman spectator . . . seeks entertainment from the wreck of some other life, and she sits through the most revolting evidence outwardly placid, inwardly indulging in an orgy of unhealthy sensation. . . . [At the Fahmy trial, women] sit and nod to their friends with the self-satisfied smirk of those who enjoy privileges not granted to less influential persons. Among them was more than one matron accompanied by a girl who appeared not to be of the age to vote at the polling booths.
>
> The study of their faces was a lesson in feminine psychology. The more unprintable the evidence brought forward, the more they rejoiced in listening to it.

The two women who *had* to be present, Madame Fahmy and a wardress ("whose neat and kindly personality suggested"—to the *Daily Graphic*'s reporter—"a ministering angel of the V[oluntary] A[id] D[etachment]"), had ample elbow room, for the dock in the main Central Criminal Court was large enough to accommodate a score of burly men. The defendant dressed differently each day; though it was at least two months since she had bought any clothes, she always looked fashionable.

Before the indictment was read, the judge gave permission for an interpreter—one of two, working turn and turn about—to sit near Madame Fahmy. The interpreter's first task was to put into French the Clerk's question, whether she was guilty or innocent of the murder of her husband. *"Non coupable,"* she replied—quietly but sounding as though she meant what she said. If she was capable of relaxing, she was allowed to do so for the rest of that day and the whole of the next: she would not be asked further questions until Wednesday morning.

After Percival Clarke had outlined the case for the prosecution, a few minor witnesses gave evidence. Then came the second Big Moment: the calling of Said Enani—"a short dapper figure in a well-tailored blue suit" (*Daily Express*). It came as a surprise to him, though he didn't show it, that the first questions he was asked came, not from Clarke, examining-in-chief, but from Marshall Hall. No sooner had he taken the oath than defence counsel rose—majestic and as awe-inspiring as an eagle in his black gown—and demanded to know:

"On what book were you sworn?"

"The Bible."

"Does the oath on the Bible bind you?"

"Yes."

The judge intervened: "You regard an oath taken on the Gospels as binding on your conscience?"

"Yes, sir."

Rigby Swift twitched his eyebrows at Marshall Hall, wondering if he was satisfied. And the latter sighed hugely, shrugged extravagantly, shook his lovely head at the jury, and sagged back into his pew. He had scored thrice—by raising a doubt about the witness's veracity, by putting him off his stroke, by treating the jurors, all twelve of them, as allies.

Freke Palmer had brought from Cairo, and was treating royally, either as kings or queens, two exquisite young men who had been intimates of Ali. The couple, each daintily coiffured and cosmeticised, flanked the solicitor in unwitting mimicry of porcelain bookends when, directly after the luncheon adjournment, Said Enani stood in the witness box, waiting to be cross-examined. Keeping him waiting a while longer, Marshall Hall turned to Palmer, whispered something, then bowed to each of the Egyptians. His intention was to ensure that Said Enani noticed the young men and associated them with the defence; his hope was that the secretary would be influenced to speak with some candour about aspects of his dead master's social life by the belief that loyal reticence was pointless, since gaps in his testimony would be filled by the young men, defence witnesses to be. Actually, Marshall Hall did not mean to call them; they had been pumped by the defence and were now just intimidatory props; as soon as Said Enani had left the witness box, they would be shipped back to Egypt, the chinking of their trinkets accompanied by the clinking of pieces of silver from Palmer's petty-cash box.

It is hard to make out whether or not the intimidatory ploy worked. During the four hours of the cross-examination, Said Enani rarely feigned ignorance of matters that must have been within his knowledge—but his stated recollections were less dramatic than the defence would have liked; as each question was put to him, his mind started censoring the whole-truth answer that he had sworn to tell. That was no bad thing for the defence: so long as a person being cross-examined consistently diminishes the truth, sensible members of a jury will amend all the footnote-sized answers to a larger font, perhaps of bold type. Marshall Hall had to be careful that, in attacking Ali's character, he delivered no more than glancing blows against that of the witness: an overt attempt to discredit him would bring into play the tit-for-tat rule of legal combat, entitling the prosecution to "dish the dirt" about the defendant. Marshall Hall's first few questions were risky, and one wouldn't be surprised if Curtis-Bennett, sitting next to him, sent up a nose-blowing, brief-riffling or even gown-tugging signal, causing him to change the subject.

Q. How long did you know Fahmy?
A. For seven years.
Q. Before he came into his money, you lived together?
A. No.
Q. He had no money then? He was poor?
A. He had £100 a month.
Q. What was your employment at that time?
A. I was employed by the Minister of the Interior.
Q. At what salary?
A. £22 a month.
Q. And when you became Fahmy's private secretary, was there a clause in the agreement providing that you should be paid at £35 a month for ten years' service, whether you served all that time or not?
A. That is so.

The best instance of Said Enani's diminished responses is his answer to a question, one of several, regarding Ali's physical ill-treatment of the defendant: whereas Marshall Hall spoke of "a heavy blow across the face," the witness preferred "a smack."

He recalled, but in faint light, many of the public arguments and fights between the Fahmys. There was, for example, an incident during the prior-to-London stay in Paris:

Q. Following a visit to the Folies Bergeres, did Fahmy seize her by the throat?

A. I do not know that. I did see him take off a bracelet which she had given him and throw it at her.

Q. On that occasion I suggest that she was bleeding from the mouth from a blow given by her husband?

A. I remember a small mark near her nose.

Q. *switching from the particular to the general:* Was he a bully?

A. He was rather shy.

Q. You know what "a bully" means? Was he a man in the habit of beating women—not only one woman, but women?

A. No, sir. He would dispute with them, but I have never seen him beat them.

Q. You have known of his intimacies with many women?

A. Yes, sir.

Q. Do you know that he treated them brutally, one and all?

A. No, sir; I cannot say brutally.

Near the end of the day, Marshall Hall referred, for the first and only time during the cross-examination, to Madame Fahmy's plan to enter a nursing home for an operation. He suggested that Said Enani had heard his master tell her to "go to the devil" when she broached the subject.

A. I do not recall his saying that.

Q. Was she always crying?

A. No.

Q. Was the Madame Fahmy of 1923 totally different from the Madame Laurent of 1922?

A. Perhaps—but she did not cry.

Q. Had every bit of life been crushed out of her during those six months?

A. I do not know.

Q. From an entertaining and fascinating woman, had she become miserable and wretched?

A. They were always quarrelling.

Q. And did she say that you and Fahmy were always against her, and that it was a case of two against one?

A. Yes.

Q. Did you say that if she would give you £2000, you would clear out of her way?

A. I said that if she would discharge me, I should be pleased to go. I did not say anything about money.

Q. Did you give her presents?

A. Yes; but they were not expensive.

Q. At supper on the night of the tragedy, did Fahmy say, "I will disfigure you so that no one else will want you"?

A. I do not remember.

To preface his last question, a risky one, Marshall Hall produced an enlarged copy of a cartoon that had appeared in a Cairo satirical magazine called *Kachkoul*. The drawing was of three profiles, each of two of them set back from the one below, and the caption read: "The Light, the Shadow of the Light, and the Shadow of the Shadow of the Light." The topmost profile was of Fahmy, the next of Said Enani, and the bottom one of the secretary's own secretary.

"I suggest," Marshall Hall thundered, "that the association between yourself and Fahmy was notorious in Egypt."

"That is not so," Said Enani replied softly.

Still scowling at him, Marshall Hall sat down.

Percival Clarke was on his feet at once—not to reexamine but to protest to the judge that the cartoon that had been flourished to his entire surprise reflected on the witness's moral character.

Patting a yawn, Rigby Swift responded, "It does not reflect on anybody's moral character—except, perhaps, the artist's," and before Clarke could say another word, adjourned the proceedings until the following day . . .

. . . when "the other Mr. Churchill"—Robert, the gunsmith of Agar Street, off the Strand—gave evidence. Macdonald Hastings, who wrote Robert Churchill's biography (London, 1963), says that the gunsmith's appearance at the trial

was a routine affair. Madame Fahmy admitted that the pistol was hers, and that she had fired the shots—whether intentionally or otherwise it was for the court to decide—which had killed her husband.

But Marshall Hall, partly because the winking mechanism of a gun fascinated him in the same way that he was fascinated by jewellery, partly because it was most important to his case to impress the jury that he knew more about firearms than anyone else in court, used his friend Churchill in a subtle way to underline the reasonableness of the case he was planning to make. Cross-examining him in the witness box, he got Churchill to explain the workings of an automatic pistol; how for the purpose of emptying a loaded cartridge out of the breech it was necessary to pull back the breech cover to dribble it out. He suggested that a person inexperienced in firearms—as most women are—might not know this, might think that to empty the gun the only way was to fire the round in the barrel; indeed, might well be ignorant of the fact that, in an automatic, the recoil of one round lifts another round out of the magazine into the firing position. Churchill agreed that that was true.

For the defence it was a little step forward. One shot, out of the three that had to be explained away, had been accounted for; provided that is, that the prosecution didn't pooh-pooh the suggestion by pointing out that the pistol was Madame Fahmy's personal property, not her husband's, and that it was unlikely, if not highly improbable, that a woman who thought it necessary to have a pistol for the protection of her jewels wouldn't have taken the trouble to find out how it worked.

Churchill was one of a number of men from the neighbourhood of the Strand who appeared as prosecution witnesses that day. The others were—in ascending order of importance at the Savoy—John Beattie, Arthur Mariani, and Thomas De Bich. And Dr. Edward Gordon—who, having answered questions from Percival Clarke about, among other things, his after-the-shooting consultation with Madame Fahmy, was asked by the judge:

"Did Madame Fahmy explain what she meant by her husband having brutally handled her immediately prior to the tragedy?"

"She told me that he took her by the arms in the bedroom." (But *which* bedroom? *Hers?*—as she had stated, through an interpreter, to Inspector Grosse when he interviewed her at the police station. Or *her husband's?*—as may have been indicated by Grosse's earlier observation of crushed white beads on the floor by Fahmy's bedside.)

The doctor's reply to the judge's question left Percival Clarke with no choice but to ask: "Did you see any marks of bruising on her arms?"

"She showed me a scratch on the back of her neck, about an inch and a half long, probably caused by a fingernail. She said it was caused by her husband." Adding to Clarke's misery, Gordon added: "When I saw her on 4 July [six days before the day he had been asked about], she had bruises on her arm and leg, which she said had been caused by her husband 'fighting her.'"

Cross-examining, Marshall Hall asked: "Was the mark on the neck consistent with a hand clutching at her throat?" And he was delighted with the positive reply, the unrequested, ideally worded addenda: "It was. Madame Fahmy complained that her husband was very passionate, and that his conduct had made her ill. Her condition was consistent with conduct she alleged against him."

With a little help from friendly witnesses like Gordon, Marshall Hall had already given excellent value for the 652 guineas marked on his brief.[3] His speech to introduce the case for the defence made the sum inadequate (and, as will appear, his closing speech, on its own, was deserving of more than any other barrister has ever been paid). He began the opening speech at three o'clock on the Tuesday afternoon, and, careful with the timing, only sat down when he saw the judge looking at the clock in a wistful-for-adjournment way. During the speech, he referred to Madame Fahmy's contention that the shooting was accidental—but devoted most of his efforts to making the jury think that if ever a man had deserved to be killed, that man was her husband:

"Fahmy Bey, shortly before he was shot, attacked his wife like a raving, lustful beast because she would not agree to an outrageous suggestion he made—a suggestion which would fill every decent-minded person with utter revulsion. Almost throughout their miserably tragic life of six months, this treacherous Egyptian beast pursued his wife with this unspeakable request, and because she—immoral though she

3. If Curtis-Bennett's fee was in the same region, and supposing that Roland Oliver was receiving the usual fee to a junior of two-thirds of that of leading King's Counsel, the bill for the three defenders (excluding any "refreshers" that were paid to them) amounted, in present-day terms, to about £40,000 (close to $65,000).

may have been—resisted him, he heaped cruelty and brutality on her until she was changed, by fear, from a charming, attractive woman to a poor quaking creature hovering on the brink of nervous ruin."

First thing next day, the jury's entrance was delayed while Percival Clarke submitted to the judge that he should be allowed "to dispel the idea that the defendant was a poor child dominated over by this man." He went on to explain: "I want to prove that she associated with men from an early age, and that she is a woman of the world in the widest sense. I submit that I am entitled to ask her how she treated other men. I do not want it to be thought that all the fault was on the husband's side."

Mr. Justice Swift: "Sir Edward [Marshall Hall] has said that she was an immoral woman, but he said it in such a way that he gave the impression to everyone who listened to his speech that she was an innocent and most respectable woman. It is a difficult thing to do, but Sir Edward, with all that skill we have admired for so long, has done it." Rigby Swift then seemed to contradict himself by ruling against Clarke's submission. Marshall Hall must have thought to himself, "Hoorah, Rigbah," or something to that effect.

Once the jurors were settled, he requested Madame Fahmy to leave the dock and go to the witness box—which she did, so unsteadily that her VAD chaperone needed to give her a hand. Until now, the spectators in the gallery had looked exhausted and bedraggled, for they had had to queue for their slight spaces since before two in the morning; but the progress of the prisoner perked them to become as one, an oblong of unblemished alertness, an organ that went ooh and ah, that throbbed with expectancy.

I hate to say this—and not because I have it in me to feel sorrow for the spectators—but the show did not live up to advance publicity. Everything would have been fine if only Madame Fahmy had bothered to learn English in the period between her arrest and the trial. But no: she still couldn't even say please or thank you. And so every single question put to her was followed by the rigmarole of translation of it into French by an interpreter, her answer in that language, the interpreter's English version of what she had said. Tedious.

And irritating to those who believed that there was such a thing as the *whole* truth—for the word structure of a witness's reply is sometimes almost or as revealing as the meaning of the reply; and, of course, there was the chance of a forensic variation on the military tale of the message to "send reinforcements, we are going to advance" that, muddled by middlemen, finished up at headquarters as "Send three and fourpence, we are going to a dance." Why, even the oath-taking ceremony was unsatisfactory. Marshall Hall had queried Said Enani's acceptance of the Bible—but when Madame Fahmy used the same volume, no one for the prosecution pointed out that, unless a Holloway-visiting priest had officially returned her to Catholicism, she was still a Muslim and that, in any event, it was surely unsafe to assume that she considered herself bound by an oath on a book of words, sans that of Dieu, that were complete gibberish to her.

Going by the translations of her answers, she stuck pretty much to her story as we know it. In cross-examining her, Percival Clarke achieved only a few, minor successes. For instance, she had agreed with Marshall Hall that she had been "terrorised" by several of Ali's employees, including a black valet—but she had to admit to Clarke that the valet was a youth of eighteen who was only five feet tall. She quite often wept, and once or twice swooned. The big dramatic moment was during examination-in-chief, when Marshall Hall asked that a pistol like her own be handed to her. The *Daily Express:*

> The drooping, slim figure in black, almost hidden in the witness box, rose slowly, and a small black-gloved hand stretched out to take the pistol held over the ledge of the witness box by the court usher.
>
> Then in a flash, the small gloved hand recoiled as if it had been touched by an electric current, and was pressed over two tear-rimmed eyes in which revulsion flashed. The pistol fell on the ledge of the witness box, and in the tense silence it seemed that some great weight had crashed on the wood.
>
> "Come, Madame Fahmy, take hold of the pistol; it is harmless now," came Sir Edward Marshall Hall's soft voice reassuringly across the court, and the small black-gloved hand of the trembling woman in the witness box closed on the pistol.

The questioning of her went on throughout Wednesday and was continued next day, until about noon. Between that time and the luncheon recess, three other defence witnesses were heard.

First, Yvonne Alibert, the defendant's sister, who said that during the Fahmys' visit to Paris she had seen bruises on Madame Fahmy's face and body and had heard her husband threaten her. She added that prior to the visit she had received two letters from Ali: "I regarded them as improper. In one letter he asked me to place his love at the feet of a lady who was in Paris, and requested me to become acquainted with nice women so that he might be introduced to them."

Second, Amy Pain, Madame Fahmy's maid, who remembered that, "on one occasion, when Madame wished to wear an evening dress at Luxor, she had to use a great deal of cream and powder to hide the bruises on her neck and back." Amy created a stir in court—and a collective shudder of defenders—by tagging on to one of her answers a recollection that she had never mentioned before—"because I was so upset. Between eight and nine on the night of the tragedy, I heard a shot, and saw Madame Fahmy put a pistol on the arm of a chair." Perhaps because, clearly, she was wrong about the time (by eight o'clock, the Fahmys, with Said Enani, were watching, if not enjoying, *The Merry Widow*), Percival Clarke did not express interest.

Third, Eugene Barbay, auxiliary chauffeur to the Fahmys in Paris, who, as well as commenting on "Madame's bruises," recalled that during an argument between his master and mistress, the former had said—well, had said *something*. The interpreter declined to interpret, explaining between blushes that "the certain expression is so bad that even in court it cannot be uttered." Coaxed by Rigby Swift, the interpreter gave a clue: "It is usually indicated by an initial"—but refused point-blank to narrow the possibilities from twenty-six.

On that demure note, the morning session ended.

Straightway after lunch, Marshall Hall began the greatest defending speech of his life.

Having sought to simplify things for the jury by telling them, "Either this was a deliberate, premeditated and cowardly murder, or it was a shot fired by this woman from a pistol which she believed was unloaded at a moment when she thought her life was in danger." He used racism in what he believed was a good cause:

"She made one great mistake," he said quietly—"possibly the greatest mistake any woman of the West can make. She married an Oriental."

A pause to allow that thought to sink in; then, still quietly, he went on:

"I dare say the Egyptian civilisation is one of the oldest and most wonderful in the world. I do not say that among the Egyptians there are not many magnificent and splendid men. But if you strip off the external civilisation of the Oriental, you have the real Oriental under-neath—and it is common knowledge that the Oriental's treatment of women does not fit in with the idea the Western woman has of the way she should be treated by her husband."

After suggesting that Said Enani epitomised "Eastern duplicity," and asking the jury if they did not think that Madame Fahmy had reason to fear "Hercules, the great black blackguard who owed his life to Fahmy," Marshall Hall reverted to the never-the-twain theme:

"The curse of this case is the atmosphere of the East which we can-not understand—the Eastern feeling of possession of the woman, the Turk in his harem. This man Fahmy was entitled to have four wives if he liked. For chattels. Which to us Western people, with our ideas of women, is almost unintelligible—something we cannot deal with.

"Picture this woman, inveigled into Egypt by false pretences—by letters which for adulatory expression could hardly be equalled. *And which make one feel SICK.* At first, everything is honey and roses. He shows her his beautiful palace, his costly motor-cars, his wonderful motor-boat, his retinue of servants, his lavish luxuries, and cries, "Ah, I am Fahmy Bey—I am a prince!"

There was more, much more, along much the same lines: contempt for Ali—for all but a few Orientals, for virtually the entire adult male population of Egypt. (Following the trial, the attorney general re-ceived a long cable of protest from the Bâtonnier of the Egyptian Bar; the foreign and colonial secretaries had to placate ambassadors and high commissioners from places east of Greece—and Marshall Hall was persuaded to write, or put his signature to, a letter saying that he hadn't said any of the anti-Oriental things that he had said.)

When Mr. Justice Swift adjourned the proceedings—earlier than usual—on the Thursday, Marshall Hall had not finished. Continuing the speech next morning, he cheekily told the jury: "While your de-cision must not be governed by sympathy, still less must it be gov-erned by prejudice." Then he got angry with Percival Clarke for having framed a question to Robert Churchill in such a way as to suggest that if Madame Fahmy really had fired her pistol out of the hotel win-dow before the shooting, she had done so not with the intention of rendering it harmless but to make sure that it was in working order: "The suggestion is that this wicked woman, this murderess, shot her husband like a dog. I regret—I reject—that suggestion, because there is absolutely nothing but the suggestion." Calming himself, he whispered a description of the thunderstorm. Then:

"Imagine its effect on a woman of nervous temperament who had been living such a life as she had lived for the past six months—outraged ... abused ... beaten ... degraded." Grasping a pistol—it may have been the real one—he went into a crouch; no one in court had much doubt that it was the crouch of "A Stealthy Oriental," but Marshall Hall confirmed this by explaining, "In sheer desperation—as he crouched for the last time, crouched like an animal, like an Oriental, retired for the last time to get a bound forward—she turned the pistol and put it to his face. And ... to her horror ... the thing went off."

While speaking, he had pointed the pistol toward the jury.

Now he dropped it.

The clatter as it hit the floor and bounced was not that at all to the people in court. To them it was a series of explosions. And as Marshall Hall, no longer crouching, crooned, "Sweetheart, speak to me!," he was a translated Madame Fahmy to a T.

Himself again, he roared: "Was that deliberate murder? Would she choose the Savoy Hotel for such an act?"

"No," shrilled a woman in the gallery. "Of course not," another, more talkative, piped up.

Coming toward the end of his act, Marshall Hall spoke of "that wonderful work of fiction by Robert Hichens, *Bella Donna,*" and continued:

"You will remember the final scene, where this woman goes out of the gates of the garden into the dark night of the desert. Members of the jury, I want you to open the gates where this Western woman can go out—not into the dark night of the desert but back to her friends, who love her in spite of her weaknesses; back to her friends, who will be glad to receive her; back to her child, who will be waiting for her with open arms."

Right on cue, a shaft of sunlight pierced the glass dome of the court. Pointing his whole hand at it, Marshall Hall ordered the jury, "You will open the gate and let this Western woman go back into the light of God's great Western sun."

Then he sat down; almost fell down, having taken so much out of himself. There was no applause. Or rather, there was that greatest of all applause, which is utter silence.

Poor Percival Clarke, having to speak next, showed, at least, that he had attended better to *Bella Donna* than had Marshall Hall. The work was, he said, "a strangely unfortunate one to recall to mind. The woman who went out into the desert, out into the dark, was the woman who planned and nearly succeeded in murdering her husband. In that respect, it may be that the simile between the work and this case is somewhat close." The main thrust of Clarke's speech seems to have been toward reminding the jury that they were "trying the woman in the dock, not the dead man."

Late in the afternoon, Mr. Justice Swift began to sum up, commenting that he had been "shocked, sickened and disgusted" by some of the evidence. Continuing next morning, he told the jury that they had to decide on one of three verdicts: guilt of murder or of manslaughter or innocence; but he gave no clues to which of the verdicts he considered most apt.

The jury retired just before half past noon and returned a minute or so after half past one. The foreman had to speak loudly to make the words "not guilty" audible above the weepy moans of one of the jurywomen, the drama too much for her, and the stentorian soothing of her by the stiff-upper-lipped other.

Madame Fahmy must have taught herself at least one English word, that being "not." Prior to the foreman's utterance of it, she stood with her elbows on the rail of the dock, her hands giving further cover to her veiled face—but the moment the word came out, her fingers pinched the muslin and flicked it atop her cloche, revealing a beaming face.

There was great rejoicing in the gallery: the cheers, whoops, screams, and shouts made a din loud enough to be heard by the hundreds of Madame Fahmy fans blocking the street outside, and the resultant racket from them could be heard in the courtroom like an echo of the galleryites' delight. Outraged, Rigby Swift snarled an order for all spectators, including the few unhysterical ones, to be removed. Once the only sounds were external, he said to the interpreter (a French woman barrister who had replaced a regular interpreter at Marshall Hall's request): "Tell the defendant that the jury have found her not guilty and that she is discharged."

The translation of those words had a bad effect on Madame Fahmy: the joyfulness dwindled from her features and she swayed as if about to swoon. There were two wardresses in the dock today, and they both grabbed the woman who was no longer in their charge, volte-faced her, and half-carried her down the steps to a reception room—where Dr. Gordon revived her with the aid of a jolter more expensive, to his patients, than sal volatile. Though she was soon all right, she accepted advice not to leave the building for an hour—during which time, it was reckoned (rightly, as it turned out), the rabble would disperse. When she eventually slipped through a side door and into a waiting cab, only reporters and a few other people, desperate to see her or with nothing better to do, noticed her going. Either appropriately or quite inappropriately, her destination was the Prince's Hotel, smaller and smarter than the Savoy, in Jermyn Street.

There, instead of taking an après-ordeal *sieste,* she gave an audience to a "special representative" of the Sunday paper that had made the winning bid in Freke Palmer's auction of her first "exclusive inter-view." The journalist, bashful compared with most of his or her kind, "hesitated to disturb Mme. Fahmy in view of her wrought condition. But she was so glad to meet me that I felt she would be offended had I neglected the chance, on behalf of the readers of *The People,* to give her a word of sympathy and encouragement. 'You may stay with me for five minutes,' she said in her delightful French." (One wonders if the translation is complete. Did she also point out that *The People* had purchased only five minutes of her time and that a servant had already started a stopwatch?)

"Giving me her tiny hand, she invited me, with a wan smile, to sit and talk to her. Her room was glowing with colour. There were the choicest of flowers everywhere—a tribute from the enormous number of her compatriots, as well as English folk, who did not hesitate to show their sympathy in her trying hour. There were many mascots, too, sent by people of all classes as a magic solace.

"Madame told me she is not leaving London yet. 'My doctor abso-lutely forbids me to travel, and so I must be patient,' she said." (Was Gordon nearby, nodding frantically, fondling his wallet the while?)

"Her wonderful eyes grew dim with tears as visions arose before her of the dreadful past. 'Marriages between East and West can hardly ever turn out happily,' she said.

"Madame Fahmy spoke of the splendid encouragement she had received from many unknown English women and girls in all stations in life. 'They are like the mountains that look cold and stately with the white snow on them—white, like their English skin, but they are full of fire.'

"When the possibility of her receiving a large fortune from her hus-band's estate was broached, she said the subject was painful and distasteful to her." (So painful and distasteful that, though *The People*'s person still had a few seconds to go, she shut up like a clam.)

"As I bade adieu to this pathetic woman, she sank back with a sigh among the luxurious cushions on her couch."

The size of Madame Fahmy's portion of the estate of the man whom she had, maybe unintentionally, punctured with three bullets was never revealed: not by her; nor by any member of either of the packs of civil lawyers—hers and the Fahmy family's—that, after a deal of dickering, one with the other, came to "an equitable agreement." If her negotiators were unworthy of their fees, and she got only the basic widow's entitlement, under Egyptian law, of one-sixth of the estate, it meant that her annual income was increased by not less than £8000 (now close to £200,000, over $300,000).

Reasonable compensation, or not, for nine months of different sorts of suffering? Making it all worth while?

I don't know the answers—but, in pondering the questions, I found a meaning of an old Gaelic saying that had perplexed me previously: "He [or she] that eats a slice of his [or her] spouse may, with great propriety, relish the soup that is made of the same."

For a few days following her trial, she was busy in the West End of London: partygoing and interview-giving—and, it is nice to know, finding the time to pop in to see Marshall Hall at his chambers in the Inner Temple as well as sending him brief messages expressing her gratitude. Then she went to Paris, where, of course, she received a heroine's welcome. After two or three years, press stories about her doings appeared, not on news pages, but, aptly, in gossip columns; then, after a couple more years, the dropping of her name seems to have ceased.

I am grateful to my friend and fellow crime historian Andrew Rose (author of *Scandal at the Savoy* [London, 1991]) for the information that the widow Fahmy lived, prosperously and unspectacularly, latterly in the fashionable Paris suburb of Neilly, which was where she died, aged eighty, in January 1971. The announcement of her death— apparently in only one French newspaper, presumably paid for by her executor—stated only that the burial had taken place, "in the strictest privacy," nearly a fortnight before. Not a word about an incident on the fourth floor back of the Savoy Hotel, London, England, during a thunderstorm that my father and some others who were kept awake by it would recall whenever the weather became markedly inclement.

A POSTSCRIPT ON A SUBSEQUENT MURDER AT THE SAVOY

At about nine o'clock on the tranquil night of Wednesday, 1 October 1980, a young man—slim, dark, with curly hair cascading over the collar of the trendy garment he was wearing rather than a jacket—booked into the Savoy Hotel; for that purpose, he called himself D. Richards and claimed that he hailed from the Handsworth district of Birmingham. The booking clerk allotted him single room No. 853 and mentioned—in the casual, but prepared-to-blame-inflation manner prescribed by his trainer—that the charge was £78 a night. (Comparatively speaking, not exorbitant: now the lowest charge is well into three figures.)

At 10:15, a female employee of the hotel, doing something or other in a room on the eighth floor, was alarmed by screams issuing from room 853. She peeped into the corridor and saw a man—his trendy garb stippled with blood—emerge from room 853 and enter a lift. She waited until the position indicator by the lift glowed G, then scampered along the corridor, pushed open the door of room 853, and looked within. What she saw caused her to make noises not unlike those that had made her curious. As a result, security men arrived; and one of them, shocked into forgetfulness of priorities, telephoned the police prior to speaking to a hotel executive.

Room 853 would need extensive redecoration, partial refurnishing, and entire replacement of the wall-to-wall carpeting.

The corpse of the woman who had screamed was lying near the bed. It was only partly clothed. An inventory of the garments on the body and lying about showed that when the woman had entered the room, some time after nine, she was wearing a white skirt and—each item black—a jumper, an unconventional sort of brassiere, a suspender belt, fishnet stockings, and high-heeled shoes. And she was carrying a large black handbag made of glistening stuff called, inappropriately, leatherlike.

This, too, was part of the mess. And so was something that, presumably, had come out of the bag: a wig of black hair, far more luxuriant than that of the dead woman. Among the paraphernalia still in the bag were articles indicating that it belonged to Ms. Catherine Russell of 729 Chelsea Cloisters, London SW3. Until the blood from fifty-five stab wounds in the dead woman's body had been wiped away, it was difficult to make out whether a snapshot in the bag was of her; but that turned out to be so. The Savoy's public relations people heaved small sighs of relief when early press reports of the crime referred to the victim as a masseuse; the relief was short-lived, though, for subsequent reports noted that massage was but one of several skills, to say nothing of knacks, that Ms. Russell, aged twenty-seven when she died, had practised upon or simply displayed to male clients, to the evident satisfaction of the great majority, during a career in prostitution that had stemmed from a pastime that she had indulged in, just for fun, when she was teenaged.

Room 853 contained not only clues to the identity of the victim but also clues to that of the culprit. A clasp knife—one of those with a superfluity of accessories—lay, with its four-inch blade exposed, just inside the door. The whole contraption was smothered in blood, and the blood on the handle was dabbed with fingerprints. A tribute to the housemaid: when the polished tops of tables were examined, few fingerprints were found, but nearly all matched those on the handle of the knife. A further clue—a rather good one, this—was a pocket diary. The entries were of less interest to the police than a preliminary page, printed like a form and completed in pencil by the diarist—

NAME	Tony Marriott
HOME ADDRESS	XX Highland Avenue,
	Horsham, Sussex
EMPLOYER	(blank)
AGE	Twenty-two

—and so on, right down to collar size, name and address of next of kin, sign of the Zodiac. Fingerprints on the diary matched those already mentioned.

Soon after the arrival of the first policemen, one of them returned to the foyer and commandeered as evidence the registration book (the handwriting of the man who had signed in as D. Richards was similar to that in the diary); he also quizzed the booking clerk, ascertained that Tony Marriott, aka D. Richards, had not settled his bill, and enquired of foyer staff and porters whether they had noticed a conspicuously bloodstained man leaving the hotel at about 10:15 (none had).

Marriott's movements after he walked out of the Savoy would be pieced together as follows: turning right, he hurried along the brightly lit and crowded Strand, crossed it, and proceeded up Kingsway and onward, until he reached the President Hotel, next to the grander Imperial in Russell Square.[4] The President's booking clerk—a short-sighted or unparticular individual, it seems—accepted the blood-stained, dishevelled, and breathless man as a guest. Marriott must have been carrying a spare knife, for after entering the room allotted to him on the fourth floor, he tried to cut his left wrist, and then, having failed to pierce the artery, tried to cut his right wrist, but again without the determination that his apparent purpose required. Next day, he quit the President, without paying his bill, and travelled to Liverpool Street railway station, where he boarded a train to the Essex resort of Southend-on-Sea. In the evening, he visited the Britannia public house on the Esplanade.

The bloodstains, dried and dark by now, might have been taken by some for intended embellishments of trendy clothes—but the land-lord of the Britannia, a middle-aged, untrendy man named James Locke, peered at them, raised his gaze to the customer's face, thought that it was a bit like a photograph of a face that he had seen on a tele-vised news programme, and decided that he had better ring the police. Thus it was that Tony Marriott's postmurder odyssey ended.

He admitted—no, insisted—that he had killed Catherine Russell. Musing in an interview room, he murmured, confusingly to the lis-teners: "The real problem, I feel, is that I seem to develop a resent-ment of normal sexual relationships." He had booked a room at the Savoy with the express intention of killing a prostitute: *any* prosti-tute; he had never met Catherine Russell before—had simply learnt that she was on the game, phoned her, agreed her price and fixed an appointment, and, a minute or so after her arrival, when she was get-ting ready, opened his knife and plunged it into her, and thereafter plunged it into her fifty-four times, at first frenziedly, then, when she was dead, with metronomic regularity, and then, toward the end of his mission, exhausted by it, as if in slow motion.

During the six months between his arrest at Southend and his trial at the Old Bailey, he was questioned, maybe more than once, by a psychiatrist, who concluded that he was suffering from "a persistent psychopathic disorder leading to abnormally aggressive behaviour."

---

4. Presently the home of Our Society, called "the Crimes Club" by those who know no better.

His counsel argued that as his, Marriott's, responsibility was diminished, he was guilty of manslaughter, not murder; the jury agreed; and the judge sent him to Broadmoor Hospital for the criminally insane "without limitation of time."

If his legal aid stretched to a subscription to a press-cutting agency, allowing him to see all of his reviews, and to while away wet afternoons at Broadmoor by making a scrapbook, he may have wished that he had chosen a different scene for his crime: Claridge's, Brown's, even the Arabic Dorchester—any hotel other than the Savoy would have been better in terms of himself-centred coverage. As it was, many reporters assigned to the second Savoy Killing gave less space to it, to him, than to reminders of the first Savoy killing, done nearly sixty years before by a pretty Parisienne called Marguerite Fahmy.

Hers was a hard act to follow.

Slaughter at the Governor's Lodge

SLAUGHTER AT THE GOVERNOR'S LODGE

hroniclers of crime (who, if they are at all good at the job, are basically novelists telling a truth) are vastly underprivileged compared with fictionists of crime. They cannot skirt a writer's block by, for instance, changing a method of murder in midscream, replacing a dull character with a quaint one, removing the scene of a crime from a semi-detached in suburban Tooting to a five-star hotel in the West End, ironing out nonsenses in a plot, altering a murderer's licit occupation from that of butler to that of butcher for the simple reason that, as everyone knows by now, it is never the butler whodunnit. And they cannot—or rather, should not—have characters talking Capotely-precise prose or thinking *at all*. (The latter constraint means that the chronicler worth his salt is adrift from the cosy mooring that Ogden Nash termed *HIBK,* standing for *Had I But Known*—which, as Jacques Barzun and Wendell Hertig Taylor explain in their wonderful *A Catalogue of Crime* (New York, 1971; revised and enlarged edition, 1989), "sums up the heroine's mind as she repeatedly ponders her failure to see the obvious traps laid for her by the villains, or as she recurrently regrets not having acted with ordinary judgment and spoken out in time, for reasons never stated to herself or the reader"; and it bars the chronicler from membership of what the book-dealing Jack Hammond of Ely called the He-Must-Have School—e.g., "As Tom Brown set about the grisly task of dismembering the late Mrs. Brown, his thoughts must have turned to their wedding night.")

And writers about *English* crimes suffer from the ordinariness of what most of the people concerned are called: the fictionist can tell his characters apart just by his christening of them (there is no chance of a novel-reader confusing the apparently blameless Marigold Sunbeam with the plainly deceitful Hortense Garrotte, or the privately investigating Nick Sharp with the constabularian Aloysius Plodd)—but, nine times out of ten, the chronicler is stuck with Janes and Johns, such names preceding indiscriminately distributed ones such as Brown, Jones, Patel, and Smith.

Writers about American crimes are better off—chiefly because natives of and settlers in that land tend to be ornately designated, but also because some American parents and priests and registrars of births go by drawled or mumbled sounds when spelling, and so add oddity to perfectly ordinary names (thus, an intended Barbara goes through life as Barbra, a Candice as Candace, a Deborah as Debra, a Justin as Dustin, an Elizabeth as Lizabeth—whose father, one guesses, was a lectrician); and even forename/surname combinations that are drab by American standards—Oscar Hammerstein, for instance—are, if passed down, given uniqueness by the tagging on of sequential numbers, II, III, IV, and so on, until the latest in the line of parents, not knowing the Roman numeral that comes next, break the baptismal monotony.

An instance of the truth of the saying that, in the United States, clarity of characterisation begins at home is provided by what became known, maybe unfairly to a woman called Candace, as the Candy Murder Case.

Candace's husband, who played the nonspeaking role of victim in the affair, had originally been called Jakella Moscovitz, but long before becoming a dead millionaire, had made his name as Jacques Mossler. Among others in the large cast were John V. Handwerker, who was the first of several doctors who looked at the corpse (he was not the pernickety one who counted thirty-nine stab wounds in the torso and upper limbs and half a dozen blows to the head from a blunt instrument, and who made the neat observation that Mossler "could have died from the stabbing, even if there had been no blows, and could have died from the blows if there had been no stabbing"); Melvin Lane Powers, the widow's favourite nephew; Earl C. Martin and Freddie Duhart, each of whom swore that Powers had offered him a fee to commit murder, the former saying that the offer was made—and turned down—a year or so prior to 30 June 1964, the date of Mossler's demise, and the latter saying that he had received—and rejected—the offer only a month before that date; Billy Frank Mulvey, who stated that Candace Mossler had given him the first installment of a payment for killing her husband but that he had welched on the deal, and Virgil Nelson Halford, who sought to cast doubt on Billy Frank's statement; Clyde Woody, senior spokesman for Candace when she and her nephew stood trial for her husband's murder; and Nathan Greenbaum, Leroy P. Grigley, and Clarence McQueen, members of an all-male and quarter-black jury that, because of peremptory challenges and challenges for cause by the aforementioned Mr. Woody and Melvin's leading counsel, the renowned though unimpressively named Percy Foreman, took nine and a half working days to amalgamate. The fact that three of the other nine jurors had surnames starting with Z—Zeller, Zellner and Zoller (making them sound to a reporter of the trial "like Siamese Triplets")—indicates either that the queue of prospective jurors was in alphabetical order, and was just about exhausted by the time the jury was complete, or that Dade County, Florida, which was where both the murder and the trial took place, had more, far more, than its fair share of Z-initialled residents.

Candace's maiden name was Weatherby. She was the sixth of a dozen children born to a small-time farmer and his wife, residing and toiling near the small town of Buchanan in the state of Georgia, just north of Florida. A record of her birth puts it in February 1920; but she, when grown up, insisted that she was not delivered until seven years later. If her insistence was justified, then she was a tender twelve when, in 1939, having been urged to marry a civil engineer named Johnson by one of her grandfathers, a bishop of the Mormon Church who had looked after her following the death of her mother and the decampment of her father, she did so. Whatever her age when she became Mrs. Johnson, her golden hair had grown long, her features were pretty in a pert sort of way, and her build, though small (perhaps because she had been stricken with polio; for five years she exercised her body to complete recovery), was pleasingly proportioned.

She gave birth to a son, called Norman, after his father, in 1943; to a daughter, called Rita, probably because Rita Hayworth was all the rage, a year later. Before Rita had mastered toddling, her father became ill; and her mother, forced to be the breadwinner, did a crash course in dressmaking then departed the family home for New York City, where she set up—and, it seems, prospered—as a fashion designer. After but a year or so of designing, she turned to the task of being photographed for advertisements and was soon specially in demand on behalf of dental products, for her front teeth, all her own, were immaculate. Her husband, well enough by now to have gone engineering in Canada, suggested a "friendly divorce"; she having agreed, the formalities were completed; like it or not, she had custody of the children.

In 1949, when she was at least twenty-two, she moved to New Orleans, there to set up, all in one go, the Candace Finishing School, the Candace Modeling School, and the Candace Modelling Agency. In the first-named establishment, she tutored pupils toward becoming Southern (but not too Southern) belles; in the second, graduates of the first were taught tricks of the modelling trade; the third hired out well-endowed alumni of the second for dressing and undressing assignments. Years later, reminiscing about her days down upon the Mississippi, she said:

"I was doing so well, I had time for art and culture. I volunteered to help raise money for the New Orleans Grand Opera Company. They gave me a list of businessmen to call on. Jacques Mossler, who had an office in New Orleans that year, was on my list."

"*That year.*" Just one? Well, yes.

Indeed, only a few months of it. As an indirect result of the contribution-requesting call on Mr. Mossler, she became Mrs. Mossler before May was out. Having given some of his riches to her predecessor, he was "down to four little finance companies." He was fifty-four—and so thirty-two or twenty-five years older than Candace.

If what, when widowed, she said of the marriage night was true, Jacques had a faulty sense of time and place for revelations about himself that were liable to startle those in whom he confided. "He told me . . . that women had made trouble for him—tried to blackmail him. To protect himself, he had undergone a sterilisation operation. He could never be victimised by a paternity suit."

According to her recollections of postnuptial discoveries concerning her husband's sexual inclinations, sterilisation had not impeded, may even have increased, his versatility. So far as I can tell, there was no corroboration of her allegations; but neither that nor the trial judge stopped Percy Foreman, the loudest of the defenders she bought for her nephew, from declaring that, "except for the shoe fetish, Mossler had 'em all—transvestite, homosexuality, voyeurism, masochism, sadism, all the perversions mentioned in *Psychopathia Sexualis,* Krafft-Ebing's great masterpiece."

I may be showing my unsophistication by saying that the picture of Mossler as a Jacques of all errant traits is hard to reconcile with the seemingly firm fact that he was, nicely, a lover of children. When he divorced his first wife, the four daughters she had borne him were, at his legal pleading, allowed to stay with him; and one of his stipulations before marrying Candace was that his daughters and her Norman and Rita were to be treated as *their* children, equal recipients of their love and largesse. Wanting more children, but incapable of seeding any, he told Candace that they would adopt some—and amply fulfilled that intention in 1957, when a six-year-old girl and her three younger brothers were made waifs by the action of their father in shooting dead his wife and a still younger child, having mistaken them (so said psychiatrists who subsequently spoke up for him) for Japanese soldiers who had somehow missed the news that World War II was over. The four children were added to the Mosslers' six, and Jacques straightway amended his will so as to ensure that each of the resultant ten would, when he died, receive no more, no less, than the others. As the diversification of his business interests—to include, as well as credit-finance houses, insurance companies, and banks—was making him pots of money, the children had the prospect of becoming fatherless or stepfatherless millionaires.

In case I have misled you into thinking that the children's ten-way split would account for Mossler's entire estate, I must explain that the arrangement applied only to part of what he would leave. His widow would be well provided for.

During the fifteen years before he was taken from her, he gave her, sexual requirements apart, everything she desired: jewels, flashy automobiles, bespoke clothes, an Egyptian maid who spoke three languages other than Egyptian—one, just as well, being English. There were other servants at her beck and call, some stationed in or around a twenty-eight-room house in the least undesirable part of Houston, Texas, that he bought for her, or on his present to her of a ranch southeast of Houston, just inland from the Gulf of Mexico, and some portable between the house and the ranch.

But for voluntary work in aid of a cause she considered worthy, she and Jacques would not have come together, and so it may be that he, not congenitally benevolent, was spurred by sentiment to put a little exertion and a lot of money behind her campaigns in support of cultural and social organisations (for instance, respectively, the Houston Grand Opera Association and a boys' club in the city) and of individuals who had fallen foul of the law.

It is hard to make out what attracted her to the cause of one person of the latter category, a disagreeable young man named Howard Stickney who had, perfectly properly, been sentenced to death for a specially barbaric double murder. Not only were her efforts in vain (after thirteen stays of execution, all wholly or partly financed by Mossler, Stickney went to the electric chair), but as a result of them she met a man named Billy Frank Mulvey, a prison-mate of Stickney's, who, a few years later, when she herself stood in peril of legal extinguishment, did his best to point her toward that end.

More understandable than her espousal of Stickney's cause, when Johnny Will Ford, a black worker on her ranch, was sentenced to three years in prison for having habitually carried a concealed weapon, she took up the cudgels on his behalf, first of all arranging for his release on bond, and then talking the governor of Texas into ordering his parole. Governor Daniel (his first name was Price—apt to the generality of politicians) was running for reelection. Those local newspapers that favoured one or other of his opponents were so vociferous in their condemnation of the clemency that he felt obliged to revoke the parole. While the police scoured Mossler property for the now-fugitive Ford (one officer, bespectacled, so irritated Candace by his insistence on peering in every nook and cranny that she gave him an uppercut to the chin, sending his spectacles flying he knew not where, and so causing him to grope his way home, there to search for his contact lenses), Governor Daniel issued press statements that he, his advisers, and theirs had been taken in by lies told by the parole-seeking Mosslers and their lawyers. Already upset by Daniel's reneging on a deal, Candace and Jacques were made revengeful by his besmirching of their reputations. They set about besmirching his, at the same time extolling virtues they perceived in one of his foes—contributing to his defeat by John Connally (who thereby acquired a mite of immortality, for it was he, proud governor of the Lone Star State, who, seated in a car with, among others, President John F. Kennedy, was wounded by a bullet fired by Lee Harvey Oswald). Just prior to the poll, Johnny Will Ford surrendered to the police; when he was released from prison after serving a little of his sentence—no time tacked on for the inconvenience he had caused by his disappearance—he went back to his job on the Mossler ranch.

Another of what Candace termed her "fights for justice" was a family affair. A brother, DeWitt Weatherby, proprietor of a gambling establishment called the Silver Dollar Club in her native town of Buchanan, shot to death a regular customer, and, despite his explanation that he had acted self-defensively, was charged with murder. Candace rearranged her appointments so as to be free to attend the trial but didn't seek to interfere with the legal process until (much to her surprise: thinking that acquittal was a foregone conclusion, she hadn't even offered to buy DeWitt top-notch defenders) her brother was found guilty and sentenced to life imprisonment. Thereupon, she collected Georgian lawyers much as poorer people collect Penny Blacks—at least fifty, it was reckoned by Governor Marvin Griffin, who was in the best position to keep count, since he was the target of their supplications. The trouble, from Candace's point of view, was that her collection was indiscriminate, including politico-lawyers who were not of Griffin's party: if he had granted the particular favour asked by them all, cronies and adversaries alike, the latter's cries of victory would have drowned out the former's tributes to his mercy. And so he refused to make DeWitt's durance briefer or less vile. "But they got him out anyway," Griffin subsequently grumbled, referring to the fact that DeWitt was released after serving only four years of his life sentence. Griffin's successor as governor was the lawyer who had worked hardest on behalf of DeWitt. Most of his electioneering expenses had been covered by Jacques Mossler.

Among others of Candace's kin to whom she gave succour was a nephew named Melvin Lane Powers, the son of one of her older sisters. He was born in 1941, which means that he was either twenty-one or fourteen years younger than his wealthy aunt. He was tall and well-built and had jet-black hair, specially noticeable as eyebrows, a disheveled nose, thick lips, and cheeks and a chin that, as well as being creased, were pitted with the scars of acne. He lacked social grace and displayed an arrogance that he surely cannot have felt.

Candace doesn't seem to have paid much heed to her nephew until 1961—though at some time during his late teens she may have gone out of her way to visit him: a subsequent business acquaintance of Melvin's recalled his saying "that he was in jail in Chicago—fraud for selling property or some stock or something, embezzlement, and that she [Candace] came to visit him or came to visit his cell-mate, and that's the way he got to know her." Having been allowed to leave Chicago, Melvin hawked magazine subscriptions door-to-door in Arkansas on behalf of a company run by an ex-convict named Arthur Grimsley. Late in 1961, he forsook Mr. Grimsley and, after traipsing southwest, turned up at his aunt's house in Houston. She and her husband told him to make himself at home, which he did. Once he had put on weight, was chic in garments paid for by Candace, and was no longer able, credibly, to blame his sluggard behaviour on footsoreness, Jacques Mossler fabricated a job for him in one of his Houston-based finance companies.

About a year and a half later, Jacques came to the definite conclusion that Melvin had overstayed his welcome. Having imparted his conclusion to both Melvin and Candace, without receiving a cooperative response from either of them, he sacked Melvin and, since the latter still refused to find other accommodation, enlisted legal assistance in kicking him out of the house. Candace was most upset. Understandably so, in the view of those who, early in 1966, prosecuted her and her nephew on the charge of having murdered her husband: they believed that her distress at Melvin's eviction was occasioned by the fact that she had grown partial to incest.

According to one of the aforementioned prosecutors, Candace's distress was not prolonged. Shortly after the eviction of Melvin, Jacques travelled on his own to Europe, stayed abroad until the autumn of 1963, and then resided not at the house in Houston but in an apartment in Miami. The prosecutor:

"Upon moving to Miami, he lived over his office at the Allen Parker Company, located on 36th Street. Powers and Candace remained in Houston. On 1 October 1963, Powers [who was now self-employed, trying, none too successfully, to sell recreation vehicles] rented an apartment and introduced Candace as his fiancée. She, Candace, would constantly visit the apartment, and witnesses saw them necking, kissing and hugging. Powers expressed to people how much he loved Candace, and that she was having marital complications and was in the process of obtaining a divorce, and that he, Powers, was going to marry her. On occasions Powers would refer to Candace Mossler as Miss Johnson, and on other occasions he even introduced Candace as his wife. Powers also told people that he loved her so much that he would kill for her."

Earl C. Martin, one of the several witnesses for the prosecution who testified to having been approached by one or other of the defendants with offers of cash for the rendering of a lethal service, also swore that, on a date that he couldn't fix precisely—some time toward the end of 1963—he, at Melvin's invitation, had listened in on an extension to a telephone conversation between Melvin and Candace, from which he had gathered that the former was keen on a pastime that he called "eating pussy," and that the latter, possessor of the "pussy," delighted in the former's "eating" of it.

In the first week of June 1964, Candace, accompanied by her daughter Rita (on vacation from a university) and three of the adopted children (none older than thirteen), went to stay with Jacques, who had rented a small but luxurious apartment on the second floor (which in England would be termed the first) of a block called the Governor's Lodge, situated on Key Biscayne, a slight island close to Miami and connected to it by a stilted thoroughfare known as the Rickenbacker Causeway. The stay extended until the last day of the month, a Tuesday—early in the morning.

Early on three previous mornings, those of the 24th, 26th, and 28th, Candace, complaining of migraine, had driven to the Jackson Memorial Hospital in Miami, there to beseech a palliative.

At about 1:30 A.M. on the 30th, she again drove to the mainland—this time (so she later told a policeman) not only because she felt a migraine coming on but also because she had some mail to post. She took the children with her.

That meant that her husband—who had celebrated his sixty-ninth birthday a few weeks before; had, at about the same time, been assured by his doctor that he was in tiptop condition—was left alone in the apartment. Alone, that is, apart from a recently acquired dog, a boxer called Rocky after one or other of the so-known pugilists, Graziano or Marciano: a highly strung beast, sparked into barking by the slightest sound that was uncommon.

One of the ubiquitous fictions of crime novels is that the time of a person's death can be established, give or take a minute or two, by feeling the warmth or otherwise of the skin, observing the extent and whereabouts of stiffening, peering at a thermometer that has been prodded into the rectum, and/or comparing stomach contents with the last menu. The notion has been accepted as gospel by many lay readers of made-up crime tales—and, occasionally to the detriment of justice, by some people with medical diplomas. It is piffle.

Pleasingly, none of the doctors associated with what came to be called the Candy Murder Case needed to guess the time of Jacques Mossler's death.

For consider: shortly before 1:30, Mrs. Peggy Fletcher left her apartment across the corridor from Mossler's. She would be described by reporters as a "socialite," which, considering that she worked as a typist for an insurance broker, suggests that that word has a less swell meaning in America than it has in England. One of the reporters would note that her dead-of-night emergence was "to keep from being caught short in the morning"—a further cause of confusion for English readers, to whom I must explain that she had run out of cigarettes. She went down to the parking lot and started her car but found the exit blocked by Mossler's red Pontiac convertible, which she noticed contained all but Candace of the visiting members of his family. As soon as the Pontiac had been obligingly reversed by Rita, Mrs. Fletcher drove to a shop that she thought would be open but which was not. When she returned, still cigaretteless, to the Governor's Lodge, there was no sign of the Pontiac.

She went up to her apartment, undressed, and got into bed—and had been there "perhaps five minutes" when she was disturbed by the barking of a dog. Then: "I heard the sounds of a scuffle. There was a distinct thud, and someone cried out, "Don't do this to me!" I heard another thud. The dog continued to bark. Then I heard footsteps running down the corridor—heavy footsteps. Without a doubt, it was a man."

The barking had awoken Herbert House, tenant of the apartment directly above Mossler's. It was not the first time that he had been vexed by the noisiness of Rocky; over the past few weeks, he had complained to Mossler and to a manager of the Governor's Lodge. Now he switched on the bedside lamp and, thinking to get exact data for a letter of furious complaint, looked at his watch: 1:45. House got out of bed, scampered across to the balcony, and, looking down, saw that the abominable Rocky was skittering about on Mossler's balcony, impounded there by the closed glass doors of the apartment. "I heard those sliding doors open, and I called down to ask if they were going to take the dog in. I heard a voice answer, "Yeah." It seemed to be the voice of a young man." House went back to bed and straightway fell into a sleep of such soundness that, despite forthcoming noises, he did not stir until his accustomed breakfast time.

One may assume that House had only just returned to the land of Nod when Mrs. Irene Durr, night manager of the building, was awoken in her first-floor apartment by a scream. Sitting up in bed and switching on the light, she heard barks—which cued drowsy surmise that Rocky had nipped his master, causing him, first, to scream, then to retaliate, causing Rocky, in turn, to raise a rumpus. Before turning off the light and settling down again, she looked at her watch and saw that it registered 1:30. (A subsequent checking of the watch showed that it was fifteen minutes slow.)

No sooner had she settled down than she heard running footsteps on the stairs. Deciding that she had better do some night-managing, she arose and stepped into the lobby just in time to espy someone leaving the building by the back door. Through the glass panel in that door, she could see an area of the parking lot: the area reserved for Mr. Mossler's vehicles. "The person went to a white Chevrolet in the lot. The walk didn't seem like a woman. The person got in the Chevrolet and drove off." (The apparent uniformity of American cars to English eyes makes it surprising to Englishmen that Americans are so good at telling one make from others: it seems as ophthalmically acute as finding a needle in a haystack and, without reliance on a law of probability, declaring that the needle found is the needle that was sought.)

A moment before Mrs. Durr had stepped into the lobby, a homecoming tenant, Martin Tavel, manager of a Miami radio station, had entered the lobby by the front door, and so he got a longer look at the person hurrying out at the back than did Mrs. Durr. He would tell the police that the person was definitely a man—a tall man whose dark hair was so long that no skin was visible between it and the collar of his dark shirt.

Tavel and Mrs. Durr walked out of the front door. The white Chevrolet was coming round the corner of the building, its headlamps on. As the car came closer, the lamps were switched off, only for a few seconds, though: the lamps came on again before the car turned into the street and sped in the direction of the Rickenbacker Causeway.

Rocky's barking caused Tavel to look up, to notice that lights were on in Jacques Mossler's apartment. He and Mrs. Durr took the elevator to the second floor. As they emerged into the corridor, so did Peggy Fletcher. The three became a whispering trio by the door of Jacques Mossler's apartment, and then Mrs. Fletcher, who loved dogs, even Rocky, and seems to have had a way with them, cooed through the keyhole until the boxer was lulled into silence. Pleasure at the peacefulness taking over from interest in what had excited the dog, the three retired to their respective beds. The time was close to two o'clock.

∽

By then, presumably, Candace and her charges were in Miami—a city that was still safe to visit, even in the small hours: not yet ineradicably contaminated by people whose migration from Cuba made that island a nicer place. The pain in Candace's head cannot have been severe, for after buying stamps and posting whatever she stuck them on, she escorted her children to a public lounge in the DuPont Plaza Hotel, tarried with them there until about four o'clock, and only then made her way to the emergency room in the Jackson Memorial Hospital for her regular, alternate-nights dose of a balm that she must have considered more potent than anything available from an all-night chemist.

She left the hospital at five minutes past four. That time is of less interest than the reason for its being known. Only a moment after she had gone, Maida Loretta Kolodgy, the clerk in the emergency room, took a telephone call from a man wanting to speak to Mrs. Mossler— the same man, Ms. Kolodgy felt sure, who had called twice before, making a similar request, during the previous hour and twenty minutes. Ms. Kolodgy looked outside; but, returning to the telephone, told the caller that there was no sign of Mrs. Mossler.

Who was the man? Why was he so keen to speak to Candace? And—most intriguing of all—what gave him the idea that she might be reached at the hospital? After all, unless the regularity of her previous attacks of migraine had forewarned her that another was imminent, and she spoke of what was to come, how she would deal with it, to a male acquaintance prior to about one o'clock, when—so she subsequently said—she experienced the first twinges, her husband seems to have been the only man who could have known that she was going to Miami and that the hospital was one of her destinations there. Of course, the man may have telephoned or called at the apartment soon after her departure and learned of her proposed hospital visit from Jacques.

For various reasons, none of the questions was provided with a sure answer. Jacques could not help. Candace expressed mystification. The caller never revealed himself.

༈

4:30 or thereabouts. Mrs. Durr, roused by the sound of a car pulling up in the parking lot, and made wide-awake by the patter of five pairs of feet in the lobby, turned on the light and looked at her unreliable watch.

4:45 Dr. John V. Handwerker, a physician of Key Biscayne, heard from an answering-service girl that Rita Mossler had requested his presence at the Mossler apartment, where there had been "trouble—maybe a killing." He told the girl to ring the police, then dressed and drove to the Governor's Lodge.

4:49 James Jorgenson, a young deputy sheriff who had recently applied for leave of absence so that he might study criminology at Florida State University, knocked on the door of the apartment and was admitted by Candace, who told him, "He's over there," indicating a yellow-blanketed mound in a corner of the living room. Noticing much blood as he crossed the room, Jorgenson tried to prepare himself against horror when he lifted the blanket. It was as well for him that he did so, for the sight of the stabbed and battered body of Jacques Mossler, clad only in a once-white undershirt, would shock and sicken even those subsequently arriving older officers who believed that their emotions had been used up. (At the trial, the judge refused to let the jury see photographs of the body, saying that they were "inflammatory.") Remembering that he was duty-bound to put his fingers where there had once been a pulse, Jorgenson touched below the right ankle, one of the few unbloodied parts of the body, before replacing the blanket. Then he telephoned his headquarters. He noticed that "the room did not appear to be ransacked. There was a large dog in the kitchen. Rita and one of the children took the dog into one of the bedrooms."

4:53 Dr. Handwerker arrived. In terms of handiwork, he did no more than confirm Jorgenson's conviction that Mr. Mossier was dead. But he observed the widow, wondering, without coming to a conclusion, whether or not she was in clinical shock. She was dry-eyed. "She kept herding the children in and out."

An hour or so passed. It would be nice to know what happened in the apartment meanwhile, but neither Jorgenson nor Handwerker seems to have considered any incidents worthy of mention. In England, someone would have made tea; but the result of a later examination of work surfaces in the kitchen indicates that nobody made a hot beverage of any kind. The thought that someone may have passed round cans of a fizzy drink is too distasteful to contemplate.

6:10—and all of a sudden the already crowded apartment became claustrophobic, with the advent of two members of the homicide division of the local constabulary, several scene-of-crime officers, laden with apparatus, and the medical examiner for Dade County.

One of the homicide detectives, Lieutenant Jerry Evans, cleared a bedroom of occupants, then invited Candace and Rita into it for a talk. He asked Candace if she had any idea who might have committed the murder, and she replied that her husband—a ruthless, at times vicious businessman—must have made many enemies, adding that a used-car dealer in Miami, whom she named, had a severe grievance against him. She went on to say that she believed that the apartment had been ransacked. When asked if she had any grounds for the belief, she pointed at two unzipped hold-alls in a closet in the bedroom; also she said that her husband's wallet was empty of cash, that some of her jewellery was missing, and that two hundred-dollar bills that she had left in the bathroom were gone.

Enquiring about the jaunt to Miami, Lieutenant Evans mentioned that he had had a few words with Peggy Fletcher. She had told him, he said, that when she had left the building at 1:30, intending to buy cigarettes, she had seen the four Mossler children sitting in a red Pontiac—but not their mother.

Rita explained that Candace had just popped back to the apartment to pick up something that she had forgotten. Evans asked Candace to amplify her daughter's recollection but received what he later called a "noncommittal answer."

Evans, who seems to have been a most unassertive detective, requested Candace's presence at the sheriff's office later that morning. She arrived on time, chaperoned by a lawyer, and made a brief formal statement in which, perhaps unintentionally, she added a possible motive for the murder to those which she had earlier supported or suggested. The new possibility (which would, never mind its lack of corroboration, entrance the legal defenders of Candace and Melvin) was that Jacques Mossler, having turned to homosexuality, had been slain by one of his own male lovers whom he had slighted, disappointed, or something of that frenzy-encouraging sort, or by the lover of one of them, wanting to eradicate competition. Evans paraphrased the relevant part of Candace's statement as follows: "She told me that she felt her husband had boyfriends. She said he had received calls from Texas from a male voice that had feminine tones."

As Candace and her lawyer were leaving, Evans asked her for details of the jewellery that she had told him was missing from the apartment, and she promised to send him a list. During the two following days, he telephoned Candace nine times and Rita five, invariably pleading for the list, but never did get it. After Candace's departure from the sheriff's office, he had no direct contact with her. Until the trial, his only glimpse of her was over the heads of reporters and cameramen outside the premises of an undertaker who had arranged for her husband's body to be shipped to Washington, D.C., for burial in the Arlington National Cemetery.

By then, other officers of the law—some far-flung from Florida—were getting quite excited over what one of them was audacious enough to describe as "evidential developments of an incremental nature that are confidently expected to nail the Mossler malefactor—singular or plural."

⌒

The knife that was used to inflict thirty-nine wounds in Jacques Mossler's body was never identified. The blunt instrument that was used to bludgeon him may have been either an empty soft-drink bottle, found in the kitchen by a scene-of-crime officer, or a heavy glass swan, one of a pair in the apartment, that was lying in pieces on the living-room carpet, the head and neck of it so close to the body that what would otherwise have been a puddle of blood was turned into two serpentine streams.

Of all the surfaces in the apartment that were examined for fingerprints, the most immaculate was a Formica-covered counter that abutted the kitchen sink. It had been scrubbed by Roscoe Brown, a black servant of Mossler's, during the afternoon preceding the murder. The scene-of-crime officers found only one blemish on it: the print of the palm of a hand. In every particular, the print matched that of the palm of one of Melvin Lane Powers's hands.

The search for the white Chevrolet seen by Irene Durr and Martin Tavel took investigators to the Miami offices of the Allen Parker Company, the agency used by Mossler for his credit-financing activities in southern Florida. There they learned that on 23 June, a week before the crime, Candace had asked to borrow any one of the cars repossessed by the company from clients who had fallen far behind with repayments. A four-year-old white Chevrolet having been picked out, it was, at her request, delivered to her at the Miami International Airport. The deliverer—who also handed over $125 that she had asked the company manager for—was the already mentioned Roscoe Brown. He had been employed by Jacques Mossler for seventeen years and was so grateful for the employment that he had had his son christened Roscoe Mossler Brown. Candace gave him a lift back to within a block of the Parker offices then went on to some unknown destination with her other passenger, who had been waiting with her at the airport. Roscoe was loathe to identify that person to the police but eventually succumbed to their blandishments and said that it was Melvin Lane Powers.

The Parker Company's records showed that the borrowed car had not been returned. Rather than ask Candace if she knew where it was, the investigators at once circulated a description of it among their own and neighbouring organisations. It was soon noticed, parked a yard or so away from the police station at the airport. The doors were unlocked. The keys were resting on a sun visor. And so was a parking slip, dispensed by a machine at the entrance to the lot: the slip had been stamped at 5:19 on the morning of 30 June—about three and a half hours after someone had driven if not this car, then one very much like it, away from the Governor's Lodge on Key Biscayne. The car was towed to a garage and there examined—presumably for transferred bloodstains as well as for fingerprints. None of the former was found, but there was an extravagance of the latter, including nineteen belonging to Melvin Lane Powers.

The police amassed documentary and eyewitness evidence that Powers had flown from Houston to Miami (a distance of almost a thousand miles, east-southeast) on the afternoon of Monday, 29 June, arriving shortly before six o'clock. Similarly, that he had made the return trip the following day, leaving Miami after nine o'clock in the morning.

Information regarding Powers's whereabouts during the hours between his arrival from Houston and the murder was fragmentary. It seems that the only persons who subsequently recalled seeing him were Badar Shehan and Marshall Klein, respectively a bartender in and the manager of the Stuft Shirt Lounge of the Holiday Inn at the Miami end of the Rickenbacker Causeway. According to Shehan, he served Powers with a drink between half past six and seven on the Monday evening; Powers asked for and was provided with an empty soft-drink bottle but did not take it with him when he left. According to Klein, Powers returned a few minutes later, saying that he had forgotten to take the empty bottle, was given it or another, and walked out. According to Shehan, Powers reappeared just before the closing time of one o'clock, ordered and paid for a double Scotch, quickly downed it, and left.

Paul Peter O'Neill, Powers's only full-time employee at his recreational vehicles sales establishment near Houston, said that when Powers left for the airport on the 29th, he was wearing dark clothes but that when he returned next day he was wearing clothes of a light colour, the trousers so inadequate to his inseam measurement that they barely overlapped his socks. (Months after the murder, a dark jacket and pair of trousers, both stained with blood, were found by police in the Mosslers' Houston house; an eyewitness to Powers's presence at Miami airport on the morning of the 30th was shown the garments and stated, apparently without hesitation, that they were those he had seen Powers wearing.)

Several persons swore that, during the period between Powers's eviction and firing by Jacques Mossler and the latter's sudden death, they had, each apart from the others, had conversations with Powers or with his aunt, or with both, in the course of which they had been sounded as to whether, if the price was right, they would commit a contract killing; and one of those persons, Billy Frank Mulvey, went so far as to say that Candace had given him an advance payment toward a fee agreed between them for his murder of her husband, but that he had simply grabbed the money and run.

Not all of the above-outlined evidence had been garnered by the police by 3 July. But by that date they believed they had sufficient evidence to justify their arrest of Melvin Lane Powers.

His aunt heard of his detention within hours of its beginning—as soon as she disembarked at Houston airport from the airplane that had brought her from Washington, D.C., where she had been chief mourner at a funeral. The news was screamed at her—obliquely, in the form of personal questions—by a foregathered pack of reporters. Ignoring the impertinence, she trotted to a limousine and was sped to her home. There, she straightway made her best efforts to ensure Melvin's protection. It may have crossed her mind that by protecting him, she was also protecting herself.

The suspicion that that was so would inspire an anonymous versifier to compose a couplet:

> Candy is dandy;
> But, for mercy, yells: "Percy!"

The surname of the Percy to whom Candace yelled was Foreman. He was a Texan defence lawyer, skilled at, among other things, recognising intelligent prospective jurors, ensuring that few of them served, and concentrating the minds of those he allowed into the jury box on irrelevancies and side issues. That he didn't give a cuss for justice seems to be indicated by this statement: "You should never allow the defendant to be tried. Try someone else—the husband, the lover, the police, or, if the case has social implications, society generally. But never the defendant." And that he believed that he was worth every penny of his fees, which were among the highest in the land, is shown by his comment: "It's not that I'm vain, proud, or egotistical. I just don't have anything to be modest about."

His asking price for looking after Melvin was $200,000. Candace guaranteed part of that amount by handing over to Foreman the choicest items in her recently depleted collection of jewellery and signing a document saying that he could sell all of them if his bill was not met within a week. Then she up and went to Rochester, Minnesota, where, having booked sessions with a specialist on migraines at the Mayo Clinic, she rented two apartments, one for herself, the other in which her children could squeal to their hearts' content without exacerbating pains in her head.

Foreman's first action toward earning his fee was to apprise press and television news editors that, once their representatives were outside the jail in which his client was incarcerated, he would be there too, blustering newsworthily. Having performed, he threatened the jailers with all sorts of dire consequences if they were foolish enough to argue against his interpretation of his and Melvin's rights, and then he spoke privately with Melvin, saliently for the purpose of ordering him not to say anything to anyone unless he, Foreman, had rehearsed him in an utterance and told him when to utter it.

For almost a year, Foreman resisted efforts by the Floridian authorities to have Powers extradited from Houston to Miami. Meanwhile, the police strengthened their case against both Powers and Candace—and she, acting on her own initiative or in response to suggestions from paid advisers, sought to diminish the police case and to lend apparent substance to her assertion that her late husband was homosexual.

Hearing that Roscoe Brown had made an additional statement—to the effect that the white Chevrolet she had borrowed had been in the parking lot at the Governor's Lodge in the afternoon prior to the murder—she wrote to the faithful retainer, asking him to telephone her, reversing the charge. Roscoe obeyed. He had two long conversations with Candace, during which she did her utmost to persuade him to retract his statements. Every word of the conversations was tape-recorded by the police.

She actually did persuade a man named William Measamer, who worked at the Houston branch of the Allen Parker Company, to swear that Jacques Mossler was homosexual. Soon afterward, however, Measamer suddenly suffered a severe attack of cold feet, probably a side effect of a district attorney's dissertation to him on the penalties for perjury, and declared on his oath that, so far as he knew, Mossler was as heterosexual as the day was long, and that he would never have said otherwise had not Candace, generous to him to a fault, pleaded with him to do so on a number of occasions, most urgently when they were in bed together in her apartment in Rochester.

On 20 July 1965, in Miami, a grand jury returned an indictment of murder in the first degree against Melvin Lane Powers and Candace Mossler. Melvin had recently settled in at a local jail. Candace, having surrendered voluntarily, was escorted to another. Percy Foreman, retained by her to represent Melvin, conferred with lawyers she had retained for herself, and it was agreed that though he and they should give the appearance of being separate forces, they would regard him as the chief defence lawyer. The Foreman Alliance soon scored a spectacular success by getting the prisoners released on bail of $50,000 each.

On 17 January 1966, the trial proceedings at last began. It took the lawyers until the last day of that month to gather twelve jurors and three reserves. The forensic farce was made more farcical by the judge's decision that, as neither defendant was in custody, it would be unfair on the jurors if he were to stick to the convention that jurors in such a case should be kept to themselves, night and day, for the duration of the trial; his admonition to them that, while their time was their own, they were not to read press accounts of the case, listen to radio broadcasts about it, or watch items on it in televised news programmes, seems to have passed unheeded, going by the fact that on the morning after a newspaper report referred to their general lack of sartorial elegance, each and every one of them turned up in his Sunday best.

The trial, which rambled on until Sunday, 6 March, brought disgrace upon the American legal profession. But, perhaps because so many members of that profession had already brought disgrace upon it, no one expressed much concern. Throughout the trial, lawyers on both sides, prosecution and defence, knowingly broke the most elementary rules: every few minutes, a lawyer said something that he knew perfectly well he had no right to say, an opponent objected, and the judge ordered the offending words stricken from the record—adding, ridiculously, that the jury was to ignore them. Perhaps the most blatant instance of a "professional foul" was when Percy Foreman, wanting to discredit a prosecution witness, spoke loudly to himself, wondering whether or not the judge would allow him to introduce evidence pertaining to the witness's criminal record. (Having used the sporting term "professional foul," let me suggest to Americans who feel that the Law should have something to do with Justice that they might campaign for judges to be given one of the powers of English football referees: a forensic equivalent of a yellow card would be shown to a persistent offender, who if he fouled thereafter, would be shown a red card, indicating a set period of debarment from advocacy, starting as soon as the current trial was over.)

The prosecution lawyers seem to have been so intent on thinking up ways in which they themselves could cheat and on listening for objectionable remarks from the defenders that they quite failed to notice any of the umpteen illogicalities that Foreman & Company fed to the jury. The most glaring of these concerned the solitary palm print, undoubtedly Melvin's, found on the sink-side counter in the kitchen of the apartment at the Governor's Lodge. Ignoring the fact that the print showed—unequivocally, if Roscoe Brown's evidence as to his charring was accepted—that Melvin was in the apartment within hours of its becoming the scene of a crime, Foreman contended that since some of the prints found on comparatively grubby surfaces in the apartment had not been identified, one or several of them might have been deposited by the "true culprit": ergo, Melvin's (timed) print was no more suspicious than any of the unattributed ones.

Needless to say, neither defendant ventured to the witness stand.

The jury took sixteen and a half hours, spread over two and a half days, to agree on the verdicts; they spent the nights at a hotel where one of them normally worked as a bellhop.

The judge, whose name was Schulz, seemed to be surprised by what he read on the verdict-recording slips passed to him, via a bailiff, by the foreman of the jury. He told the clerk of the court to read the verdicts aloud. Melvin uttered one word—"Beautiful"—when he heard that he had been found not guilty. And Candace, knowing that her nephew's acquittal meant that she was free as well, started sobbing with relief before the clerk read from the other slip.

∽

Some months after the trial, Candace and Melvin announced that they were engaged to be married. Nothing came of it, however. Early in 1969, Candace took Melvin to court, accusing him of having beaten her up after ordering her to "stay home where I belonged." She subsequently married a tall Texan.

She and Melvin stuck together in one respect. They fought a long-running battle with Percy Foreman over his bill, saying that the collateral that each of them had put up (jewellery from her, a land deed from him) had not only been misappropriated but, what with inflation, had grown in value, putting the lawyer in their debt. Foreman countered: "Mrs. Mossler would not have inherited one penny had she not been acquitted. I was charged with the ultimate responsibility of seeing that both clients were successfully defended against the murder charges. Lawyers often work on a fifty-fifty contingency-fee basis. Therefore, I feel I have a 50-50 percent interest in whatever amount Mrs. Mossler profited by the acquittal. I will settle for any reasonable amount between 4.5 million dollars and 16.5 million dollars." Later, he said that he hoped that the argument would be aired in court: "As an outcome of such a trial and evaluation of my services, the public might have a better opinion than it now has as to who killed Jacques Mossler." How the argument was resolved, if it ever was, doesn't appear to have been reported.

I think that Candace should have the last word. When a journalist vulgarly reminded her of some of the terrible things that had been said about her, and asked if she wished to comment, her reply was, "Well, sir, nobody's perfect."

The Death of the Devil's Disciple

The Death of the Devil's Disciple

*D*ue to circumstances beyond anyone's control, the ruthless theatrical tradition that the show must go on was broken on 16 December 1897 at the Adelphi Theatre, London, where William Terriss, the most idolized of matinee idols, was starring as Captain Thorne, alias Lewis Dumont, in an American melodrama called *Secret Service*.[1]

The play was utter hokum (Bernard Shaw, reviewing the first production, had pointed to any number of incredible plot contrivances, noting in particular that "before half an hour has elapsed the heroine quite forgets . . . an act of fratricide on the part of the hero"); but still, the show was as great a hit as any of William Terriss's earlier ones at the Adelphi—a theatre that, though owned by the Italian restaurateurs, the Gatti brothers, had become known over the past several years as "Terriss's domain."

Terriss, whose real name was William Charles James Lewin, was born at St. John's Wood, North London, in 1847. His father, a barrister, claimed kindredship with the Earl of Zetland; his mother was

---

1. By the actor William Gillette. The play was first presented in London by an American cast headed by Gillette, and including Ethel Barrymore in a small role, on 15 May 1897; the production ran for three months. The revival starring William Terriss opened at the Adelphi on 24 November. Gillette is best remembered as the author (with help by W. G. Postance) of the play *Sherlock Holmes,* mainly derived from Conan Doyle's tales "A Scandal in Bohemia" and "The Final Problem." He himself played the Master Detective in the original production, which opened at the Garrick Theatre, New York, on 6 November 1899, and in the first London production, at the Lyceum from 9 September 1901. While the play was still at the Lyceum, four companies were formed to take it around the provinces; the twelve-year-old Charles Chaplin played the part of Billy on one of the tours. Gillette continued to play Holmes—on stage, in a silent film, and on radio—until 1935, two years before his death. Conan Doyle commented in his autobiography: "I was charmed both with the play, the acting and the pecuniary result." *Sherlock Holmes* was successfully revived by the Royal Shakespeare Company at the Aldwych Theatre, London, on New Year's Day, 1974, with John Wood as Holmes and Philip Locke as Professor Moriarty.

a niece of George Grote—so noted an historian of Greece that his remains were buried in Westminster Abbey and a bust of him placed in a proximate niche. At the age of seven, Terriss became a Bluecoat boy at Christ's Hospital; three or four years later, he moved to another school, then to another. He was already stagestruck; but, his parents refusing to countenance the idea of any son of theirs being a vulgar thespian, his first job was as a midshipman in the Royal Navy. While he was on leave in March 1865, an elderly aunt took him, wearing his uniform, to the Somerset seaside town of Weston-super-Mare.[2] The visit had to be cut short because he was mistaken for Victoria and Albert's second son, Prince Arthur, Duke of Edinburgh, who was a lieutenant in the navy and attracted cheering and national-anthem-singing crowds wherever he went; according to a report in the *Bristol Times and Mirror,* the vicarious prince's smiling acceptance of the rowdy homage during his walkabouts greatly increased royalism in Weston. When William's aunt decided that they must leave and ordered a cab to take them to the railway station, the vehicle that eventually arrived was a beribboned carriage and pair, guided by postillions.

Receiving a small bequest on his eighteenth birthday, Terriss left the Royal Navy and took passage on a merchant vessel bound for Bengal, in northeastern India, where he meant to become a tea planter. Owing to a shipwreck, the journey took longer than he had expected; once there, he soon grew bored with planting tea at Chittagong, and so, after dabbling in the wine and tobacco trades in Calcutta, he returned to England within a few months of his departure. He tried banking, then went abroad again, this time to Louisiana, where he worked on a cotton plantation—briefly, because almost as soon as he arrived there, he decided that he had to be an actor. In New Orleans, he joined the crew of a cargo ship that was collecting bales of cotton from Southern ports before sailing for Liverpool. He afterward recalled that while scrubbing the deck, he dreamed of treading the boards.

In the summer of 1867 (he was now twenty), he found cheap digs in London and set about earning his living on the stage. Easier said than done. The theatrical profession was almost as overcrowded then as it is today; and there was no Actors' Equity Association to set minimum rates of pay. Terriss's first stage appearances—fleeting ones—were dur-

2. If you persevere, you will come across this place later in this collection, as the setting for a dreadful coincidence.

ing a season of plays starring Madame Celeste at the Prince of Wales Theatre, Birmingham; he was paid eighteen shillings a week. Toward the end of 1868, he played a minor role in a London revival of T. W. Robertson's comedy *Society*. After two years—two years in which he was more often "resting" than working, and in which the parts he did get were of the cough-and-a-spit variety—he came to the conclusion that an actor's life was not for him. However, he had one thing to be happy about: he had fallen in love with an actress named Amy Fellowes, and she had agreed to marry him—even though he had told her that he intended to emigrate to the Falkland Islands.

The young couple's honeymoon, if one can call it that, was spent on board a small ship travelling the 8,000 miles to the South Atlantic. Arriving at Port Stanley, they took a room at the Ship Hotel, and Terriss at once began working from dawn until dusk as a sheep breeder and tamer of wild horses. About a year later, in April 1871, Amy gave birth to a daughter, named Ellaline. The child was only a couple of months old when her parents decided to return to England. The reason for the decision is not clear: it may be that William and Amy had simply grown tired of eking out a meagre existence in the bleak Falklands . . . or perhaps William's yearning for a stage career had become strong again, to the extent that, when recalling his first attempt, the many periods of despair were misted in his memory, while the few good times were dazzlingly limelit.

In any event, on the very first day he got back to London, he bought a copy of a theatrical newspaper, scanned the audition advertisements and the reports of shows that were being cast, and then started a tour of producers' offices. A short tour, as it turned out. After making only a few calls, he found himself in the right place at the right time. A producer seeking a young (and inexpensive) actor took one look at Terriss and was so impressed by his handsome face and fine physique—both attributes enhanced by the stay in the Falklands—that he engaged him on the spot for a show that was just going into rehearsal. When the play opened, Terriss received excellent notices; talent-spotters for other producers admired his gusto and charm: his name spread through the theatrical grapevine.

Before the end of the run, he had offers of parts in forthcoming productions. He was able to pick and choose. And, with advice from Amy, he chose well, resisting the temptation to accept the highest-paid job and instead taking a part that truly suited him. So it went on. In a remarkably short time—a matter of a year or so, for in those days any production that notched up more than a couple of hundred performances was reckoned to have had a long run—William Terriss was being talked of as a rising star. Subsequently, a reporter for the stage weekly, *The Era,* noted:

> During an extended engagement at the Strand Theatre[3] in 1873–4, Mr Terriss played Doricourt, in *The Belle's Strategem,*[4] 250 times, winning golden opinions. He was then in the Drury Lane production of *Richard Coeur De Lion,*[5] playing Sir Kenneth. On the withdrawal of this play, Mr Terriss appeared as Romeo to the Juliet of Miss Wallis, and when in September, 1875, *The Shaughraun* was produced, Mr Terriss was the Molyneux, both Dion[6] and Mrs Boucicault appearing in the production. Mr Terriss's Molyneux suggested to the late Henry S. Leigh a charming set of verses, in which a pretty miss from the country, seeing Molyneux from her seat in the pit, is moved to a pretty confession of love for the handsome officer and jealousy of fortunate Claire. *The Shaughraun* was transferred to the Adelphi, and with it Mr Terriss. Here, and at the Princess's, he appeared in several revivals.

Terriss's really big chance came in March 1878, when he played opposite Ellen Terry, the most distinguished member of the famous theatrical family that was subsequently represented in the person of John Gielgud (Ellen Terry's great-nephew).

Terry . . . Terriss. The similarity between the names must have caused confusion to some readers of the playbill. More to the point of this story, the similarity would create a motive for murder.

The play, presented by the actor-manager John Hare, was *Olivia,* an adaptation of Goldsmith's *The Vicar of Wakefield* by W. G. Wills (who was an extraordinarily industrious turner of novels into plays; a few years before, Terriss had played Julian Peveril in a short-lived Drury

---

3. Renamed the Novello in December 2005. The composer and matinee idol Ivor Novello occupied the apartment above the theatre for many years, until his death in 1951.

4. The Restoration-style comedy by Hannah Cowley, first produced in 1780 at Covent Garden.

5. Adapted by James Burgoyne from a French romance; first produced in 1786 at Drury Lane.

6. Not to be confused with his same-named and even more successful son.

Lane production of Wills's version of Scott's *Peveril of the Peak*). In *The Story of My Life* (published in 1908), Ellen Terry remembered:

> Like all Hare's plays, *Olivia* was perfectly cast. Where all were good, it will be admitted, I think, by everyone who saw the production, that Terriss was the best. "As you stand there, whipping your boot, you look the very picture of vain indifference," Olivia says to Squire Thornhill in the first act, and never did I say it without thinking how absolutely *to the life* Terriss realized that description!
>
> As I look back, I remember no figure in the theatre more remarkable than Terriss. He was one of those heaven-born actors who, like kings by divine right, can, up to a certain point, do no wrong. Very often, like Dr Johnson's "inspired idiot," Mrs Pritchard, he did not know what he was talking about. Yet he "got there," while many cleverer men stayed behind. He had unbounded impudence, yet so much charm that no one could ever be angry with him. Sometimes he reminded me of a butcher-boy flashing past, whistling, on the high seat of his cart, or of Phaethon driving the chariot of the sun—pretty much the same thing, I imagine! When he was "dressed up," Terriss was spoiled by fine feathers; when he was in rough clothes, he looked like a prince. He always commanded the love of his intimates as well as that of the outside public. To the end he was "sailor Bill"—a sort of grown-up midshipmite, whose weaknesses provoked no more condemnation than the weaknesses of a child. . . .
>
> Terriss had had every sort of adventure by land and sea before I acted with him at the Court Theatre. . . . He had, to use his own words, "hobnobbed with every kind of queer folk, and found himself in extremely queer predicaments." The adventurous, dare-devil spirit of the roamer, the incarnate gipsy, always looked out of his insolent eyes. Yet, audacious as he seemed, no man was ever more nervous on the stage. On a first night he was shaking all over with fright, in spite of his confident and dashing appearance. . . .
>
> When he had presents from the front, which happened every night, he gave them at once to the call-boy or the gas-man. To the women-folk, especially the plainer ones, he was always delightful. Never was any man more adored by the theatre staff.

And children, my own Edy included, were simply *daft* about him. A little American girl, daughter of William Winter, the famous critic, when staying with me in England, announced gravely when we were out driving:

"I've gone a mash on Terriss."

There was much laughter. When it had subsided, the child said gravely:

"Oh, you can laugh, but it's true. I wish I was hammered to him!"

. . . His conversation was extremely entertaining—and, let me add, ingenuous. One of his favourite reflections was:

"Tempus fugit! So make the most of it. While you're alive, gather roses; for when you're dead, you're dead a d—d long time."

Soon after Ellen Terry's first appearance with Terriss, she became the leading lady of Henry Irving's company at the Lyceum. Terriss accepted an engagement at the Haymarket, where he played a number of leading roles, including that of Captain Absolute in *The Rivals,* and then, in the winter of 1879, rejoined John Hare for a season at the St. James's.

In 1880, seemingly at Ellen Terry's insistence, Henry Irving invited Terriss to join the Lyceum company to play the villain, Château-Renaud, in a revival of *The Corsican Brothers* (adapted from the French by Dion Boucicault). Terriss stayed with the company for five years, appearing most notably as Cassio in the production of *Othello* (May 1881) in which Irving and the American actor Edwin Booth (an elder brother of John Wilkes Booth, assassinator of Lincoln) alternated as Othello and Iago; as Mercutio to Irving's Romeo and Ellen Terry's Juliet (most critics felt that the production would have been improved if Irving and Terriss had swapped roles; a play-going politician commented. "As Romeo, Irving reminds me of a pig who has been taught to play the fiddle. He does it cleverly, but he would be better employed in squealing. He cannot shine in the part like the fiddler. Terriss in this case is the fiddler"); as Don Pedro in the production of *Much Ado About Nothing* which the dramatist Arthur Wing Pinero considered "as perfect a representation of a Shakespearian play as is possible" (the production ran for 212 performances and would have continued but for the fact that arrangements had been made for the company, including Terriss, to tour America, starting in the autumn of 1883).

In her autobiography, Ellen Terry cited Terriss's performance as Don Pedro to support her conviction that, when playing Shakespeare, "he often did not know what he was talking about":

One morning [during rehearsals] we went over and over one scene in "Much Ado"—at least a dozen times, I should think—and each time when Terriss came to the speech beginning: "What needs the bridge much broader than the flood," he managed to give a different emphasis. First it would be:
"What! Needs the bridge much broader than the flood." Then:
"What needs the bridge much broader than the flood."
After he had been floundering about for some time, Henry said:
"Terriss, what's the meaning of that?"
"Oh, get along, Guv'nor, you know!"
Henry laughed. He never could be angry with Terriss, not even when he came to rehearsal full of absurd excuses. One day, however, he was so late that it was past a joke, and Henry spoke to him sharply.
"I think you'll be sorry you've spoken to me like this, Guv'nor," said Terriss, casting down his eyes.
"Now, no hanky-panky tricks, Terriss."
"Tricks, Guv'nor! I think you'll regret having said that when you hear that my poor mother passed away early this morning."
And Terriss wept.
Henry promptly gave him the day off. A few weeks later, when Terriss and I were looking through the curtain at the audience just before the play began, he said to me gaily:
"See that dear old woman sitting in the fourth row of the stalls—that's my dear old mother."
The wretch had quite forgotten that he had killed her!
He was the only person who ever ventured to "cheek" Henry, yet he never gave offence, not even when he wrote a letter of this kind:

ᔕ

"My Dear Guv.,
"I hope you are enjoying yourself, and in the best of health. I very much want to play "Othello" with you next year (don't

laugh). Shall I study it up, and will you do it with me on tour if possible? Say yes, and lighten the drooping heart of yours sincerely,

"WILL TERRISS."

I have never seen anyone at all like Terriss. . . . One night he came into the theatre soaked from head to foot.

"Is it raining, Terriss?" said someone who noticed that he was wet.

"Looks like it, doesn't it?" said Terriss carelessly.

Later it came out that he had jumped off a penny steamboat into the Thames and saved a little girl's life. It was pretty brave, I think.[7]

Terriss left the Lyceum at Christmas 1885; the company gave him a silver loving cup, but he treasured more the gift of a gold-mounted riding whip from the stagehands. During the following three years, he starred in a string of melodramas at the Adelphi Theatre in the Strand, just round the corner from the Lyceum: *The Harbour Lights, The Bells of Haslemere, The Union Jack,* and—lastly, opening on 29 December 1888—*The Silver Falls.* In most of these productions, the female lead was played by the strikingly beautiful actress Miss [Jessie] Millward, whom Terriss had enticed from Irving. Naturally, and perhaps with some foundation, there was tittle-tattle that the stage love-scenes between Terriss and Miss Millward were instances of art imitating nature; tongues continued to wag, and the tongue-waggers tended to be more reckless with rumour when, for some eight months from the autumn of 1889, the couple toured America, most often playing the Haymarket success *A Man's Shadow* (which for some reason was billed as *Roger La Honte* in the States).

7. Terriss was less modest about another brave deed, going in person to the Royal Humane Society's office, which was then in Trafalgar Square, to report it. In the early evening of 6 August 1885, he and a companion were sailing off South Foreland, near the town of Deal, in Kent, when one of three boys who were swimming nearby developed a cramp. Terriss lowered his lugsail, jumped overboard fully clothed, and kept the boy afloat until the other yachtsman had thrown a line and hauled him to safety. The Royal Humane Society decided that Terriss's act merited the award of a Bronze Medal. Having recovered his modesty, he was absent from the Lyceum on 29 September, when a representative of the Society called to present him with the medal, and so it was accepted on his behalf by Henry Irving.

After his first American tour, with Irving and Ellen Terry, Terriss had been instrumental in arranging for Augustin Daly's company to visit England. As soon as he returned from the second tour, he went into partnership with Sir Augustus Harris to present an American drama called *Paul Kauvar* at Dairy Lane; without his presence in the cast, the production was a costly failure (as was another American play, *The Great Metropolis*, which he, having helped in its anglicization, put on at the Princess's two years later). Straightway, he rejoined the Lyceum company and remained with it for some two years, playing Hayston of Bucklaw in *Ravenswood*, Herman Merivale's adaptation of Scott's *The Bride of Lammermoor*, the respective Kings in *Henry VIII* and *Becket*,[8] and the eponymous hero of W. G. Wills's adaptation of Goethe's *Faust*.

In the summer of 1894, Terriss accepted the Gatti brothers' invitation to star in melodramas of his choosing at the Adelphi. The project was successful from the start (that being on 6 September, with a production of *The Fatal Card*); the House Full board was more often on display before the curtain went up than was the Standing Room Only one for shows like *The Girl I Left Behind Me* (almost as great a hit in the West End as it had been, natively, in New York), *The Swordsman's Daughter* (by Clement Scott, the Ibsen-loathing drama critic of the *Daily Telegraph*, and Brandon Thomas, whose *Charley's Aunt* had first appeared in London in 1892), and *One of the Best* (which Shaw reviewed under the heading of "One of the Worst"; it was written by George Edwardes, manager of the Gaiety Theatre, at the eastern end of the Strand, and the young comedy-actor Seymour Hicks, husband of Terriss's daughter Ellaline, who had begun her own stage career in 1888, when she was sixteen). Terriss, always the hero, rescued distressed damsels (usually depicted by Jessie Millward), foiled dastardly villains, and declaimed yard-long speeches about chivalry, honour, and suchlike.

He became known to the public by several affectionate sobriquets: "Sailor Bill" was one, "Breezy Bill" another. People who had never met him felt that they knew him well; they would wave to him in the street—and he would wave back. There was nothing false about his affability. He had a wide circle of friends, not just stage people, and on Sundays he and Amy often gave parties at their house—far grander

8. Lord Tennyson's play, arranged for the stage by Irving—who died after playing the title role at Bradford, Yorkshire, on 13 October 1905. (Ten years before, he had become the first actor-knight.)

than its name, "The Cottage," suggested—in Bedford Road, Turnham Green, on the western hem of London. Years later, a journalist who presumably had visited The Cottage wrote,

> Some of Mr Terriss's happiest hours were spent at his pretty house. The home life of the hero of so many melodramas was a model of comfort and good taste. Ferns and flowers, music and art, pleasant society, long rides upon a favourite mare, lawn tennis and quoits, much smoking and more reading went to make up the daily round from year's end to year's end. Picture-books, curios in every corner of the house, evidenced the artistic feeling of its tenant. Mr Terriss . . . welcomed his pleasant and quiet life in Turnham Green after the artificial surroundings of the stage, the more so, perhaps, that his earlier years were full of stir and vicissitude.

Terriss, as well as owning The Cottage, leased an apartment in Princes Street, off Hanover Square. On weekdays, if he was not rehearsing or playing, he could usually be found either at the apartment or at the Green Room Club in Bedford Street, close to the Adelphi Theatre. Perhaps because he didn't relish travelling the seven or so miles to Turnham Green after evening performances, which rarely ended much before eleven o'clock, he often slept at the apartment; gossip that he sometimes shared his bed with Jessie Millward seems to have started off as a guess from the fact that she also had an apartment in Princes Street, and it flourished without the aid of evidence.

Either because he was innately kind or because of memories of his own adversities when he had started in the theatre, he was very generous toward members of his profession who were down on their luck. As well as donating to and appearing in charity matinees for the Actors' Benevolent Fund, the offices of which were in Adam Street, diagonally across the Strand from the Adelphi Theatre, he always listened sympathetically to hard-luck stories from actors with whom he had worked, and almost always gave them money.

One recipient of Terriss's handouts was a man called Richard Archer Prince, a native of Dundee who had acquired the nickname— never used to his face, of course—of "Mad Archer." He was short of stature, and his most conspicuous facial distinctions were a heavy black moustache with waxed tips, and a squinting left eye. The squint doesn't seem to have diminished his belief that he was exquisitely good-looking, for he frequently bragged, "I am a member of the handsomest family in Scotland."

His stage appearances hardly entitled him to call the stage his career: subordinate roles in touring productions—from which he was often sacked for hamming or quite forgetting his one or two speeches—and nonspeaking or one-line parts in London shows, so particularly at the Adelphi that he had calling cards printed:

> Mr Richard Archer Prince
> Adelphi Theatre, Strand, London.

Since he sometimes used other names, and was sometimes denied acknowledgment in the programmes of shows in which he did little more than "dress the set," it would not be possible, even if considered worthwhile, to make up a full catalogue of his slight contributions to productions in the West End. So far as the Adelphi is concerned, it seems that he first worked there in October 1880 (when he was twenty-two, just down from Dundee), playing the taciturn role of Sligo Dan in *The O'Dowd,* which was written by, and on this occasion starred, Dion Boucicault. Five months later, he was the First Traveller in *Michael Strogoff,* a drama adapted from the French by H. J. Byron,[9] and in the autumn of that same year, 1881, he was the Groom in a revival of Charles Reade's *It's Never Too Late to Mend.* From October 1883—for more than a year, if he did not leave or was not replaced before the end of the extremely successful run—he was O'Flanigan in the large cast of *In the Ranks* by the prolific collaborators George R. Sims and Henry Pettitt. Prince's ever-tenuous association with the Adelphi continued during William Terriss's first spell at the theatre, starting in December 1885; he was a supernumerary in a couple of the early productions and had a little to say as Diego, one of half a dozen Miners, in the final play, *The Silver Falls,* which was also by Sims and Pettitt. It is likely that he played some small role in the penultimate production, *The Union Jack* by Pettitt and Sydney Grundy—though not that of Tim O'Grady, the minor character he portrayed when the patriotic drama was taken on tour in 1889, at about the time that Terriss and Jessie Millward were embarking for America.

9. Author of many stage offerings, the most lastingly influential being a burlesque, performed in the 1860s, from which the pantomime *Aladdin* is derived.

If Prince got any work at the Adelphi in the years between the closure of *The Silver Falls* and Terriss's return, his contribution was not
such as to warrant being mentioned in a programme. There seems no
doubt that he augmented crowds in at least two productions during
Terriss's second spell at the theatre, but which productions these were
is a matter for conjecture.

The longer "Mad Archer" remained a failure as an actor, the more
certain he became that he was God's gift to the stage. So as to keep
his egotism intact, he *had* to assume that his signal lack of success was
due to a conspiracy among the male stars: they feared that, if he were
given the chance, he would outshine them. It was obvious, wasn't
it?—well, *wasn't* it?—that the stars had noted, and been frightened by,
the fact that though he had never been allowed to declaim anything
more dramatic than "the carriage awaits, m'lord," his ability to make
a little go a long way caused audiences to gape and to gasp at the re-
alization that they were glimpsing genius. The stars—all for one and
one for all—were determined that he should never reign as the Prince
of Players, showing up their second-rate talents.

During an engagement at the Adelphi, Prince's jealous hatred of
the stars was turned into enmity against one in particular. The crowd-
players in the communal dressing room, sick and tired of his conceited chatter, pretended to agree that he, not William Terriss, should be
playing the leading role in the play—and added that he *might* be were it
not that Terriss had informed the Gatti brothers that he would walk
out if Prince was given a speaking part. It never occurred to Prince
that he was being "sent up," and from then on he regarded Terriss as
his implacable enemy.

Actually, Terriss felt sorry for Prince. On several of the occasions
when Prince had applied to the Actors' Benevolent Fund for financial
assistance, Terriss had spoken up for him; once, when the emergency
committee had voted against providing help, he had given money to
the secretary, Charles Coltson, to pass on to Prince.

In December of 1897, the year of Queen Victoria's diamond jubilee,
both men, the matinee idol and the nonentity, were deeply disturbed.

William Terriss was worried about his daughter Ellaline, who at
the end of November, undisguisably pregnant, had needed to leave
the Gaiety, where for the past two and a half years she had been playing leading roles, usually opposite her husband Seymour Hicks, in
George Edwardes's *Girl* series of musical comedies (*The Shop Girl, My*

Girl, The Circus Girl). Following a miscarriage, she had spent a week or so in a rest home at Eastbourne; but, her condition having deterioriated to the extent that she needed to fight for breath, she had been brought back to London to be admitted to the Charing Cross Hospital. There, the doctors expressed concern that she might not recover. Wanting to be with her as often as possible, Terriss had cancelled many daytime engagements, including activities associated with the Actors' Benevolent Fund.

Prince's worries were to do with finance—or rather, his lack of it. Having been unemployed for months, he had pawned virtually all of his belongings apart from a single set of indoor clothes, a grey Inverness cloak and a black slouch hat. He was in arrears with the four-shillings-a-week rent for his bed-sitter in the home of a bus driver at 16 Ebury Court, near Victoria Station, and the only food he could afford was bread dipped in milk; the bus driver's wife had threatened to turn him out, not just because he was behind with the rent but also because his small back room was "like a pig-sty," littered with theatrical newspapers, religious tracts, and notices of services at Westminster Abbey.

Since 1890, Prince had occasionally received small sums, never more than a pound, from the Actors' Benevolent Fund, but from early in November 1897 he had become "a weekly applicant for relief." When making the first of the weekly applications, he had produced a note from William Terriss: "I know the bearer, Richard A. Prince, as a hard-working actor." Terriss's "reference" had persuaded the emergency committee to grant Prince thirty shillings, and he had at once written to Charles Coltson:

Dear Sir,

I don't know how to thank you and the gentlemen of the Committee for your great kindness. It's worth ten years of one's life to receive such favours from one in the poor position I have always had at my art. But I hope to Almighty God my luck will change in the week to pay back such kindness. Thanking you, Sir, for the way in which you have received me at the Actors' Benevolent Fund. You do it the greatest honour. If it's ever in my power, with the help of God, to do it any good, I will.

Yours very faithfully,

With thanks,

RICHARD A. PRINCE

Apart from the use of pale-violet ink, that communication was very different from one that Charles Coltson received on 4 December—a card, posted in Paddington at 12:15 A.M. that day. The sender's address began, "8 War St," but then straggled into illegibility; though the message looked as if it had been dashed off, an attempt seemed to have been made to disguise the writing. It read:

> I am coming up to town next week, and I shall wait on your coming out, and you will have to go through with it. Odd man out you will be. After next Monday shall kill you.
> Yours,
> FIND OUT

Mr. Coltson—who was addressed as "John Colman" on the card—was sure that the anonymous correspondent was Prince, who, only the day before, had made a scene in the Fund's offices after being told that his latest plea had resulted in an award of only five shillings.

Apparently, Mr. Coltson did not worry about the threat. And he did not mention it when, on Wednesday, 15 December, Prince again turned up at the Fund's offices—only to be told that, for the time being, at any rate, he was to receive no further aid. Prince, who seemed to take the decision stoically, asked who had chaired the emergency committee that day. "One of the Terrys," he was told.

If Prince heard the first three words of that reply, he ignored them. It was a name that crowded his mind: not the plural "Terrys" that had been spoken but the singular "Terriss" that he had desperately wanted to hear. Once again, he had been victimized by the idol of the Adelphi.

As it happened, a few hours later William Terriss saw Prince in the street. He stopped to speak to him, and before saying good luck and goodbye, pressed some money into his hand.

Prince spent part of the gift—one shilling and ninepence, to be exact—at a shop in Victoria Street which specialized in butchering equipment. His purchase was a filleting knife, its handle fashioned from red teakwood, its blade, of Sheffield steel, honed on both edges and dwindling to a needle-sharp point.

Thursday, 16 December 1897, was a cold but harshly bright day. The Strand was crowded with Christmas shoppers. And long before the box office opened at the Adelphi Theatre, the foyer was jam-packed with people hoping to acquire the few remaining seats for that evening's performance of one of the biggest hits in town, the American melodrama *Secret Service,* starring William Terriss and—her name less prominent than his on the playbill—Miss Millward. By half past ten or so, the House Full board was being displayed.

The ticket holders, nigh on a thousand of them, would be disappointed, for the Adelphi's scarlet-and-gold curtain would not rise that evening. A few minutes after eight o'clock, when the performance was due to start, the slit in the centre of the curtain would be opened, and the assistant manager, George Budd, resplendent in tails but grey-faced and looking as if he had been crying, would make an announcement:

"Ladies and gentlemen, I am deeply grieved and pained to inform you that because of a serious—nay, terrible—accident, it is impossible for the performance of *Secret Service* to take place. I will ask you to be good enough to pass out into the street as quietly as possible. It is hardly necessary for me to add that your money will be returned on application at the pay-box."

During the morning of that fateful Thursday, William Terriss, with his son-in-law Seymour Hicks, had visited Ellaline at the Charing Cross Hospital. By midday, he was back at his apartment in Princes Street, keeping an appointment with an old and elderly friend, a surveyor named John Graves, who was giving him advice, presumably on a business footing, concerning his intention to enlarge or replace the fern-filled conservatory attached to his house in Turnham Green. In the early afternoon, he and Graves went by hansom cab to the Green Room Club. Having lunched—Graves with gusto; Terriss, as was his custom, but lightly—they both took a nap in the library, a room with almost as many green leather armchairs as books, and then joined in a card game of nap with three other members of the club, one of whom was Herbert Waring, a rising actor whom some critics had compared to Terriss in terms of personableness and panache. Terriss was a keen gambler (Seymour Hicks subsequently recalled seeing him lose or win hundreds of pounds during an afternoon or late-night card-playing session); but this afternoon his mind was not on the game. Every so often, he would leave the table to make a telephone call to the hospital or to The Cottage.

As the brass clock chimed 7:15, he finished off his pre-performance tumbler of whisky and water, donned his tweed overcoat and brown soft hat, and left for the theatre, intending to be in his dressing-room just in time to answer the callboy's knock and shout of "half an hour" at 7:25. He was accompanied by Graves—whose name would soon, very soon, be construed as ill-omened by superstitious stage-folk.

Graves had been one of Terriss's guests at the first night of *Secret Service* and had afterward complained to his friend that some members of the audience seemed to have come along more to be seen and heard than to see and hear. Now, strolling with Terriss down Bedford Street, he said that he hoped that tonight's audience, of which he would be a complementary part, would be less participative than the first one. Terriss told Graves that, a few years before, a controversy about first-nighters had blown up in the correspondence columns of a stage paper, and he had put his spoke in, declaring that while he much preferred to be applauded, he freely admitted the right of first-nighters to hiss or otherwise indicate their displeasure. Recalling part of what he had written, he quoted it to Graves: "It is all very well to claim the indulgence due to ladies and gentlemen, but artists should remember that they are actors and actresses when they are on the boards, and if they wish to be treated as ladies and gentlemen only, they had better remain in that privacy with which the public will not interfere, and where they will be free alike from public applause and public censure." By the end of the recitation, the two men had turned left and were entering Maiden Lane; Terriss was feeling in his pocket for a silver key

Little is known of how Richard Archer Prince spent the daylight hours and then the first hours of darkness of that Thursday. Subsequently, several people, most of them actors as derelict as Prince, claimed to have observed him walking—or, to stick to their words, "lurching," "shambling," or "wandering sightlessly"—in different parts of the West End; none had spoken to him, and he had not spoken to any of them. In the morning, at about eleven o'clock, he was close to the Adelphi Theatre—on the other side of the Strand, in the offices of the Actors' Benevolent Fund, where he pleaded with Charles Coltson for his case to be reconsidered and was told to come back next day, when the emergency committee would be meeting.

By seven in the evening, he was closer still to the Adelphi: standing in a shadowed side-doorway of Rule's Restaurant in Maiden Lane, at the rear of the theatre.[10]

---

10. Still the second-oldest eating house in London; the oldest is the Cheshire Cheese, just to the east, off Fleet Street. Dr. Thomas Neill Cream—graduate of M'Gill

The Adelphi had two stage doors. Over the years since 1880, whenever Prince was working at the theatre, supernumerarily or with a couple of lines to speak, he had used the main stage door, which was in Bull Inn Court, running down the eastern side of the building from Maiden Lane to the Strand. The other door, diagonally across from Rule's, was known as the Royal Entrance—more on account of the Sovereign's crest carved in stone above it than because it had occasionally been used by subjects-eschewing regal theatregoers. There were only two keys, both cut from silver, to this door—one was retained, but rarely used, by Arthur Latham, the manager of the theatre, and the other had been presented to William Terriss by the Gatti brothers, thus allowing him to treat the Royal Entrance virtually as his alone. Who knows? . . . perhaps the fact that there were two doors—"Gentleman" and "Players"—aggravated Prince's jealous hatred of the star.

7:23 Cold from standing so long in the shadows, his hunger made painful by the sounds from the crowded restaurant—the customers' chatter, the clatter of crockery, the chinking of glasses—and by the smells wafting through the grille of the basement kitchen, Prince slipped the brand-new filleting knife from the pocket of his cloak as, to his right, William Terriss and a man he did not know turned the corner from Bedford Street into Maiden Lane.

It seems likely that Terriss, quoting from a letter that he himself had written, spoke with more resonance than was his offstage wont; that Prince heard the end of what, because of his action, now just a few seconds away, would be Terriss's final sustained speech: "free alike from public applause and public censure."

As Terriss inserted the key in the lock of the private door, Prince lurched across the lane. He plunged the knife obliquely downward into Terriss's back. Withdrew it. Struck again. Again withdrew it. If, preparing for the act, he had thought up something dramatic to exclaim—something impeccably iambic, short and to the points of explanation and exculpation—he quite forgot the line.

College, Montreal, 1876; poisoner of four Waterloo-based prostitutes, 1891–92; one of the many, too many, people blamed by Ripperologists for the Whitechapel Murders of 1888 (when, but never mind, he was in a Chicago prison, serving a life sentence for murder)—was a regular customer at Rule's until 3 June 1892, when he was arrested, eventually to be charged with the murder of the aforementioned prostitutes. And, later, Dr. Hawley Harvey Crippen patronized Rule's and became friendly with Harry Davis, who was then the manager.

The only sound from Terriss—uttered twice—was a ragged expulsion of breath: "not unlike the blowing-out of birthday candles," it seemed to John Graves, who, for the moment, felt no alarm. He "thought that the strokes were merely hearty slaps, given in friendship."

Still clutching the silver key, Terriss turned away from the door, staggered back against it. Did he have time to recognize his attacker? Probably not. As he staggered—as he cried out "My God, I have . . ."— Prince rammed the knife into his breast.

" . . . been stabbed," Terriss whispered. He fell untidily, his body jerking as he fell: a marionette whose strings were being snipped one by one. Prince kept hold of the knife—he did not let the falling body pull it from his grasp, and as Terriss collapsed on the pavement, the tarnished blade gradually slid back into sight. Carefully, as if stowing a personal prop that would be needed at further performances, Prince replaced the knife in his pocket.

Graves stared at him, saw that he was smiling, and—perhaps because inconsequential details tend to assume a sham importance in times of stress—noticed that the light filtering through the red gas-globe fixed to the wall above the door gave an auburn tint to the waxed tips of his moustache. Only afterward did it occur to Graves that it was odd that Terriss's attacker did not run away. And then, one may surmise, he also wondered at, and was quietly proud of, the courage he himself showed by gripping Prince's arm and shouting, not screaming, for help.

Among those who responded to Graves's shouts of "Murder!" of "Police!" was a member of the Corps of Commissionaires who was making his way via the back-doubles from his headquarters in the Strand to a post office near Leicester Square. He broke into a run and was the first to arrive; but rather than tendering assistance to either Terriss or Graves, he stationed himself in the middle of the lane, ready to exert his uniformed authority in keeping spectators at bay. The first of those emerged from Rule's—among them, a journalist who the following morning would thrill readers with his "eyewitness" account of the attack.

Inside the theatre, Terriss's dresser, William Algar, dashed to the window of the first-floor dressing room to see what the commotion was about. Like the journalist, he would profess to have seen the entire incident; but for the moment all he knew was that someone—it looked very much like his master—was spread-eagled on the ground, and two other men, one making all the noise, were standing close by, seemingly hand in hand. Just to be on the safe side, Algar grabbed a dress

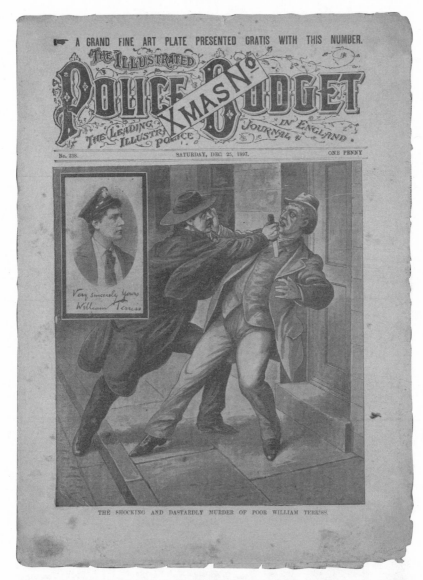

The murder of William Terriss (from *The Illustrated Police Budget*, 25 December 1897)

sword, addendum to a costume that Terriss was due to wear on stage that night, before running out of the room and down the stone steps toward the Royal Entrance. His progress was sufficiently noisy to excite the attention of other dressers, of stagehands—to bring actors and actresses, various in their preparation for the performance, from the dressing rooms. And so he was one of several men who put their

THE LATE WILLIAM TERRISS

HOUSE WHERE PRISONER LIVED

MR TERRISS'S HOME · BEDFORD PARK.

FOUL ASSASSINATION OF WILLIAM TERRISS, THE CELEBRATED ACTOR.
FROM DESCRIPTIONS BY EYE WITNESSES.

Assassination of William Terriss (from *The Illustrated Police Budget*, 25 December 1897)

shoulders or hands to the door, forcing it wide and, in so doing, pushing William Terriss toward the gutter.

It was as if the scene had been rehearsed. The people from the theatre fanned out around the fallen star. Those nearest the door shuffled aside, letting Jessie Millward come through. She was wearing a many-coloured kimono, a present from Ellen Terry. For a moment she stared down at Terriss. Then, falling beside him, she cradled his head, lifted it toward her own. She was weeping now. Her tears glistened on Terriss's cheeks. With her free hand, she loosened the knot in his tie, tried to undo his collar.

But the tableau came to an unsatisfactory end. Terriss, hardly able to breathe, muttered, "Get away . . . get away." An elderly woman—probably Mrs. Briggs, the wardrobe mistress—pulled Jessie to her feet. Some stagehands carried Terriss through the Royal Entrance and up the steps to his dressing room. Blood dropped lavishly from him. Though he was barely conscious, he still gripped the silver key.

Before following, Jessie demonstrated that she was not so overcome that she was unable to behave sensibly. As well as sending the stage manager through to the stalls bar for ice, she despatched William Algar to the Charing Cross Hospital to fetch medical aid; and she told the callboy to run to the Gaiety Theatre and inform Seymour Hicks, playing there in *The Circus Girl,* that his father-in-law had been seriously wounded. If she thought at all of Mrs. Terriss, perhaps she decided that Hicks should break the news to her.

In the dressing room, the death scene—for so it was—suffered, dramatically speaking, from the fact that the sofa of crimson velvet on which Terriss had been lain was shorter than his body, thus necessitating an unartistic lolling of his legs over an end; and from the fact that he was too far gone to speak dying words.

Down in the lane, it seemed that Richard Archer Prince had muffed his big chance of a sort of stardom. He had cast himself in the leading role of Murderer but failed to impress anyone other than John Graves, who was still clutching his sleeve. By the time Police Constable 272E John Bragg inserted himself into the half-circle of people at the Royal Entrance, having run from his traffic-directing post at the convergence of Bedford, Garrick, and King Streets, Prince, with Graves in tow, had wandered a hundred yards east along Maiden Lane, almost as far as the Bedford Head pub, on the left-hand side. After getting the gist of what had happened, the constable went in pursuit. Graves, who must have been mightily relieved to see him, called out, "I give this man in custody for stabbing." As soon as Bragg had hold of Prince, Graves let him go. "What's the matter?" Prince enquired. "You know what," Bragg replied, and straightway nudged him onward, in the general direction of the

Lyceum, the Theatres Royal of Drury Lane and Covent Garden, and, of peculiar significance, Bow Street Police Station.

It appears that Graves and Prince had not spoken to each other while they were, so to say, attached; but now they entered into conversation.

In reply to Graves's question, "What could have induced you to do such a cruel deed as that?" Prince explained, "Terriss would not employ me, and I was determined to be revenged. He kept me out of work for ten years." When Graves hummed dubiously, Prince snapped, "I should have had either to die in the streets or else have my revenge."

At the police station, Constable Bragg handed his prisoner over to Inspector George Wood; John Graves made a brief statement and was then allowed to return to the Adelphi. Perhaps because Bragg had been intent on listening to and trying to remember Prince's remarks, it had not occurred to him that Prince might still be in possession of the knife he had used on William Terriss. But that thought struck Inspector Wood at once, and he ordered Prince to turn out his pockets. As Prince produced the bloodstained knife, he murmured to Bragg (whether or not jestingly, one cannot tell), "It is a good job for you that you didn't get it." Handing the knife to the inspector, he said, "I gave Terriss due warning, and if he is dead he knew what he had to expect from me. He prevented me getting assistance from the Actors' Benevolent Fund, and I stabbed him."

The only other items in his pockets were a pair of black woolen gloves, so far beyond repair that they looked as much like mittens, and a bundle of letters, all from well-known people, most either acknowledging the receipt of verses or expressing sympathy, or both; of the rest, one was from the Duke and Duchess of York, thanking Prince for his congratulations on the birth of their son; one, on black-edged paper, was from the Princess Henry of Battenberg, saying that she was touched by his sentiments concerning her late husband, and one was from William Gladstone, noting that he was as pleased as was Prince that the River Dee was now spanned by the Victoria Jubilee Bridge.

Since Inspector Wood was unsure of the gravity of Prince's crime, he did not charge him before telling Constable Bragg to take him to a cell. As Prince was being led away, he burst into tears. The inspector asked him what ailed him, expecting the answer to be contrition for his act or fear of the consequences. Prince said that he couldn't help crying, he was so hungry. He begged for food. Once he had been assured that he would be given some, he wiped his eyes on his sleeve and apologized for having made a scene.

At five minutes to eight—the time for the call of "Act One, beginners" on any ordinary night—the silver key fell from William Terriss's hand, signifying his death. (Or so it is said. The trouble with stories that have a theatrical background is that the first tellers of them are apt to be lured into sacrificing exactness to dramatic unity: they speak of what should have happened as if it actually had. None of the three doctors who had hurried from the Charing Cross Hospital took a note, to the minute, of when, as a reporter would put it, "the light of the star was extinguished for ever.")

As has been mentioned, shortly after eight o'clock the Adelphi's assistant manager made an announcement from the stage; resultantly, the auditorium was soon empty save for its attendants.

By nine, special editions of newspapers, reporting Terriss's death, were being hawked in the West End. There was no special edition of the *Daily Telegraph,* but next morning the paper made news of the spreading of the news—

At first most people were incredulous, for tragedies of this kind are fortunately rare in the annals of our stage life, but when the fatal tidings were confirmed there was only one topic of discussion in the district occupied by the playhouses and throughout London, for the sad intelligence reached the clubs and other places where people foregather in an amazingly short time. All kinds of rumours—most of them contradictory, and some obviously absurd—were afloat as to the exact circumstances of the terrible crime, a fact which need excite no surprise when it is recollected that for some time after Mr. Terriss had been attacked the greatest consternation prevailed in the theatre, and the immediate neighbourhood was in a state of ferment. A vast crowd of the curious and sympathetic flocked to the various entrances of the theatre, in the vain hope of learning details from the officials, and at one time the Strand was impassable. Neighbouring thoroughfares whence access may be had to the Adelphi were also filled by the multitude, whose faces, it was easy to see, expressed surprise and horror. . . .

Only the briefest interval elapsed before the dreadful news extended to the general public in the neighbourhood of the

Strand. Of course, among the members of the profession it travelled apace, and general regrets and expressions of horror at the
act were heard. The actors and actresses of the Adelphi company,
as they came out of the theatre, passed away in twos and threes,
talking in subdued tones of the distressing occurrence. It was
evident that the remark of one actor to another as they came
into the street: "Good-night, old chap; I feel quite upset," voiced
the feelings of them all.

Mingling with the throng, one could easily see that, but for
the corroboration given by the darkened theatre itself, the news
would hardly have been credited. To the public, Mr. Terriss's
figure was associated with deeds of bravery; so often had he
portrayed before them the dashing, manly hero that there is no
doubt that, as chance scraps of conversation showed, they saw
him with the glamour of the stage upon him. To think of him,
therefore, as dead by the cowardly hand of the assassin gave an
intensified shock. "Poor old Bill Terriss!" said a soldier in the
crowd, "if only he'd 'ad a chance, it wouldn't have been so bad.
But it do seem a miserable death for 'im."

At ten, Prince was roused from a sound sleep to be charged "that he,
about 7:20 P.M. on Thursday, the 16th of December, 1897, did kill and
slay one William Terriss with a knife, in Maiden Lane, in the Parish of
St Margaret's." He nodded and said, "All right." Asked if he had a relative or friend living in London whom he wished to be informed of his
plight, he spoke of a married half-sister named Maggie. He said that
he had chanced upon her only a few hours before, in the Strand, and
had pleaded with her to give him ten shillings: "If she had not refused
me, this thing would never have happened." A policeman was sent to
her home. Upon his return, he told Prince that she wanted nothing to
do with him. "I didn't think she would," Prince said. "It is now clear
that she was in league with Terriss."

Shortly after midnight, Terriss's body, concealed in a basketwork
shell, was carried from the Adelphi, through the main stage door, and
transported on a covered dray to the mortuary beneath the church of
St. Martin-in-the-Fields. There, an autopsy showed that the two stab
wounds in the back were severe, and might themselves have proved
fatal, but that the wound in the breast was the cause of death. A cut

on the left wrist indicated that Terriss had tried to deflect the frontal blow—which, the surgeon believed, had been struck with "almost super-human force," for the weapon had pierced Terriss's coat, jacket, waistcoat, and chest-protector, then almost severed the fifth rib before penetrating the heart.

Throughout the night, the telephone and telegraph lines from Fleet Street were engrossed by questions, orders, and requests, all in aid of adding to the bare details of the crime. As soon as it was known that Prince hailed from Dundee, "stringers" of that city were alerted; and one of them, early from bed, learned the address of Prince's mother, Margaret Archer, and called there.

Mrs Archer evidently knew nothing of the fearful event which had taken place in London, for she was anxious to learn the cause of so early a visit.

"Oh, it was about Dick?" and a happy smile played upon her features as she mentioned the name. "He's in London, is Dick—an actor. Have I heard anything about him lately? Of course I have. My daughter had a letter from him only a day or two ago. Here it is," and she drew the envelope from a rack near the fireplace.

The missive was written in a bold, clear hand—the letter of a man who could put a sentence together. But there seemed evidence of something being amiss with the writer. After a kindly query as to his mother's health, he relapsed into a desponding tone. He referred to the difficulty of getting work in London, and went on to say that he supposed there would be little use of him looking forward to visiting Dundee at Christmas. "Just as well die in London" was the bitter observation with which he concluded.

Meantime, Mrs Archer had asked if anything was wrong with Dick, to which the only reply that could be given was that the young man had got into serious trouble in London. Intuitively, she seemed to conclude that to ask more would be to learn too much. However, she very courteously, if at times huskily, continued to answer questions regarding her son.

Dick, as she called him, had always been a curious boy. When he was quite young he evinced a passion for the play, and night after night he spent within the walls of the old Theatre Royal in Castle Street. It was a happy night when he came home and confided to his parents that he had been taken on as a supernumerary at the theatre. This situation he kept for four years, working in a shipyard during the day and carrying out his stage duties in the evening. For the latter work he was paid at the rate of nine shillings a week, and that he was neither of a wild nor spendthrift disposition his mother testified. Richard's education had not been elaborate, but he was anxious to improve his mind, and with this in view he underwent a course of study, and gradually came to be regarded as a promising young fellow. The temporary removal of the household to London was the cause of Dick's throwing up his situation in Dundee, and he went to the metropolis a short time after his father and mother. "He's a grand actor, our Dick," said the old woman, and while under less depressing circumstances one could have admired the exhibition of maternal pride, it was terribly pathetic to listen to the mother's words of praise.

Previous to leaving Dundee on the last occasion, he had been idle for a considerable time, but he was hopeful of securing a post in some of the London theatres. The engagement which he looked for never came, however, hence the despairing nature of his last letter.

Replying to a question as to whether her son had ever spoken in a threatening manner of any person, Mrs Archer declared that she was not aware of his having the slightest animosity toward anyone in theatrical circles out of Dundee, although she remembered him once saying that he would like to do for one of the local officials. She never paid any attention to this threat.

"Now," at last said Mrs Archer, "I have told you all about Dick. Tell me what they have done to him. Is he locked up?" I answered that he was in the custody of the police. She covered her face with her hands and sobbed.

The public gallery of Bow Street Police Court was packed, in the main by actors and actresses, when, at half past eleven on Friday morning, the door from the police station swung open and Richard Archer Prince made his entrance. No doubt he would have liked to pause, posing, in the doorway, but the two following constables marched inexorably, forcing him into the dock. The reception he got was uncertain at first, for hardly anyone in the audience knew him, not even by sight; however, the moment he entered the dock, there to stand pencil-straight, his Inverness buttoned to the throat and with the collar turned up, one hand holding his black slouch hat, the fingers of the other preening his moustache, a chorus of boos, hisses, and shouts of detestation filled the court. To his delight. He didn't mind being the villain; no, not at all. The important thing was that he was at last a star, standing centrestage, playing to a full house. According to the reporter for the *Daily Telegraph*:

> During the hearing of the evidence the prisoner paid the closest possible attention to every detail, and watched the witnesses or Mr Wilson, who conducted the prosecution, with eyes that grew almost beadlike with the intensity of their concentration. Prince is said to be a Scotsman, but he possesses none of the outward characteristics of that race. On the contrary, his general appearance, his accent, and manner of speech are distinctly Italian, and the style in which the hair is worn in particular gives him a foreign look. One could not avoid the thought as one watched the man's movements in the dock that he was very self-conscious, and felt throughout that he was acting a part which must command the eyes and ears of his audience. It may have been entirely unpremeditated on the part of the prisoner, but his every action appeared calculated for effect. He leant over the dock rail in a dramatic attitude for some time. When a statement was made by any of the witnesses to which he took exception, he shook his head slowly and smiled. No incident of the hearing disturbed his cool self-possession. At one point he turned round in the dock and took a comprehensive survey of the spectators, as if seeking for some familiar faces. Even the very dramatic moment when Inspector Wood slowly unfolded the fatal knife from its wrappings of paper and displayed it to the court had no effect upon him, though a perceptible shudder ran through everyone in court. A lethal weapon the knife looked. The blade had its bright steel reddened near the handle with an ominous stain.

In the prisoner's demeanour, after the cruel and terrible crime had been committed, as described by the witnesses, he showed no remorse for the deed or any desire to palliate or excuse it. Neither did he in court appear in the slightest to flinch from the consequences of it. He contradicted, in clear and unwavering tones, some of the statements of Mr Graves and Inspector Wood,

December 25. 1897. THE ILLUSTRATED POLICE NEWS.

TERRISS'S MURDERER IN COURT.
SKETCHES BY OUR SPECIAL ARTIST.

William Terriss's murderer as seen in court (from *The Illustrated Police Budget*, 25 December 1897)

and seemed to particularly resent the use of the word "revenge" that was attributed to him. He denied that he had ever used that word, and said that "blackmail" was the proper expression. . . .

He was quick to profit by the warning from Sir John Bridge [the magistrate] not to make statements. He evinced no lack of nerve or courage.

At the close of the proceedings, when the magistrate decided to remand him, the prisoner exhibited the first symptom of concern, and complained that he had no solicitor. On being told that he might consult one before the next occasion when he would be brought before the Court, he bowed to the magistrate, and walked from the dock unmoved by the unprecedented display of disgust and abhorrence of the foul crime which followed his retreating figure. Altogether the scene in court was a remarkable one. The intense eagerness of the spectators, and the sangfroid of the central figure, as the facts and circumstances of the crime were being narrated, formed a contrast not often seen in the courts, and one which must add, if possible, to the extraordinary feeling which has been excited by a dramatic crime.

In the nineteenth century, sensational murders often had commercial side effects. The potters of Staffordshire turned out presentments of culprits and of the scenes of their crimes, printers rolled off catchpenny broadsheets, trial transcripts, and victim-commemorative cards that were suitable for framing (in February 1897, a London printer made, it might be said, a killing with unofficially consecrated slices of pasteboard, Sacred to the Memory of Elizabeth Camp, a murdered barmaid, late of a pub called the Good Intent), and until the summer of 1868, when hangings in a good, legal cause were first carried out unpublicly, executioners and their reps made capital from the sale of cuttings of uniquely used hemp—at half a crown per inch if the association was reckoned to justify that top rate—to sufferers from warts or the goiter or to people who were merely acquisitive of morbid mementoes. (Subsequent to public hangings—and to the public snipping of the respective means—the market was for a while glutted with chunks of hemp described as ex-executional; but then suspicion grew, demanding of the hawkers forgery of provenance prior to the spiel, and this additional chore caused most of them to revert to three-card trickery or to the offering of acceptedly controversial splinters from the Cross.) Some murders had a depressing effect on trade: in 1871, a national partiality to chocolate creams was diminished by the news that Miss

Christiana Edmunds, who could hardly have been more genteel, had injected several of such confections with strychnine, her object being to bereave the doctor she adored of his sweet-toothed wife, leaving the coast of Brighton clear for her own pursuance of matrimony; and, if one believes the legend, Mrs. Marie Manning's choice of material for her going-away gown, remarked upon by thousands, Charles Dickens among them, who craned their necks as she was hanged on the roof of Horsemonger Lane Gaol in 1849 for the murder of a one-time beau, had an adverse effect on the fashionableness of black satin.

So far as I can tell, there is no footnote to the annals of crime, no aside from a stage person's memoirs, no parentheses in a history of the retailing of textiles, observing that on Friday, 17 December 1897, the haberdashers of the West End and its environs experienced a rush for slight offcuts of black crepe that all but the oldest of them, at least forty-five years in the business and so theoretically capable of recalling a similar rush following the demise of the Iron Duke thought unprecedented; or that, during the remaining fortnight of the year, any man noticeable in the street in any event but made more so by his wearing of an armband of mourning was, ten to one, a member of the theatrical profession. Each phenomenon, the first contributing to the second, certainly occurred. Of course, much as some people today wear sweatshirts publicizing causes that they do not support, some of the ostensible mourners of William Terriss felt no pang at his passing but had black tacked to their sleeves because they liked the idea of being labelled, albeit temporarily, as thespians.

But, no doubt of it, the counterfeit mourners were vastly outnumbered by the genuine. Headlines such as "A Profession Grieves" told a truth. The stage weekly, *The Era,* spoke for as well as to its readers in the issue hastened from the press for sale on the Friday night:

> The excitement, the agitation, have subsided; and all that remains is a deep, benumbing sorrow. . . . In all circles of society, from the mansions of the West End to the slums of the East, there are faithful friends and honest admirers mourning for the dead actor and execrating his cowardly assassin. The first feeling must have been one of awe, for it is an awesome thought that this actor, young at least in virile energy, manly spirit, and the enjoyment of life, should have been cut down in the full bloom and flower of his popularity and prosperity. We can hardly realize, even yet, that

Terriss—the hearty, honest, buoyant, breezy Terriss—lies a mere mass of still, cold clay; that the mobile features are fixed and waxen, the eloquent eyes are glazed and stony, and the strong, active body is stiffened into a spiritless corpse. And when it comes home to us as a cruel, wretched reality, the truth is too terrible and the bitterness is greater than we can bear.

The Adelphi was dark (and would remain so until the morning after Christmas Day, when *Secret Service* would be revived, with Herbert Waring playing Terriss's part and May Whitty replacing Jessie Millward, still inconsolable, as Miss Varney); but that is not to say that the theatre was a forsaken place.[11]

From early on Friday, Henry Spratt, custodian at the stage door, hardly had a minute to himself, was rarely upright between bows, as one important person after another entered, dishevelled from contact with the crowds of reporters and spectators at one end or the other of Bull Inn Court, which was kept clear by cordoning constables, to express sorrow to the Gatti brothers and, through them, to the Terriss family. Most of the visitors were connected with the stage (these included the three actor-knights Henry Irving, Squire Bancroft, and Charles Wyndham), but some were hereditarily noble, and at least one (Sir Henry Hawkins, who refused to tether his terrier outside, snapping magisterially that "Jack" accompanied him in all unecclesiastic places) was a member of the Queen's Bench.

Hundreds of telegrams, thousands of letters and cards, were delivered to the Adelphi; on some, the address was scanty or inventive, or both—to "Terriss's Playhouse, London," for instance—and nearly all were meant to be read by Terriss's widow. The latter fact turned out to contain a complication. Early on, the clerk assigned by Arthur Latham, the manager of the theatre, to sort the missives into piles, the eventually largest of these to be tidied away into sacks and transported by hansom to The Cottage at Turnham Green, noticed that the writer

11. Now best remembered as the Lady Who Vanished in the film that Alfred Hitchcock made in 1938 of Ethel Una White's novel *The Wheel Spins*. In 1918, she became the first actress to be a Dame Commander of the Order of the British Empire—though for services in connection with the Great War rather than for her stage work; the American-born Genevieve Ward was the first actress to be honoured as such, by being made a dame in 1921; four years later, Ellen Terry, who most people considered should have been the first actress-Dame (the general suspicion was that she was passed over on account of her having been thrice married), became the second.

of one card, oblivious of Amy Terriss, had assumed that the widow was Jessie Millward: a pardonable error considering that husband-and-maiden-named-wife stage partnerships were common and that during the last few years of William Terriss's celebrity, Amy had become almost reclusive, rarely venturing from the house, not even to attend her husband's first nights, and never, but never, aiding the concoctors of Green-Room Gossip columns (who, quite likely, relished her reticence, which allowed them to be venturesome with innuendo about an offstage—or rather, behind-the-scenes—relationship between the male and female stars of the Adelphi).

Apprised of the card-writer's misapprehension, Arthur Latham ordered the clerk to add censorship to the sorting task; to winkle away from the Turnham Green–intended pile any condolences to the widow that might distress her by their faulty guesswork as to who she was. As it turned out, the carefulness was unnecessary: after one consignment of mail had been delivered to The Cottage, Amy wrote to Arthur Latham, thanking him all the same, but saying that she could not bring herself to read any of the countless messages she was receiving direct, let alone forwarded ones; a day or so later, her son Tom (Ellaline's younger brother, himself a stage performer, though without distinguishment) spoke on her behalf to the press, explaining "the impossibility of replying individually to the great number of manifestations of affection and sympathy, and trusting that a general acknowledgment would suffice." It seems probable that Amy made an exception to her nonreading, nonreplying decisions—that being in the case of a message from Queen Victoria, the Widow of Windsor, who asserted that her sorrow was shared by all her subjects, in Great Britain and far-flung throughout the world: an extent of emotion that, what with the suffusion of Empire Pink on the globe, left relatively few people untouched.

Within a short while of Terriss's death, the Adelphi management had telegraphed the news to William Gillette, who was in Pittsburgh, heading a *Secret Service* road company. Gillette's immediate, wired response augmented, and confirmed a part of, the Queen's generalization: UNSPEAKABLY SHOCKED. WE MOURN DEATH OF TERRISS WITH ALL WHO LOVED HIM, WHICH MEANS ALL ENGLAND.

The press-requested comments of Terriss's native fellows tended to be quietly recollective: more in keeping with the new "natural" style of drama, leaving the audience to worry for meanings between the lines, than with the declamatory sort. But George Alexander, the actor-manager who had made himself as much at home at the St. James's as had Terriss at the Adelphi (though, two years before, he had been forced to cut short the inaugural run of *The Importance of Being Earnest* owing to the tribulations and trials of the play's author—who had once complained of him that he did not act on the stage: he *behaved*), came up with a speech that would have satisfied any of the Adelphi melodramatists:

> Will Terriss was a man to the finger-tips. Nature stood up and said it to all the world; and by his death the modem stage loses some of its virile force.
> Lie lightly on him, Earth.

George Edwardes, of the Gaiety, recalled Terriss as "one of the most generous men I knew. About two months ago, he was in my office when an application was brought to me for help from a poor actor. I showed it to him. 'Well,' he remarked with a smile, 'if you give to every one in this way, you will finish up in the workhouse.' Afterwards I had a conversation with the applicant, who admitted that only a week before, Terriss had sent him £10."

The vocalist and actress Florence St. John exclaimed, "Poor old Willie!" and went on: "The last time I saw him was when he called on me on the night of last Saturday week, after the production of *The Grand Duchess*.[12] I was feeling a bit depressed, but he cheered me up with these words, which I little dreamed would be the last I should ever hear from him: 'Never mind, Jack; so long as you have a few pals and your health, you're all right.'"[13]

12. The English libretto of this comic opera, with music by Offenbach, was written by Charles Brookfield, who, in 1895, when he was playing the small part of Phipps, the butler, in the first production of *An Ideal Husband*, moonlighted industriously as a seeker of evidence in support of the Marquess of Queensberry's assertion that the play's author, Oscar Wilde, was "Posing as Somdomite [*sic*]."

13. Terriss's words indicate that he was unaware that a probable reason why Miss St. John was "feeling a bit depressed" was that an actor named Francis Carroll, who was as unsuccessful as Prince, was threatening to murder her. In the following February, Carroll—of Buckingham Road, Brighton—was convicted of having sent threatening letters to her and to his father, a retired army officer. In default of finding sureties in the sum of £100 for his good behaviour for one year, he was given a prison sentence of six months. His first action when he was returned to his cell was to pick up a plate of food intended as his dinner and hurl it at the jailer. However, subsequent disciplining seems to have mellowed him: I can find no indication that, following his release, he used the Royal Mail objectionably.

Henry Irving's business manager, Bram Stoker, whose tale of vampirism, *Dracula,* had been published earlier in the year, thought back to 1883, "when the Lyceum company were crossing to America on the SS *City of Rome.* A rather bragging man, seeing so many landmen present, not like himself in yachting rig, pulled out a ten-pound note, and openly offered to bet that not one of the passengers would take his cap off the top of the mast. Terriss instantly covered the note, and, throwing off his coat, tightened his belt. 'Done,' he said; 'up with you and put it on. I will follow and take it off.' The offer was withdrawn."

During the week in which Terriss was murdered, the Lyceum company was at the Grand Theatre, Wolverhampton. Of course, Stoker was not the only person associated with the company to be asked for a quote. The entry for 16 December in Ellen Terry's diary records: "Willie Terriss was murdered this evening. Newspapers sent me a wire for 'expressions of sympathy'!!"

As will appear, her shock at the news may have been accompanied by a worry concerning a practical effect of Terriss's death on a friend. For the present, all she would tell the reporters was that she could not tell them anything: "The whole affair is so terrible, and I feel it so deeply, as all who knew him must, that I really cannot talk of it."

Irving—called "guv'nor" by Terriss, even when he was no longer a Lyceumite—was more forthcoming: "Some of us have his words—confident, cheery words—still ringing in our ears. Only two days ago he was with me, arranging for the production of *The Corsican Brothers* at the Adelphi—a play with which he had intimate associations in his Lyceum days—and it is strange that, with that grim drama in his mind, he should have been struck down by a murderous hand."

One of Terriss's friends at the Green Room Club must have been surprised, perhaps saddened, to learn that he had planned yet another revival of *The Corsican Brothers.* Three weeks before, just after the opening of *Secret Service,* Terriss had confided in the man: "I'm longing to appear in a new style of drama. I'm tired of being accused of murder every night, and being proved innocent about eleven o'clock."

It seems that that last comment was spoken tongue-in-cheek, because Terriss was thinking of surprising the theatrical world, not once but twice: first with the announcement that he was to star in a new play by the foremost new-style dramatist, George Bernard Shaw, who as a drama critic had lambasted Irving at the Lyceum, Terriss at the Adelphi, for squandering their talents on tosh—and then with the play itself, which would mock those melodramas, staple of the Adelphi, in which the hero made a series of mighty bounds between predicaments, at last coming to rest, clutching the girl of his dreams, and with sufficient breath left to utter a speech on some worthy topic, just before the curtain fell.

Ellen Terry was one of the few people who knew of Terriss's intention and of Shaw's play, which was called *The Devil's Disciple*. Not until more than thirty years later—in 1931, when the correspondence between Shaw and Ellen Terry, by then dead, was published—was it possible to piece together an account of the making of the play that, but for Richard Archer Prince's intervention, William Terriss might have presented in London, not only starring as Dick Dudgeon, a copy of his stage-self, but also amending the script here and there, perhaps saliently in some of the scenes. Though futile, it is fascinating to wonder how different the play would be from its published form if the actor who bespoke it had lived to trim it, Shaw approving and assisting, toward a perfect fit.

The first Ellen Terry heard of the project was from a letter that Shaw (whom she had never met) wrote to her on 26 March 1896:

Terriss (this is a secret) wants me to collaborate with him in a play, the scenario of which includes every situation in the Lyceum repertory or the Adelphi record. The best act is The Bells.[14] He is arrested either for forgery or murder at every curtain, and goes on as fresh as paint and free as air when it goes up again. I talked it over with him whilst he was dressing for a matinee at the Adelphi. I noticed that his chest was black and blue. He caught the expression of pity and horror in my eyes as I caught sight of the bruise, and said, with a melancholy smile, "Ah yes, Ellen Terry! You remember the third act of *Olivia* at the old Court? I was Thornhill. The marks have never come off. I shall carry them

14. Irving's first season at the Lyceum, in 1871, was unsuccessful until his appearance as Mathias, the unapprehended murderer who suffers from ringing in the ears, in *The Bells*, adapted by Leopold Lewis, a solicitor, from *Le Juif Polonais* by M. M. Erckmann-Chatrian. When Lewis died, in February 1890, the editor of *The Stage* wrote, "Poor fellow, at one time it was said of him that *The Bells* had made him, as he was wont to boast that the same play had made Irving. As a matter of fact, I think *The Bells* ruined him. His success was too much for him, and ever since its production he has been steadily going down the hill. One of his most faithful friends was Mr. Irving, and it is from the Lyceum manager that Mr. Lewis received many little acts of thoughtful kindness of which the world will. I suppose, forever remain in ignorance."

to my grave."[15] I did not tell him that I also had received heart wounds in those days which I shall carry to my grave. Neither, by the way, did I decide in favour of the collaboration. But I seriously think I shall write a play for him. A good melodrama is a more difficult thing to write than all this clever-clever comedy: one must go straight to the core of humanity to get it, and if it is only good enough, there you have Lear or Macbeth.

Shaw to Ellen Terry, 30 November 1896:

I finished my play today. What do you think of that? Does that look like wasting my time? Three acts, six scenes, a masterpiece, all completed in a few weeks, with a trip to Paris and those Ibsen articles thrown in—articles which were so over-written that I cut out and threw away columns.

What did I want so particularly to say? Oh yes, it was this. I have written to Terriss to tell him that I have kept my promise to him and have "a strong drama" with a part for him; but I want your opinion; for I have never tried melodrama before; and this thing, with its heroic sacrifice, its impossible court martial, its execution (imagine W.T. *hanged* before the eyes of the Adelphi!), its sobbings and speeches and declamations, may possibly be the most farcical absurdity that ever made an audience shriek with laughter. And yet I have honestly tried for dramatic effect. I think you could give me a really *dry* opinion on it; for it will not tickle you, like *Arms and the Man* and *You Never Can Tell*, not get at your sympathetic side like *Candida* (the heroine is not the hero of the piece this time); and you will have to drudge conscientiously through it like a stage carpenter and tell me whether it is a burlesque or not.

But now that I think of it, all this is premature. The play only exists as a tiny scrawl in my note books—things I carry about in my pockets. I shall have to revise it and work out all the stage business, besides reading up the history of the American War of

15. If Shaw's anecdote is true, then Terriss had already carried the marks for nearly eighteen years, an extraordinary time for bruises to remain visible. Admittedly, accounts of the Court production of *Olivia* indicate that Ellen Terry did not pull her punches. One cannot say whether Shaw was more or less impressed by the breast-beating "business," witnessed by him from the stalls in 1878, than by the lingering effects of it on Terriss's person; but, either way. he borrowed the business for a stage direction in *You Never Can Tell*, which he appears to have completed in June 1896.

Independence before I can send it to the typist to be readably copied. Meanwhile I can read it to Terriss, and to other people, but not to—well, no matter: I dont ask that the veil of the temple shall be rent: on the contrary, I am afraid, in my very soul, to come stumping in my thickbooted, coarse, discordant reality, into that realm where a magic Shaw, a phantasm, a thing who looks delicate and a boy (twelve stalls and a bittock off) poses fantastically before a really lovely Ellen. . . .

Now I have finished my play, nothing remains but to kiss my Ellen once and die.

The reading of the play to Terriss did not go as Shaw would have wished, he told an *Observer* journalist in 1930: Terriss heard little of it as he could not keep awake. However, Ellen Terry drudged remarkably conscientiously through the copy of the script that Shaw had sent to her. On 7 March 1897, she wrote,

Yes, the 2nd Act was so tremendous, it "took it out of me" as they say. So I tried to *wait* for Act III and lay flat on the dining room table for a while! Fidgeted, then got up and went at it again. "You'll rewrite it?" Oh now do like a pet. No softening. No, no. Nothing of that kind.

"Tell you how? Why, you have been working on it for months! How could I tell you "how" all in a minute? . . . I'll get someone to read it to me over and over again, and then I'll tell you what I think. And if a lot of my "thinks" could be of a wee bit of use to you, should not I be a proud lady! It struck me at once that those scenes between Burgoyne and Swindon (although they are excellent scenes *as scenes* and *for acting*) are irritating as interruptions, like Lovers talking of Ships or Icebergs that pass in the night when they dont feel quite like that. Then too 3 scenes in one act (and that the *last act*) is clumsy (Oh, excuse me! Ignorant and rude!), unfortunate. I think I've turned the corner and am getting better. But this ghastly weather is frustrating. Cant write. Oh, that 2nd Act! There has never been anything in the least like it. You *are* a Dear. . . .

People are so odd that I'm certain no one could compete with T. as Dick. The neat head and figure, and the charm, the arrogant manner. "Taking." Act II will find but the *woman*.

Another copy of the script had been sent, or would soon be sent, to the American actor-manager Richard Mansfield, who had produced and starred in two of Shaw's plays, *Arms and the Man* and *Candida,* in that country. In Shaw's letter of 26 March 1896 to Ellen Terry, letting her into the secret of what had passed between himself and Terriss in the star's dressing room, he had referred to his short play *The Man of Destiny* (in which the character of the Strange Lady was modelled on Ellen Terry), saying that he was thinking of allowing it to "be done . . . in America by Mansfield, who has had the audacity to ask me for another play, after heaping villainy on me over my *Candida.*" And Ellen Terry had added a postscript to her letter of 3 September 1896: "One word about the little play (and breathe it to a living creature, and ugh! what is there I won't do to you?). If you let the little man [Mansfield] play it, it will be of little count, for he's rather clever, but not enough clever. In the first place he'd play it as it is, uncut, and Lord help you both then! For, although I love every word of it, it is too long in certain places to play-act as it now stands. All well, as it stands, to read, but not to play-act." Mansfield presented *The Devil's Disciple* (presumably, as it was), he himself as Dick Dudgeon, at Albany on 1 October 1897, and the following week at the Fifth Avenue Theatre, Manhattan; despite poor reviews, the production became Shaw's first great box-office success, enabling him to give up regular journalism so as to concentrate on the writing of plays.

But as for a London production, Shaw told Ellen Terry on 24 December 1897:

My calculations are quite put out by the unforeseen extinction of Terriss. I was scheming to get the D.'s D. produced with him in the part and Jessie Millward as Judith. The alternative was a [Herbert] Waring and [Arthur] Bourchier combination—Bourchier to play Burgoyne. And now Terriss is only a name and a batch of lies in the newspapers, and Waring goes to the Adelphi in his place. However, Waring may need stronger plays than Terriss, who was a play in himself; so perhaps Jessie may play Judith yet.

In her reply, written two days later, Ellen Terry remarked that "the D.D. would be best now I think with [Charles] Wyndham who would I should say revel in the part," and went on: "Poor Willie Terriss, I'll miss him. That calling him 'Breezy Bill' always annoyed me. So vulgar and so very stupid to call him that. Poor Jessie M.!"

Shaw, unable to believe his eyes when he saw the suggestion that Wyndham should play Dick Dudgeon, wrote back at once: "It would be impossible: he's too old; and he has not the peculiar fascination." After allowing that the sixty-year-old Wyndham "would be admirable as the husband: it would suit him to a hair's breadth," and musing on other casting possibilities, Shaw concluded, "I should like to get the piece on at the Adelphi with Waring in order to secure Jessie's part for her."

What actually happened was not at all to Shaw's liking. *The Devil's Disciple* was not presented in England until 26 September 1899—and then tattily, without benefit of stars, at the Princess of Wales's Theatre in that drab part of London called Kennington, where it lasted only a fortnight. Eight more years elapsed before it was seen in the West End, as a component of Harley Granville-Barker's repertory season, retrospectively reckoned epoch-making for presentational style, at the Savoy, across the Strand from the Adelphi; Matheson Lang played the part of Dick Dudgeon—of William Terriss.

Richard Archer Prince—he, too, had written a play: *Countess Otto,* it was called. Penned in pale-violet ink in penny exercise-books, those sewn together at their top left-hand corners, the script had grown dog-eared from many submissions by the autumn of 1896, when Prince, saving on postage so as to afford his fare home to Dundee, delivered it, in a broken envelope marked "For the Kind Attention of Mr Fred Terry," at the stage door of the Royalty Theatre in Dean Street, off Shaftesbury Avenue. Weeks passed; and then Prince, having received only an acknowledgment from Fred Terry, began to inundate the actor with correspondence, on some days—damn the expense to his mother—posting three or four letters or cards. Terry returned the script; but, trying to soften the accompanying note of rejection, said that the play had no part suitable for himself or for his wife Julia Neilson—a comment that Prince twisted into meaning that Terry had been henpecked into turning down *Countess Otto.* The next thing was that Julia Neilson—playing Princess Flavia in *The Prisoner of Zenda* at the St. James's—started receiving missives from Dundee. However, by Christmas, Prince had run out of steam—or his mother of stamps—and Fred and Julia Terry were forgetting their pesterer.

But months later, and then for weeks to come, Fred Terry was made aware that Prince was back in town. Terry, you see, often chaired meetings of the emergency committee of the Actors' Benevolent Fund. He was the "one of the Terrys" mentioned to Prince, the denied applicant, on Wednesday, 15 December 1897.

The following night, he, like his elder sister Ellen, heard from reporters what had happened by the Adelphi and was asked for an "expression of sympathy." Off the cuff, he supplied, "Will Terriss has left us, mourned by many, regretted by all." He was now working with his wife at the St. James's. After the performance, while driving to their home on Primrose Hill, they spoke more of Prince than of Terriss; and next morning they rummaged through box files of old letters in search of evidences of the long-running *Countess Otto* correspondence. All that remained were a couple of cards, both postmarked "9:30 P.M., 23 Nov 96," and an undated letter. One of the cards read:

> 68 Hill Street, Dundee
> Sir—Please return play "Countess Otto" at once. If you are hard up for money will send it. Terriss, the Pope and Scotland Yard, I will answer in a week.—RICHARD A. PRINCE

The message on the other card, presumably written following receipt of the script, contained another mysterious allusion:

> 68 Hill Street, Dundee
> Sir—Favour to hand this morning at ten o'clock. The old story about King Charles and the two hundred thousand pounds. They sold him for a King. I'm only a Prince. But a woman, mon Dieu, a woman.—RICHARD A. PRINCE

The letter read:

> 51 William Street, Vic Road, Dundee
> Late Union Jack Tours
> To Mrs. Fred Terry
> Madam—I thank you as a "Highlander and a gentleman," and in the name of the Almighty God, our Queen, and my rights for play "Countess of Otto." I am, Madam, yours faithfully,
> RICHARD A. PRINCE

On the reverse of the sheet was a wonderfully irrelevant postscript, something to do with the troubles besetting the "Godly" King of Greece.

Though it must have struck Fred Terry that the dropping of Terriss's name, among those of more illustrious others, would intrigue the police, he chose to show the communications to a journalist on the *Daily Telegraph,* thus enabling that paper—as carefree with comment on cases that were sub judice as were its rivals—to speak most authoritatively about Prince, "a monomaniac who has gradually developed the homicidal tendency."

Following Fred Terry's lead, less-renowned members of his profession who had had dealings with Prince decided to help the press, rather than the police, with their inquiries. For instance, Ralph Croyden, manager of Miss Lena Develrey's London Theatrical Company—"presently delighting audiences at the Princess Theatre, Leith"—spoke "exclusively" to several special correspondents about his encounters with Prince, the first on the evening of Saturday, 23 October 1897, at the Amphitheatre, Newcastle-upon-Tyne. (One cannot be sure, but it seems that Prince, having heard or read of a vacancy in Miss Develrey's company, was so desperate for work that he had travelled the three hundred miles or so to Newcastle on the off chance of getting the job.) Mr. Croyden recalled that

> Prince detailed his experiences as an actor, and explained that he had played important parts at the Adelphi, London, most especially in *The Union Jack.* He had, he said, been wronged—deadly wronged—by one of the leading lights of the stage, and there was only one man in the world whom he hated, and he was Mr Terriss. In reply to a question why he left the Adelphi, Prince said that it was because Mr Terriss was a man whom he could not stand. Mr Terriss had got on purely through influence, while he, a poor dog, had to work his way up. Although suspicious of Prince on account of certain peculiarities which he presented, I engaged him.
>
> It had been arranged that the company were to appear at the theatre in Hetton-le-Hole, twelve or fourteen miles out of Newcastle, on Monday evening, the pieces to be played being *Nurse Charity* and *Parson Thorne,* and the parts—they were minor parts—assigned to Prince being Sir Leycester Lightfoot in the former and Sir Geoffrey Dashwood in the latter. Prince received copies of his parts for the purpose of studying them, and before he left I invited him to tea on the Sunday afternoon. My wife belongs to Scotland, and when Prince arrived I told her that a Scotsman had come to see her. She expressed delight, whereupon

Prince, assuming a melodramatic attitude and waving his right arm, exclaimed, to the surprise of everyone present, "My name's MacGregor, and I'll smoke a clay-pipe if I like." He had, he subsequently explained, been with another theatrical company, and had been discharged because he smoked a clay-pipe instead of a cigar. He scarcely ever ceased speaking of and vowing vengeance on Mr Terriss, and the party came to the conclusion that he was mentally deranged.

We had reserved five compartments of the train that was to take us from Newcastle to Hetton. Prince duly turned up and joined the party at the station, but he declined to travel with any of us and occupied a compartment to himself. On reaching our destination, we at once proceeded to the theatre for a rehearsal. Then it appeared that Prince was utterly incompetent to speak anything. He, in turn, tugged at the hair of his head, rolled his eyes in a wild fashion, and pressed his temples.

In the circumstances, I found myself in a rather awkward predicament. At length, I told Prince that he had better go away. On this, Prince raved over his experiences at the Adelphi, declared what a fine actor he was, and pleaded that the performance might be postponed until the following evening. This, of course, was out of the question, and eventually I and some associates got rid for the time being of our disagreeable companion.

Next morning, Prince was early astir. He called at the house where my wife and I were staying no less than five times before I found it convenient to see him. When admitted into the room, he demanded some money. The fact of the matter was, he said, that his head went wrong at times, and he could not think what he was doing, thinking of his vengeance. Naturally enough, I declined to give him any money. Thereupon he became more excited than before, and used threatening language. He remarked that he was "Not strong enough to fight with you now, but tomorrow I will come and have my vengeance." I ordered him out of the house as a madman, and he retaliated by raising his walking-stick, and saying:

"Mad, mad, mad! You will hear of my madness. The world will ring with it."

By the time twilight fell on Monday, 20 December, the eve of the funeral, the conservatory of The Cottage was unseasonably floral, crammed with tributes in many forms and from all sorts of people.[16] Nosegays from Terriss's humble friends, admirers, and servants drooped in the crevices between ingenious creations ordered by those who could afford to express themselves extravagantly: ladders, globes, masks of Tragedy, lyres, haloes (one from the Prince of Wales), hearts, prosceniums, and books (or were they playscripts?), both open and closed. Not all of the tributes were waiting there; some had gone straight to Brompton Cemetery—among those, Jessie Millward's, which was a cushion of white chrysanthemums with the words "To My Dear Comrade" spelt out in purple anemones.

Ellen Terry kept company with Jessie that night. She afterward wrote to Shaw: "Poor little Jessie . . . seemed so wee and crumpled up. I hope she will get good work. She will need help now."[17]

16. Financial contributions toward a Terriss Memorial poured in to the organizer's office at the *Daily Telegraph:* £1,126 in all (roughly the equivalent of 60,000 present-day pounds, close to $100,000).

Ellaline Terriss wrote in *Just a Little Bit of String* (London 1955), "There was no thought of a statue or something which would do little or no good. Instead of that, to the memory of the man who had loved the sea, and sailed it, who had saved life from its clutch, who had been a hero of *Harbour Lights,* they erected a lifeboat house at Eastbourne, bearing his name. And from that house his lifeboat saved many lives. My father would have been overjoyed at that."

From the *Eastbourne Local History Society Newsletter,* No. 26 (ca. 1975): "The foundation stone of the William Terriss Lifeboat House was laid by the Duchess of Devonshire . . . on 16 July 1898. . . . The new lifeboat house was to be built at the foot of the eastern slopes of the Wish Tower Hill, and a marquee was erected over the spot where the foundation stone was to be laid. Gaily decked with bunting, the lifeboat, with the crew aboard, was drawn by horses from the old boathouse at the rear of the Wish Tower grounds. The band of the Sussex Artillery Militia played and the Eastbourne Cadet Corps formed a guard of honour. After the Duchess arrived in her carriage, the ceremonies began. Many letters and telegrams were read from friends and associates of William Terriss. . . . After a brief religious service, the Duchess tapped the stone with a mallet and declared the stone well and truly laid. . . .

"Until 1924 the William Terriss Memorial Lifeboat House housed an active boat. For thirteen years after that, it only held a boat for demonstration purposes. On 22 March 1937 it was opened as a lifeboat museum, the first of its kind in the country. It was opened by Sir Godfrey Baring, chairman of the Royal National Lifeboat Institution. Ellaline Terriss attended and made a short speech." The museum still exists.

17. Reporting her death, at the age of 71, in July 1932, the *Times* noted that "after the murder, it needed a great force to compel or cajole Miss Millward to enter a theatre again. That force was at hand in [the American impresario] Charles Frohman. In 1898 he persuaded her to go to the United States of America, and there she stayed until 1913, with only one short break in 1906. After her return, she played a little in suburban theatres and on tour."

The cortege set off on its five-mile journey, timed by Terriss's stage manager to take an hour, at noon. Right at the start, something happened that one of the dozens of reporters scribbled down as "an incident unrehearsed by Man that yet seemed too perfectly theatrical to be ascribed to coincidence." As the head of the cortege was passing beneath the railway bridge by Turnham Green Station, a train was passing, just as slowly, overhead. "It was filled with soldiers, and the redcoats, bent upon adding their tribute to the rest, gave three lusty cheers for the actor upon whose words and deeds they had so often hung."

The *Daily Mail:*

Few could have anticipated the remarkable demonstration of interest and respect which imparted to the funeral the dignity of a public ceremonial. Throughout the route to the cemetery the streets were lined with people who silently watched the procession pass, while in the cemetery it is computed that the sorrowing assembly numbered many thousands.

Long before the cemetery was reached, dense crowds lined and blocked the streets. And the multitude which thronged the avenues and was dispersed over the vast burial ground was

AN ORDERLY MASS,

patient and silent in the eager east wind; not deeply moved, perhaps. Indeed, it would be misleading to assert that any such wave of emotion was perceptible as often sways a multitude when one of its idols goes untimely to his death.

But its deep respect was shown in many striking ways. There was a kindliness abroad. Not even the biting cold and the long hours of weary waiting could affect that. The people were mostly drawn from the lowlier ranks to whom the dead actor's art specially appealed. They had come to be present at the final scene, to see his last part played in deathly silence.

And when the open hearse drawn by four horses had passed, and the long string of mourning coaches and carriages had filed slowly by, many thousands quietly re-covered their bared heads and sadly wended their way home.

Around the oak coffin, as it stood within the chapel, upon a catafalque draped with purple velvet, as around the open grave, well-known faces were to be seen on every side. Actors, managers, singers, playwrights—the London stage had sent all the most

famous of its favourites to discharge the last debt of comrade-
ship to their dear friend. They went

FOR THE MOST PART UNRECOGNIZED

by the huge concourse which gazed across the large roped-in enclosure around the grave, but many eyes were centred on the tall,
stately figure of Sir Henry Irving escorting Miss Millward, both
stricken with grief.

Some people had dreaded, and others had looked forward to, a con-
frontation between Terriss's widow and his "dear comrade"; but this
did not take place, because Amy was not among the visible mourners.
Though, of course, her absence gave rise to unkind rumours, it is probable that she was either too ill to attend or ordered not to by a doctor:
eight months later, she died from cancer. One gathers that Shaw, himself an absentee, read an account of the funeral but was too taken by
the vignette of Irving and Jessie to observe the omission of Amy's name
from the columns-long list of mourners. He wrote to Ellen Terry:

H.I. scored nobly by standing by Jessie at the funeral: had it been
his funeral, Lady Irving would have been in the position of Mrs
Terriss; and you would have been—probably taking a nice drive
through Richmond Park with me, or perhaps with that villain
you persuaded me you were going to marry the other day. Jessie
must have been consoled a little; for she adores H.I. and always
reserved his claims, as an intellectual prince, before Terriss's,
greatly to William's indignation; for he knew that Henry was in-
tellectually an imposter, nothing like so hardheaded as himself.

One of the lyre wreaths was from Ellaline Terriss; the attached card
read, "To darling old father, from his devoted, heart-broken daughter,
Ellie." Directly after the murder, Seymour Hicks had considered keeping it secret from her for the time being, fearing that the shock might
cause a relapse; still undecided when he next went to the hospital, he
was left with no alternative but to tell her by the sight of a pack of
reporters roaming near her ward.

The last card to her father was written from the hospital, but
shortly afterward she was deemed well enough to leave. By the following August, when her mother died, she was touring as the Girl in a
Gaiety musical. Her share of the estate amounted to a substantial sum

(William Terriss's will was proved at £18,809, the equivalent, roughly speaking, of over half a million present-day pounds), and this, added to over the next few years from her increasingly high earnings as a stage performer and from those of her husband as both playwright and actor, enabled Hicks to team up with Charles Frohman to build two theatres in the West End: first, the Aldwych, near the Gaiety and intended to be its competitor as a musical-comedy house, which opened in December 1905 with a revival of *Bluebell in Fairyland,* Hicks's "musical dream-play," starring himself and Ellaline (and with a girl called Gladys Cooper, just seventeen, playing a small role), and second, the Hicks, in Shaftesbury Avenue, which opened almost exactly a year later, the first production being *The Beauty of Bath,* partly written by Hicks and with his wife starring, which was transferred from the Aldwych; in 1909, the Hicks was rechristened the Globe, and then, very recently, the Gielgud.

The husband-and-wife stage partnership lasted for half a century, until 1949, when Hicks died; he had been knighted fourteen years before, and then it had been said that the honour was actually a joint tribute, earned equally by "Lady Ellie." As if making up for the curtailment of her parents' lives, she lived to be a hundred, qualifying for a congratulatory telegram from the Queen. Upon her death in June 1971, obituarists mentioned that she was the daughter of an actor known as William Terriss, and felt the need to explain that he too had been a star.

The last act of what most of the papers entitled "The Adelphi Tragedy" was played out at the Theatre Royal, Old Bailey—correctly called the Central Criminal Court—on Thursday, 13 January 1898. No; that date, four weeks from that of the commission of the crime, is not a misprint. Nor is there error in the indication that the proceedings were completed within a day. If you are surprised or, being liberal, shocked by such speeds, then you have been taken in by the legal profession, which has only since the 1950s made an ersatz virtue of both dilatoriness in the preparation of criminal cases for trial and elongation of the proceedings, thereby profiting many of its members at the expense of, inter alia, Justice.

Following the tryout at Bow Street, Richard Archer Prince had been lodged, with other prisoners on custodial remand, in the hospital wing of Holloway Gaol. There, he had eaten, if not well, with unaccustomed frequency and regularity, and so had put on weight. He had received a variation on fan mail: correspondence from clergymen, autograph collectors, admiring maniacs, and people who were just plain puzzled by what he had done. (One of the last-mentioned category was Mr. George Astley, proprietor of the toff's tobacco shop in Burlington Arcade, to whom Prince responded, "Had Mr Terriss only spoken to me, he should have been alive now, and the poor Prince would have been in Scotland. He asked for it, and he got it. That's why I killed the cur who could only fight a gay woman and a starving man.[18] Sent on tour to ruin my character. . . . I must see a doctor. I should like one of the best in London. If you can do this for me God will reward you. My soul is all right. . . . Bring or send a white shirt and collars, $15^1/2$ or 16, a tie, and handkerchief, and one stud. I would ask my sister Maggie again. She sent the last, but I don't think she is in London. She sent me a lot of under-things last week and ten shillings.") As well as giving consideration to his costume in the dock, he had decided, early on, to assist his characterization with a beard of the Mephistophelean kind. If it had occurred to him that he could, on account of local prejudice, request a change of venue for the trial, from the West End to some provincial place, he had, one may safely assume, given no second thought to an option that, if taken, might result in his appearing in a forensic equivalent of the Bijou Pavilion, Hetton-le-Hole.

---

18. A reference that may have seeded a story that, with artistic deletions and additions, was told as if it were true for many years. In 1930, Harry Davis, the recently retired manager of Rule's, gave his version of the story to the *Daily Herald:* "At the Adelphi was a very charming and pretty girl, the daughter of an assistant stage carpenter named Prince. She used to tidy up the dressing-rooms every morning. One day when Terriss came in earlier than usual to collect his letters he found her in his room. Her freshness, charm and vivacity made an immediate appeal to the somewhat jaded senses of the actor. He began to make love to her—violent, passionate love that left the girl dazed and bewildered. His grace and gestures, his art, his voice, the commanding presence that was his, carried her off her feet. A few months later the girl had to leave the theatre. In her despair, she told her parents that the actor was to blame. . . . That night Prince, the girl's father, tackled Terriss in the theatre. Burning rage against the betrayer of his daughter filled his heart and he reviled Terriss as no one had ever dared to revile the actor before. There was a violent quarrel. Terriss, in a fury, his vanity wounded and his conceit shaken, went to W. Brumsden, who was in charge of the stage hands, and demanded the dismissal of Prince that very minute. Prince was popular at the theatre. And he had justice on his side. But such was the power of Terriss, such was his voice in the affairs of the Adelphi, that Prince had to go. The Princes had suffered. The daughter had lost her good name; and the father had lost his job." As the continuation of the story is tamely proximate to the real denouement, it can be left to moulder.

On the morning of the trial, London was smothered by a pea-souper. The yellow-grey fog cloaked the tall windows lining the wall to the left of the bench in the principal court of the Old Bailey; intruding within, it dwindled to a mist that, from the gallery, crowded with people who had queued since the early hours, detrimentally to their lungs, and gave the impression of a stage scene viewed through gauze.

Adding minutely to the feeling of theatricality, the judge, Mr. Justice Channell, sported a sparkling monocle and treated as a versatile prop—baton, italiciser, toothbrush, ear probe, itch resister—the quill pen that he seemed rarely to use for its intended purpose. There was nothing stagey about the leading prosecutor, Charles Gill, senior counsel to the Treasury, who spoke with an Irish brogue but often stumblingly, never with eloquence or wit; epitomic of civil servants, he appeared to wear wig and gown unwillingly, as if he felt that they constituted a practical joke that tradition should have known better than to play in a serious place like a court of law.[19] Gill was assisted by Horace Avory: twig-thin, his gown drooping from his shoulders as if from a wire hanger, his features pursed to assemble an expression that in later years, when he was a judge, would help toward earning him the nickname of "the acid-drop." Avory's father had been clerk of the court at the Old Bailey, and his elder brother was the clerk of arraigns for the trial of Prince.

A Mr. Sands and a Mr. Kyd had been assigned to defend Prince. Neither of these barristers was (or ever would be) eminent. There was equality of numbers between the sides, prosecution and defence, but the imbalance of skills, of experience, was extreme. If any of the stage people in the gallery whispered among themselves about the opposing castings, perhaps there was recollection of the brief tale of two actors, one famed for a tour de force, the other unknown and forced to tour.

Waiting for his call, Prince fretted that, as he had been so often in the past, he was going to be let down by inadequate supporting players. Having made his escorted entrance through the trap in the floor of the dock, he gazed around the court, satisfying himself that he had drawn the town, and paid attention as Horace Avory's brother Kemp read the indictment and gave him his first cue, the question, "Are you guilty or not guilty?"

"I am guilty—with provocation," he replied. Then, turning his

---

19. Four weeks later, Gill was the prosecutor of Francis Carroll: see note 13, on page 268.

gaze toward the judge, he continued: "I have to ask a favour. I believe the law of England allows an accused person the right to a Queen's Counsel. I have counsel, but I should like a Queen's Counsel to watch the case on my behalf."

MR. SANDS (*rising from his seat below the dock*): I am instructed, with my friend Mr. Kyd, to defend the prisoner.

PRINCE (*affecting not to have noticed the interruption*): I understand that by the law of England I can have a Queen's Counsel. (*He lowers his head, his voice.*) I have no friends. My mother cannot help me with a penny for the defence. If you will not allow me to have it, I insist on saying that it must be paid by the people who drove me to do this crime.

MR. JUSTICE CHANNELL (*quietly but firmly; dotting the air with his pen at full stops*): You are not entitled by law to the services of a QC. On the contrary, if you desire the services of a QC, he would have to take out a licence to appear for you. You are entitled to have the benefit of counsel if you desire it. You are, of course, also entitled to defend yourself.

PRINCE: Thank you, my Lord.

MR. JUSTICE CHANNELL (*indicating by his tone that he doubts the prisoner's ability to make wise decisions*): Assuming you are in a condition to indicate what you will do. (*He points his quill towards MR. SANDS.*) There is a gentleman here who is prepared to conduct your case. I should advise you to accept his services.

PRINCE (*having had his attention distracted by the thought that it is some time since he groomed his rudimentary beard*): So long as I am allowed to defend myself, that is all I wish.

MR. JUSTICE CHANNELL (*trying to be patient*): You cannot be allowed to defend yourself in a general way as well as being defended by counsel. You may be allowed to make a statement to the jury in addition to being defended by counsel. I shall allow that, but nothing more. You may suggest anything to counsel.

PRINCE: That is all I wish.

MR. JUSTICE CHANNELL (*just to make sure*): Then you will be defended by counsel?

PRINCE (*certainly*): Certainly.

MR. JUSTICE CHANNELL *taps the writing end of his quill on the bench to attract the notice of* THE CLERK OF ARRAIGNS *and mutters at him*

to repeat the question regarding PRINCE'S *plea. This* THE CLERK OF
ARRAIGNS *does.*

PRINCE: I plead guilty—with the greatest provocation.

MR. JUSTICE CHANNELL (*less patiently*): You have told me you
will be defended by counsel.

PRINCE: Yes.

MR. JUSTICE CHANNELL: Then you had better take their advice
before you plead.

MR. SANDS *and* MR. KYD *rise and slant towards* PRINCE; *he leans over
the wooden shelf of the dock toward them. There is a sotto-voce conversation,* PRINCE *waving his Invernessed arms the while. Ultimately,*
MR. SANDS *and* MR. KYD *subside, while* PRINCE *returns to an upright stance and addresses* MR. JUSTICE CHANNELL.

PRINCE: I have been advised to plead "not guilty"—so I plead
"not guilty."

The curtain-raiser over, Charles Gill took little more time to outline
the case for the Crown. The first prosecution witness was Tom Terriss.
Examined by Horace Avory, he said that he had last seen his father alive
on 15 December. The following night, shortly before eleven o'clock, he
had seen him lying dead at the Adelphi. He did not know the prisoner.

PRINCE: I saw you once during *The Harbour Lights,* in the dressing
room. Perhaps you will remember that.

Ralph Croyden, manager of Miss Lena Develrey's London Theatrical
Company, was called next. The reporter for the *Daily Telegraph* noted
that when he came into the court,

the unfortunate man in the dock squared his shoulders and assumed a histrionic smile, which was clearly intended to convey
how little he thought of his quondam employer. This facial by-
play was continued through the witness's evidence. His statement that the accused described himself when he applied for
employment as having played big parts at the Adelphi was the
occasion for a confident glance at the jury. The sequel that Mr.
Croyden found that he could not play any part was met with a
reproachful smile directed at the speaker. All this time the prisoner was busy with memoranda for his counsel, and he changed

his position as the whim took him, now standing, now sitting. He had not tired yet of his miserable attempts to make an impression. The recall of his statement that "the world would ring with his madness" was the signal for another quiet display of self-satisfaction, strangely incongruous with the awful position in which the verification of that prophesy had placed him.

Among the following witnesses were Charles Coltson (who, incidentally, had arranged for the briefing of a barrister to watch the proceedings on behalf of the Actors' Benevolent Fund); Charlotte Darby, Prince's landlady at Eaton Court; John Graves; and Constable Bragg.

At noon—by then, the fog had cleared from the streets, the mist from the court—Charles Gill announced that the case for the Crown was closed. After an adjournment, Mr. Sands asked the jury "to disabuse their minds of all that had been said outside, and to pretend ignorance of the sympathy that was felt at the loss of one whose name had become almost a household word"; having explained how, as it seemed to him, madness was defined by the law, he said that he was confident that the forthcoming evidence would convince the jury that Prince was insane.

The *Telegraph*'s man again:

For an hour and more the cultivated and polished accents of counsel and the rugged Doric of Dundonian witnesses were interwoven in comical medley. It was far from plain sailing for either side, differences of dialect leading to constant misunderstanding.

As Mrs. Archer, the prisoner's mother, passed slowly toward the witness box and climbed laboriously up its steps—she was old and frail—the fixed smile faded for a time from her son's face, his eyes shone brighter, and one was fain to hope that natural affection was not entirely gone from that strange mind.

The idea received a shock a few moments later. The poor old lady, who, it may be mentioned, suffered from extreme deafness, spoke in a very low voice, and on counsel complaining that they could not catch her words, her son shouted from the dock, "Speak louder, Mother, they can't hear you."

She was very Scotch, and very canny, referring counsel on one or two points to other witnesses with the remark, "She'll tell you that," but withal was ready to sacrifice her mother tongue to the vocabulary of the "southern English." Prince was "never right" from his birth, she said, and swiftly terminated a pause of puzzlement with the addendum, "He was born mad." When he was a baby, she had occasion to leave him in the harvest field. When she came to him she found him blue in the face. He had received a sunstroke. Her son was "dour to learn"; then she tried again with "bad in the uptake," and finally achieved success with "slow at learning." Her next problem in Scotch was more difficult. Speaking of the accused's bursts of rage, she said, "They pit him rang in his mind, his passions," Two jurymen by her side could not understand her, though she repeated the phrase more than once, and then the prisoner interposed, "She said they put me wrong in the mind, my passions. That is the "English of it."

Speaking of times when he was unemployed and living with her, she said that he was sometimes not very well pleased; he used to think she doctored his food. He had told her a Mr. Arthur had kept him from getting work in the Dundee Theatre, and in saying so he used the word "blackmailing." This was eight years ago. He had told her he himself was the Lord Jesus Christ and that she was the Virgin Mary, and had charged her with adulterating his tea. When he was affected with what she described as "his turns," he would sing songs and hymns, and his eyes would stare out of his head. He had left Dundee for the last time five months ago. His father was formerly married, and a son by that marriage was mad from his birth but never locked up: he was silly.

Other Dundonians spoke of Prince's oddities of behaviour. And so did Arthur Ellison, the manager of a theatre at Southport, in Lancashire, who recalled, "While in my employ, and afterwards, I received postcards from him which spoke of blackmailing and horse-whipping. He charged me with thwarting him in getting an engagement, and called me a hell-hound."

PRINCE: Shut up! Shut up!!
WITNESS: If I am not mistaken, I discharged him.
PRINCE: If I am not mistaken, you are wrong.
MR. GILL: He had a very exalted opinion of his powers?
WITNESS: Actors in his position usually have.

MR. GILL: Can you remember a particular part he played?

WITNESS: The sergeant who led on the soldiers.

PRINCE: (*provoked by sniggers from the gallery*): It was a very good part.

The final witnesses were doctors: the medical officer at Holloway Gaol, who said that he had paid close attention to Prince during his stay, and two "experts in lunacy," both of whom admitted to Charles Gill that their evidence was based chiefly on their observations of the prisoner's demeanour in the dock. The three were unanimous in the opinion that Prince had been mad when he murdered, and was still. When one of the specialists remarked that "a person of sound mind would display, or at least feign, remorse at having committed such a dreadful deed," Prince cried out, "Why should I? Terriss blackmailed me for ten years."

After the closing speeches, the first for the defence, neither lasting more than a quarter of an hour, Mr. Justice Channell summed up, and at 6:30 the jury retired to consider their verdict.

Shortly before the trial, Henry Irving had told a friend, "They will find some excuse to get Prince off—mad or something" and had added what he considered an explanation: "Terriss was an actor, so his murderer will not be executed."

Whatever Irving meant by that last comment, his prophesies were made true at seven o'clock, when the foreman of the jury announced that "although the prisoner knew what he was doing and whom he was doing it to, upon the medical evidence he was not responsible for his actions."

Prince's look of puzzlement was replaced by a broad smile as the judge explained the import of the verdict: "That the prisoner shall be confined in a criminal lunatic asylum until Her Majesty's pleasure be known."

"Shall I be allowed to make any thanks to the Court for that?" Prince asked—and, without waiting for a reply, went on: "I should like to thank the gentlemen who have assisted me in the case. Of course, I did not bring my defence properly forward after the medical evidence, because I did not think it necessary. I will only say that I have had a very fair trial."

"I cannot allow any statement," Mr. Justice Channell snapped. "You had better not make any."

"Well, the only thing I can say, my Lord, is that I thank you very much."

"That is all." Without further ado, Mr. Justice Channell turned his pen into a magic wand, and Richard Archer Prince was made to disappear.

He spent the next thirty-nine years, the rest of his life, in the Broadmoor Criminal Lunatic Asylum. There, he was accorded celebrity status. Not because of the act that had resulted in his confinement. And not, as you might have thought, because he filched all the star parts in productions by the Broadmoor dramatic society. Giving up acting in favour of musicianship, he appointed himself conductor of the inmates' orchestra. He had a fine time, waving his baton with great panache, gesticulating, shouting things like *apassionato* and *agitato,* and every so often looking over his shoulder to see how the audience was responding to his performance. Marringly for many, the concerts lacked concertedness. Each of the instrumentalists played a different tune, and none took the slightest notice of the man who had once dreamed of being the Prince of Players.

A Wolf in Tanned Clothing

A Wolf in Tanned Clothing

ccepting that Sweeney Todd didn't happen, the trade of barbering seems to be less blemished by murderers in its midst than are nearly all others that are comparable in terms of number of traders.[1] Generalising psychiatrists, which means nearly all of them, will deduce from that comment that the 9-to-5 plying of scissors and cutthroat razors works "cathartically" upon barbers, turning them against using those tools lethally from 5 to 9. Until 1987, the public relations officer of the Hairdressing Council could, if he or she had wanted to, have proclaimed that there was a sort of minus-quantity of illegal dangerousness attributable to barbers—a deduction arising from the perception that there had been more deaths caused by barber-hangmen than by barber-murderers. (The most household-named of the former were James Billington, who executed during the last ten years or so of Queen Victoria's reign, meanwhile running a barbershop in Farnworth, Lancashire; his sons, William and John,

---

1. Prior to Stephen Sondheim's musicalising of the tale, the man most associated with stagings of it was Tod Slaughter, author of *Sweeney Todd, The Demon-Barber of Fleet Street*, and, from about 1922 until the late 1950s, the almost invariable player of the eponym. "Slaughter" really was his name (his brother, Ernest Slaughter, was a Fleet Street reporter for almost as long as he himself was an actor-manager), but "Tod" was a replacement for "N. Carter"; his secrecy about what lay behind the initial suggests that it stood for a name as innocuous as Noel. The moment that audiences of his playing of Sweeney Todd most savoured came when, after dropping a customer, chair and all, through the trapdoor and then exiting to "finish him off," he reentered, his hands drenched with "blood" (a mixture of olive oil and cochineal), and ruminated: "The old Jew—hmf—I thought he was anaemic." His repertoire of melodramas included some that were loosely based on the doings of real mass-murderers: *Landru, Jack the Ripper* (which he presented at, among many other theatres, the Granville, in the South London suburb of Fulham, while an uncle of mine was its manager), and *The Wolves of Tanner's Close* (he as William Hare). A special friend of mine, Richard Carr, stage-directed the last of his "farewell tours." I had tea with him once—which is to say that I drank tea; he was abstemious of that beverage, fearing that it might mar his fine-tuned taste for Scotch, of which he drank the equivalent of a bottle a day, none during performances.

who followed in both sets of his footsteps, William for the longer in the executional set; and John Ellis, who combined the same occupations—the barbering one in Rochdale, also in Lancashire—between 1907 and 1923, and who, eight years after retiring as a hangman, committed suicide with a razor that he had used professionally.) However, the outcome of proceedings at the Old Bailey in the summer of 1987 would have prompted the public relations person to put any proposal for a "You're Safe and Sound When Your Barber's Around" press release on what public relations people refer to as the back burner.

§

Michele de Marco Lupo was born to working-class parents, his father a bricklayer, in the northern Italian city of Bologna, which should be famous for things other than a spaghetti sauce and a sort of sausage, in 1953 or thereabouts.

Lupo, a not uncommon Italian surname, is the Italian word for *wolf.*

As soon as Lupo was old enough to be a choirboy in the cathedral, he became one; and, as his voice took longer to break than is normal, he grew to be the leading juvenile chorister. When he left school, meaning to go to a college of art, his form-master gave him a reference: "A boy of high quality whose morality is beyond question." Since hardly any boys of school-leaving age have proved that they are more or less moral than other boys (or girls, for that matter) of the same age, the teacher's tribute may actually have been a retort to rumours or a groundlessly optimistic prophesy that Lupo's morality would become unquestionable. I must emphasise that that is only a guess. In 1971, he was conscripted. To anyone who remembers World War II jokes about Italian servicemen but did not fight any of those servicemen, the idea of that country subsequently having commandoes will seem as preposterous as the idea of Switzerland having sailors; but Italy did, and perhaps still does: in 1971 there were at least twenty-two Italian commando units. Private Lupo was assigned to the 22nd.

One gathers that he served his time untroublesomely—that, while doing so, he was taught how to kill with efficiency and, if necessary, without the aid of blunt or sharp or explosive instruments—and that, also while serving his time, he either discovered or had a preconscription suspicion confirmed that he was unequivocally homosexual.

The latter knowledge, so it is said, worried him only as his parents—rigid adherents to Catholic doctrines, including some regarding matters that a growing number of Catholics believed that God had no strong feelings about—would be shocked, shamed, even made to feel guilty if they learned of his condition. With the intention—again, so it is said—of preventing that, he, demobilised from the army, decided to emigrate, at first with no particular other country in mind. He could speak, with varying degrees of fluency, four languages in addition to Italian, and so he believed that he had a wider choice of other countries than the average educated intending emigrant. English was one of the foreign languages he could speak.

In the end, it was a tossup between the United States (or rather, some of them: he excluded Alaska, Hawaii, those in the rather un-Catholic Bible Belt, and also those that were predominantly rural) and England—or rather, London. His choice, which was London, may be blamed upon the time when he was choosing, which was in the early 1970s, closely following the decade when London was supposed, mostly by people not living there, to be an especially "swinging" city. Small incidents sometimes have large effects: Lupo may have been lured to London because of an article about it in a once-glossy magazine that he picked up in a Bolognese dentist's waiting room. London had swung in a number of directions, several toward destinations that were either downright sleazy or attractive to sleazy people. Not only in Soho, there had been an uncontrolled infestation of establishments offering pornography on the premises or to be taken away; the word "kinky" had been coined as a replacement for "perverted," and shops specialising in merchandise appealing to kinky people had opened, not unlike sores, on prime sites in high streets, juxtaposed with branches of Woolworth's and Marks & Spencer's and of the brand-new chains of stores selling "natural Swedish pine" (unpainted Taiwanese chipboard) furniture and "farmhouse" (heavy and lopsided) crockery; transvestites had transvested in public, for money, in certain pubs and membership-at-the-door clubs, and some of those pubs and clubs, and others that provided no advertised entertainment, had become "in places" for people who needed drugs or desired to meet male or female prostitutes, etcetera.

By 1973, when Lupo arrived in London, it had swung in more directions, and further in those directions, than most founder-members of its "permissive society" had ever, in their wildest, wettest dreams of 1959, dreamed possible. It lived down to Lupo's expectations. He was enchanted. There is no accounting for taste.

Quite as enchanted as he was by what he saw were many natives (leaving out greengrocers, milkmen, people like that, but not excepting one or two heterosexual wealthy men) who caught sight of him. He was darkly handsome, he wore his white shirts, always white, open to the button above his Gucci belt, as if forgetful of buttoning and irrespective of nippy weather, and his jeans looked painted on; those lucky spectators who got close noticed that he smelt only of antiperspirant; and those luckier ones who struck up a conversation found it hard to continue, having been thrilled so by his funny accent, his charming smile, his lovely manners.

He soon had many male friends, and as each of them already had many gregarious male friends, he was almost as soon friendly with the friends of the first friends, and as each of them had other gregarious male friends, it wasn't long before he was friendly with them as well; and so on. I understand that there are marine protozoa that have a similar colonially multiplying facility, though I don't understand how, in their case, each of the ever-increasing multitude of organisms is able, as the fancy takes it, to adjoin any of the others. Lupo did not have sexual relations with all of the friends. Not quite all.

If he needed to rent a flat or bed-sitter when he arrived, I don't know where it was. He had no trouble in finding a job—doing something at a London branch of the French fashion and cosmetics firm Yves Saint Laurent. (Most of the other male employees took to him— he, showing slight discrimination, only to most of those.) He did not stay there long because, meanwhile, having been advised—wrongly, as it turned out—that the easiest way for him to make lots of money was as a hairdresser in an elegant "salon," he trained to be a hairstylist. The training must have been extremely unarduous, considering that he completed it in a month or so while he was working five or six days a week for Yves Saint Laurent and either enjoying the gay social whirl or recuperating from it at most other times. He then practised shampooing, snipping, and setting in one small salon after another, and eventually was engaged to perform in a large yet chic unisex salon in Belgravia. The total of his tips there, only a small percentage of which he declared to the Inland Revenue, dwarfed his properly taxed salary.

After a couple of years, he bought—apparently without the need of a mortgage—a flat in Roland Gardens, a select, dog-legged turning off Old Brompton Road, within easy walking distance of his daytime workplace.[2] Though some of his friends who were interior decorators gave him ideas, his initial furbishing of the flat was fairly convention-al. Over the years, however, as he sought more and more idiosyncratic sexual pleasures, and as he entertained more and more men who were as sexperimental as he was, he added a number of fixtures and fittings that were so unconventional that he cannot, surely, have had them fixed or fitted by workmen who were at all narrow-minded or inquisi-tive of the items' intended purposes; suffice it to say that among the items were shackles, either suspended from a ceiling (more depend-able than most) or attached to posts of Lupo's four-poster bed. Lying loose about the flat, much as in bourgeois living rooms, copies of *The Official Sloane Ranger Handbook* and pottery souvenirs of places on the Costa del Sol were deposited as if casually, were whips, riding crops, and unequestrian but just as hurtful implements, several of which had been bespoken by the occupant. By no means all of the visitors who, shackled or not, were given a taste of Lupo's leather or ironmongered bric-a-brac received the treatment on the house: as a moonlighting trade, drummed up by small ads in which he used the business name "Rudi" and which he inserted under the headings of "Esoteric" or "Bondage—No Holds Barred" in "homosexual-contact" weeklies, he tortured for cash (paid in advance by the torturees; Lupo's period of operation was one of high inflation, and so the best idea of his tariff is given by what he charged for the deluxe treatment in 1985, toward the end of the period, which was £100; I cannot tell whether his satisfied customers, not knowing that he was also a hairdresser and therefore expectant of tips, gave him any—but even if none of his regulars did, some of them must, like some drug addicts, have needed to thieve so as to afford their habits). Every so often, one or other of Lupo's neigh-bours complained about his loud playing of records (especially those made by his friend, a singer known as Freddie Mercury), but none of the neighbours seems to have complained about, or even commented upon, the thwacking sounds, the screams of pleasure and/or pain, the cries for mercy or greater punishment, which frequently disturbed the peace of that part of the Royal Borough of Kensington & Chelsea.

2. Fewer than two hundred yards west of the Onslow Court Hotel—the residence, until 18 February 1949, of Mrs. Olivia Durand-Deacon, the only one of the heaven knows how many victims of John George Haigh, the "acid-bath murderer," with whom he was charged with having dissolved.

Lupo was insatiable. Not content with his sexual busyness at home and in the London homes of friends, he travelled far and wide in the pursuit of being sadistic to masochists—for instance, a ballet dancer in Amsterdam, an unemployed aristocrat in West Berlin, a dress designer in Paris, a commercial artist, a shop assistant, a stockbroker, and a fashion photographer in Manhattan. And he exhibited himself, gossiping with old acquaintances while keeping his mascaraed eyes open for prospective friends or clients, in London clubs popular with homosexuals, such as a place called Heaven (owned by a company called, oddly enough, Virgin), underneath the arches that the music-hall act of Flanagan & Allen had made respectably famous many years before. On one occasion, in one of the clubs, he caused an especial stir by popping up, dressed to some extent as a nun, out of a coffin, and then made everybody laugh by lifting his skirt, to reveal that he was wearing fishnet tights, and doing a bump-and-grind dance. It would be interesting to know whether that act was witnessed by an acquaintance of his, a radio disc jockey who had turned to slapstick comedy, for the act was of a kind that would be performed by the versatile entertainer in his own series of television shows.

Lupo had a penchant for dressing up, and black leather was the material he most favoured for his costumes. He seems to have had only one *all*-black-leather costume, and that costume he wore only at home, tête-à-tête, and then only in the company of one or other of the friends or clients who were prepared to go to almost any lengths in aid of getting goose pimples all over. The outfit consisted of a hood, slitted so that he had no difficulty in seeing, breathing, and speaking (but, as it was not slitted at the sides, requiring whoever else was present to speak clearly), and with thongs, a little like spring onions, planted in and drooping from it; a leotard that had large holes in it, so that Lupo must have resembled a negative of a Henry Moore statue; a wristband, just one, that was embellished with and clasped by iron studs and bits of chain; boots of the type associated with wine treaders and soccer hooligans. There were no smalls. One of the clients for whom Lupo often donned that costume often brought along a costume of his own, which was that of a prewar preparatory-schoolboy—monogrammed cap, blazer, Aertex shirt, striped tie, short trousers, socks that were kept up by rubber bands, plimsolls, and an accessory satchel—and I hope that most readers will find it hard to imagine the scene of the elderly schoolboy and the leathered Lupo doing whatever it was they did.

Until fairly recent times in England, any white woman who wore a thin gold-looking anklet was advertising that she was a prostitute, any white man or woman whose hair was of fairground colours was to be pitied, and kept well away from, because that could only mean that he or she was being treated for fleas or lice with something like gentian violet, any white woman wearing an earring through her nose almost certainly had one black parent, and any man of any colour who wore an earring on an ear was undoubtedly a merchant seaman. But such decorations are no longer sure signs. It won't be long before diminutive men—and certain women too, perhaps—take to wearing the necktie of the Brigade of Guards, simply because the combination of blue and red goes nicely with a shirt or blouse. I must warn any heterosexual and occasionally slovenly man who possesses leather clothes or jeans that have come apart anywhere that he should either have them mended or throw them away—the reason being that, in some homosexual circles (which are sometimes unwittingly trespassed into), the wearing of such torn garments is interpreted as an indication that the wearer is "into violent sex."

It is at this point that the story of Michele Lupo becomes appropriate to a book about murder.

For months, maybe years, before the spring of 1986, he had sometimes worn leather clothes that he had torn to signify that he was into violent sex—to act as a tacit invitation to like-minded men. During a short period before that spring, he was able to buy leather clothes at a discount price, for he had left the unisex salon in Belgravia and become manager of a clothes shop, Tan Guidicelli, in Beauchamp Place, about halfway between Harrods and the Brompton Oratory. He had flaunted himself, and the gaps in his leather clothes, in clubs and pubs in various parts of London, some of the parts very seedy indeed, and the violent sex that he had enjoyed with some of the men whom he had met on those premises had whetted a desire to extend violence to mutilation and murder.

On Saturday, 15 March 1986, he visited the Coleherne pub in Old Brompton Road and picked up, or was picked up by, James Burns, a railwayman in his midthirties. They did not go to Lupo's home, only a stroll to the east, but about the same distance north, to the derelict basement of a house in Warwick Road, near the Earls Court Exhibition Building. Shortly afterward, two tramps entered the basement, meaning to make themselves unconscious with methylated spirit, and found the body of James Burns, who had been strangled with his own Burberry-check scarf and, either before or after death, savagely bitten, as if by a rabid wolf. Perhaps surprisingly, the tramps reported their discovery at the Kensington police station, in the parallel Earls Court Road. An investigation was begun. No one who had noticed Lupo and Burns conversing in the Coleherne, and leaving the pub together, imparted that information to the police.

On Thursday, 3 April, Lupo visited the Prince of Wales pub in Brixton Road—south of Elephant & Castle, and still farther south of Blackfriars Bridge, over the Thames. There he met Anthony Connolly, a twenty-six-year-old native of Newcastle-upon-Tyne who had had brief spells of employment as a waiter but was presently on the dole, and who considered himself fortunate to have been given accommodation in a nearby council flat, the registered tenant of which was a carrier of AIDS. Lupo left the pub ahead of Connolly—who, as he left, remarked to friends at the bar, "I have just met the most beautiful man." Two days later, his body was found in a disused railway shed even closer to the Prince of Wales than to the council flat which he had shared. He had been strangled and, either before or after death, savagely bitten, as if by a rabid wolf; the most noticeable difference between his murder and that of James Burns, less than three weeks before, was that, in his case, the strangling ligature had been taken away by the criminal.

An investigation was begun by detectives working from the police station in Kennington Road, to the north of Brixton Road. Strangely, and worryingly, the Kennington detectives were unaware that the Kensington detectives were investigating a similar crime—and vice versa. The Kennington ones were hindered by a forensic-medical delay: when Connolly's erstwhile flatmate went to Southwark Mortuary to identify the body, he happened to mention that he was a carrier of AIDS, and the mortuary staff, frightened that Connolly might have contracted that disease from him, refused to let a postmortem examination be conducted, and were supported by colleagues in other mortuaries, who refused to cross the picket line as stand-ins; and so a fortnight passed before a pathologist was able to venture within the vicinity of the body.

By then, Lupo had strangled (and, before or after, bitten) Damien McClusky, an Irish hospital-porter, just past his majority, whom he had lured to the derelict basement of a house in Cromwell Road, South Kensington, between the Victoria & Albert Museum and the Baden-

Powell House, the headquarters of the Scout Association. There was no serendipity in this case—no one stumbled upon the body. Officers of Special Branch who, knowing that McClusky belonged to the Irish Republican Army, had been keeping tabs on him, took his sudden disappearance concernedly, suspecting that he was lying low alive, making ready to use his membership in the IRA as the excuse for doing something psychopathic.

On Friday, 18 April, Lupo left Heaven late at night and started walking across Hungerford Bridge, which is meant as much for trains as for wayfarers. His intended destination can only be guessed at; the bridge leads, from Heaven's side, toward, among other districts of South London, Brixton—nowhere near Roland Gardens. Halfway across the bridge, he was accosted by a male vagrant, ostensibly "bumming for a fag" (but hoping for greater generosity—much as, when an October comes, children pleading for "a penny for the Guy" to celebrate Guy Fawkes Night are actually so contemptuous of that coin that they are liable to mug any literal-minded donor). Lupo—who was not only a nonsmoker but also an ardent supporter of the ASH antismoking organisation because he considered smoking to be a filthy habit—enticed the vagrant across the bridge and, on waste ground in the region of the Royal Festival Hall, strangled him with a black stocking which he, Lupo, happened to be carrying. There appears to be no information as to whether it was the stocking he had used on Anthony Connolly and Damien McClusky, or one of them, or fresh hose; a matter relating to a subsequent incident suggests that he did not use one stocking murderously more than once. The body was soon found, but the identity of the vagrant is still unknown. It is understandable that the detective or detectives who dealt with this case did not connect it with either of the cases that the respective detectives of Kensington and Kennington had not yet connected, for Lupo had not bitten the vagrant. He would say that, try as he might, he could not explain what possessed him to commit this particular murder: "I just decided to do it," he would remark with a shrug—adding, so that none of the audience ran away with the idea that his libido was grateful for even the grubbiest of small mercies, "I certainly did not get any sexual feelings—certainly not," and then uttering an afterthought that sounds suspiciously like a misquotation from William Burroughs, Jean Genet, or Barbara Cartland, or all three of them: "Something inside me was screaming to the world."

Presumably, something inside him was still screaming twenty-four hours after the murder of the vagrant, when, having coaxed or been coaxed by a young cook named Mark Leyland to one of the increasing number of public conveniences in Central London from which water had been cut off, he attacked Leyland with a length of iron adrift from the redundant plumbing. Leyland, unpartial to sex as violent as that, fled—eventually to a police station, where he told a no doubt dubious detective that he had gone to the loo simply and solely to relieve himself and had suffered attempted *robbery* with violence.

Less than three weeks later, between one and two o'clock in the morning of 8 May, a Thursday, Lupo was in or loitering near the Market Tavern, Nine Elms, which is about a mile and a half northwest of the Prince of Wales, Brixton. The Market Tavern is so named because of its proximity to the New Covent Garden wholesale fruit market; and because of that proximity—the law being sympathetic of the fact that much marketing is done in unsocial hours and that some marketing is thirsty work—the tavern was entitled to be open when most others had to be shut. The law ignored the fact that comparatively few of the people who took advantage of the Market Tavern's entitlement were marketers of fruit. David Cole, one of the early-morning regulars there, was—as James Burns had been—employed by British Rail; he was in his late twenties; he is homosexual.

According to his recollection of events in the small hours of 8 May, he got to talking to Lupo, whom he knew only by sight, and, at Lupo's suggestion, walked with him from in, or near, the Market Tavern to the market's main lorry-park. Lupo or Cole produced and broke an ampoule of amyl nitrate, a drug whose primary proper use is to relieve angina but which is used improperly, and dangerously, as an aphrodisiac. Squatting in a space shadowed by banana lorries, they sniffed the drug. Neither was quite recovered from its physical effects when Lupo pulled what he thought was a black stocking from one of the pockets of his black-leather trousers. It appears that he had come out in rather a hurry: he had pocketed, not a black stocking, but a black sock. In the darkness, he realised his error only when he tried to circle the sock round Cole's neck and found that it was nowhere near long enough. By then, his efforts to make a little go a long way were starting to make Cole suspicious of his intent. Cole's suspicion was confirmed when Lupo gave up with the sock and made a noose of his beautifully manicured hands. Cole's heart, still thumping as an effect of the drug, thumped even harder, faster, from fear. He chiselled his hands through the noose made by Lupo's, scrabbled it apart, shoved Lupo back, staggered to his feet, and ran all the way home—though, even before he was out of the lorry-park, his heart felt as if it might burst.

He rested. He wondered what he ought to do. And having decided what he ought to do, he wondered if that was wise. He telephoned an organisation that offers guidance to homosexuals, gave a counsellor an account of his experience, and was told that he should not inform the police. (A spokesman for the organisation has denied that Cole was given such negative counsel. Well, yes.) He had read of the murder of James Burns, and the more he now thought about it, the more firmly he believed that the murderer and the man who had tried to strangle him were one and the same. He telephoned Scotland Yard, and was told to telephone Kensington police station. A Kensington detective took a statement from him and decided that the man who had tried to strangle him was not the man who had succeeded in strangling James Burns; however, the detective had heard of the strangling of Anthony Connolly, and so he sent Cole's statement to Kennington police station. By the time it arrived there, the "Connolly-murder squad" was working from a police station in Stockwell, closer to the scene of the crime. Cole's statement was sent to that station—and eventually read by Detective Superintendent John Shoemake, the officer in charge of the Connolly murder investigation. Shoemake interviewed David Cole. Fortunately, Cole's memory of the events in the small hours of 8 May had not been dimmed by time.

In the early evening of 15 May, four undoubtedly heterosexual male members of the Connolly-murder squad paraded in black leather clothes that they had begged, borrowed, or hired, and, after being inspected by Shoemake and Cole, set off with the latter on a tour of places frequented by homosexuals; Cole had had to be cajoled into acting as lookout for his assailant and was so apprehensive of success that he often trembled and then had to be "jollied along" by the largest of the imperfectly disguised detectives. The posse cannot have looked as strange as it sounds; the detectives must have marched separately, pretending that they were not in one another's company, otherwise the progress of a "heavy mob" of men dressed as they were would surely have caused beat policemen along the route who had not been let into their secret to band together and trail them precautionarily. The tour began north of the Thames, taking in such places as Heaven and the Copacabana Club (which, despite its name, is in the Australian part of London), and continued on the south side: the Royal Vauxhall Tavern, adjacent to the plain Vauxhall Station of British Rail, the Market Tavern—and the Prince of Wales, Brixton. It was in that hostelry that David Cole spotted the man who had tried to strangle him, first with a black sock, then with his bare hands. Cole began trembling so violently that his escort knew at once that they were at journey's end—that the one man in the bar whom he was now determined not to look at was the man they were after.

Lupo came quietly. If any of the other customers guessed that the men leading him out were, in the argot of most of them, "pigs," none was intrepid or tipsy enough to utter the word "harassment" above a whisper. One surmises from Superintendent Shoemake's subsequent comment that his officers had "acted exemplarily in the face of harrowing and difficult experiences" that they would have reacted roughly to rudeness or ridicule of the slightest kind.

During his accompanied walk to the Stockwell police station, and for some time following his reception there, Lupo insisted that he didn't know David Cole from Adam. But then, as if orgasmically, he spilt out such a diverse confession that Shoemake and anyone else who was present must have been somewhat taken aback. Yes, he *had* tried to strangle David Cole—and yes, he *had* murdered Anthony Connolly—and oh, by the way, he had also murdered James Burns and the unidentified vagrant and Damien McClusky. He needed to give directions as to where McClusky's body was decomposing. A few days later, Mark Leyland, having read of Lupo's arrest, suggested to the detective who had taken his statement regarding the attempt to "rob" him that Lupo might be the culprit—and when that suggestion was eventually mentioned to Lupo, he agreed that it was so.

By then, Shoemake had visited, and some of his subordinates had taken stock of, Lupo's flat in Roland Gardens; Shoemake had also visited a flat in Chelsea which Lupo had cited as a "temporary residence," explaining that he had stayed there for some weeks, looking after the occupant, an elderly Italian widow whose daughter was married to an art director who was best known for his work on many of the James Bond movies. The daughter said that Lupo was "a lovely man who was very kind to a lonely old lady."

Among other possessions of Lupo's that Shoemake took from the guest bedroom in the Chelsea flat were some leather-bound volumes:

albums of snapshots, not all of which Lupo would have dared show the old lady, appointment registers (in which the handwritten word *Surgery* recurred), and address books. Leaving no stone unturned, Shoemake got a subordinate to count the entries in the address books: there were over seven hundred (a total considered insufficient by all of our comic daily papers, the least untrustworthy of which reported it as a thousand). Several of the entries were incomprehensible; perhaps they were in code, or perhaps they had been scrawled, Ouija-fashion, by Lupo while he was under the influence of an hallucinogenic drug. A number of the decipherable names were of much-publicised persons, one or two of whom so relished publicity that they employed press agents to buy them more. Included in that entire number were the names of smart photographers (it would be interesting to know whether any of them had taken any of the snaps in Lupo's albums), transvestites and transsexuals, dress designers (one of them peculiar in that he had become famous without having designed anything for either of our newest princesses by marriage), far-distant relatives of royal rulers of negligible places like Monaco, and society ladies (one of them best known by her nickname of Bubbles, which seems more likely to have been derived from a Shirley Temple perm that Lupo gave her than from her being associated with the song about bubbles which begins, "I'm forever blowing"). Speaking only of male names in Lupo's address books, he had entered an unrepresentatively large number of social workers.

I cannot tell you why the law's usual delays were added to in Lupo's case. More than thirteen months passed between his arrest and his trial, which was held in Court No. 7 of the Old Bailey, before the Recorder of London, Sir James Miskin, and a jury on Friday, 10 July 1987. Part of the unusual delay may have been due to if-at-first-we-don't-succeed efforts by psychiatrists, none successful, to find that Lupo was suffering from "a recognised mental illness or personality disorder." His claim, made to most of the psychiatrists, that he had had four thousand sexual partners since his arrival from Italy (which works out, on the basis of six-day weeks, and without allowing for holidays, as an average of one conquest per diem) is unlikely—as it would be impossible to verify—to get into the *Guinness Book of Records;* if it did, the editor might add a footnote to the effect that the slang word *baloney* is a corruption of the place-name *Bologna*.

Lupo's trial counsel, Lord Gifford—not for the first time, poor fellow, defending a defendant who had no defence—said little more during the proceedings than did his client, who, apart from saying "Guilty" to all of the counts of the indictment, said nothing. The recorder, illustrating the illogic of post-capital-punishment legal arithmetic, sentenced Lupo to life imprisonment on each of the four murder charges, and to consecutive terms of seven years for the two attempts, and told him, "I am confident that you will never be released until it is totally safe for the public at large."[3]

But Lupo was unlikely to live that long. He had contracted AIDS. It is reasonable to guess that his greatest punishment was that the prison authorities did their utmost to keep him away from other convicts, even those who were affected by the same disease. That was a punishment that came close to being fitting to his crimes.

3. In November 2006, I wrote to the Prisoner Location Service, asking whether Lupo was still imprisoned, and was told, wonderfully unhelpfully, that their records "did not disclose him to be in prison custody." Dead, then? Please God, yes. Even I, suspicious of psychiatrists, cannot believe that any of them would have decided that it was totally safe to release Lupo.

A Coincidence of Corpses

If they say that it rains
Or gives rheumatic pains,
    'Tis a Libel (I'd like to indict one.)
All the world's in surprise
When *any one* dies
    (Unless he prefers it)—at Brighton.
        —*"Arion,"* Blackwood's Magazine, *1841*

Dear Brighton, in our hours of ease,
A certain joy and sure to please,
Why have they spread such tales as these
    About thy smells?
            —*Anonymous, Society, 1882*

A Coincidence of Corpses

By midsummer of 1934, that year had the stench of decay about it. It was the sort of year that is remembered for what most people who lived through it would prefer to forget.

In Callander, Ontario, an accident of fertility called the Dionne quints was perverted into a multimillion-dollar industry. Only a day or so after the births on 28 May, while it was still touch-and-go whether any of the babies would survive, the father received an offer for them to appear, a constellation of stars outshining singular freaks of nature, at the Chicago World's Fair; he signed the agreement after consulting the local priest, who gave his advice in return for a commission on the deal. But, before long, other offers, and more lucrative ones, poured in, giving ample reasons to welch on the bargain with the Chicago promoters, ample funds to contest their claim. The Dionne Quints (yes, with a capital Q by now) went on to become an advertising symbol, a public relations exercise, a product to boost sales of other products. It never occurred to anyone that they might need protection against anything other than breach of contract.

On the sweltering-hot Sabbath day of 22 July, John Dillinger—"Public Enemy No. 1" and the first gangster to have a fan club—was shot to death by an impromptu firing squad of FBI agents as he left the Biograph Cinema, Chicago, after seeing *Manhattan Melody*, in which a prosecutor (played by William Powell) convicts his friend (Clark Gable) of murder. Following the shooting, the most human gesture was that of a policeman so delighted to see Dillinger dead that he shook hands with the corpse. Spectators dipped hankies in the blood; some lady onlookers went so far as to kneel and soak the selvedges of their skirts in it. As soon as the inquest was over, a queue-shaped mob surged past the body as it lay in state in a mortuary. A crowd even more dense—five thousand strong, it was reckoned, many carrying picnic hampers—was locked outside the cemetery (and was drenched but not depleted by a thunderstorm—"God's tears," according to someone who was prevented from attending)—while Dillinger's remains were interred. Those remains, for which Dillinger's father had turned down an offer of $10,000, weren't quite complete: during the autopsy—a select, all-ticket affair—a light-fingered person with a quaint taste in mementoes had pocketed the brain.

30 June ended as The Night of the Long Knives: Adolf Hitler, self-styled as "the supreme court of the German nation," organized the massacre of ninety or so people whose political views and morals did not coincide with his own. And on 25 July, over the border in Austria, the Heimwehr Fascists attempted a coup d'état. The timing was awry, though: the Nazis turned up at the Chancellery just after the Cabinet had gone to lunch. Still, Dr. Dollfuss was shot as he tried to escape. The Nazis refused to allow anyone out of the building to summon medical help, and the "little Chancellor" bled to death on a red leather couch.

Few people in Great Britain seem to have been specially concerned about the atrocities in Germany and Austria—least of all Oswald Mosley's black-shirted, fascist biff-boys, who were far too busy carrying out atrocities of their own, all in the name of King and Country. On 8 June, members of parliament expressed disquiet at the scenes of well-drilled thuggery they had witnessed at a Nuremburg-style rally at the Olympia exhibition hall the night before, and the home secretary recited an assurance that "the situation is under most careful scrutiny." Maybe it was some consolation to victims of Blackshirt brutality to know that the Home Office was watching what was happening.

A casual scanning of newspapers of 1934 gives an impression of a year that had more than its fair share of death; but this is probably an optical illusion induced by a large tally of banner-headlined accounts of bizarre deaths and postmortem occurrences. On a blustery day at the recently opened Whipsnade Zoo north of London, a man seeking to retrieve his bowler hat from the lions' den fell on the fatal side of the barrier; the first man to be hanged in Austria for fifteen years was a half-witted hobo who had set fire to a hayrick; the wife of the Nepalese Minister to Great Britain, having died, was cremated at an alfresco, coffinless ceremony at Carshalton, South London; in America, a resident of the Buckeye State of Ohio suffered a slapstick-comedy death by slipping on a banana skin. And in Brighton—addendum to attractions that were part and parcel of the holiday season—bodies were treated as baggage.

BRIGHTON. County borough, Sussex, 51 miles south of London (3rd-class return rail-fare, 12/10d.); on English Channel; magnificent promenade (3 miles) with two piers; fisheries. Pop. (1933 census) 146,700.

Its fortune founded in the middle of the eighteenth century by Dr. Richard Russell, of Lewes, who enticed rich sufferers from scrofula (otherwise known as the King's Evil) to bathe in—and even to quaff—the seawater at Brighthelmstone, a fishing village whose sole claim to fame until then was as the place where Charles II embarked for France following his defeat at Worcester, Brighton owed much of its subsequent prosperity and growth, and all of its architectural splendour, to the morally insane but aesthetically inclined George, Prince Regent, who was a regular visitor in summers from that of 1783 until that of 1820, shortly before he was crowned King, and in half a dozen summers afterward. The First Gentleman's influence was at least twofold: his presence acted as a magnet to others, and aspects of his taste were mimicked in the design of houses and hostelries that were erected to cope with the rush.

In 1934, Brighton was still the most resplendent seaside resort in England, perhaps in Europe. Pebbledashed and Tudorbethan residential nonentities were already blemishing the hem of the town, and office blocks, posing as architecture, degrading the skyline, but these were just first symptoms of a disfiguring rash. The general impression was of the Regency: of bowfronts and balconies, of faded stucco, of snooty squares, terraces, and crescents (some of which in propinquitous Hove had conveniences for dogs, few of which took advantage of them).

In this setting—and, by a perverse visual alchemy, seeming to be apt to it—there were all the gaudy trappings of a trippers' town: red, blue, and predominantly white seafood stalls, assailing the nostrils with the intermingled scents of vinegar and brine; fortune-tellers' booths, their velveteen-curtained windows patched with pictures of customers as celebrated as Tallulah Bankhead, Isaac Hore-Belisha (whose lollipop-like traffic-controlling beacons appeared on the streets that year), and aviatrix Amy Johnson; arcades crammed with penny-in-the-slot peepshows and pin-tables; a display of waxwork dummies; hundreds of greasy-spoon cafes ("Thermos Flasks Filled with Pleasure") and near as many pubs; dance halls; an aquarium; and souvenir emporiums that did a roaring trade in miniature-chamber-pot ashtrays, sticks of rock candy, straw boaters with ribbons that extended invitations such as "KISS ME QUICK," and naughty postcards painted by Donald McGill. There was even, on the prom, a store that offered not only rhinestone jewellery and strings of paste beads but also—unsurprisingly, come to think of it—"Ear Piercing While-U-Wait."

Since the days of the Prince Regent and his corps d'amour, Brighton had enjoyed a reputation as a place where sexual illicitness was allowed, expected, invited even; when the town was mentioned in conversation, a knowing wink was very nearly implicit. "A dirty weekend at Brighton" was a catchphrase so familiar as to suggest that the town had cornered the market as a venue for sexcapades—that weekends were never at all grubby at resorts like Lytham St. Anne's and Bognor Regis. As is often the case, with people as well as with places, the reality was less exciting than the reputation.

Brighton had acquired more nicknames over the years than anywhere else in the land. In the decade or so following the Great War, when the racecourse and the town were infested by villains, "Doctor Brighton," "London-by-the-Sea," "Old Ocean's Bauble," and other chamber-of-commerce-nurtured sobriquets were joined by "Soho-on-Sea" and "The Queen of the Slaughtering Places." But the preposterous coincidence of the town's being the scene of three of the five known trunk crimes in Great Britain made "Torso City" perhaps the most deserved nickname of all.

The first trunk murder was committed in 1831 by John Holloway, a twenty-six-year-old labourer on Brighton's Chain Pier, who was assisted in his post-executional chores by the fact that his victim—his wife, Celia—had stood only four feet three inches tall. His crime was brought home to him at Lewes Assizes on 14 December, and he was hanged two days later.

The next two trunk murders were London sensations.

In 1905, Arthur Devereux, a chemist's assistant, poisoned his wife and two-year-old twin sons with salts of morphine and crammed the bodies into a tin trunk fitted with a homemade airtight cover, which he deposited in a warehouse at Kensal Rise. Three months later, in April, his mother-in-law got permission to have the trunk opened. Arrested in Coventry, Devereux was tried at the Old Bailey in July; the jury rejected his plea of insanity (which was supported by a clergyman who asserted that Devereux was "a little bit off the top"), and he was hanged in August.

The third trunk-employing murderer was John Robinson, an estate agent who in May 1927 did away with an aspiring prostitute called Minnie Bonati in his office facing Rochester Row Police Station and afterward dismembered the body, packed the portions in a trunk, and deposited the trunk in the left-luggage office at Charing Cross Station. Robinson, who had scattered incriminating evidence as if it were confetti, was, like Devereux, hanged in the month of August and at Pentonville Gaol.

So far as is known, there was a lull of nigh on seven years before Brighton, home of the inaugural trunk crime, became the main setting for more than one.

៚

17 June 1934, the day when a large amount of the first-discovered body came to light, was a Sunday: a bright, tranquil day, one of many that summer, with the temperature on the south coast rising into the seventies by early afternoon. In Brighton's railway station, on the brow of Queen's Road, the sunlight, softened by its struggle through the grimy glass of the vaulted canopy, descended in dust-dotted, steam-flecked columns that emphasized the shadows.

Four o'clock: the median of a busy day at the station; a hiatus of calm between the arrival of the last of the special trains that had brought thousands of trippers to the town and the departure of the first of the trains that would take most of them—moist, pink-faced, salty-lipped—away after A Nice Day by the Sea.

It was stuffy in the left-luggage office. Occasionally, the movement of a bus, cab, or car in the forecourt of the station would send a breeze scuttling across the linoleum-surfaced counter; but this merely rearranged the stale air. And it certainly had no deodorizing effect on an item of luggage that, at that moment, was being discussed in unflattering terms—and not for the first time—by William Vinnicombe and James Lelliot, the attendants on the two-till-ten shift.

The plywood trunk was brand-new. Its covering of light-brown canvas was clean, unscratched—marred only by the counterfoil of the threepenny ticket, number G.1945, that had been dabbed on the lid when the trunk had been left for safekeeping eleven days before, on 6 June.

The trunk stood solitary on the stone floor, as if shunned by the pieces of luggage on the tiers of wide, slatted shelves. Actually, it had been left on the floor because of its weight. Harry Rout, the attendant on the other shift who had accepted the trunk, had told Vinnicombe that he remembered saying how heavy it was to the man who had handed it in. The only other thing that Rout had recalled of the transaction was that it had taken place some time between six and seven on the Wednesday evening. In his memory, the depositor of the trunk was faceless, formless; he might, just might, recognize the man if he saw him again—doubtful, though. After all, 6 June was Derby Day, and crowds of racegoers returning from Epsom Downs had combined with the usual early-evening commuter rush to overcrowd the station.

Now, standing as distant from the trunk as the confines of the left-luggage office would allow, Vinnicombe and Lelliot agreed that the smell from it—which they had first noticed a couple of days before and wrongly attributed to a shoulder of lamb insufficiently wrapped in sheets of the *Brighton Argus*—was growing stronger, more pungent, with every minute that passed. Before long—and in no time at all if the fine weather persisted—the odour would be unbearable.

Something was rotting within the trunk; there was no doubt about that. But what? The smell, as well as being noxious, was unique in their experience. In all probability, both men surmised what was causing the smell. Neither of them, however, was prepared to put the thought into words.

"Whatever it is," William Vinnicombe prevaricated, "it's definitely not lilies of the valley."

The conversation about the trunk drifted on; aimlessly, repetitively, uncertainly. At last—spurred, perhaps, by a specially rich whiff—Vinnicombe decided that enough was enough. Leaving Lelliot to hold the fort and to endure the smell alone, he went in search of a railway policeman.

As it happened, the officer he found was hidden from the public's gaze, having a chat with the constable of the Brighton police force assigned to uphold law and order in the environs of the terminus. Neither officer was pleased at having his unofficial tea break interrupted, but when Vinnicombe explained the reason for his own absence from his post, both of them accompanied him back to it. Having sampled what troubled the attendant, they agreed with him—and with the more talkative Lelliot—that the trunk gave cause for suspicion; they only nodded their agreement, then hastened from the left-luggage office and began breathing again. Talking to each other, they concluded that the trunk had to be opened and its contents examined, but that the adding together of their respective years of service did not equal the authority to take on the task. The Brighton policeman "got on the blower" to his station, which was a section of the town hall, and within a few minutes (the town hall being just over a quarter of a mile away, close to the sea) they were joined by Detective Constable Edward Taylor. The latter, a man of action, borrowed his uniformed colleague's truncheon and used it to prise open the two catch-locks on the side of the trunk. Then he flung back the lid. And then, his need for resuscitation easily overcoming his curiosity, he staggered out on to the concourse. Perhaps it was his imagination, but he was sure that the fumes from the trunk had seeped into his clothing. (Perhaps not imagination at all: even a year later, the trunk, sans contents and having had dozens of drenchings with disinfectant, gave off such a disgusting odour that the spare room at the police station where it was kept was dubbed the "stink-hole.")

Taylor was joined by another detective constable, Arthur Stacey (whose slight delay is explained by the fact that, having been ordered to proceed to the terminus, he had decided to wait for a tram rather than make himself intolerably sweaty by walking). The two of them dashed into the left-luggage office, stared into the trunk, observed a large brown-paper parcel tied with cord of the type that was used in Venetian blinds, scrabbled some of the paper away, sufficient to reveal a female torso, and dashed out again. Having recovered, Stacey telephoned the police station to request—no, to insist upon—the despatch of the head of the Criminal Investigation Department (never mind if it was his Sunday off), other senior detectives, an undertaker's shell, canvas screens, the police surgeon, and a posse of uniformed constables to what he described as "the scene of the worst crime we've had in donkey's years."

By the time the rush of homeward-bound day-trippers got under way, the left-luggage office was obscured by decorators' sheets; a scribbled notice apologized for the inconvenience of temporary closure. The offensive trunk, contents and all, had been removed to the mortuary. Its floor space had been scrubbed with boiling water and lye soap, and half a dozen detectives (known in Brighton as "splits") were perusing the remaining left-luggage for indications of the presence of the limbs and head that had been detached from the torso. No such parts were discovered. (But the search did reveal other human remains. A battered Moses basket, on the lid of which the initials VP

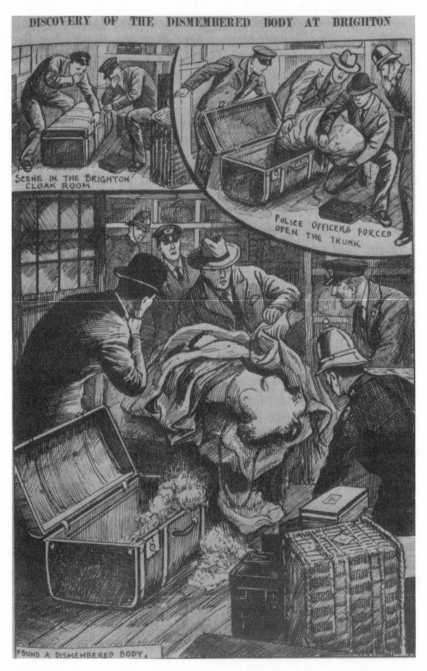

The discovery at Brighton (from *The Illustrated Police News,* 28 June 1934)

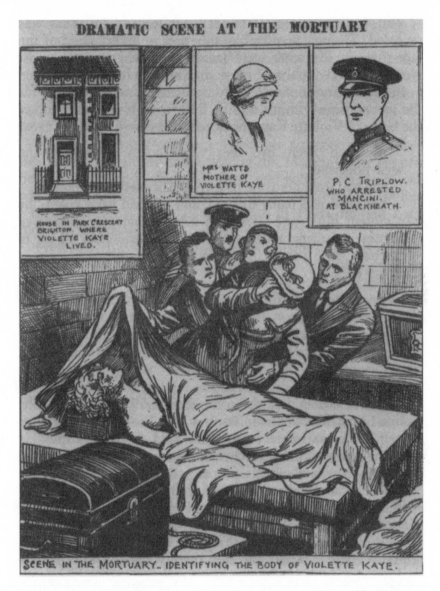

Mortuary scene identifying the body of Violette Kaye (from *The Illustrated Police News*, 26 July 1934)

had been partly scratched away, was found to contain the body of a baby—a girl who, if she had lived at all, had survived no longer than a few days. As the basket had been deposited as far back as 23 February, Detective Inspector Arthur Pelling, the officer in charge of the investigation, felt confident in saying that there was "no possible connection between this discovery and the trunk case.") The search was still going on when Captain W. J. Hutchinson, the ex-soldier who was chief constable of Brighton, got in touch with the duty officer at both Scotland Yard and the London headquarters of the railway police to ask for all left-luggage offices in the south of England—in coach depots as well as railway stations—to be scoured for suspicious baggage.

At the mortuary, the trunk was unpacked by the police surgeon. Not all at once, but over the next couple of days, the following facts were established apropos of the contents:

> Excepting the wounds of decapitation and dismemberment, the torso appeared to be uninjured; a small pimple below the left breast was the sole distinguishing mark.
>
> As well as the brown paper and the venetian-blind cord (19 feet of it; disappointingly unpeculiar, available from thousands of hardware stores at a halfpenny a yard), there were some hanks of cotton wool (used to soak up the blood?) and a once-white face flannel with a red border. Written in blue pencil on one of the sheets of wrapping paper were letters that looked like f-o-r-d; there seemed to be a preceding letter—*d*, perhaps, or a hasty *l*—but this was only just visible, on the right-hand edge of a patch of congealed blood. Was "ford" the end of a surname? Or of a place name?—Dartford, Guildford, Stafford, for instance. Or was "ford" a misreading? Were the letters actually h-o-v-e?—and, if so, was there a connection with the so-named western continuation of Brighton? (None of those questions would be answered. Toward the end of the week, the sheet of paper would be sent to the government laboratories in Chancery Lane, London, but none of the newfangled tests, using chemicals and ultraviolet rays, would bring to light the letter or letters that lay beneath the blood; and later, any number of people practising as graphologists would come up with any number of different readings of the visible letters.)

On Monday morning, Inspector Pelling enlisted the help of the press. "What I should like," he said, "is that members of the public, particularly those residing in the Southern Counties, including London, should contact the Chief Constable of Brighton if a female relative or friend disappeared without explanation on or prior to the 6th of this month." (The response to the appeal was over-gratifying:

by the beginning of September, twelve thousand letters, cards, and telegrams—not to mention many telephone calls—had been received; more flowed in during the autumn and winter, but no one at the police station bothered to count these.)

While Arthur Pelling was talking to reporters—guardedly concerning the crime itself—some of the policemen assigned to the investigation were scanning the Brighton and Hove missing-persons files, others were trying to establish whether those files required deletions or additions, and others were at the railway station, working in the left-luggage office or quizzing staff and travellers in the hope of finding people who had been there between six and seven on Derby Day and noticed a man who, perhaps with assistance, was carrying, pushing, pulling, or in some less conventional way transporting a trunk.

And at other stations, policemen of other forces were sniffing unclaimed baggage or, more fastidious, standing by or back while left-luggage attendants sniffed on their behalf. One of these stations was, of course, King's Cross, London, a primary metropolitan terminus of the London North Eastern Railway. There it was, on Monday afternoon, that William Cope, a porter deputizing for an attendant who was on holiday, sniffed and then unhesitatingly opened a cheap brown suitcase. Crammed inside the case were four objects wrapped in brown paper and copies of national newspapers, those wrappings soaked from within by blood and from without by olive oil. Cope looked no further before hailing a constable, who, having taken a fleeting glance at the discovery, blew his whistle to summon other, more senior officers, one of whom felt obliged to pay greater heed to the parcels. Finding that two contained a human leg apiece and that the other two each contained a human foot, he assumed that the feet had been cut from the legs, and that this had been done because, whereas the four parcels fitted snugly inside the case, two larger ones, roughly L-shaped, could not have been accommodated.

The first of those assumptions was confirmed by Sir Bernard Spilsbury, the honorary Home Office pathologist, who, once the legs and feet, still in the case, had been removed to the St Pancras mortuary, went there to examine them. As well as noting that the legs and feet were, so to say, a matching set, he concluded that they had been chopped, from the body of a woman—a natural blonde, he believed, basing that opinion on a microscopic examination of the faint down on the legs. The state of the feet—free of corns or other blemishes, the nails expertly trimmed—led Sir Bernard to believe that the woman had worn decent shoes (size $4^1/_2$, he reckoned) and that she had paid regular visits to a chiropodist, the final visit being shortly before her death.

By the time the police received the pathologist's report, officers at King's Cross had learned that the suitcase had been deposited round about half-past one on the afternoon of 7 June, the day after the trunk was left at Brighton station; they had interviewed Cyril Escott, the attendant who had issued the ticket, but had been unable to jog from him the slightest recollection of the person to whom he had issued it. However, the newspapers that had been used as wrappings—one dated Thursday, 31 May, the other Saturday, 2 June—seemed to provide a small and very general clue: after looking at the blood-and-oil-sodden sheets, a newspaper printer said that the "make-up," and "compositor's dots" on a front page, showed that the papers were copies of editions distributed within about fifty miles of Fleet Street.

Sir Bernard Spilsbury travelled to Brighton to examine the torso. He was occupied for three hours (during which time a crowd gathered outside the mortuary—a few locals, several reporters, and many holidaymakers, including "jazz girls," some conspicuous in beach pyjamas, some of those and others rendering the hit song, "It's the cutest little thing, got the cutest little swing—hitchy-koo, hitchy-koo, hitchy-koo," over and over again) and then informed Inspector Pelling that

> internal examination of the torso had not revealed the cause of death;
> the legs and feet found at King's Cross belonged to the torso;
> the victim had been well-nourished (which, put with the chiropody, suggested to Spilsbury "a middle-class background"); she had been not younger than twenty-one and not older than twenty-eight, had stood about five feet two inches, and had weighed roughly eight and a half stone;
> she was pregnant at the time of her death.

        ᔐ

On the Monday afternoon, Brighton's seaward newsboys, standing at corners on the promenade or crunching through the pebbles on the front, had a cry in common:

"Horrible murder in Brighton! Dead body in trunk!"

The cry gave a man known as Toni Mancini the worst shock of his twenty-six years of life. Since the start of the holiday season, he had been employed as a waiter and washer-up at the Skylark Cafe, which took up one of the manmade caves beneath the promenade, entered from the beach. On this particular day, his attention had been almost wholly directed at the kitchen sink. Therefore, he had heard nothing of the discovery at the railway station.

"Toni Mancini" was not his real name but just the current favourite among an accumulation of aliases that included Jack Notyre, Luigi Pirelli and Antoni Luigi. He had committed a few petty crimes, but the Italianate aliases, rather than being inventions aimed at misleading the police, were symptoms of his Valentinoesque dreamworld; so was the way he slicked his dark hair diagonally back from a central parting, and so was his attitude toward a string-thin moustache, which was there one week, gone the next. Actually, he was a native of the South London borough of Deptford, where he had been born on 8 January 1908 to an eminently respectable couple—his father a shipping clerk—with a determinedly unforeign surname; the parents had borrowed from the nobility for his Christian name and made the mother's middle name his, thus arriving at Cecil Lois England.

Still, to save confusion, we may as well refer to him as Toni Mancini. He was already calling himself that when, in 1932 or thereabouts, in London, he met up with and soon moved in with a woman sixteen years older than himself. Though her first name was Violet, and despite the fact that she was still married to a man named Saunders, she insisted on being called Violette Kaye, which was the name she had used during an unprosperous career as a dancer in chorus lines—first, "Miss Watson's Rosebuds"; finally, "The Parisian Pinkies"—at tatty provincial music halls. Subsequent to terpsichory, she had turned to prostitution, and she was well versed in that trade when Mancini joined forces with her, soon to add business to pleasure by appointing himself her pimp. The partners moved from London to Brighton in the spring of 1933. Occasionally, slumps in the never great demand for the forty-one-year-old Violette's services forced Mancini to work; but more often than not he spent afternoons and evenings in dance halls, usually either Sherry's or Aladdin's Cave, for he was as much a master of the tango and the fox trot as Violette had ever been mistress of tap- and clog-dancing routines. They shared a succession of small furnished flats, the last being in the basement of 44 Park Crescent, almost opposite the Race Hill Inn on the main Lewes Road.

That was their residence on Wednesday, 10 May 1934, when (according to the account given by Mancini a long time afterward) he finished a stint at the Skylark Cafe, went home for tea, had a flaming row with Violette, who was the worse for drink or drugs, and, in the heat of the moment, threw a coal hammer at her—with such unintended accuracy as to kill her. Flummoxed, he left the body lying on the floor, close to the fireplace. When he eventually thought that he must put it out of sight, rigor mortis was complete, which meant that he had the devil's own job fitting it, standing in an upright pose, into a wardrobe (within which, as the rigor wore off, it dropped in fits and starts, making rather alarming noises while Mancini was trying to sleep). To forestall the arrival of Violette's sister, who was looking forward to spending a week in Brighton, sleeping on the Put-U-Up, in the basement flat, he sent her a telegram:

> GOING ABROAD GOOD JOB SAIL SUNDAY
> WILL WRITE VI

A week or so later, he decided for some reason to move from Park Crescent to the diminutive basement flat at 52 Kemp Street, the southern bit of a dingy thoroughfare that, after being crossed by a main road, became Station Street—so named because its western aspect was the blind side wall of Brighton's railway terminus.

In preparation for the move, he purchased a black fibre trunk from a dealer in secondhand goods, not haggling at the asking price of ten shillings. Having stowed his and most of Violette's belongings in cardboard boxes and suitcases, he transferred the corpse from the wardrobe to the trunk, packed the crevices with female garments that remained, scattered a bag of moth-balls over the contorted body, closed and locked the trunk, and threw away the key. As, on his own, he could hardly shove the trunk, let alone lift it, he borrowed a wheelbarrow, then persuaded two acquaintances, a blind piano-accordionist named Johnnie Beaumont and a kitchen porter named Tom Capelem, to help him lug the trunk to the barrow and trundle the barrow to Kemp Street. When Capelem enquired, "What yer got in 'ere—a body?" Mancini replied, with every appearance of nonchalance, "Silver and crockery do weigh surprising heavy, don't they?"

He involved himself in additional expense in the basement flat, for he decided that as he intended to use the trunk as a makeshift seat when he had more than one teatime guest, he needed to cover it with something: he bought a square of pretty, primrose-patterned American cloth from Woolworth's. Though, as the weeks went by, the trunk became increasingly malodorous and began to leak body fluids, Mancini continued to have visitors. He was fortunate at least in one respect: the landlady had no sense of smell—and when she commented on the fluids seeping into the floorboards, he told her that they were a unique blend of French polishes, so were enhancing the boards rather than disfiguring them, a reply that pleased her so much that she asked for a quote for spreading the stuff wall-to-wall. On one occasion, a lady guest broke off from munching a muffin to say, "Do excuse my curiosity, but I'm wondering if by any chance you breed rabbits or . . . um . . . skunks." "That funny smell, you mean?" Mancini asked. "I must apologize for it. And when I have a minute to spare, I'll remove the cause—which (I hesitate to admit this) is an old pair of football boots, reminders of my lost youth: Queen's Park Rangers were keen to sign me on, you know. Won't you partake of the raspberry junket? I made it with my own fair hands, and it would be such a shame to let it go off."

When, on the afternoon of Monday, 17 June, Mancini was allowed a five-minute break from his chores in the kitchen of the Skylark Cafe, he sauntered between the white-painted cast-iron tables and out on to the beach. There he heard the newsboys' cry. Assuming, reasonably enough, that he was the only person in or anywhere near Brighton who had lately put a body in a trunk, he furthermore assumed that Kemp Street was at that moment a hive of police activity; and, once he was able to hear his thoughts above the beating of his heart, he registered surprise, astonishment even, that the only uniformed person within arresting distance of him was a deck-chair attendant. Extending his five-minute break, he staggered across the pebbles to where the occupant of a deck chair was reading a copy of a special edition of the *Brighton Argus*. Forcing himself to look over the man's shoulder, he read the headlines above, and stared at the picture illustrating, the report of the trunk crime. *Of a trunk crime that was quite independent of his own.*

At last believing the unbelievable, he strode back to the cafe. And he whistled a happy tune.

ᔕ

You will recall that when Toni Mancini first heard of what came to be called "Brighton Trunk Crime No. 1"—differentiating it from the death and subsequent bundling of Violette Kaye, which was billed as "Brighton Trunk Crime No. 2"—Sir Bernard Spilsbury was toiling over the torso in the mortuary. Also, policemen were traipsing the town, some checking on whether women reported missing were still astray, others looking in empty premises and even burrowing in rubbish dumps on the off chance of happening on the head and arms to augment the portions found fifty-one miles apart; and, at police headquarters, a trio of detectives was considering the first suggestions from the public regarding the identity of the victim (who, by the way, had already been dubbed "The Girl with the Pretty Feet" by a London crime reporter—the same man, perhaps, who would call Violette Kaye "The Woman with Dancer's Legs" and her terminal souteneur "The Dancing Waiter"). And, some time during the same period, Captain Hutchinson, the chief constable, had a word with Inspector Pelling and then telephoned the Commissioner of the Metropolitan Police to request that Scotland Yard detectives be sent to Brighton to take control of the investigation; by making the request promptly, Captain Hutchinson ensured that the cost of the secondment would not have to be met by local rate-payers.

The "murder squad" detective chosen for the assignment was Chief Inspector Robert Donaldson, who was, in comparison with most other policemen, quite short. His relative diminutiveness and neat apparel might have led people to believe that he was a "desktop detective," also that he lacked endurance. Both notions would have been far from the truth. Not only had he taken part in a number of murder investigations, but on several occasions he had "gone in mob-handed" to arrest violent criminals, some carrying firearms. Any doubts about his stamina would be dispelled by his sojourn in Brighton, during which he worked eighteen hours a day, seven days a week, for months on end.

The detective sergeant who accompanied Donaldson to Brighton was Edward Sorrell, who at twenty-six had only recently joined Scotland Yard. Donaldson had not worked with him before but chose him as his assistant after talking to him and getting "an impression (proved accurate) of intelligence and alertness." (That and subsequent otherwise unattributed quotations are from letters that Robert Donaldson wrote to me from his home in New Zealand in the 1970s.)

Donaldson knew that it was vital to get the support of Arthur Pelling, who might feel put out at having had control of the investigation taken away from him. This he succeeded in doing; indeed, the two men became friends. Donaldson considered Pelling "a very competent detective. A Sussex man whose father had been in the force, he was serious-minded and conscientious. He showed no resentment that Scotland Yard were summoned to the inquiry, and it was largely through his efforts that the Brighton Constabulary, as a whole, were most co-operative."

Captain Hutchinson arranged for Donaldson to have a team of a dozen detectives and uniformed officers and promised that additional manpower would be provided if and when it was required. As no large offices were available to be turned into "trunk-crime headquarters" at the police station, Captain Hutchinson asked the town clerk if there was space to spare in any council-owned premises, ideally in the centre of Brighton.

Thus it was that the investigators occupied three apartments adjoining the music salon in the Royal Pavilion; and there, amidst the chinoiserie bequeathed by King George IV, and sometimes to the muffled accompaniment of string quartets and of choirs eager with hosannas, they got on with the task of trying to identify the Girl with the Pretty Feet, of trying to establish who had gone to such lengths to make that task difficult.

The police did all the things one would suppose they would have done and many that were out of the ordinary. The investigation, uniquely thorough, comprised a myriad of activities, some of long duration, others of a day or so or a matter of hours. For instance, as a result of what the press called "the great round-up," 732 missing women were traced. A questionnaire was sent to every hospital and nursing home in the country. Hundreds of general practitioners and midwives were interviewed. At Queen Charlotte's Hospital, London, the main one for maternity, five thousand women, some from abroad, had received prenatal advice or treatment between the beginning of February and the end of May; all but fifteen were accounted for.

Statements were made by several residents of Worthing, just along the coast, to the effect that a man who had until recently owned a seagoing vessel had offered them the opportunity of seeing a rather unusual double bill: first, the murder of a woman, then her dismemberment. The would-be exponent of Grand Guignol was tracked down, interviewed, and dismissed as being "all mouth and no achievement." Much the same description was applied to the several men and two women who insisted, despite clear evidence to the contrary, that they were the "trunk criminals." Donaldson's men took notes but little notice of what clairvoyants, water diviners, teacup readers, numerologists, vivid dreamers, and people who had been given Ouija boards for Christmas had to say. (One or the clairvoyants, known to his many fans as Grand Wizard of the Past and Future, told a Brighton detective—and, after being shown out of the Royal Pavilion, a reporter for the *Sunday Dispatch*—that "the trunk criminal is probably called George; he has busy hair, works in a wholesale seed-store, and originally used the brown paper found in the trunk for wrapping up tyres.")

Police throughout the country asked register-office clerks whether in the past few months couples had given notice of marriage but not turned up to complete the transaction. The thought behind this question was that whoever had made the trunk victim pregnant may have bolstered the conning of the girl with indications of legitimizing intentions.

Of the many people who responded to repeated appeals that anyone who was at Brighton railway station between six and seven on the evening of Derby Day should come forward, two women and a man, the latter a retired warrant officer of the Royal Engineers, claimed to have seen the—or *a*—trunk being transported toward the left-luggage office. The trouble was that, whereas the women—fellow Tory travellers from a garden party at North Lancing—were convinced that they had seen just one man coping with a trunk, the ex-soldier was sure that he had seen two men sharing a similar load. Still, his description of one of the men—"about forty-five, tall, slim, dark, clean-shaven, and quite respectably attired"—came close to the description arrived at (perhaps after much "No, you're wrong, Mabel" "I'm certain I'm right, Edna" discussion) by the women; and as all three witnesses had been at the station within a period of a few minutes, it was reasonable to hazard a guess based on the station master's notes of the actual times that trains had reached Brighton—that if the trunk was brought to the station by rail, its journey was short, probably from the west and no further away than Worthing. An artist was called in to make a portrait from the witnesses' specifications, and copies of this were shown to staff at local stations; but though one or two railwaymen raised hopes by saying that the drawing slightly resembled someone or other who at some time or other had entrained to somewhere or other, the eyewitness evidence led nowhere.

An imperfection was observed in the serration of a piece of brown sticky tape affixed to part of the wrapping that had been round the torso. Therefore, policemen called on every single stationery supplier in London and the Southern Counties, trying—but without success—to find a saw-blade cutter with one tooth blunted in a peculiar way.

So as to check a London suspect's alibi, particles of sand found in his car were compared with samples of sand from near Brighton and from sandy-beached resorts east of Bournemouth and south of the east coast of Yarmouth. The sand turned out to be unique to Clacton, in Essex—a fact that lent support to his story.

Upon completion of one of the early begun tasks—the interviewing of residents of Brighton who might help to establish the whereabouts of women who had suddenly become conspicuous by their absence—Donaldson ordered that the interviews be repeated. A roster was prepared, its aim being to ensure that everyone already interviewed was revisited—and by a different officer.

Right at the end of the first sweep, one of Violette Kaye's customers had called at 44 Park Crescent and, having been told by the landlady that "Mr. and Mrs. Mancini" had gone, she knew not where, reported the prostitute's departure to the police. On Saturday, 14 July, a constable had traced Toni Mancini to the Skylark Cafe and, not liking the look of him, decided to take him to the Royal Pavilion rather than question him at his place of employment. But after Mancini, ostensibly quite at ease, had said that his "old friend Vi" was trying her luck in France, Germany, or somewhere like that—and that she was forty-two, at least fourteen years senior to the trunk victim—he was allowed to leave.

But Mancini did not return to the Skylark Cafe; nor did he go to the house in Kemp Street—the front of which had since the day before been latticed with scaffolding, put there on behalf of a firm of decorators who were to start repointing the brickwork on Sunday. No; he sought out a girlfriend and treated her to a plate of cod and chips at the Aqua Cafe, which was at Old Steine, near the Palace Pier. He was not his usual cheery self. Ever the perfect gentleman, though, he commented that the girl looked rather nice in her new dress (which was not new at all: once the possession of Violette Kaye, Mancini had presented it to the girl a week or so after Vi's demise, suggesting that it could do with dry cleaning). The girl was still eating when Mancini abruptly asked for the bill, paid it, left an over-generous tip, and, muttering something that the girl didn't catch, walked out of the cafe. The waitress scurried across to bag the tip. Lifting the cup of tea that Mancini had barely touched, she pointed out to the girl that he had left her a message, scribbled in blue crayon on the tablecloth: SEE YOU LATER, DUCK.[1]

Mancini was already on his way to the northern outskirts of the town, where he would hitch a ride to London.

On Sunday morning, just as one of Donaldson's team was about to leave the Royal Pavilion to start a round of repeat interviews, including a second chat with Toni Mancini, at his home this time, a telephone call was received from a foreman-decorator, who insisted that the police come to 52 Kemp Street at once. Why? Well, for the simple reason that he and his mates, repointers all, needed gas masks against the dreadful smell coursing into the street from the nether regions of the dilapidated house.

The detective with 52 Kemp Street on his list of addresses was told to delay his departure. When he left the Royal Pavilion, he was accompanied by colleagues, one of whom was Detective Constable Edward Taylor—who, you may recall, was the officer who had opened the stinking trunk at the railway station exactly four weeks before. Arriving outside the house, the detectives at once followed the example of the waiting decorators and turned up their noses; Taylor afterward expressed mystification that the smell, which must have been polluting the outside air for days, had not offended any of No. 52's neighbours, nor the scaffolders, into complaining about it to a health officer. As there was no reply when the detectives banged on the front door (it turned out that the landlady and her husband—he as senseless of smell as she was—had arranged to be away on holiday while the external decorations were being done), they broke it down.

Having descended the uncarpeted steps to the basement, the detectives first of all flung open the windows, front and back. Then the highest-ranking of them pointed an accusing finger at the black trunk and twitched another finger in Taylor's direction, indicating that he had volunteered to open it. The detectives, every one of them,

---

1. "Duck," a term of endearment in the 1930s, seems to have died out. (In and around Newcastle-upon-Tyne, and in parts of Scotland, the term of endearment "hen" survives.)

Brighton Trunk Crime No. 2 (from *The Illustrated Police News*, 26 July 1934)

were sure that the trunk contained the missing head and arms. Taylor grabbed a sharpening iron from among the stuff on the draining board and, his head reeling from a blend of stink and déjà vu, prised open the locks and pulled back the lid.

You will be aware—basically at least—of what was revealed. Though predictable, mention must be made of the fact that the contents were lavish with maggots, the most gluttonous of which were more than an inch long.

In the afternoon, Sir Bernard Spilsbury visited Brighton for the second time within a month. Following his examination of the body of Violette Kaye, he noted on a case card that

> she had been five feet two inches in height and well-nourished;
> she had used peroxide to turn her brunette hair blonde;
> her head was badly bruised, and she had been killed "by a violent blow or blows with a blunt object, e.g. head of hammer, causing a depressed fracture extending down to the base, with a short fissured fracture extending up from its upper edge."

Even before Spilsbury's arrival, Robert Donaldson—depressed that he now had two trunk crimes to deal with, though "Brighton Trunk Crime No. 2" seemed to be virtually solved—broadcast a message to all police forces, giving a description of Toni Mancini and asking that he be apprehended.

At about eleven o'clock on the night of Wednesday, 18 July, Police Constables William Triplow and Leonard Gourd were sitting in a patrol car near the Yorkshire Grey pub in Lewisham, South London, close to Mancini's birthplace. All at once, Triplow nudged his partner and pointed through the windshield in the direction of a well-lighted roundabout. A man was walking toward an all-night cafe. "So what?" Gourd muttered. "Look at his walk," Triplow said. Gourd looked. Yes, there *was* something odd about it: it was more of a prance than a walk; the feet merely dabbed the ground, making one think of a liberty horse—a tired liberty horse. "I reckon it's the Brighton-trunk bloke, the 'dancing waiter,'" Triplow said. With that, he left the car and ran toward the man.

"Excuse me, sir," he said, "but do you happen to be Mr. Marconi?"

"Mancini," he was corrected. "I couldn't half go a cup of tea and a sandwich or something."

Triplow and Gourd took Mancini to the local police station. A phone call was made to Scotland Yard, and from there a message was sent to Brighton police headquarters, saying that Mancini would be arriving under escort in the town in the early hours of the morning.

The arrest was front-page news on papers that reached Brighton at about the same time as did Mancini. The reports heaped praise on William Triplow, one going so far as to call him "the sharpest-eyed policeman in the Metropolis." (When I met him at his home in Lewisham in the 1970s, he had been blind for several years.)

Presently, a queue began to form outside the magistrate's court. Most of the queuers were young women, some of whom bragged of having partnered Toni on the dance floor, others of whom went farther in boasting of their knowledge of him. Soon there were more than fifty people in the queue. As there were only fifty seats in the gallery of the court, the thousand or so latecomers disorganized themselves into a cheering, singing, waving-to-press-photographers mob. Mounted policemen were needed to bisect it when Mancini, flanked by detectives, made his first public appearance as a celebrity. He looked as if he had been allowed to shave, but his clothes—dark blue jacket, grey shirt, white tie, flannel trousers—were crumpled. He smiled in response to the shouts and screams of "Hello, Toni," "Keep your pecker up," "Don't worry, love, all will be well," and frowned concernedly when a woman in beach pyjamas fainted, either from sheer emotion or from absence of underwear on a rather chilly morning. The girl he had treated to fish and chips at the Aqua Cafe stood apart from the mob; she was again wearing the dress he had given her.

Similar scenes were enacted when he left the court, having been remanded into custody, and when, over the next few weeks, he was brought from Lewes Gaol, first for further remands, then for the committal proceedings, at the end of which he was ordered to stand trial at the forthcoming Lewes Assizes.

The trial lasted four days. Beforehand—perhaps on his own initiative, perhaps at the suggestion of his counsel, Norman Birkett—he had done some preparation:

"I had carefully rehearsed my lines like an actor. I had practised how I should hold my hands and when I should let the tears run down my cheeks. It might sound cold and calculating, but you have to remember that my life was at stake."

Toni Mancini's acquittal (from *The Illustrated Police News*, 20 December 1934)

His story—in its essentials, entirely false, as he admitted when the rule against double-jeopardy protected him—was that he had found Violette Kaye lying dead when he returned to the basement flat in Park Crescent on 10 May. As he had a record of convictions for petty crimes (none involving violence—an important point in his favour, Birkett contended), it would not have occurred to him in a month of Sundays to report the matter to the police: "I considered that a man who has been convicted never gets a fair and square deal from the police." So—very silly of him, he now understood—he had bought the trunk, wedged the body in it, and moved, trunk and all, to a different basement.

Birkett brilliantly abetted the lies, saliently by patching together disparate answers from prosecution witnesses so that they seemed to support the theory that Violette Kaye had either taken a mite too much morphine and fallen down the area steps or been pushed down them by a dissatisfied, over-eager, or jealous client—and that, whatever had caused the fall, she had struck her head on a projecting rail or a pilaster of masonry.

Holes gaped in both Mancini's story and Birkett's theory: but the jury, having stayed out for some two hours, returned to the bijou court with a verdict of "not guilty."

Was Mancini surprised? One cannot tell. When he entered the dock to hear the verdict, he was wearing an overcoat—indicating that he expected to walk out into the high street a free man—but when the foreman of the jury spoke two words rather than the fatal one, he staggered and stared, and when he was at last able to speak to his counsel, he muttered, "Not guilty, Mr. Birkett—not guilty?" as if he were a character in someone else's dream.

(The following summer, Mancini toured fairgrounds with a sideshow featuring a variation on the trick of sawing a woman in half. Instead of a box, he used a large black trunk; his "victim" was his wife, whom he had met at Aladdin's Cave shortly before his flight from Brighton and married a week after his acquittal. He did not draw the crowds for long, and was almost forgotten by 1941, when he was serving in the navy. In that year, a man who really was named Toni Mancini was hanged for a gang murder in Soho, and people recalled the earlier case, the self-styled Toni Mancini, and said, "Now there's a coincidence.")

While Brighton Trunk Crime No. 2 had been delighting the populace, Robert Donaldson and his eventually reduced team of helpers had been working hard to solve Trunk Crime No. 1. Donaldson had reason to believe, but was never able to prove, that one or both of the missing arms had been burned on the Sussex Downs, close to a place where, after the Great War, the bodies of Hindu soldiers who had died in hospitals in or around Brighton were cremated. As to the whereabouts of the head—well, perhaps Donaldson obtained a general indication of its resting place when, early in September, he was put in touch with a young man of the town. The latter stated that "shortly before the discovery at the railway station, he and his girl had been walking along Black Rock, to the east of Brighton. In a rock pool they found a head. It was the head of a young woman. The man explained to his sweetheart that they should leave it alone as it was probably the remains of a suicide and that the police had removed all they needed of the body."

As soon as Donaldson received this information, he caused a search to be made of the whole beach: "Nothing relevant was found, so I consulted various marine authorities on the question of where the head might be; the sweep of the tides indicated that it could have been taken out to sea and then swept ashore at Beachy Head, but nothing was found there either."

The courting couple's silliness was just one thing among many that Donaldson had to hide his anger about. His greatest reason for anger was the action of a high-ranking policeman stationed at Hove.

By early July, Donaldson had garnered indications that the person directly or indirectly responsible for Trunk Crime No. 1 was Edward Seys Massiah, a man in his midfifties who hailed from the West Indian island of Trinidad. One of Massiah's parents had been white, the other black, thus making him a mulatto, his skin dark but not ebony, his hair more wavy than crinkled, his lips quite thin. He had an impressive collection of medical qualifications: MD, MB, BCh, DTM. All but the last of those designatory letters, which stood for Doctor of Tropical Medicine, were scratched larger than his name on his brass shingle, which in 1934 gleamed beside the imposing entrance to a slightly less imposing house within sight of the sea at Hove: 8 Brunswick Square.

The fact that he lived as well as practised there was something he stressed in conversation with prospective patients and with gentlemen whose lady-friends were pregnant or at risk of becoming so; he was, so to speak, open all hours, and that convenience was allied with a guarantee of confidentiality. No doubt you will have guessed that he was an abortionist; and it will have occurred to you that abortion was then a criminal offence.

Now, a likely cause of the death of the Girl with the Pretty Feet was a mishap during an attempt to abort her embryonic child; if that was the cause, then a person who had been involved in the arrangements for the abortion or the person who had tried to perform the operation, or both, would have been most anxious that the transaction and, more important, their roles in it remained secret.

When Robert Donaldson had put together diverse reasons for being suspicious of Edward Massiah (whose qualification of BCh was, by the way, a shortened form of the Latin *Baccalaureus Chirurgiae,* meaning Bachelor of Surgery), he found a sum greater than its parts. But as that sum did not equal justification for making an arrest, he came to the obvious conclusion that efforts were needed to ascertain whether there were additional reasons for suspicion—or whether there was a single exculpatory fact. Toward that end, he gathered a number of people together in one of the apartments at the Royal Pavilion; among those present at the meeting were Captain Hutchinson, Inspector Pelling, key members of the trunk-crime team, and a senior officer from Hove. Donaldson enumerated the points that seemed to tell against Edward Massiah, invited discussion of them, and then—speaking specially to the man from Hove—requested covert collection of information regarding the doctor's background, his present activities and acquaintances, and his movements on Derby Day. He emphasized the word covert.

However, that emphasis was overlooked or ignored by the Hove policeman. Having come upon—and kept to himself—a further unflattering fact about Edward Massiah, he went, uninvited and unexpected, to 8 Brunswick Square and laid Donaldson's cards on the consulting-room table. Massiah paid attention, smiling the while, never interrupting. The sun shining through the tall windows glistened on the ranks of surgical instruments, on the green and crystal-clear pots of medication, on the framed diplomas; tinctured the red-plush couch; nestled in the careful creases of the doctor's pearl-grey cravat, black jacket, and striped trousers; flashed from the unspatted parts of his patent-leather shoes. Toward the end of the policeman's speech, the doctor took a silver pencil and began jotting on a pad. Notes of what he had said and was saying, the policeman guessed.

But no, he was wrong. When he had quite finished and, pleased with himself, was feeling in a pocket for his own pad—he would need that to record the doctor's exact response—he was nonplussed by what the doctor was doing: carefully tearing the sheets from the pad on the ormolu table, turning them round, and using one manicured finger to prod them toward him. He looked at the writing. Names. Addresses, too. Telephone numbers following some of the addresses. Many of the names he recognized: they belonged to important personages of Sussex, or to national celebrities, members of noble families, or extravagantly wealthy commoners who gave financial support to worthy causes. The doctor explained. These were people who, if he were ever threatened with court proceedings and, in turn, threatened them with publicity relating to services he had rendered them, would do all in their power to protect him and ruin his accuser or accusers. The list of names was only a small sample—come to think of it, he had omitted the name of Lord So-and-So, of the member of parliament for the Such-and-Such constituency, of the owner of the Thingummyjig group of newspapers.

It seemed to the policeman that the sun had gone in: all of a sudden, the consulting room was a place of sombre shadows. The doctor was speaking again—quoting the forewarned-is-forearmed adage, thanking the policeman for revealing each and every fact known to Donaldson, adding that he was much obliged since he could now set about sanitizing most of those facts. And, needless to say, he would make blessed sure that Donaldson—whom he would be delighted to meet some time—made no further headway toward his objective of foisting responsibility for Trunk Crime No. 1 on a quite innocent person: himself, he meant. Could the officer find his own way out?

The officer could. And did.

Of course, he didn't volunteer an account of the interview to Robert Donaldson. The latter learnt of the visit from one of the people named by Edward Massiah. The doctor had just happened to mention it—casually, with all the humour of a hyena to that person, whose consequent fear was manifested as a quietly spoken threat to Donaldson. The threat didn't worry Donaldson; but the disclosure of the Hove policeman's action made him very angry indeed. Even so, though he got the full story of the interview from the policeman himself, and berated him for "putting ambition before professionalism," he did not instigate disciplinary action.

(Shortly afterward, Edward Massiah left Hove and started practising in London. There, a woman died following an illegal operation that he had performed. It would be wrong to say that there was a cover-up, but somehow or other he managed to escape retribution; his name was not erased from the medical register. By 1938, he had left England and was living in a fine house, "Montrose," near Port of Spain, Trinidad. Not until December 1952 did the General Medical Council strike his name from its register, and then only because he had failed to respond to letters.)

At about the time of the Massiah incident, Robert Donaldson brought his family to Brighton: "Not wanting this to be found out by a gossip columnist, we lived in a private hotel under the name of

Williams. I was supposed to be an engineer. My wife and I briefed the children as to their new surname and we thought all would be well. However, my six-year-old younger son, not realizing what was at stake, would solemnly ignore the injunctions of 'Andrew Williams, come here,' etcetera, and would tell all and sundry that he was a Donaldson. My cover was quickly blown."

Months later, the strain of the inquiry took its toll on Donaldson: "I found that I was having trouble with my eyes. I went to an oculist in London, and after extensive testing he said there was nothing organically wrong with my eyes. He recommended that I see a nerve specialist. His diagnosis was that I had been overworking. Under the circumstances, that was somewhat self-evident. However, I was then given a Detective Inspector; Taffy Rees—to help me. But Taffy too became a casualty with a stomach ulcer."

There is a final—one could say unforgivable—coincidence to be mentioned. In September 1937, Robert Donaldson took a well-earned holiday. He went motoring in Scotland. On the way home, he parked his car near the border town of Moffatt and sat on the bridge over Gardenholme Linn for a quiet smoke. Beneath the bridge, tucked well out of sight, were some of the neatly parcelled remains of Dr. Buck Ruxton's common-law wife, his children's nursemaid, Mary Rogerson. By the time Donaldson reported back to Scotland Yard, those parcels and others had been discovered, and it goes without saying that it was he who was put in charge of the London end of the inquiry into the north-country variant on bodies-as-baggage. Though not a superstitious man, he must have been at least slightly worried when he learnt that Dr. Ruxton, guilty beyond doubt, was to be defended by Norman Birkett, the trial barrister who had been so helpful to Toni Mancini. But no: this time Birkett's client was found guilty and was duly hanged.

A Postscript on Mr. England's Surprising Autobiography

It must have been in the mid-1980s, soon after "A Coincidence of Corpses" was first published, that I received an affable phone call from Cecil Lois England (also known as Toni Mancini). He explained that he had written his life story: would I like to read it, perhaps help to get it published?

I asked him to send me the script. It arrived a week or so later, having been mailed promptly but by second-class post, in an envelope that had been used so many times previously that my address on it must have needed astute sorter's eyes to be recognised as the most recent.

The script was handwritten. That was not unexpected. What *was* surprising was that it contained no reference, not a word, to Brighton Trunk Crime No. 2—none to (as I happened to know) Mr. England's checkered, often petty-villainous, subsequent career. Yes, I knew that autobiography is said to be the purest form of fiction—but this was ridiculous.

I had not quite finished reading the haloed account when I got another phone call from Mr. England. Irate from the moment he started talking, leaving no gaps for me to have a say, he accused me of plotting to steal his literary work—adding that I had better return the script *at once,* as he, though for some years retired from criminality, was still chummy with many Metropolitan "hard men" who would be only too happy to do nasty things to, among more sensitive parts of me, my kneecaps. That sort of talk, so at variance with the all-sweetness-and-light tone of his nonlife story, persuaded me, admittedly a coward, to return the script to him that very day, by express mail, in a Jiffy bag bought specifically for the purpose.

Some time afterward (months?—a year or so?—I wish I had been less slovenly with my personal archive), I received a letter from a woman who said that she had good reason to believe that she was Mr. England's daughter: could I put her in touch with him? Having weighed selfish risks—after all, he was likely to wish his whereabouts be mysterious—I divulged his address. He must be dead by now, so I can be ostentatiously proud of myself for having done a slight good deed courageously.

THE FIRST TRUNK MURDER

It was not until the long hot summer of 1934, when Brighton played host to two trunk crimes, independent of each other apart from the mutual employment of luggage, that the southcoast resort gained the nickname of Torso City. However, the place was not just doubly deserving of that name, but trebly so—though, admittedly, none of the 1934 Brightonians involved in, or merely intrigued by, the concurrent sensations was anywhere near old enough to have firsthand knowledge of an earlier trunk murder: so far as is known, the inaugurator of the genre in the British Isles.

It happened in 1831. The pioneering murderer was John Holloway, a twenty-six-year-old labourer on Brighton's Chain Pier.[2] Brought up strictly as a Nonconformist, he had dabbled in crime since his teens and was an industrious lecher, possessed of what he termed "a kind of natural love, or it may be called a lustful desire, which some men have towards every woman they look on."

The victim was his estranged wife, Celia, whom he had felt constrained to marry in 1825 as a consequence of having made her pregnant. One can understand that the advertised morality of the time left him little alternative—but, even allowing for his indiscriminate lewdness, it is hard to explain why he put himself at risk in the first place. Consider this contemporary description of Celia:

> She was only four feet three inches, being in reality almost a dwarf, so that when either washing or ironing, she was obliged to be placed on a high stool before she could perform her work. Her head was of an extraordinary size in proportion to the rest of her body, and her hands turned outwards, like the paws of a mole. Her features had not the slightest pretension to anything allied to beauty, and on the whole she was rather a repellent object.

It appears that, his aesthetic distress at Celia's appearance apart, Holloway had more than one motive for disposing of her.

First, there was the question of money. He had been ordered by the Brighton magistrates to pay his "deserted wife" two shillings a week. This was easier said than done, as he was keeping a woman called Ann Kennett, whom he had bigamously wed, and his weekly take-home pay from the Chain Pier rarely exceeded three shillings and sixpence. Both women were seven months pregnant, and Holloway feared that, additional to the impending expense of Ann Kennett's baby, he would be ordered to increase the payments to Celia—despite the fact that, as he claimed, he was "not responsible for her sick condition."

There was also a motive of revenge—not only on Celia but on her kin, whom he blamed for most of his misfortunes.

2. The pier was so called because its deck, nearly a quarter of a mile long, was partly supported by chains hanging from towers; opened in 1823, it was destroyed by fierce storms in 1896.

Another motive was jealousy. Like many married philanderers, he felt that his own "mere jokes," as he called his dalliances, were no excuse for his wife "to invite other men to shake her bed." In his printed confession, he told of an occasion when he visited Celia late at night:

> She had come down without a candle. She had nothing on but her nightgown, and the landlord came down nearly naked. I could not help noticing that he made as free with Celia in her nightclothes as if he had been her husband, and the more free he made himself, the more pleased she appeared to be. I walked away, to tell the truth, in a great rage.

In July 1831, Holloway rented a house in North Steyne Row for the sole purpose of doing away with Celia. "I went and told her to keep herself in readiness, for in a few days I should come for her to go and live with me. She appeared much delighted at the news." Perhaps to justify the expense, before carrying out the murder plan Holloway took "a nurse-maid that frequented the pier" to the house and attempted to seduce her—"but when we were there and I took a little too much liberty, she showed symptoms of alarm, which caused me to desist."

After moving Celia's few paltry belongings to the house,

> I desired Ann Kennet to be on hand. To that she agreed. But the next thing to be thought of was where was the best place for her to be when I returned. I at last proposed for her to get into the cupboard under the stairs, so that she might be ready in case I should need her assistance.
>
> The plan being thus laid, I went away for Celia, and got some beer on the road. When I got to her lodgings, I found her quite ready; and for dinner she had got a kind of batter-pudding baked. I ate some, but not with a good appetite.
>
> I had made up my mind how I intended to murder her; I was resolved to strangle her. But I had not provided anything for the purpose. I went downstairs and found the child at play with a small bit of cord. I asked for it and then got another small bit. I tied them together and then went upstairs for Celia.[3]

---

3. I am reminded of the rather dotty Lady Bland-Dutton. When she died, a large box was found among her effects, carefully labelled "Pieces of String Too Small to Be Used."

Shortly after, we left the house together. We went through the streets with scarcely a word passing between us, until we came to the bottom of Edward Street. I desired her to stop there till I returned, saying I was going to call a mate of mine that lived there and he was going with us to the house where we were going to live. With that, I ran along to the house, and when I had seen Ann Kennett in the cupboard, I laid the small bit of cord on the window. Then I went to the door and waved my hand for Celia.

She came along and looked so innocent that I was ready to drop before she came to the door.

When she got there, I said my mate was not up yet and desired her to step in, for we would not wait for him; and I shut the door and went upstairs, pretending to hurry him.

When I came down, she—poor dear girl—was standing against the window where the fatal cord was lying. I went up to her and placed my arms round her neck, at the same time taking the cord in my hand. I fondled her as if I loved her. I kissed her several times: at the same time I tried to pass the cord round her neck, unobserved by her, as she stood by the window. But I could not succeed.

I then asked her to go and sit down on the stairs; which she did. I kept my arm around her neck, to prevent her seeing the cord as we moved from the window to the stairs. She sat down, and I sat down beside her. My heart was once or twice ready to fail; but I would not allow pity nor compassion to have any room in my breast. I sat with her some minutes, pretending to love her, and was on the point of giving up my purpose many times, and then I again took courage many times. At last I found I must either do it or give it up altogether.

The devil said: "Do it: it will not be discovered."

My keeping her there so long caused her, however, to suspect something not right. She looked at me very innocently and said:

"How—how much longer will he be?" meaning the mate who, she thought, was above stairs.

The last words she ever spoke were: "Come, my dear, let us go."

These words were scarcely from her lips when, watching my opportunity, I, unknown to her, passed the cord round her neck.

It was then some minutes before I pulled it tight.

At last, I lost all natural feelings and pulled the cord with all my might. She never spoke nor groaned, but immediately sprang to her feet; but the attack was so sudden that she appeared not to have the power so much as to lift her hands to her neck.

I held her myself a few seconds; but the appearance of her face shocked me and, my arm beginning to ache, I called Ann Kennett. When she came out of the cupboard I desired her to come and assist me, which, God knows, she did, by taking hold of each end of the rope with me; and she held the rope with me until the poor girl dropped on the stairs.

We held her there until we judged that she was dead, and then Ann Kennett let go of the cord.

After that, I found that she was not dead.

Ann Kennett desired me not to let my heart fail me but to put her [Celia] out of her misery as soon as possible. I dragged her from the stairs to the middle of the kitchen. It would not do to let her remain, for she began to revive. I then tied the cord as tight as I was able, and then dragged her into the cupboard and hung her up on some nails, so that she was then hanging by the neck.

Having at last accomplished the fell deed, Holloway took Ann Kennett for a drink and then went home for a nap before returning to the house with the intention of hiding the body in Celia's own trunk. But although Celia was small, the trunk was smaller, and so Holloway—who at one time had worked as a butcher—set about cutting off the head and the limbs. (In an especially macabre passage of the confession, he recalled "taking off the legs at the knees without taking off the stockings"—oh my, think [no, *don't* think] of the juddering of the saw as it caught against the opposing weft.)

Once the torso and thighs had been stowed in the trunk, and the trunk wrapped round with Celia's spare outfit of clothes, he parcelled up the head with the limbs and carried the package to his lodgings in Margaret Street, near the sea front, where he undid the package and emptied the contents into the privy.

That night we went again to the house to wash away the blood, which we did without much trouble: the floor being brick, the blood never dried in as it might have done had it been boards.

The next day I borrowed a wheelbarrow, a pickaxe and a shovel and took them down to the house. Then Ann Kennett met me at the house at dusk. I put the trunk on the wheelbarrow and

Kennett took the pickaxe and shovel and came after me, just keeping in sight of me. Although the night was beautifully bright, yet I felt, at times, an involuntary shudder come over me when I looked at the trunk that I was conveying to its place of secrecy.

Holloway had decided to bury the trunk in a copse beside "Lover's Walk," a footpath near the village of Preston. One can assume that he chose this location because of his intimate knowledge of it. But here he again encountered problems:

I began to try to dig. I found it too dark: and what made it more difficult were the roots of the trees, which were very thick. Consequently I was obliged to drop the attempt for that time, and after putting the tools and the trunk in a place of security we returned home. . . .

On the following morning, as soon as it was light, we returned to the spot, intending to bury the trunk and all, but had not time to dig the hole deep enough. In my hurry, I took off the lid and turned it bottom uppermost, spilling the contents into the hole. I covered it over as soon as possible. I then broke the trunk into several pieces and threw most of it into the standing corn, while some I put under some bushes.

Still nothing went smoothly for Holloway. A week or so after the untidy burial, a violent storm washed away the top covering of earth on the shallow grave, revealing part of Celia's dress, and some passersby—one of them a Mr. Sherlock—informed the High Constable of Preston. The *Brighton Gazette* reported,

As soon as the murder was confirmed, the copse was visited by a great number of people from Brighton. . . . Some lace, said to have been part of the cap, was picked up, and, with fragments of the gown, was handed about and sold. To attempt to describe the consternation which the knowledge of this event caused at Brighton were a faint effort. Rumour, with its thousand tongues, was busy to exaggerate every circumstance. . . .

During Sunday, the little village of Preston was crowded with people visiting the copse and barn where the body was deposited. Indeed, so eager were some persons, many of them females, to view the body that a hole was made in the barn door. The effluvia made many of them regret their curiosity.

Despite its incompleteness, the body was easily identified as that of Celia Holloway by its diminutive proportions and its clothing, which was recognized by Celia's mother. Ann Kennett was arrested at once. Holloway, who had gone into hiding, gave himself up after swallowing a rumour that the body had been identified as that of another missing woman.

The evidence against him was formidable, and he was committed to Horsham Gaol to await trial. There, having added to his inefficiencies by making a hash of an attempt at suicide, he "turned his face Zion-ward" and whiled away the time by dictating confessions and writing sanctimonious, moral-drawing epistles to relatives:

Dearest Mother and Sister,

I, your unfortunate and unhappy son, once more out of prisson take up my pen to right to you, hoping it may find you well, I know not happy. I hope, my deare Mother, you will not fail to pray for me without ceasing, that God create in me a cleane heart, and renew a right spirit with me, for now is the expected time, and none but now is the day of Salvation.

I do not expect, dear mother, that you can send me anything but I shall take it hard if my sister do not help me the few hours I have to live, yet I know she will, for I know she loveth me.

Dear Mother,

You said you hoped that I would, for your sake, make a candid confession. Could I do anything more than what I have to convince you, and to appease offended justice, I would gladly do it; but as I have shook hands with the world, I cannot do anything to satisfy the curiosity of any man no further than what is consistent with divine justice. If the world will persist in judging the innocent I cannot help it, I have not failed to tell them that I am guilty, that I am the murderer; and if the innocent are judged let them bare with patience, but let those that judge them tremble at the following words spoken by Our Lord Himself:—"Judge not that ye be not judged!"

This last quoted letter indicates that Holloway's mother was anxious to protect Ann Kennett—or, more likely, the baby that was now almost due. Subsequently, Holloway made what was probably the one chivalrous gesture of his life, ingeniously exculpating Ann Kennett by saying that he knew any number of women of that name and that the Ann Kennett mentioned in his early confessions was not necessarily the woman to whom he was bigamously married. Afterward, however (as evidenced by the second paragraph of the following letter), his determination to be a martyr seems to have made him forgetful that the saving of Ann Kennett was his mother's idea.

Dear Mother,

I hope you will not be offended at what I am going to say, but to tell you the truth, I feel rather surprised that you said you was afraid you should lose your character and that you might as well lose your life. Have you forgot yourself or do you know against whom you speak, and do you not profess to trust in God? O my dear mother and sister, let not my punishment trouble you; for my soul's sake cease not to cry night and day that the Lord may receive my soul at last. Make it known to the minister of the Methodist Society that I desire an interest in all their prayers.

I hope you don't think that because that poor innocent and unfortunate woman was living with me at the time that I committed this, and on that and no other evidence she is to be accused. I tell you I have been the ruin of the girl, *and how can I seek to take away her life also.*

To reverse the proceedings, let me say that Ann Kennett, tried separately, was acquitted—more on account of the fact that she was big with child than that the prosecution was short of evidence—and that Holloway, tried at Lewes Assizes on 14 December, was found guilty. His execution, carried out two days later, was described thus by the *Brighton Gazette:*

The hangman drew the cap over his eyes; and the chaplain continued to pray, concluding with the Lord's Prayer, during which Holloway, with great solemnity, repeatedly ejaculated, "Lord, receive my spirit," until the signal, when the bolt was withdrawn, and the wretched culprit's life was at an end. He appeared to suffer but little. There was no manifestation of feeling in the crowd, nor could we perceive any tokens of commiseration.

Fifteen minutes or so after Holloway had been launched into eternity, a superstitious rustic from the village of Cowfold haggled with the hangman to have a wen, or cyst, on his forehead rubbed by the hanged man's hands. Having reached a bargain, the hangman escorted the afflicted man on to the scaffold, undid the manacles, and placed Holloway's hands on the wen. He kept them there for some time, while the rustic knelt, eyes closed, lips moving, body trembling; then, really giving value for money, he untied the man's kerchief and thrust it inside Holloway's shirt, proximate to the still heart, and in one deft movement transferred the kerchief to the wen. The treatment over, the man descended the steps—not without some difficulty, for he was holding the kerchief to his forehead with one hand, searching his purse for the hangman's fee with the other.

Two women spectators, both with wens, pled for similar Laying On of Hands, but their transactions with the hangman were curtailed by the undersheriff, who, worried that his breakfast was getting cold, ordered them to take themselves and their wens elsewhere. The undersheriff was understanding, though, about the hangman's traditional perk, and merely stood sighing impatiently while that worthy gave the rope that had hanged Holloway to a gentleman of Lewes in exchange for half a crown.[4]

---

4. Osbert Sitwell, born in 1892, recalls in his autobiography *Left Hand, Right Hand* (London, 1946) that when he was about three, his mother, Lady Sitwell, allowed him, at set times on certain mornings, to wander unchaperoned around her room. He says that he "recognised all the detail on the bed-side table; but I did not understand one thing, a loop of thick rope, a foot or two long, twisted in a knot round the head of the bed. . . . Eventually, after many implorings, I was told what it was. 'It's a bit of a hangman's rope, darling. Nothing's so lucky! It cost eight pounds—they're very difficult to get now. Old Sir William got it for me.' . . . And, suddenly, I was back in a world, instinctively comprehended, of Hogarth and Gay."

Consider, friends, George Joseph Smith,
A Briton not to trifle with;
When wives aroused his greed or wrath,
He led them firmly to the bath.
Instead of guzzling in the pub,
He drowned his troubles in the tub.
  —*Ogden Nash, "They Don't Read De Quincey*
  in Philly or Cincy"

ALSO KNOWN AS LOVE

lthough two hundred miles separate 16 Regent's Road, Blackpool, from 14 Bismarck Road[1] in the North London suburb of Highgate, and sixty miles separate the latter address from 80 High Street, in the Kent town of Herne Bay, the three places have a gruesome fact in common—a fact that, with others, came to light early in 1915, capturing the attention of newspaper readers to such an extent that reports concerning hostilities with the Boche were on some days, in some papers, given second billing on the front page.

One supposes that the most avid readers of the accounts of how people had taken a bath but not lived long enough to dry themselves were women, young and not so young, about to embark on matrimony; and their mothers, fearful that, in gaining a son-in-law, they might be losing a daughter for good and all. Perhaps some of the more apprehensive mothers added to their birds-and-bees advice the warning that, at least during the nuptial period, their daughters should forget that cleanliness is next to godliness and steer clear of bathtubs.

The man whose activities had caused the maidenly and maternal worries about the cause-and-effect relationship between personal hygiene and sudden death was born in Bethnal Green, a sleazy district of East London, in January 1872. He was christened George Joseph Smith.

His first name was also that of his father, who was an insurance agent. If the father was at all good at his job, presumably he was a slick talker—and if so, then George junior's power to charm the birds was partly inherited. Only partly, though. Considering how, by the time he was in his midtwenties, he was using—or rather, misusing— women, he must have practised the deceit of blandishment, learning from trial and error, so that an innate talent was disciplined and refined into something akin to genius.

1. Now called Waterlow Road. During the Great War, all Bismarck-entitled thoroughfares in the capital patriotically were renamed.

You may sneer at the notion, but I am inclined to believe that the fatal fascination Smith exercised over women (truly fatal, so far as some of his victims were concerned) was in part measure optically induced. According to one of the lady-friends who lived to tell the tale, "He had an extraordinary power. . . . This power lay in his eyes. When he looked at you for a minute or two, you had the feeling that you were being magnetized. They were little eyes that seemed to rob you of your will." Other women said much the same thing. And Edward Marshall Hall, the great barrister, once broke off an interview with Smith because he believed that an attempt was being made to hypnotize him.

But if Smith was a hypnotist, he either developed the skill in manhood or, possessing it earlier, displayed it only as a party trick during his formative years. Hypnotism, mesmerism, call it what you will, can hardly have played a part in his fledgling criminal schemes, the unsuccessfulness of which might have caused a less dedicated apprentice crook to make the best of some thoroughly bad jobs and seek a licit calling. Its final act apart, the story of the life and crimes of George Joseph Smith provides an object lesson to all aspiring villains: if at first you not only don't succeed, but fail abysmally, try to find a novel method of fleecing.

᠁

By the age of ten, Smith had committed such an assortment of misdemeanours that it was decided that the community—and he, too, perhaps—would be far better off if he were in a reformatory. He was despatched to one at Gravesend (a name that might be considered portentous of his way of breaking off relationships in later life), and there he stayed until he was sixteen. Drawing no righteous morals from the experience, he was no sooner back with his mother—who was now living alone, whether widowed or deserted I cannot be sure—than he was being troublesome again. A small theft was punished by a sentence of seven days' imprisonment. Out again, he took a fancy to a bicycle, and so was soon back in gaol, serving six months with hard labour. He was released in the late summer of 1891.

Perhaps, as he subsequently claimed, he spent the next few years in the army. That might explain why, during that period, no further entries appeared on the police record sheet headed "SMITH, George Joseph." On the other hand, he may have been more discreet in his criminal activities—or simply fortunate not to be caught. Another possibility is that his transgressions were recorded on record sheets bearing names other than his own: distinctly likely, this, for when he was arrested for his final, dreadful offences, the list of his aliases looked not unlike an electoral roll for a small town.

He was "George Baker" when, in July 1896, he was sentenced to a year in prison for three cases of larceny and receiving. The fact does not appear to have been included in the evidence against him, but by now he had latched on to the idea of using members of the fair sex unfairly: he had persuaded a domestic servant to become a job-hopper, misappropriating her employers' property shortly before each hop.

The following year, once he was free, he moved to the Midlands town of Leicester. As a sort of "in-joke," so esoteric that he allowed no one else to appreciate it, he called himself "Love." Caroline Thornhill, a teenaged native of the lacemaking town, fell under the spell of "Love"— but not to the extent of accepting his suggestion that they should live in sin. So in January 1898, when he was just twenty-six, he married Caroline. The wedding was a quiet affair, for the bride's relatives so disapproved of "George Love" that they boycotted the ceremony.

The relatives were soon able to remind Caroline that they "had told her so." Within six months, life with "Love" became intolerable, and Caroline sought refuge with a cousin in Nottingham. But her husband pursued her; and persuaded her to accompany him south, where—first in London, then farther south, in the seaside towns of Brighton, Hove, and Hastings—he wrote references, posing as her last employer, which helped her to obtain domestic posts. Perhaps needless to say, each house in which she worked was less well stocked with trinkets by the time she moved on to the next position George had chosen for her. The crooks' tour ended when the Hastings police arrested "Mrs. Love." Smith managed to evade capture. He travelled to London, booked into a boarding house, and, rather than fork out money for his digs, "married" the landlady at a register office near Buckingham Palace. That was in 1899.

About a year later, Caroline chanced to spot Smith window-shopping in Oxford Street. She informed a constable. As her husband was led away, she called after him, "Treacle is sweet—but revenge is sweeter." Found guilty of receiving stolen goods, Smith was sentenced to two years' imprisonment.

Upon his release, he stayed a few days with the landlady-"wife," then set off for Leicester to find Caroline—whether in the hope of making things up or with the intention of harming her, one cannot be sure. Either way, it was a choice of evils for Caroline. Luckily for her, she had some loving and brawny brothers, who chased "Mr. Love" out of town. But by now Caroline was a bundle of nerves. Deciding that she needed to get far away as fast as possible, she boarded a ship to Canada.

Thirteen years passed before she was summoned back to England to identify as her legal husband the man who had illegally married a number of other women, latterly for the purpose of acquiring a quick profit from a self-imposed state of widowerhood. Caroline was unfortunate in being George Joseph Smith's first, and only real, wife—but she could console herself with the thought that at least the marriage had lasted.

I am not making an original observation but am merely passing on a remark made by others when I say that, exceptional to the law of averages, a number of mass-murderers have ostensibly earned their living from trade in secondhand goods.

Of course, this raises an egg-and-hen question: which came first? Did the need for used items, as stock or to satisfy the stated requirements of customers, cause the dealers to turn to crime—or did these men, criminals first, drift into the trade, perhaps seeing it as a means of reducing their reliance on "fences" for the disposal of loot? Sadly for criminologists who like neat, cut-and-dried findings (and who have been known to fashion them by ignoring details that don't conform), some dealers become criminals . . . and some criminals become dealers.

George Joseph Smith took the latter course. It seems that he started dealing, travelling the country in search of both secondhand wares to buy (or, better, pilfer) and people to buy them, soon after his release from prison in October 1902.

As a profitable sideline to the trade in used goods, he preyed on unused women—virginal spinsters who, with a little flattery, a few promises, a taste of what they had been missing, could be induced to part with a dowry that would lift them off the shelf. As soon as the fleecing was accomplished, Smith made himself scarce. He enjoyed this work, finding in it a mixture of business and pleasure—the pleasure being twofold, derived partly from the satisfaction to his ego of a playacting job well done, and partly from what was then referred to as "gratification of strong animal propensities."

Not all of his victims were spinsters. To amend a line of a then-pop-
ular song: oh, he did like to be beside the seaside. Many of his exploits
occurred in coastal resorts. In June 1908, when he was in Brighton
(one of the towns on the south coast where, nine years before, he had
forced his wife Caroline to filch), he struck up a conversation with a
widow whom he "just happened to encounter" on the promenade.
Mrs. F. W. (her name was never revealed) told Smith that she was in
Brighton only for the day and that she lived and worked at Worthing,
a few miles along the coast. Unfortunately for Mrs. F. W., she also
gave Smith her address.

The very next day, she received a "gentleman caller." Yes, it was
Smith—who, unusually, was using his real name. While Mrs. F. W.
was still recovering from the shock of seeing him again, he shocked
her still more—most pleasurably—by blurting out his belief that the
meeting on the front at Brighton had been engineered by Kismet,
with some assistance from Cupid, and that, if she did not find him
utterly repulsive, she must accept Destiny's word for the fact that she
should become his nearest and dearest. Delightedly flabbergasted, the
widow murmured something about the need for a period of court-
ship. But—ever so politely—Smith noted the silver threads among the
gold of her hair, said that they ought not to waste a single precious
moment, and, his masterfulness making Mrs. F. W. reach for the sal
volatile, enquired if she had made any engagements for a date three
weeks hence that were more pressing than the register-office wedding
he had in mind.

Oh my, such a rush of words. Such a rush that Mrs. F. W. treated
Smith's question about her worldly goods as an unimportant aside.
Having agreed to plight her troth, she introduced George (yes, they
were on first-name terms by now) to her best friend—who took an instant and violent dislike to him. Ascribing the friend's reaction to sour
grapes, Mrs. F. W. travelled with Smith to London. Such a kind man,
he insisted on carrying all her baggage; far from complaining of the
weight, he fretted that she might have left something of value behind.

In London, they shared an apartment (maybe very properly, maybe
with some premarital hanky-panky—Mrs. F. W. did not subsequently
divulge the sleeping arrangements). The widow was taken on two out-
ings in the metropolis. First, to the north of the city, where Smith
insisted on showing her round an interesting new post office—and,
while they were there, persuaded her to withdraw her savings—and to

give the cash to him for safe keeping. Second, to the western outskirts, where Smith treated her to an evening of greyhound racing—and after telling her that he would only be gone a minute, dashed back to the apartment. By the time she got there, not only was there no sign of Smith but there was an entire absence of her belongings.

With money realized from these, together with the widow's savings, Smith opened a secondhand furniture shop in the West Country city of Bristol. In a house just a few doors along the road, a young woman named Edith Pegler lived with her mother. Learning that she was seeking a job, Smith asked her to be his housekeeper. Edith soon discovered that her new employer could not afford to pay her wages; but even sooner than that, she was under his spell.

They were married—Smith for the umpteenth bigamous time—on 30 July 1908. I give the exact date only to illustrate the speed of Smith's romantic conquests, the brevity of the period between his first meeting with a woman and, if he felt that the journey to a register office was really necessary, the wedding ceremony: Mrs. F. W.'s withdrawal of her savings from the North London post office was effected on 3 July, less than four weeks before Edith Pegler became—or *thought* she had become—Mrs. Smith.

"Mrs. Smith" is correct: at the Bristol register office, Smith was for the first time "married" under his real name—perhaps because, for once in his life, he felt a slight affection toward a woman. Edith was less cruelly treated than were the rest of his dupes. Aside from the fact that Smith actually provided her with a trousseau (he didn't let on to Edith that it had come from the bottom drawer of a young skivvy he had fleeced in the seaside town of Bournemouth), he never, not once, used her as a criminal accomplice; so far as she knew, when for long stretches he was away from home, he was "about the country dealing." In the year following the wedding, while doing some deals in Southampton—another coastal town, notice—he met and went through a form of marriage with a girl who was quite nicely off. After a honeymoon of a few hours, he left her penniless.

His next port of call was the Essex seaside town of Southend, where he invested most of the Southampton girl's money in a house. The transaction completed, he returned to Bristol.

One day during the summer of 1910, while he was sauntering in Clifton, on the western outskirts of Bristol, his predatory gaze fell upon a girl named Bessie Mundy.

She was destined to be his first murder victim. Or the first so far as is known.

෨

A slim, plain-featured spinster, Bessie Mundy was thirty-three: five years younger than the man with the icicle-blue eyes who introduced himself as Henry Williams when she was out walking near her home in Clifton. Her father, a bank manager, had died a year or so before, leaving her well provided for; she had £2,500 in gilt-edged securities— the equivalent of some £75,000 ($120,000) today.

That made her irresistibly attractive to Smith. He wooed her, won her, and wedded her (or so she thought; she was not to know that the ceremony at Weymouth registry office did not legitimize the relationship, for the simple reason that Smith, not yet a widower, never divorced, had gone through the same ceremony any number of times before).

On the very wedding day, 26 August 1910, Smith wrote to Bessie's solicitor, requesting a copy of her late father's will. When this turned up, Smith may have muttered a few rude words, because the document showed that the bequest to Bessie was protected; she received an income of a mere £8 a month. Still, he was slightly cheered to learn that the solicitor held £130-odd to cover emergencies. So far as Smith was concerned, an emergency had just arisen: he inveigled the liquid funds from the solicitor.

Not content with these, he rifled Bessie's handbag before absconding. The next morning, she received a letter—bearing no return address, of course—that began,

> Dearest, I fear you have blighted all my bright hopes of a happy
> future. I have caught from you a disease which is called the bad
> disorder. For you to be in such a state proves you could not have
> kept yourself morally clean. . . . Now for the sake of my health
> and honour and yours too I must go to London and act entirely
> under the doctor's advice to get properly cured of the disease.

In fact, Smith took a train to Bristol, not London, and there rejoined Edith Pegler. He did not stay in Bristol long, but, with the faithful Edith in tow, went on a circular tour, wheeling and dealing as he travelled, returning to Bristol toward the end of 1911.

After seven weeks—reasonably happy ones for Edith, despite Smith's frugality with housekeeping money—his wanderlust took him away again. Though Edith was left virtually penniless, she somehow managed to survive on her own for five months; then she returned to her mother.

In March 1912, Smith's travels took him to the Somerset coastal resort of Weston-super-Mare. By a dreadful coincidence, Bessie Mundy was staying at a boardinghouse in the town. One morning, she went out to buy some flowers as a gift for the landlady, Mrs. Sarah Tuckett, who was also a family friend. As she walked along the front, she saw Smith (or Henry Williams, as she knew him) staring at the sea.

Certain criminologists subscribe to the theory of "victimology"—a belief that, in many cases, particularly of murder, the victim is more or less responsible for his or her own plight. I can think of no person who more blatantly supports the theory than Bessie Mundy. Considering how Smith had deceived her, robbed her, divested her of self-esteem, and, adding acid to the lemon, accused her of infecting him with a venereal disease, one would suppose that she had but two choices when she saw him—to rush back to the sanctuary of the boarding house or to report her sighting to the police.

But no; she did neither of those things. Incredibly, what she did was to approach Smith, timidly cough to announce her presence, and, once he had recognized her, ask how he was keeping. The moth, wings seared by fire, had returned to the flame.

Mrs. Tuckett received a bunch of daffodils—not from her excited guest but from Bessie's "long-lost husband." The flowers did not help to dispel the landlady's dislike or suspicion of Smith. When he said that he had been scouring the country for his dear Bessie for over a year, Mrs. Tuckett enquired why he had not got in touch with her relatives, whose addresses he knew, or with her solicitor. There was no answer to that. Mrs. Tuckett told Smith that she intended to send a wire to one of Bessie's aunts. He left Weston-super-Mare that night. And Bessie, who earlier had informed the landlady that she had "forgiven the past," went with him.

The reunited couple travelled around, staying in lodgings, until late in May 1912, when they turned up at Herne Bay, Kent, and rented a house, No. 80 in the High Street, for thirty shillings a month.

They had been in the town for only a few days when Smith consulted a local solicitor about Bessie's "protected" £2,500. Was the protection absolute? What if Bessie were to make a will in his favour? Would all her money be his if she died?

The solicitor received counsel's opinion on 2 July.

It was Bessie Mundy's death warrant.

Less than a week later, she and Smith made mutual wills.

Next day, Smith went into an ironmonger's shop, and after some haggling, agreed to buy a £2 bath for £1.17s.6d. Though he didn't pay for the bath on the spot, the ironmonger agreed to deliver it that afternoon.

Smith's purchase would have surprised Edith Pegler, for in all the time she had lived with him, he had only taken a bath once, perhaps twice. And he had advised her, "I would not have much to do with baths if I were you, as they are dangerous things. It has often been known for women to lose their lives in them, through having fits and weak hearts."

One wonders how Bessie viewed the acquisition. Perhaps, poor creature, she thought back to the letter that had accused her of transmitting a venereal disease, in which a line following those I have quoted said that she had either "had connections with another man . . . or not kept [herself] clean." Maybe she inferred that Smith, concerned at the insufficiency of her personal hygiene but no longer wishing to offend her, had bought the bath as a tacit hint. Did she vow to herself that she would plunge into the bath morning, noon, and night, scouring her meagre body of all perhaps contagious impurities?

There is no way of answering such questions. Bessie herself was the only person who could have said what went through her mind. But she was alone, friendless, far from anyone in whom she might confide; Smith had seen to that. In any case, she had precious little time left in which to speak of matters involving her husband; to speak of anything.

After the arrival of the bath, Smith was as busy as a bee in creating the impression that he feared for the life of his beloved Bessie.

The ironmonger delivered the bath during the afternoon of Tuesday, 9 July. Next morning, Smith took Bessie to see Dr. Frank French—who, as it happened, was the least-experienced medical practitioner in the town. Smith said that his wife had had a fit. The young doctor may have wondered whether Bessie was suffering from amnesia as well as epilepsy, for she did not remember having a fit. French prescribed a general sedative.

Two days later, Smith called the doctor to the house. Bessie was in bed—unnecessarily, it seemed to French, who could see nothing wrong with her. Still, just to be on the safe side, he went back to the house later in the day. Bessie looked "in perfect health." And she felt fine, she told the doctor—just a touch of tiredness, but that was probably because of the heat wave.

The touch of tiredness must have evaporated soon after the doctor's departure, for she then wrote a letter to an uncle in the West Country. The letter, which went off by registered post that evening, spoke of two "bad fits," and continued,

> My husband has been extremely kind and done all he could for me. He has provided me with the attention of the best medical men.... I do not like to worry you with this, but my husband has strictly advised me to let all my relatives know and tell them of my breakdown. I have made out my will and have left all I have to my husband. That is only natural, as I love my husband.

At eight o'clock next morning—Saturday, 13 July—Dr. French received a note: "Can you come at once? I am afraid my wife is dead."

As soon as the doctor arrived at the house, Smith ushered him upstairs. Bessie was lying on her back in the bath, her head beneath the soapy water. Her face was congested with blood. French lifted the body from the bath and, simply because he thought it might be expected of him, went through the motions of applying artificial respiration, with Smith assisting by holding the dead woman's tongue.

An hour or so later, a coroner's officer took a statement from Smith, and in the afternoon a neighbour, Ellen Millgate, came to the house to lay out the body. Though she was practised at the task, this was the first time that she had found a corpse lying naked and uncovered on bare boards behind a door. Odd, she thought.

Just as odd, when one comes to think of it, was the fact that the doctor had found the body still submerged, the face staring up as if through a glass darkly. Surely the natural thing for Smith to have done when he first entered the room was to lift his wife, or at least raise her head, from the water.

But neither of these oddities, nor any of the several others, perplexed the coroner or his jury, whose verdict was relayed to Bessie's relatives in a note written by Smith on the Monday, soon after the proceedings: "The result of the inquest was misadventure by a fit in the bath. The burial takes place tomorrow at 2 P.M. I am naturally too sad to write more today." Until they received this note, the relatives were not even aware that an inquest had been held. And there was no time for them to travel from Bristol to Herne Bay to attend the funeral (which Smith arranged "to be moderately carried out at an expense of seven guineas," the body being interred in a common grave).

Within forty-eight hours of the funeral, Smith sold most of the furniture in the house, returned the bath (which he had not paid for) to the ironmonger, and, most important, instructed the solicitor who only nine days before had drawn up Bessie's will to obtain probate.

By the middle of September, Smith was better off by about £2,500 (in present-day terms, about £100,000–$160,000). He was then back in Bristol, again living with Edith Pegler. It appears that, no more than a month or so after his return from Herne Bay, Smith came close to letting Edith in on the secret of how he made money from matrimony: he enlisted her aid in arranging insurance on the life of a young governess, but then for some reason decided not to go ahead with whatever scheme he had in mind.

If that scheme had been carried through, requiring him to remain in Bristol, he might never have met Alice Burnham; and she, a twenty-five-year-old nurse, rosy-cheeked and ample-bosomed, would probably have attained the age of twenty-six.

Smith first encountered Alice in Southsea on a late-summer day in 1913. Having quizzed her about her financial situation, he proposed marriage and was delightedly accepted. Whereas he had gone out of his way to avoid meeting relatives of his earlier victims, he insisted on visiting Alice's father, a fruit-grower living at Aston Clinton, Buckinghamshire, northwest of London. His insistence was entirely due to the fact that Charles Burnham was looking after £100 of his daughter's money. The visit, at the end of October, was not a success. Contrary to Alice's starry-eyed, rose-coloured view of her beau, Mr. Burnham considered Smith a man of "very evil appearance—a bad man."

But Alice, ignoring her father's fear that "something serious would happen" if she went ahead with the marriage, became "Mrs. Smith" (yes, George was using his real name this time) on 4 November. The day before, her life had been insured for £500.

Owing to some irritating holdups (to do with the nest egg Alice had left with her father, the life insurance, and the making of her will), Smith had to wait over a month before he could become a widower again. Choosing Blackpool as the scene of his crime, on Thursday, 10 December, he knocked at the door of 25 Adelaide Street, a guesthouse run by Mrs. Susannah Marsden, and, while Alice loitered by the luggage, asked the landlady if there was a bath in the house. As the answer was no, Smith enquired whether Mrs. Marsden knew of a nearby establishment offering bed, board, *and bath.*

On Mrs. Marsden's recommendation, the couple took lodgings at 16 Regent's Road, where the landlady was Mrs. Margaret Crossley. As soon as they had unpacked their bags, they walked to Dr. George Billing's surgery at 121 Church Street. Smith, who did all the talking, explained that his wife had a nasty headache. The doctor gave Alice a pretty thorough examination, found nothing wrong, prescribed tablets for the headache and a powder to clear the bowels, and requested a fee of three shillings and sixpence—which Smith, would you believe, paid at once, without haggling.

It may be that Mrs. Crossley was willing to make allowance for the transgressions of out-of-season boarders, for at about eight o'clock the following night, Friday, when she saw water pouring down a wall in her kitchen, she did not rush upstairs to complain about the overfull bath. Five or ten minutes later, however, she was summoned upstairs by Smith, who said that he could not get his wife to speak to him. The reason for Alice's taciturnity was that her head was submerged in soapy water.

In many respects, the events that followed were reproductions of those following Bessie Mundy's abrupt demise. Dr. Billing was called; he, in turn, called the coroner's officer; on the Monday, an inquest jury took just half an hour to return a verdict of accidental death. Smith negotiated a cheap funeral, took the first steps toward collecting his bequest and the payment from the insurance society, and left the town.

Just before his departure, he reluctantly gave Mrs. Crossley part of what he owed her and handed her a card on which he had written a forwarding address in Southsea. The landlady scribbled on the back of the card: "Wife died in bath. I shall see him again some day."

She was right.

How many women did George Joseph Smith marry? And how many did he murder?

One cannot give a sure answer to either question. Certain of his exploits are well documented; but it is quite possible that he committed crimes that were never ascribed to him. For one thing, he was such a busy rogue that even if he could have been persuaded to tell the truth, the whole truth, and nothing but the truth, some of his matrimonial misdeeds might have slipped his mind; for another, some of his female dupes who remained extant may have decided that discretion was the better part of valour; and for yet another, when he was at last brought to book, some of his victims, or their surviving relatives or friends, may not have connected him with the man they had known under an alias other than those listed in press reports—*Love . . . Williams . . . Baker . . . James . . .* and so on.

"Charles Oliver James" was the name he was using in the late summer of 1914, when, all within a fortnight, he met, "married" and left impoverished a young domestic servant called Alice Reavil.

A month or so later, he was "John Lloyd." That was the name he gave when introducing himself to Margaret Lofty, a thirty-eight-year-old spinster with pouting lips and dark hair that she arranged in kiss curls over her negligible forehead. The daughter of a parson, she eked out a meagre existence as a companion to elderly women residing in tranquil cathedral cities. Sadly appropriate to her fate, it was in Bath that she first encountered Smith.

As her savings of £19 were ludicrously inadequate to Smith's purpose in marrying her, he added to his proposal instructions regarding life insurance. Once the first—and, as it turned out, only—premium was paid, he married Margaret at a register office. The date was 17 December, a Thursday—almost exactly a year after the death of Alice Burnham; two and a half years since the death of Bessie Mundy.

That evening, after Smith had been refused lodgings at one house in North London (because the landlady was frightened by his "evil appearance"), he took a room for himself and his bride at 14 Bismarck Road, Highgate, having first ascertained that there was a bath in the house.

The grim routine began. Before unpacking, Smith took Margaret to see a Dr. Bates and told him that his wife was suffering from a bad headache. It seemed to the doctor that she was terrified to speak. Next morning, the couple visited a solicitor for the making of Margaret's will, then went to a post office to withdraw the balance in her savings account.

In the evening, just after eight o'clock, Louisa Blatch, the landlady, was doing some ironing in her kitchen. She heard "a sound of splashing—then there was a noise as of someone putting wet hands or arms on the side of the bath . . . then a sigh."

His mission accomplished, Smith crept down the stairs. He entered the parlour, seated himself at the harmonium, and began to play "Nearer My God to Thee."

After the short recital, Smith wandered into the kitchen to ask Mrs. Blatch if she had seen anything of his wife. He then went upstairs, "found" Margaret lying dead in the bath, and shouted to the landlady for help.

Subsequent events were almost carbon copies of those that had followed the drownings in Herne Bay and Blackpool. But there was one important addition: the inquest, with its verdict of accidental death, was reported in the *News of the World* Sunday paper under the double headline,

FOUND DEAD IN BATH
BRIDE'S TRAGIC FATE ON DAY AFTER WEDDING?

Though the bereaved husband's name was given as "Lloyd," two readers of the report were so struck by similarities between the tragedy in North London and the death of Alice Smith (née Burnham) in Blackpool a year before that they decided to communicate with the police. One of the persons who put two and two together was Joseph Crossley, the husband of the Blackpool landlady; the other was Charles Burnham, the Buckinghamshire fruit-grower whose daughter had drowned in the bath at Mrs. Crossley's boardinghouse.

Detective Inspector Arthur Neil was put in charge of the investigation. In seeking to untangle the web of Smith's deceits over a period of some sixteen years, Neil and his helpers made inquiries in forty towns, took statements from 150 witnesses, and traced some of the proceeds of Smith's crimes to more than twenty bank accounts.

It didn't take the detectives long to find sufficient evidence to justify Smith's arrest—but the fact that at the time of his arrest the investigators knew nothing of the death of Bessie Mundy at Herne Bay adds point to Neil's subsequent observation that there would probably never be a full account of the life and crimes of George Joseph Smith.

At his trial, which was held at the Old Bailey in the summer of 1915, the indictment referred only to the case of Bessie Mundy—who, so far as was known, was the first of Smith's brides to die a watery death. His fate was sealed when the judge, Mr. Justice Scrutton, allowed the prosecution to introduce evidence relating to the deaths of Alice Burnham and Margaret Lofty, so as to prove his "system" of murder.

Smith was an unruly defendant. He flung abuse at witnesses (describing Mrs. Crossley as a lunatic, Inspector Neil as a scoundrel), and when one of his counsel advised him to be quiet, pounded the rail of the dock with his fist and shouted, "I don't care what you say!"

He was silent, however, while Bernard Spilsbury, the pathologist, was giving evidence. Before the trial, in seeking answers concerning the method used for the three murders, Spilsbury had enlisted a nurse as a human guinea pig—with near-fatal effect, for when he had suddenly lifted the nurse's legs so that her head was immersed in bathwater, she had instantly lost consciousness. This experience had convinced Spilsbury that Smith's trio of victims had died from shock rather than drowning.

Smith did not exercise his right to give evidence on his own behalf— but that does not mean that he remained silent after the case for the Crown had been presented. He muttered and moaned during the closing speeches and often interrupted the judge's summing-up, claiming at one point, "I am not a murderer—though I may be a bit peculiar."

The jury was out for only twenty minutes. After stating that he thoroughly agreed with the verdict of "guilty," the judge told Smith that he would spare him the usual exhortation to repent: it would be a waste of time.

The sentence of death was carried out on 13 August, a Friday. Before he was hanged, Smith asserted, with evident conviction, "I shall soon be in the presence of God"—a prophecy that, for God's sake, one trusts was over-optimistic.

YOURS—TRULY?

Writing in the *Daily Telegraph* recently, Sir Ludovic Kennedy, who in the past has pronounced on what constitutes worthwhile evidence and what doesn't, came up with another pronouncement. Having said that the first things he wants to see before deciding whether or not to look into any alleged miscarriage of justice in a murder case are post-sentence letters from the convicted person, he explains his reason for that primary consideration: if anyone found guilty of murder continues to insist, in sincere-sounding prose, that he is not guilty, then it is painfully obvious that he must be innocent.

So as to keep my blood pressure in check, I managed, though it took some doing, to forget Kennedy's pronouncement—till a day or so ago, when I came across some letters from a Mr. George Smith that were published in the correspondence columns of the *Bath & Wiltshire Chronicle* toward the end of 1911.

Mr. George Smith—who, he? Well, before telling you, let me quote from three of the four letters, leaving out one that must have put the fear of God into hypochondriacal residents of Twerton, on the southern outskirts of Bath, for it raised the spectre of a multidisease plague thereabouts, all because the local council had reduced the frequency of refuse collections from that village.

The other letters deal with extra-Twertonial issues. Passages in them bring on a feeling of déjà vu: their tone and content have been echoed over the years and still are, thereby making Mr. Smith seem both ancient and modern.

The first of the letters reads, in part, "If the new system of education be far more serviceable and substantial than it was 20 years ago, how is it that we do not see the fruits in the general behaviour of children? Can any grown-up person deny the fact that when they themselves were children, their obedience to parents and superiors was more observed than it is today? Take, as another instance, the coarse manner, the lack of true brotherly and sisterly feeling, and the late hours indulged in by children. Then there is the vast amount of objectionable literature, such as the 'penny dreadfuls,' read by children. In conclusion, the training of children is undoubtedly a great problem, and cannot be solved by the State alone. Thus it becomes the duty of parents to do their share, in as much as there are two educations—the one which is taught at school, and the other which comes from parents, the latter being as important as the former."

In December, Mr. Smith launched a further attack upon penny dreadfuls and more expensive "objectionable publications": "I maintain that they are doing more harm and are accountable for more law-breaking than excessive drinking, and that unless our shops are cleansed from such a living curse—and the young prevented from obtaining such poison—our new generation, instead of rising to credit us, will only live to disgrace us."

Between those two letters, Mr. Smith had his say on the subject of reformation of criminals: "It is impossible to purify any sphere of society while the hardened unreformed criminal is in our midst. Yet the public, as a whole, seldom, if ever, turns its attention toward this downfallen class, never troubling as to what system the authorities are using in order to reform, as well as punish, these unfortunate beings. It is only when the public is reminded from time to time by the astounding revelations made known through the Press by some of the more intellectual of discharged prisoners that any regard is paid in that direction, and the whole matter, unfortunately, soon falls into oblivion."

A clue to the identity of Mr. Smith: a *private* letter, written by him some two years after the published ones, replying to a request for information about his antecedents from Mr. Charles Burnham, who had just heard that his daughter Alice had suddenly and surreptitiously become Mrs. George Smith: "My mother was a Buss horse, my father a Cab-driver, my sister a roughrider over the Arctic regions—my brothers were all gallant sailors on a steam-roller. This is the only information I can give to those who are not entitled to ask such questions."

That letter was written by George *Joseph* Smith, the so-called brides-in-the-bath murderer. And so were the published ones "painfully obviously" penned by a concerned citizen, a conscientious churchgoer, a pillar of the community. The address on those letters—91 Ashley Down Road, Bristol—was George Joseph's. Though it was his permanent home, tended by his only permanent "wife," Edith Pegler, he was more often than not away from it, travelling the country as a dealer in secondhand merchandise, meanwhile pursuing the far more profitable sideline of snaring shelved spinsters, "marrying" them, and ditching them the moment he had appropriated their assets. His career as a ubiquitous bigamist seems to have begun at the turn of the century, when, still in his twenties, he had served three terms of hard labour for larceny and receiving.

Shortly before his flurry of Letters to the Editor, he had "married," fleeced, and deserted Bessie Mundy; three months after writing the last of those letters, he would, quite by chance, meet her again, easily persuade her to forgive and forget, also to sign a will, then buy a bath and drown her in it. The same ostensibly accidental fate befell Alice Burnham; likewise in 1914, Margaret Lofty. But the third sudden death turned out to be one drowning too many; it was compared to the earlier bath-night tragedies, to decide that the evidence of Smith's system was overwhelming.

In sincere-sounding love letters to Edith Pegler, he insisted that he was a victim—of "perjury, spite, malice, vindictiveness." On the morning of Friday, 13 August 1915, minutes before (to quote his own words in a different context) he fell into oblivion, he stated, "I shall soon be in the presence of God—and I declare before him that I am innocent."

Oh, sure. Of course, no one (but Sir Ludovic Kennedy) can doubt that Smith's protestations were untrue. He appears to have placed undue reliance upon a version of the drama-school maxim: "Success as an actor is all down to sincerity—so if you can fake sincerity, you've got it made."

Doubts about Hauptmann

Doubts about Hauptmann

*T*he Lindbergh case has been turned into a sort of fiction.

That has been achieved mainly through the efforts of certain authors of books about the case, makers of television programmes about it, writers of plays said to be based upon it, and a woman who for nearly sixty years did her utmost to make people disbelieve the truths of the case. Early in 1993, the fiction was strengthened when, in an episode of a no-expense-spared BBC television series, *Fame in the Twentieth Century,* the presenter, the very Australian writer Clive James, told millions of viewers that the man executed for the kidnapping and murder of the Lindbergh baby "was almost certainly innocent."

Mr. James's reference to the case was a postscript to comments on the immense fame of Colonel Charles A. Lindbergh, all because he had made the first solo airplane flight across the Atlantic. That was in May 1927. Two years later, the "secret" marriage of Lindbergh, the Lone Eagle, to Anne Morrow, a daughter of a rich politician, was given front-and-subsequent-pages coverage throughout the world. And so was the birth of their son, Charles Jr., in June 1930. Long before the arrival—the "perfect landing"—of the "Eaglet," Lindbergh had grown tired of being a public show. Seeking a refuge from fame, he bought a wooded estate a few miles from the small town of Hopewell, in the desolate Sourland region of New Jersey, and had a two-storeyed house built, to his precise specifications, in a clearing at the end of a long curving driveway from the road. Believing the publicity that he had come to despise, which made him out to be *everyone's* hero, and therefore inviolable, he did not consider the fact that so secluded a residence was ideally suited as the setting for a crime.

Apart from some finishing touches—including replacement of a shutter on one of the nursery windows, which had warped, making it impossible to fasten—the house was complete by March 1932. The Lindberghs had taken to spending long weekends there, the rest of the time at the Morrows' home at Englewood, fifty miles or so to the northeast, looking across the Hudson River to the Bronx, the northernmost borough of New York City. But that routine was broken on Tuesday, 1 March: as it was a miserable, blustery day, and the baby, now twenty months old, was suffering from a chill, Mrs. Lindbergh decided to remain at the new house. Lindbergh, who spent part of the day in New York City, drove back in the evening, arriving at half past eight; on his way through the servants' quarters, he paused to ask Betty Gow, the Scottish-born nanny, about his son's slight illness. The other servants, butler and cook, were a married couple, Oliver and Elsie Whateley, who were both from England.

At about ten past nine, soon after the Lindberghs finished dinner and went into the living room, they heard a noise—sounding to Lindbergh "like the slats of an orange-box falling off a chair." Supposing that the noise had come from the kitchen, they resumed the conversation that it had briefly interrupted.

At ten o'clock, Betty Gow went to the nursery to check that the baby was still sleeping as soundly as when she had left him two hours before, swaddled against the merest draught with a sleeping suit, a woollen shirt, and a sleeveless garment she had sewn together earlier in the evening with distinctive blue thread that she had got from Mrs. Whateley: "a proper little flannel shirt to put on next his skin." Leaving the door open so as to give some light from the landing, she groped her way to the crib. The baby was not there. Betty Gow felt no alarm, for she assumed that Mrs. Lindbergh, perhaps hearing the child crying, had taken him from the crib. She went to Mrs. Lindbergh's room, found her on her own, and, fearful now, ran in search of Lindbergh, hoping against hope to see him holding his son—and, finding him in the library, alone, screamed to him to follow her back to the nursery. They searched the room, then every other part of the house, now with Mrs. Lindbergh and the Whateleys helping—and then Lindbergh shouted to the butler to phone the police, grabbed a hunting rifle, and ran through the front door, around the clearing, and along the driveway to the road.

He had returned, had gone back to the nursery, before the first policemen arrived: the entire force of Hopewell, numbering two. He pointed to an open window, the one with the warped shutter, and to a white envelope on the muddied sill, saying that he had not touched it in case it bore the kidnapper's fingerprints. When the envelope was eventually opened, having been dusted without result, it was found to contain a single sheet of white paper, also free of prints, on which a message was written in blue ink:

Dear Sir
Have 50000$ ready 25000$ in 20$ bills 15000 in 10$ bills and 10000 in 5$ bills. After 2–4 days we will inform you were to deliver the mony We warn you for making anyding public or for notify the police. The child is in gut care. Instruction [or "indication"] for the letters are singnature

The "singnature" was of two interlocking circles, with three holes near the perimeters.

Lindbergh and the local policemen went outside. Shining their torches on the muddy ground below the open window, they saw two indentations made by the ends of a ladder. The ladder itself was lying some twenty yards away. Obviously homemade, it was of three sections, each seven feet long. The two lower sections were connected (with dowel pins pressed through matching holes in the rails), and the top section, which the kidnapper had not needed so as to reach the window, was nearby. There were splits in the rails of the connected sections, almost certainly caused during the kidnapper's descent with a burden weighing thirty pounds, making a combined weight that overstrained the timber, particularly where the sections were held together with the dowel pins. Again almost certainly, the noise the Lindberghs had heard at about ten past nine was the splitting of the ladder rails.

By midnight, the investigation was being carried out by officers of the New Jersey State Police, directly led by Colonel H. Norman Schwarzkopf, who had been in charge of the semimilitary force since its formation eleven years before. (In the Gulf War of 1991, the Allied forces were commanded by his son, General Norman Schwarzkopf.) By daybreak, there were more state policemen at Hopewell than in the rest of New Jersey put together. Even so, they were outnumbered by reporters and cameramen, who were themselves outnumbered by sightseers. The early stages of the investigation, the most important ones, were a complete shambles. It has been said that Schwarzkopf and his aides "suffered, under the sudden spotlight, from a bad attack of stage-fright," but the truth of the matter is that the spotlight showed them up as incompetent detectives. None of them thought to measure, let alone make a plaster cast, of a footprint, probably the kidnapper's, below the nursery window; the inspection of the nursery was superficial; dozens of people, not only policemen, were allowed to handle the ladder although it had not been thoroughly tested for fingerprints.

Three days after the crime, Lindbergh received, by post from Brooklyn, a second note from the kidnapper, repeating the warning against involving the police, saying that the baby was in "gut health" and raising the ransom demand to $70,000. The following day, another note, similar in tone, was delivered at the Manhattan office of Lindbergh's legal adviser. Lindbergh issued press statements to the effect that he was eager to negotiate, without bringing in the police. He also announced that, in case the kidnappers (plural, though there were several reasons, including the comparative modesty of the ransom demand, for believing that the crime was the work of an individual) did not wish to deal with him personally, he had authorized two New York bootleggers, Salvy Spitale and Irving Bitz, to act on his behalf. Among many other persons who offered their services as go-betweens were the presidents of Columbia and Princeton universities; Al Capone, whose offer was contingent upon his being given leave of absence from the prison where he had recently begun serving an eleven-year sentence for tax evasion; and John F. Condon, a retired schoolteacher who had lived all of his seventy-two years in the Bronx, which he considered "the most beautiful borough in the world."

A week after the kidnapping, Condon's local newspaper, the *Home News,* printed a letter from him in which he pleaded with the kidnapper to communicate with him, promising both secrecy and the addition of a thousand dollars—"all I can scrape together"—to the ransom money. Next day, he received a letter, containing a sealed enclosure, which said that if he was willing to act as go-between he should "handel incloced letter personally" to Lindbergh and then remain at home every night. He phoned the Lindbergh house, read the letter to the person who answered, and, when told to open the enclosure, read that out as well: explicit instructions regarding the parcelling of the ransom money were followed by the circles-and-holes signature. Condon, asked to come to Hopewell, got a friend to drive him there. Comparison of the letter and the enclosure with the letters that had definitely been written by the kidnapper showed that the handwriting was much the same, there were similar errors of spelling and grammar, and the signatures matched. It was agreed that, in accordance with the kidnapper's instructions, a small ad should be placed in a New York paper, saying that the money was ready; the message would be signed "Jafsie," an acronym of Condon's initials.

Three nights later (Saturday, 12 March), a letter was delivered to Condon by a cabdriver who had received it, together with a dollar for the "fare," from a man who had flagged him down a short distance away. Following the instructions in the letter, Condon went to a deserted frankfurter stand, where he found a note directing him to Woodlawn Cemetery, in the Bronx. After wandering around there for some minutes, he was approached by a man who, speaking with a strong Germanic accent, said that he was one of a gang of five kidnappers, two of whom were women. Condon and the man, who called himself John, talked for over an hour, meanwhile moving from place to place in and near the cemetery. The man said that the baby was alive and well, receiving constant care aboard a boat. Just before he hurried off into the cover of woodland, he promised to send Condon "a token" that would prove beyond doubt that he was not a hoaxer.

The token—the baby's sleeping suit, parcelled and sent by post—was delivered to Condon on 15 March. The negotiations continued, with Jafsie ads bringing replies through the post—till Saturday, 2 April, when final arrangements were made for payment of the ransom. The serial numbers of the bills had been taken; at Condon's suggestion, the money was in two packets, one of $50,000, the original asking price, and the other of $20,000. That night, Condon, in a car driven by Lindbergh, followed a trail of messages, at last to a dirt road beside St Raymond's Cemetery, where "John" was waiting. Lindbergh heard him calling out to Condon to follow him into the cemetery. After some argument, the kidnapper agreed to accept the $50,000, and handed Condon a "receipt" which, so he said, gave instructions for finding the baby. He ran off into the cemetery, and Condon returned to where Lindbergh was waiting. The note read:

> The boy is on the boad [*boat*] Nelly. It is a small boad 28 feet long. Two persons are on the boad. The [*they*] are innosent [*sic*]. You will find the boad between Horseneck Beach and Gay Head near Elizabeth Island.

Early next morning, Lindbergh began flying over that area, off the coast of Massachusetts. He continued the search till late on the following day, long after he had accepted that the "boad Nelly" was a figment of the kidnapper's imagination.

On Thursday, 12 May, while Lindbergh was searching for another "kidnap boat" (the invention of a man named John Hughes Curtis, whose motive for concocting the complicated hoax remains obscure), the decomposed body of a baby boy was found, quite by chance, lying facedown in a thicket beside a little-used road five miles from the Lindbergh home. Any slight doubt as to whether the body was that of the kidnapped child was dispelled by Lindbergh, who, returning in response to a radio message, viewed the body in a mortuary and recognized several physical characteristics, particularly a malformation of the bones in one foot; also by Betty Gow, who identified garments, one of which was the flannel shirt which she had stitched together with unusual blue thread. According to the local coroner, the principal cause of death was "fractured skull due to external violence."

At last released from constraints imposed by the possibility that the baby was still alive, law officers, not only of New Jersey, set about tracing the man who had committed the double crime against "the first family of America." Not that there was much to go on. The best hope seemed to be that the criminal would be caught through his spending of the ransom money. The list of the serial numbers was circulated to banks, and cashiers were given an incentive to watch out for the bills by the offer of a reward of seven dollars, partly contributed by Lindbergh, for the spotting of any of them. They soon started to appear, usually in deposits made by shops, cafes, and filling stations; depositors were interviewed in the hope that they could connect the particular bills with specific transactions and recall something about the customer. As each bill, or batch of bills, was spotted, the location of the place where it had turned up was marked on a map, which soon showed a preponderance of transactions in the Bronx and the contiguous northern part of Manhattan.

Part of the ransom money was in gold notes, and in May 1933, following President Roosevelt's order that all such notes were to be exchanged for ordinary currency at a Federal Reserve Bank, someone signing himself J. J. Faulkner exchanged nearly three thousand dollars' worth of them at the bank in New York City; soon after it was noticed that they came from the ransom (they constituted the largest transaction ever spotted), it was found that no one named Faulkner lived at the address given by the exchanger, whom the cashier could not describe at all.

Later in the year, the police sought help from attendants at filling stations, saying that whenever a customer paid with a bill of ten or twenty dollars, the attendant should write the licence number of the customer's vehicle on the bill. That initiative would produce the vital break in the case.

While the "Lindbergh squads" of detectives doggedly stuck at their respective tasks—each acting virtually independently, and some of them as if in competition rather than cooperation with the others—a most unconventional detective was at work.

His name was Arthur Koehler. He was a "wood technologist" of the Forest Service of the Department of Agriculture. Shortly after the kidnap case became one of murder as well, he began trying to establish where the criminal had bought the timber to construct the ladder.

Having identified the types of timber, he concentrated on that which was of North Carolina pine. Microscopic examination showed marks made by a particular kind of mechanical plane; the records of manufacturers of such machines revealed that twenty-five were in use; most of those were ruled out because they were used only to dress other types of timber. After months of searching, Koehler found the plane he was looking for at a mill in South Carolina; because a non-standard pulley had been installed in the autumn of 1931, the machine made additional marks that were uniquely the same as those on some of the ladder rails. Koehler visited all of the timber companies to which the mill had shipped ladder-size boards of North Carolina pine during the five months between the pulley-changing and the kidnapping. Only at one of the yards—that of the National Lumber & Millwork Co., in the Bronx—did he find a remnant on which there was an "extraordinary mark," resulting from the temporary nicking of one of the frequently sharpened blades of the mechanical plane, that he had detected in his examination of the ladder. He was sure that he had found the yard at which most of the timber for the ladder had been bought. Not quite all of it: four apparently old nail holes at one end of the rail he designated as No. 16, as well as the fact that the rail was grubbier than the rest, indicated that the timber was secondhand, that it had been used for some other purpose before becoming part of the ladder; the most likely explanation for the presence of Rail 16 was that the kidnapper, finding that he had not bought quite enough timber, had made up the deficit with an old piece that happened to be nearby. Koehler, whose achievements had set him among the greatest forensic investigators, could do no more—for the time being, that is.

On Tuesday, 18 September 1934, more than two and a half years after the kidnapping, a cashier at a branch of the Corn Exchange Bank in the Bronx spotted a ten-dollar ransom bill in a deposit from the Warner-Quinlan Company, a local filling station. A vehicle licence-plate number—4U-13-14-NY—was written on the margin of the bill. The filling-station manager and his assistant said that the bill had come from a customer driving a blue 1930 Dodge sedan, who had bought five gallons of petrol, costing just under a dollar. The licence bureau provided the name and address of the owner of the car: Bruno Richard Hauptmann, 1279 East 222nd Street, the Bronx. The registration card showed that he was almost thirty-five, of medium build, with blue eyes and "muddy blond" hair, German-born, and a carpenter by trade.

Further inquiries revealed that he was an illegal immigrant (and it was subsequently learned that he had served a five-year prison sentence in Germany for burglaries and a highway robbery—in which he had threatened to kill two women wheeling prams—and that he was wanted by the German police, who considered him "exceptionally sly and clever," because in 1923 he had escaped from custody while awaiting trial for other burglaries, and fled to America). In 1925, he had married Anna Schoeffler, a waitress, also German-born, who in November 1933 had given birth to a son, named Manfred in homage to Baron Manfred von Richthoven, the German air-ace of the Great War.

At nine o'clock on the morning of the 19th, Hauptmann was arrested after he had backed his car out of the garage in the yard of his house and started driving toward Manhattan. He was searched before being taken to a police station, and a twenty-dollar ransom bill was found folded in his wallet.

Much more of the ransom money—$14,600 of it—was found in various hiding places, including holes burrowed through a block of wood, in his garage. Faintly scribbled in pencil on the inside of a closet door in the house were John F. Condon's phone number and address; also what appeared to be the serial numbers of banknotes—none corresponding with that of any of the ransom bills.

According to Hauptmann, the ransom money had come into his possession in December 1933—though without his knowledge at that time. He had, he said, agreed to look after a shoebox for a friend and business associate, Isidor Fisch, who was about to take a trip to Germany. Fisch had died during the trip. Hauptmann said that he had forgotten about the box till the summer of 1934, when rainwater had seeped into the closet where he had stowed it; the box, damaged by the water, had been further damaged, to the extent that the contents were revealed, when he had accidentally hit it with a broom. Without saying a word to his wife, he had hidden the bills in the garage. As Fisch had died owing him money, he had felt justified in dipping into the small fortune, unaware that it was criminal loot.

Hauptmann had worked regularly as a carpenter till 2 April 1932, the day when the ransom was paid, but had done only a few odd jobs since; his wife had given up her job as a waitress in December 1932. Their joint earnings since April 1932 amounted to just over a thousand dollars. And yet during that time, though Hauptmann had bought several luxury items, gone on hunting trips, and paid for his wife to visit her relatives in Germany, his capital had risen from just under five thousand dollars to just over forty thousand—including the money in the garage. He attributed his recent affluence to successful dealings in the stock market, but examination of his brokerage accounts showed that he had made a total loss of nearly six thousand dollars. Many of his bank deposits in the same period consisted largely or wholly of coins (two deposits of about four hundred dollars were made up entirely of silver), which suggested to the investigators that he had systematically "laundered" ransom bills by using them for small purchases and getting lots of change. There was nothing to indicate that Isidor Fisch, a small-time dealer in cheap furs, was better off after April 1932 than previously: he had continued to get by without a car, had remained in the cheapest of digs, had borrowed money and tried to borrow more—and apparently would not have been able to afford the trip to Germany from which he did not return if Hauptmann had not stepped in at the last minute with a loan of $2,000.

When Hauptmann was interviewed by the district attorney of the Bronx (with a shorthand writer taking down the questions and answers), he was shown the detached closet door and asked, "Your handwriting is on it?" "Yes, all over it," he replied. He said that he could not make out some of the notations and could not explain some of the others. Why had he made a note of Condon's address? "I must have read it in the paper about the story. I was a little bit interest, and keep a little bit record of it, and maybe I was just on the closet and was reading the paper and put down the address. . . . It is possible that a shelf or two shelves in the closet, and after a while I put new papers always on the closet, and we just got the paper where this case was in and I followed the story, of course, and I put the address on there. . . . I can't give you any explanation about the [*Condon's*] telephone number." (At a subsequent interview, he said that he was in the habit of jotting down notes of important events on walls in the house.) He said that the serial numbers on the closet door were of large bills that Fisch had given him to buy shares.

Handwriting experts compared the kidnapper's writing (on the demands to Lindbergh and on the ransom-arranging letters to Condon) with specimens of Hauptmann's writing before his arrest. In the summer of 1932, detailed analysis of the notes had proved that, as was to be expected, the writing was disguised; but the analysis had picked up many repeated letters and words that the kidnapper had failed to disguise—also a number of misspellings and peculiar locutions. Since the analysis, one of the experts had examined the writing of more than three hundred men questioned by the police, without finding a single specimen with sufficient resemblances to the notes. The kidnapper/Hauptmann comparisons left the experts in no doubt that no one but Hauptmann could have written the notes. Their conviction was based not only upon matching formations but also upon Hauptmann's writing of a dictated "test paragraph" containing words that the kidnapper had misspelt—for instance, "anything" and "something" as "anyding" and "someding," "our" as "ouer," "were" as "where," "later" as "latter." Hauptmann misspelt every one of the "trick words" in exactly the way the kidnapper had.

Almost a year before, Arthur Koehler had suggested to the police that they should interview every customer of the National Lumber & Millwork Company in the months preceding the crime; the suggestion had not been followed up. But by the time that Koehler was summoned to Hauptmann's house, a few blocks from the timber yard, a checking of the company's records had shown that Hauptmann had bought ten dollars' worth of timber there at the very end of 1931. Hauptmann either could not or would not say what he had used the purchase for. Koehler inspected the woodwork in and of the house—lastly, that in and of the attic. There, he immediately noticed that part of one of the flooring boards was missing; that it had been sawn off was evident from the fact that sawdust clung to the lathes at the end of the truncated board. He compared Rail 16, the odd one out, with the board. Not only were the two pieces of the same type of wood and the same lateral dimensions, but the graining and the annual rings corresponded. And when an end of Rail 16 was placed near the end of the board, the four nail-holes in the rail exactly matched four nail holes in the joist below; two of the holes in the rail had been driven in diagonally, at the selfsame respective angles as the matching holes in the joist. With the holes aligned, there was a two-inch gap between the rail and the board, indicating to Koehler that the maker of the ladder, having sawn off rather more than he needed, had sawn the rail to the required length. Seeking further evidence that Hauptmann had made the ladder, Koehler examined the contents of the carpenter's chest in the garage-cum-workshop, paying particular attention to the planes, the blades of which he examined under a microscope, scrutinizing them for nicks and other imperfections. He used the planes on blocks of "neutral wood" and found that one of them left ridges that coincided exactly with the ridges he had observed in hand-planed surfaces of a side of the ladder and all of its rungs; the matching of the ridges, as unique to a particular plane blade as fingerprints are to a particular hand, was apparent to the naked eye. Proving that the plane was Hauptmann's, a bracket in the garage bore the same ridges.

At identification parades, Hauptmann was picked out by various eye-witnesses—and, though not on a parade, by an ear-witness, Lindbergh, who said that Hauptmann's voice was that of the man he had heard calling out to Condon at St. Raymond's Cemetery on the night when the ransom was handed over. Condon was both an eye- and an ear-witness, saying that Hauptmann was definitely the "Cemetery John" with whom he had negotiated on two occasions, for nearly two hours in all. Among others who claimed to recognize Hauptmann were the cabdriver to whom the criminal had given a letter for delivery to Condon; a woman who said that, during the "Jafsie period," she had seen Hauptmann watching Condon at a Bronx railway station; a box-office girl at a Manhattan cinema, who said that he was the man who in November 1933 had paid for a ticket with a ransom bill; and two men living near Hopewell—one an illiterate hillbilly with an unsavoury reputation, the other an octogenarian whose eyesight had deteriorated—who said that they had seen Hauptmann near the Lindbergh estate shortly before the kidnapping. Condon was the only one of the eye/ear-witnesses whose evidence was stronger than doubtful.

The trial of Hauptmann began on the second day of 1935 in the pretty courthouse in the small town of Flemington, New Jersey, which was jam-packed throughout the trial with journalists (including Damon Runyon, Walter Winchell, and Ford Maddox Ford), press photographers and movie cameramen, and sightseers (including show-business personalities such as Jack Benny and Clifton Webb, and members of high society, some accompanied by their publicity agents). The prosecution was led by David T. Wilentz, the pugnacious attorney general of New Jersey, the defence by Edward J. Reilly, "the Bull of Brooklyn," who had been briefed in more than two thousand murder trials and whose fee in the Hauptmann case was partly paid by a newspaper in return for "exclusives" from the defendant and his wife. The trial dawdled on till 13 February, when the jury of eight men and four women, all local people, each now famous wherever newspapers were circulated, having deliberated for just over eleven hours, returned a verdict of "guilty of murder in the first degree," without recommendation of life imprisonment.

There were, of course, any number of appeals, each postponing the execution. Meanwhile, Anna Hauptmann went on a fund-raising tour of places with large populations of German Americans and told audiences at Hauptmann-is-Innocent rallies what they wanted to hear: that her husband was the victim of a frame-up, chosen as such simply because he was German. Near the end of 1935 (shortly before the Lindberghs, wanting to get away from it all, sailed for England with their second son, Jon, intending to settle there), Harold G. Hoffman, the governor of New Jersey, who happened to be planning a bid to become the Republican candidate for the presidency, got himself on to front pages and into editorials by saying that he had visited Hauptmann in his cell and that he had grave doubts as to whether the case had been solved. Hoffman kept himself in the news for the next couple of months—by declaring his faith in Hauptmann's Fisch story and pooh-poohing Koehler's findings, by announcing that he had hired private detectives to reexamine the case, by talking of "new evidence" (all of which turned out to be worthless, either because it was immaterial or because it was proved to have been fabricated), and, in January 1936, by granting Hauptmann a thirty-day stay of execution—during which a vainglorious detective named Ellis Parker, a friend of Hoffman's, entered the case. A few days before Hauptmann was again scheduled to die, Parker and his son produced a detailed "confession" signed by Paul Wendel, a disbarred lawyer—but refused to produce Wendel until Attorney General Wilentz insisted on knowing where he could be found: in a mental institution, where he had been confined for some weeks on Parker Senior's orders. The execution, rescheduled to take place on the last day of March, was postponed while a grand jury pored over Wendel's "confession" and discussed his account of how he had been kidnapped by a gang, kept in a cellar in Brooklyn, where he had been tortured till he was ready to sign anything, and then taken to the mental institution.

On Friday, 3 April 1936, shortly after the grand jury voted to drop the Wendel case, Hauptmann, still protesting his innocence, was executed in the electric chair at Trenton Prison.

That necessarily brief account does not, of course, include every bit of the long story. But I don't think I have left out any points of real importance. If I have, the omissions are unintended, not meant to mislead. I shall, in a minute, refer to points that another writer has suggested are important but which, in fact, are not. If my account contains any inaccuracies, they must be of a trivial nature. I have not amended truths to suit a purpose.

Bruno Richard Hauptmann was guilty of the kidnapping and murder of the Lindbergh baby.

I state that, not as an opinion, but as a fact.

Harold G. Hoffman and Ellis Peters were not the first persons, nor (as I intimated when I began) the last, to try to muddy the truths of the case. For a discussion of some of the quaint theory books published before 1985, I can do no better than quote Patterson Smith, the leading American bookdealer specializing in factual crime material:

> Although it is now not often realized, the Lindbergh kidnapping attracted sceptics from the start. Just after the story broke in 1932, Laura Vitray, a Hearst reporter, rushed into print with a little-known book, *The Great Lindbergh Hullabaloo: An Unorthodox Account.* Unorthodox it is.
>
> Vitray, sensing a hoax, wrote derisively of the Lindbergh family, referring to the child as "the golden-haired Eaglet" and accusing certain vaguely defined "powers" of having "deliberately" arranged the Lindbergh "kidnapping," not for ransom, but as

a story, to divert public attention from the grave disaster that threatens this nation at their own hands today."

Laura Vitray had a sister sceptic in Mary Belle Spencer, a Chicago lawyer who seems to have had an animus against the massive law-enforcement effort that was thrown into the hunt for the Lindbergh child and its kidnapper. In 1933, after the discovery of the child's body but before the arrest of Hauptmann, she published a pamphlet bearing the cover title, *No. 2310, Criminal File: Exposed! Aviator's Baby Was Never Kidnapped or Murdered.*

Her argument was that no crime had been shown to have been committed, the infant being perfectly capable of having wandered off on its own to meet its death by animals in the woods. She presents the text of a mock trial in which she defends a vagrant "John Doe" who has been indicted for kidnap and murder. In her burlesque, she makes thinly veiled substitutions for names prominent in the case, such as "Limberg" for Lindbergh and "Elizabeth Gah" for Betty Gow. (For reasons unknown to me, on the front cover she has covered the original line of type, which read "Limberg's Baby," with a correction strip reading "Aviator's Baby.")

This curious work, which is now rare, almost had severe consequences for the trial of Hauptmann. Prior to the proceedings, copies were mailed to the panel of jurymen, causing the judge to consider granting a change in venue.

H. L. Mencken said that the Lindbergh case was "the biggest story since the Resurrection." Concerning Hauptmann's guilt there seemed to be little doubt, for he was tied to the crime by a web of circumstantial evidence which, taken as a whole, was so strong that it seemed that no one possessed of reason could challenge the certainty of his guilt.

But a challenge did come. Anthony Scaduto, in *Scapegoat* (1976), marshalled some 500 pages of evidence and argument in an attempt to demonstrate that Hauptmann, at most guilty of extortion, ended his life the victim of a judicial murder by the state. Scaduto's arguments, given additional publicity by Hauptmann's widow, seeking vindication for her husband, attracted much attention and gained many adherents.

An issue is raised here on which I wish to ruminate. In some forty-eight years of dealing in material on criminal justice history, I have had contact with many writers and researchers seeking material for new books on past crimes. Often a product of such endeavours will be the first of its kind on a given crime; often it will be a retelling, with added information or a new analysis, of a familiar crime narrative; often it will add to the literature yet another theory in explanation of a crime never satisfactorily explained.

On rare occasions, of which *Scapegoat* is one, it will offer a radically divergent theory of a crime hitherto considered settled. Of all crime books published, those posing revisionist theories tend to attract the greatest media attention. They are "news." Far from merely adding to our knowledge of a past event or re-embellishing a tale previously grown stale in the telling, they say to us, "You've been wrong about this case." And if someone is thought to have been unjustly convicted and executed, the news value is all the stronger.

It has, after all, been observed that Americans have a greater sense of injustice than of justice. When a revisionist account reaches reviewers, the arguments put forward by its author can seem extraordinarily compelling, for very often the book does not aim for balance but selects only those facts that support its divergent thesis.

Moreover—and this is very important—the reviewer of a book on crime written for the general public often has little or no background in the case which could help him weigh the author's novel contentions against countervailing evidence. The reviewer sees only one side of the story, and it usually looks good.

If you infer from these musings that I do not accept Anthony Scaduto's thesis about Hauptmann's innocence, you are correct.

Another quote, this one from the brilliant American lawyer Louis Nizer, who, having coined the term "analytical syndrome," explains:

It is possible to take the record of any trial and by minute dissection and post-facto reasoning demonstrate that witnesses for either side made egregious errors or lied. Then, by ascribing critical weight to the exposed facts, the conclusion is reached that the verdict was fraudulently obtained. This was the process by which the Warren Commission Report [on the assassination of President Kennedy] was challenged in a spate of books. To cite just one illustration, a constable deputy sheriff described the rifle which had been found on the sixth floor of the Book Depository Building, Dallas, as a Mauser, instead of a Mannlicher-Carcano, which it was. Out of this innocent error, due to ignorance or excitement, sprouted the theory that the real assassin's rifle had been spirited away and Lee Harvey Oswald's rifle planted on the scene to involve him. Multiply this incident by many others, such as someone's testimony that shots were heard coming from the mall, and the "hiding" of the death X-rays of the President (since revealed), and you have a gigantic conspiracy by foreign agents, or government officials, or New Orleans homosexuals, or lord knows what, to fix the blame on an innocent man, Oswald. Of course, all this was nonsense, and subsequent events have confirmed the accuracy of the Report.

The analytical syndrome can be used to discredit any verdict, from the commonest automobile negligence case to the most involved anti-trust or proxy contest.

Anthony Scaduto uses the analytical syndrome. And so does Sir Ludovic Kennedy, the British television personality who in 1985 published a 438-page book, *The Airman and the Carpenter: The Lindbergh Case and the Framing of Richard Hauptmann,* which must have convinced many, perhaps most, of its readers that Hauptmann was the victim of a miscarriage of justice.

Since Kennedy's is the most recent Hauptmann-was-innocent book, and since he repeats the Scaduto notions that he likes best, I shall concentrate on his view of the case.

First, though, let me quote his explanation of what invariably persuades him to produce so-and-so-was-innocent books and of what his method of investigation is. My interpolations may, at this stage, seem to be nitpicking, but I promise you that they are pertinent.

Kennedy: "I have been asked whether in cases I have investigated I have ever been convinced of the complainant's guilt. The answer is no, because I have never pursued cases where I have been uncertain about guilt or innocence." (The words "guilt or" are redundant, for Kennedy has only pursued cases where his initial instinct assured him that the persons found guilty were innocent.) "In those cases I have written about, my initial instincts that the person in question was not guilty have been fully confirmed by subsequent investigations." ("Fully confirmed"? To his own satisfaction, he must mean.) "It should however be emphasized that, contrary to popular belief, cases of guilty men proclaiming their innocence and *continuing to do so with evidence to back it up* are so rare as to be almost non-existent." (Heaven knows what that means. One assumes that the backing-up evidence refers to the proclamations rather than the innocence of the guilty men. Perhaps not: as I shall demonstrate, Kennedy, following the general example set by Humpty Dumpty, does tend to use the word "evidence" rather loosely—as a description of things that may have happened, things that are rumoured to have happened, and things that certainly didn't happen. In any event, how does Kennedy know that his statement is true, considering that he has never investigated any such cases?) Speaking of his method of investigation, Kennedy says, "My starting-point has always been a presumption of innocence, and in all my cases I have found a narrative story based on that presumption to be far more convincing than a continued assumption of guilt."

Using the Kennedy Method (which is far more complicated than he has just made it out to be), one would have no difficulty in "proving," say, that Adolf Hitler was pro-Semitic—or, having plumped for a presumption of guilt, that St. Francis of Assisi was a vivisectionist. Actually—*confirming* popular belief—the annals of crime are strewn with undoubtedly guilty persons, many of them users of the analytical syndrome, who never wavered from pleading innocence.

Here is one of Kennedy's several versions, all much the same, of how he came to the conclusion that Hauptmann was innocent:

"The place was my hotel bedroom, the time around 8 A.M. [on a day in 1981]. As one often does in New York at that time of day, I was flicking idly through the television channels while awaiting the arrival of orange juice and coffee. I did not even know which channel I was tuned to when there swam into my vision a very old lady proclaiming with vehemence that her husband was innocent of the crime of which he had been convicted. I sat up and paid attention for this was, as it were, my territory. . . . Slowly it dawned on me—for the scene had been set before I had tuned in—that the old lady was none other than Anna Hauptmann, the widow of Richard Hauptmann. . . . And then I remembered from Eton days a picture that would be seared on my mind for ever, a full-page photograph of the haunted unshaven face of Richard Hauptmann as it first appeared after his arrest and then again, on the day of his electrocution two years later.

And now, nearly half a century on, here was his widow not only proclaiming his innocence but telling Tom Brokaw (and this was the peg for the interview) that as a result of new information about the case, she was taking out a suit against the State of New Jersey for her husband's wrongful conviction and execution. . . . I felt the old adrenalin surging through me and a sense of heady exhilaration; for I thought it improbable in the extreme that an old lady in her eighties would have agreed, forty-four years after her husband's death, to have travelled all the way to New York to appear on an early morning television show to assert her husband's innocence and launch a suit against a powerful state if she knew (and she would have known) that her husband was guilty; not unless she was out of her mind, and she did not seem to me to be that.

Let us examine Kennedy's criteria for an "extreme improbability":

1. That "an old lady in her eighties would have agreed . . . to have travelled all the way to New York to appear on an early morning television show." The old lady in her eighties (as opposed to a young lady in her eighties, who really would deserve sympathy) was as fit as a fiddle. Near the end of Kennedy's book, more than four hundred pages away from his account of Mrs. Hauptmann's appearance on television, he reveals that, four years later, she was "still amazingly active and mentally alert." Her journey "all the way to New York" sounds a very long way indeed; but, in fact, she had only come from Philadelphia (which is a shorter distance from Hopewell than Hopewell is from New York); all her expenses were paid, all arrangements made, by the television company, who no doubt also paid her an appearance fee. With no disrespect to her, it is reasonable to think that she would have been glad to put herself out far more than she did in order to appear on a popular television chatter show, doing her utmost to sway public opinion in favour of her claim that her husband had been "Wrongfully, Corruptly, and Unjustly" executed—and, incidentally, that she was entitled to damages of a hundred million dollars.

2. That unless Mrs. Hauptmann was out of her mind (and she seemed perfectly sane to the perfectly sane Kennedy), she would not have gone to such trouble "if she knew (and she would have known) that her husband was guilty." Excluding Kennedy, Scaduto & Co. (and Mrs. Hauptmann's lawyer, who was presumably working on a contingency-fee basis that

he would receive a percentage of any profits from the legal action), it is impossible to think of any campaigning pro-Hauptmannite whose utterances on the case should be taken with more salt than those of Mrs. Hauptmann. Following her husband's arrest, she too was grilled; her questioners were unable to break her story that her husband had told her nothing of the ransom money hidden at first in the house and then in the garage, she had never chanced on any of it, and she had accepted his explanations as to how he, though hardly ever working, was able to pay the domestic bills, buy luxury items, and send her off to Germany for a three months' holiday. Supposing her story was true, then there is no doubt whatsoever that Hauptmann, if he was the kidnapper, never told her that he was, and never gave her the least reason for suspecting that he was. Therefore (and quite apart from the fact that it would be most unexpected if she, a determinedly trusting and loving wife, no less determinedly trusting as a widow, were ever to speak of any suspicion of Hauptmann that may have crossed her mind against her will), all that she can say firsthand in defence of her husband is that, until his arrest, she had no reason for thinking that he was connected in any way with any crimes committed in the spring of 1932. The best one can say of that is that it is negative evidence—about as useful as the evidence of an eyewitness who claims that he didn't witness anything. A proverb seems apropos, not only of Mrs. Hauptmann but also of her confederates: "There are none so blind as those that will not see."

In every complex criminal case, the evidence for the prosecution can be divided into two sorts: *salient* and *secondary*. If the salient evidence stays intact, no amount of doubt concerning any, even all, of the secondary evidence has the slightest weakening effect upon the strength of the salient evidence—which, in the case of Hauptmann, was this:

1) He had spent some of the ransom money and was in possession of a large part of the remainder, which he had hidden away in his garage, some of it in specially carpentered hidy-holes.
2) He was the writer of the ransom notes.
3) Part of the ladder specially carpentered for the kidnapping had been sawn from the floor of carpenter Hauptmann's attic.
4) He had written John F. Condon's address and telephone number on the inside of a closet door in his home.

5) He had given up full-time work on the very day that the ransom was paid.

Let us look at the first four points one by one—leaving out the last, which was and is undisputed.

1) Hauptmann's explanation for his possession of the ransom money was that a shoebox had been left with him by Isidor Fisch, who had since died, and that, after Fisch's death, he, Hauptmann, who meanwhile had given no thought to the box, let alone been at all curious as to what it contained, had accidentally opened it and found a small fortune, which—without thinking twice, and without saying a word to his poor, hardworking wife—he had treated as a windfall (but one which, though it never occurred to him that he might be handling "hot money," he felt that he needed to stash away in various hiding places, some of which he used his long-unused carpentry tools to create).

There isn't a scrap of evidence that supports Hauptmann's Fisch story. But Kennedy does his best—or rather, worst—to lead readers up a garden path to a belief that the story was corroborated. Some of those readers will have been taken in. One of Kennedy's methods is to state something with complete assurance in the hope that readers will assume that they must have missed or forgotten his earlier proving of the statement and will therefore accept his statement as gospel. His first more than slight reference to Isidor Fisch appears on page 134 and is given particular emphasis because it is at the start of a subchapter: "Of all the diverse characters who people the Lindbergh kidnapping story, the most mysterious, the most enigmatic, the most sinister is undoubtedly Isidor Fisch." It is safe to say that Kennedy would feel that he had been treated disgracefully, unfairly, improperly, if the author of an article about him began by saying: "Of all the diverse characters who have written about the Lindbergh kidnapping case, the most mysterious, the most enigmatic, the most sinister, is undoubtedly Ludovic Kennedy"—and that he would be still more upset if the author, continuing, failed (as, of course, he would) to substantiate the statement. Yet Kennedy doesn't seem to care that he fails to substantiate his statement about the dead Fisch.

The most Kennedy is able to *pretend* to prove in his efforts to bolster the Fisch story concerns Hauptmann's best friend, Hans Kloppenburg. On page 243, he says, "A key witness in the matter was Hans Kloppenburg, who had seen Fisch arrive at Hauptmann's home with the shoe-box, hand it to Hauptmann, and the two of them go into the kitchen with it." A few of those readers who have frail memories, and most of those with a healthy suspicion of anything that Kennedy says as if stating a fact, will thumb back a hundred pages to the account of the "handing over the shoe-box" incident: "on December 2 [1933], the Hauptmanns gave a farewell party for Fisch [who was sailing to Germany on the 6th]. . . . When Fisch came he brought a package wrapped in paper and tied with string which Kloppenburg, who was standing by the door, described as a shoe-box." Kennedy then says—but without explaining that he is now quoting, would you believe, from *Hauptmann's* story—that "Fisch asked if Hauptmann would look after the package while he was away . . . and Hauptmann readily agreed."

So between Kennedy's two accounts, a package wrapped in paper, tied with string, and described by Kloppenburg as a shoebox becomes "*the* [my italics] shoe-box"; and the package, only carried by Fisch in the first account, is handed over to Hauptmann in the second. Perhaps Kloppenburg did describe the package as a shoebox when interviewed by Kennedy or his researcher half a century after his fleeting glimpse of it; but at the trial, answering a question from his best friend's counsel, he described it only as a package and gave a rough idea of its dimensions—which made it as likely to have been a boxed strudel, Fisch's contribution to the party fare, as a shoebox filled with ransom money. Under cross-examination, Kloppenburg admitted that he "did not remember seeing Fisch leave the Hauptmann home on the night of the farewell party, and therefore could not say whether Fisch took the package away with him." Imagine what Kennedy would have made of it if Kloppenburg had testified that Fisch left empty-handed: he could have turned that into "clinching evidence" that the shoebox story was true—as easily as anyone disagreeing with him, and willing to swallow the shame attached to resorting to a similarly fallacious way of arguing, might use the empty-handedness to turn the strudel possibility into the strudel "fact."

2) Whoever kidnapped the Lindbergh baby also tricked the $50,000 from John F. Condon. There is conclusive proof of that in the fact that all of the ransom notes, including the one left in the nursery, bore the overlapping-circles "singnature"; if anyone, like Kennedy, insists upon having incontrovertible corroboration of that conclusive proof, there is the fact that the baby's sleeping suit was mailed to Condon by the ransomer. Kennedy may, without thinking, protest

that there is a possibility that more than one person took part in the kidnapping—that the person who left the note in the nursery was not the writer of that note or the subsequent ones. All right—but I doubt if he, inventive as he is, can conjure that point around to make an ersatz semblance of help for his argument that Hauptmann was neither *a* kidnapper nor *the* ransomer—just a poor, framed illegal immigrant who, having been given a small fortune to look after, decided, as any sensible person would, to keep it for himself.

At Hauptmann's trial, the prosecution called eight handwriting examiners, all of whom were convinced that the ransom notes had been written by the defendant. Before those examiners gave evidence, the defence had half a dozen examiners prepared to say the opposite; but by the time the latter were needed, all but one had dropped out, some admitting that they had done so because they had completely changed their minds. The defence touted around for replacements, but, unable to entice a single one, were left with the only steadfast member of the original half-dozen—and had difficulty in persuading the judge that he, John Trendley, of East St. Louis, was qualified to give evidence as an expert witness.

One doesn't need to be a handwriting examiner to know, from looking at the hundreds of word and letter comparisons presented at the trial, that Hauptmann wrote the ransom notes. The resemblances between words and letters in the notes and words and letters in documents written by Hauptmann cannot be explained away. And, as if further proof were needed, words and letters in a "farewell declaration of innocence" that Hauptmann sent to Governor Hoffman demonstrate his guilt.

What does Kennedy make of this? Not a lot. Though he includes J. Vreeland Haring's classic and massive book, *The Hand of Hauptmann*, which is packed with illustrations of the comparisons, among what he claims are the "sources" of his book, he makes no obvious use of its contents. Despite the fact that he includes seventy-five halftone and line illustrations in his book, not one is of a handwriting comparison—which surely means that he was unable to find a single comparison which he thought doubtful enough for him to pooh-pooh. What does he say about the prosecution's handwriting examiners? Not a lot. Inter alia, this: that they looked "like senior members of an old folks' bowling club." (In fact, only one of the eight was older at the time of the trial than Kennedy was when he published his book.) What does he

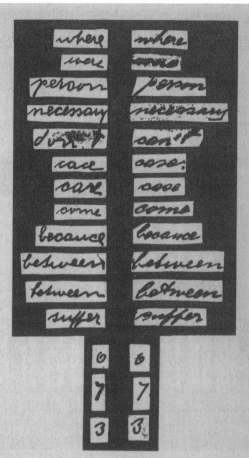

Kidnapper's handwriting on left, Hauptmann's on right

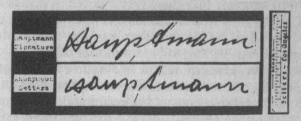

Top: Hauptmann's normal signature.
Bottom: A 'signature' composed of letters cut from the ransom notes.

Handwriting sample of Bruno Richard Hauptmann and kidnapper (from *The Modern Murder Yearbook*)

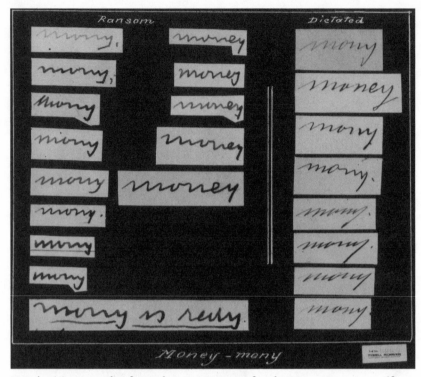

Handwriting samples from the ransom note for the Hauptmann case (from *The Modern Murder Yearbook*)

say about the handwriting evidence? Not a lot—indeed, even less. This: "As the combined testimonies [of the handwriting examiners for the prosecution] run to some five hundred pages of the trial transcript and are much concerned with technicalities—the shape of a 't' or the curl of a 'y'—and as their conclusions were later challenged by the defence's lone expert using the same material, it is not proposed to go into these in any detail." *Five hundred pages* of evidence against Hauptmann, and he does not propose to go into it in any detail!—(a) because much of it is technical, as much expert evidence at most trials is—does he mean, then, that all such technical expert evidence can be disregarded by jurors? and (b) because the defence had a "lone expert" so reckless or desperate for a fee that, having glanced through fifty documents in the space of two and a half hours (under cross-examination, Trendley was forced to admit that that was the extent of his prep), he was willing to be a minority of one.

So far as Kennedy would like us to be concerned, the fact that

Hauptmann's handwriting was the same as that of the ransom notes is irrelevant to the question of whether or not Hauptmann was the ransomer. Forget about that, he says hopefully—let's concentrate on the all-important matter that words misspelt in the ransom notes were similarly misspelt by Hauptmann in his "request writings." Those similarities, every single one of the many of them, are easily explained away by Kennedy. Speaking of all investigators, he says, "When contradictory evidence appears, they ignore it, unwilling to admit that their original belief was false; and the longer the original belief is held, the more difficult it becomes to shift. When no corroborative evidence appears to reinforce the belief, it has to be manufactured." Ergo, the investigators who got the request writings from Hauptmann forced him to misspell certain words in the same way that those words were misspelt in the ransom notes. Isn't that obvious? Well, it might be— but what of the fact that many of the misspelt words appear in the same misspelt way in documents written by Hauptmann *before* his arrest? I doubt if you will be surprised to learn that Kennedy tries to gloss over the obvious answer to that question. Rather surprisingly, he does not seek to reincarnate a notion that the defence had at the start of the trial but dropped once it was established that Hauptmann and Fisch were not introduced till after the kidnapping: the notion was that Fisch had, for some reason or other, forged Hauptmann's writing on the ransom notes. One last point about those notes: proof that they were not written by Fisch is as undoubtable as the proof that they were written by Hauptmann.

3) Even if only in terms of persistence, Arthur Koehler's work in tracking the kidnap ladder to the man who made it is among the most admirable pieces of detection of all time. There is not a scrap of evidence to suggest that Koehler (who completed the legwork part of his investigation nearly a year before anyone had any reason to suspect Hauptmann) was not entirely honest. The same can be said of Koehler's helper, Lewis Bornmann, of the New Jersey State Police. Kennedy, irritated by such honesty, sneers at "these two jokers." On the same page as that sneer (221), he *states* that Koehler's discovery that ladder rail No. 16 was from the floor of Hauptmann's attic is completely discredited by the fact that he did not instantly "proclaim it [the discovery] to the world." On the same page as the sneer and the statement, he speaks of a defence "trump card" (in fact, a trumped-up card: it was some nonevidence of an alibi, which I shall refer to shortly)—and does not consider

that it is at all devalued by the fact that the defence kept it up their sleeve for months. Heads, he wins—tails, honest investigators lose.

He is forced to use the chestnut ploy of asking the reader to be as reasonable-minded as he is: is it likely that a sensible person (Hauptmann) would do a silly thing (cut timber from his attic for a kidnap-ladder rail)? Since almost all sensible criminals who are arrested are found out because they have done silly things, if all defence counsel used the ploy with invariable success, almost all sensible criminals would be acquitted. That might please Kennedy, but I would venture to suggest that all other sensible law-abiding persons would take a dim view of it. The fact that Hauptmann made the ladder from different sources is no more strange than the fact that, rather than finding or making one hiding place for his "windfall," he found or made more than one.

Kennedy, incidentally, accepts Hauptmann's description of the ladder as "ramshackle"—meaning that it must have been made by someone without carpentering skills. Kennedy has seen the ladder. So have I. Even if I spent months trying to, I certainly couldn't make as good a job. Could Kennedy? If he says yes, and has a few months to spare, would he mind putting his manual mastery where his mouth is? If he likes, he can appoint a noncarpenter proxy. Is that a fair challenge?

As part of Governor Hoffman's reexamination of the case, a so-called wood expert visited the attic—and told Hoffman that he could prove that Rail 16 had not come from there, saying that his conclusion was partly based on the fact that when nails were pressed through the holes in the rail and into the holes in the joist, they protruded a quarter of an inch. Koehler was summoned to the house, and it was discovered that, since his last visit, quarter-inch wooden plugs had been pushed into the holes in the joist. Kennedy ascribes the post-trial jiggery-pokery in the attic to an act of nature—or rather, he accepts without question Hoffman's subsequent comment that an unidentified someone had told him that the plugs were just "fibrous fragments" that, in the abnormal course of dead-wooden events, had sort of congealed together to look the spitting image of plugs. Still relying on Hoffman, he quotes him as saying (in 1936), "I have in my possession a photograph of the ladder made the day after the commission of the crime. It is a clear photograph, in which the knots and grains are distinctly shown, and Rail 16 can be easily identified; but neither in the original nor in a copy magnified ten times can the alleged nail-holes be found." Has anyone ever seen the photograph or the enlargement? Has Kennedy? Had Hoffman? The four nail holes are clearly visible in police photographs among those taken of the ladder on 8 March 1932. It is all very well for Kennedy to admit (well away from the Hoffman quote) that Hoffman was posthumously proved to have embezzled $300,000 from the state he governed—and almost as well to comment that Hoffman's crooked-ness "in no way diminishes the courageous stand he took in champi-oning the cause of Hauptmann's innocence"—but it is reasonable to assume that if anyone who contributed to the verdict at Hauptmann's trial had afterward turned out to be crooked, even only slightly so com-pared with Hoffman, Kennedy would have used that fact as a reason for disbelieving any anti-Hauptmann evidence from that contributor. Come to think of it, one doesn't need to assume: Kennedy, in seeking to discredit the eyewitness evidence of the Hopewell hillbilly I mentioned on page 223 (whose evidence was, surely everyone agrees, dubious), re-ports that, a couple of months after the trial, the hillbilly was "clapped into jail for stealing a road grader and selling it for $50."

Kennedy doesn't seem to have understood all of Koehler's evidence. For instance, there are times when he speaks of Rail 16 when what he is really talking about is the board in the attic from which, according to Koehler, Rail 16 was cut. In his account of the quizzing of Koehler in the attic on 26 March 1936, he says that Hoffman's "wood expert," Arch Loney (can anyone doubt that Loney was the plug-ugly?), "pointed out that Rail 16 [actually, the board] was a sixteenth of an inch thicker than the other boards, but Koehler didn't have an answer to that." The statement that Koehler was stumped is untrue. Having already an-swered questions from Loney that showed that the latter's knowledge of carpentry was rudimentary, Koehler patiently explained that "as the attic was unfinished, uneven flooring was to be expected." After a cou-ple more questions from Loney, and immediate answers from Koehler, an observer said to Attorney General Wilentz, speaking loudly enough for everyone to hear, "I can't believe that Koehler has been brought all the way from Wisconsin for this!" That exclamation seems to have prompted Hoffman—not Loney, you notice—to demonstrate that nails pushed through the holes in Rail 16 and into the holes in the joist did not go all the way down (because, as was proved later in the day, plugs had mysteriously become inserted in the holes in the joist).

4) During the week after Hauptmann's arrest, he twice, on separate occasions, neither of them a third-degree session, admitted that he

had written John F. Condon's address and telephone number on the inside of a closet door in his home. At the trial, when cross-examined about the writing, he got into a hopeless tangle in trying to explain away his original explanation. One can understand why. Clearly, when Hauptmann was first asked about the writing—shown it—he, flustered because he *knew* that the writing was his, *believed* that the writing was undoubtedly identifiable as his, felt that there was no point in lying that he had not made the notations, and gave the only explanation for them that he could invent: that he was in the habit of jotting down references to important events on doors (a habit of which there was no other sign in the house).

Kennedy, who gets angry about hearsay that doesn't suit his purpose, is only too happy to accept hearsay that does. On page 204 he says, no ifs or buts, that a *Daily News* reporter, Tom Cassidy, "planted" the writing "as a joke . . . either late on September 24 [1934] or on the morning of the 25th. . . . He then smudged the writing as though an attempt had been made to wipe it out." Well, that's sure enough, isn't it? Isn't it? Well, no—because it turns out that "Cassidy's joke" is something that in the late 1970s was rumoured to have been rumoured toward the end of 1934: rumoured both times, what's more, by reporters—the 1934 ones among those who, so Kennedy says four pages later, "went overboard completely, not hesitating to print all sorts of allegations and rumours as fact." Not satisfied with the little that the reporter-rumourers of the 1970s had to say, Kennedy adds one of his own, that "Cassidy got word to the Bronx police"—presumably so as to make his joke hilarious. According to all three of the 1970s rumourers, Cassidy was too pleased with his joke to worry that, if he had really perpetrated it, he could be imprisoned: "Hell, he bragged about it all over town." "He admitted it to me and Ellis Parker, he told everybody about it." "He told a bunch of us." Like most rumourers, these protested too much: if the joke was such common knowledge, how is it that the defence lawyers were never let in on it? Kennedy doesn't explain that (not even when, exactly a hundred pages later, he speaks of a moment during the trial "after Wilentz had been questioning Hauptmann about *Tom Cassidy's writing* [my italics] on the inside trim of the closet").

Perhaps he believes that Hauptmann's leading counsel, Edward J. Reilly, did hear about the joke and decided that it must not be mentioned, for fear that it might help to get his client acquitted. Kennedy, you see, suspects that Reilly was actually a mole-type extra counsel for the prosecution. If ever a statement deserved to be followed by several exclamation marks, that one does. Kennedy's suspicion is based on two things, one being the fact that part of Reilly's fee had been guaranteed by "the anti-Hauptmann Hearst Press" (in return for exclusives from Hauptmann and his wife), the other being Kennedy's feeling that Reilly did not ask all the questions he should have asked. If Kennedy knew anything about the art, which it is, of cross-examination, he would know that the reason for virtually all of the Reilly unquestions which he cites is covered by a maxim of cross-examination: never ask a question if you don't already know the answer.

It is surprising if Kennedy has never heard that maxim, for he himself, as an investigator, pays great regard to a variation on it: never ask a question if there is the slightest risk of getting an answer that does not accord with your preconception.

Twenty pages after "proving" that Tom Cassidy was a psychopathic joker, Kennedy reinstates Cassidy as an upright citizen, his word even better than his bond, the last person in the world one would suspect of fabricating evidence. This reinstatement is in aid of "proving" that Hauptmann did a full day's work at the Majestic Apartments, Manhattan, on 1 March 1932, in the evening of which the Lindbergh baby was kidnapped. Cassidy, so Kennedy says, unearthed payroll records showing that Hauptmann worked at the Majestic Apartments till 5 P.M. (A few Kennedy sentences later, "5 P.M." becomes "5 or 6 P.M.") Finding Kennedy's Majestic argument incomprehensible, even after umpteen attempts to fathom it, I gave photocopies of the pages to four friends—a barrister, a coroner, a forensic scientist, a book-publisher's editor—and was relieved to hear from all four that they too were baffled. The trouble, I think, is that Kennedy, for once believing that he has a lot of evidence that needs no help from him, presents all of it—so much that one cannot see the wood for the trees.

But supposing that the Majestic argument is valid, the documentary evidence for it untampered with by pro-Hauptmann researchers, it certainly doesn't mean that Hauptmann had a sort of alibi. Kennedy is guessing again when he says, on page 173, "The police realized that if he [Hauptmann] was working at the Majestic Apartments until five or six [*sic*] on Tuesday, March 1, it was unlikely that he was putting a ladder up against the nursery window at Hopewell three or four hours later." Let us allow Kennedy his unsubstantiated assumption that Hauptmann worked an hour of overtime, from five till six. Even if Hauptmann had driven the sixty miles from the Bronx to Hopewell at the dangerously slow average speed of 20 mph, he would have arrived at the Lindberghs' house with ample time to spare before the kidnapping, at about ten minutes past nine. Not that he would have *wanted* ample time: the longer he loitered near the house, the more danger there was that he or his parked car would be observed.

Kennedy, as well as saying that Hauptmann almost had an alibi for the time of the kidnapping, claims that Hauptmann had a complete alibi for the night of Saturday, 2 April, when Condon handed over the ransom money to "Cemetery John": "It being the first Saturday of the month, Hauptmann and Hans Kloppenburg had their regular musical get-together." At the trial, under direct examination, Kloppenburg testified that he "recalled being at the Hauptmann home on the night of 2 April 1932, it being a custom to gather for an evening on the first Saturday of each month." (Kloppenburg's helpfulness to Hauptmann is rather hard to reconcile with the tale he told half a century after the trial, which was that he had first been grilled by detectives—"They were trying to scare me with the electric chair so that I wouldn't testify"—and then by David Wilentz: "A day or so later, I think it was the day before I testified, there was a story in the newspapers that police were about to arrest a second man in the kidnapping. That was me they were talking about. They were trying to scare me so I would shut up. And I *was* scared.") Under cross-examination, Kloppenburg "admitted telling the Bronx District Attorney, shortly after Hauptmann was arrested, that he could not remember when he saw Hauptmann in March or April 1932, because 'that is too long ago.'" Under redirect examination, he gave two further reasons for remembering the date of the evening of music: "There was some sort of April Fool joke" and "Mrs. Hauptmann spoke of wanting to go and see her niece the following day." (Did anyone else, even Tom Cassidy, play April Fool jokes after April Fools' Day? So far as anyone seems to know, Mrs. Hauptmann may have paid frequent Sunday visits to her niece—or frequently, on Saturdays and other days, spoken of wanting to see her niece.) Under recross-examination, Kloppenburg admitted that he had "talked with Detective Sergeant Wallace, of the New York City

Police, shortly before Christmas 1934, and at that time said he could not recall any dates upon which he saw Hauptmann in March or April 1932." Can anyone be as certain as Kennedy claims to be that the Hauptmanns and their best friend Hans were musically trio'd when, in a cemetery not far away, the ransom was paid?

Four years after the publication of his book on the Lindbergh case, Kennedy published his memoirs, *On My Way to the Club* (London, 1989). Meanwhile, in 1987, a book by Jim Fisher, *The Lindbergh Case,* was published by Rutgers University Press (New Brunswick). Kennedy makes a chapter of his memoirs from how he came to the conclusion that Hauptmann was innocent and from what he considers most important of the things he subsequently found, so as to give ostensible support to his conclusion. And he then, in the space of a page, launches an hysterical attack on Fisher—all because, so he says, Fisher doesn't pay enough attention to "information . . . used by Mrs Hauptmann's lawyer, Tony Scaduto and myself." It is the most despicable page of writing that I have come across in a very long while.

I hold no brief for Fisher—whom I have never met and who has written me just one letter, that in reply to a single letter I wrote to him—other than that his book is honest, any errors in it that I have noticed being slight and unintended. Which is more than can be said for some books.

I shall not comment on those parts of Kennedy's attack on Fisher which are gratuitous, entirely irrelevant to the Lindbergh case—for I could only do so after repeating them. They should never have been published. Since Kennedy also makes a snide remark about Rutgers University Press, I shall express my surprise that his publishers, known to be reputable, permitted him to say such things.

Kennedy states, "So concerned were the New Jersey authorities by Mrs Hauptmann's suits and the books by Tony Scaduto and myself that they gave their backing to . . . *The Lindbergh Case.*" That is untrue.

Kennedy states, "The police officer in charge of the Lindbergh room at [the New Jersey] police headquarters became consultant to [Fisher's] project." That also is untrue. Fisher received no more help from the policeman-curator than Kennedy would have been offered if he had requested help. (Incidentally, the untrue statement is pretty rich, coming from Kennedy—who employed Anthony Scaduto's wife as his researcher.)

Near the foot of the page, Kennedy says that, round about the time when Fisher's book was published, he was "disappointed to hear that a [television] treatment based on my book and submitted to all three American networks had been turned down. Professionally, I was told, they all thought it a fascinating story that would make a gripping screenplay, but as network producers they did not feel they could support a programme whose conclusions were contrary to those arrived at by the American courts, and not yet reversed by them. The New Jersey establishment had triumphed again!!" Of all the many ridiculous comments made by Kennedy, that one takes the biscuit. Before writing his book, he cobbled interviews with pro-Hauptmannites into a television programme, *Who Killed the Lindbergh Baby?*, which was shown in Britain and America; soon afterward, a television movie based on the case, starring Anthony Hopkins as poor Bruno, was shown in both countries; in 1989, Mrs. Hauptmann and her lawyer, with other pro-Hauptmannites, appeared in a documentary that was shown throughout America.

Right to the end of *The Airman and the Carpenter*, Kennedy omits facts that don't appeal to him. Apart from slight mentions in passing, none value-judgmental, all that he says about either Paul Wendel's retracted confession or Ellis Parker is this:

> [During the weekend before the execution,] there had been a new and extraordinary development in this most extraordinary of cases in that all members of the New Jersey Court of Pardons had received a twenty-five-page confession to the Lindbergh baby kidnapping and murder by a fifty-year-old disbarred Trenton attorney and convicted perjurer (who was also wanted for fraud) by the name of Paul Wendel. This was not as crazy a confession as at first thought, since it had been made to none other than Ellis Parker, Hoffman's friend and the chief of Burlington County detectives [earlier described by Kennedy as a "brilliant investigator"]. Ellis was instructed to deliver Wendel to Mercer County detectives who took him before a Justice of the Peace to be arraigned for murder before being lodged in the Mercer County Jail. Once there he immediately repudiated the confession, claiming that he had been kidnapped by Ellis Parker and his son Ellis Junior, taken to a mental hospital for a number of days, tortured there and forced to sign the confession under duress. It seemed to many

that this, if true, was a last desperate effort by Parker, convinced that Hauptmann was innocent, to save him from the chair.

That, so far as Kennedy is concerned, is, importantly, all. Any reader of his book who has not read other books on the case must be left thinking that Wendel may have committed the crimes for which Hauptmann was executed.

The continuation of the Wendel/Parker story (which Kennedy, if he had felt like it, could have recounted in his last chapter, which deals with those post-execution events which he did feel like recounting) is as follows: Wendel's account of his being abducted and tortured into making a false confession was investigated by the district attorney of Brooklyn and proved true. Four of the gang of six confessed; one of the four died before the trial, but the others were sentenced to twenty years' imprisonment in Sing Sing. As Governor Hoffman refused to extradite the two ring-leaders, Ellis Parker and his son, to Brooklyn, Wendel got the U.S. attorney general to agree that the charges were the concern of New Jersey's federal grand jury, which handed down an indictment charging the Parkers with conspiracy under the Lindbergh Law (the statute, enacted in 1932, which made the kidnapping and transportation of a person across state lines punishable by imprisonment for life). Ellis Parker was sentenced to six years' imprisonment, his son to three, in a federal penitentiary. (And so the only law enforcement officer influentially involved in the Lindbergh case whom Kennedy does not accuse of crookedness, and the only one about whom he has a nice—"brilliant"—word to say, was the only one proved to be a crook.) By using appeal procedures much as Hauptmann had done, the Parkers managed to remain at large till the summer of 1939, when they were imprisoned at Lewisburg, Pennsylvania. Early in the following year, Ellis Parker died of a brain tumour in the prison hospital; his son was released a few months later.

There is a saying that "no one suddenly becomes a murderer." More likely to be true, it seems to me, is a saying that I have just invented: "No writer on criminal cases suddenly becomes an unreliable writer." It would be valuable to crime historians, and others, if someone with the time and the research resources were to examine the miscarriage-of-justice books published by Kennedy before he published *The Airman and the Carpenter*. Let me be absolutely clear: I don't know much about any of the cases covered, and so have no particular grounds for wondering if any of those books may have helped toward the miscarriage of justice that a guilty man was prematurely freed from imprisonment and/or pardoned and/or given compensation.

I applaud an idea mooted in the January 1988 edition of the journal of the American Academy of Forensic Sciences as a direct reaction to *The Airman and the Carpenter:*

> There are positive steps that the Academy can take to educate the reviewing press and the public when a book such as *The Airman and the Carpenter* presents the document or other scientific evidence in an unfair or biased manner. Each section of the Academy would appoint a book-review editor charged with reviewing those chapters of new books dealing with his particular discipline. If he found the information to be fairly presented, nothing further would be required. However, should the information prove to be deceptive, inaccurate, or incomplete, the reviewer would contact the major newspapers and magazines with his critique of the offending portion. This would seem to be one of the ways a forensic science group can fight back against the misinformation disseminated in books like *The Airman and the Carpenter.*

An Anatomy of Murders

*P*erhaps to some extent because some writers of social history are financially dependent upon patrons (usually, these days, state-funded research-subsidising councils or large companies that, needing to gloss their image, sponsor academic projects as well as sporting competitions) and so feel that they must try to elevate their trade above its proper purposes, few writers of social history take notice of the nine days' wonders that occupied the minds of people who lived during them, leaving little or no room for interest in what was happening in parliament and other important places.

But nine days can be a long time in social history; and if the writing of such history is to meet one of its purposes, which is to give an idea of how it *felt* to be a supernumerary member of the cast of a period, then the wonders—provoking oohs of abhorrence or ahs of admiration from the mass of men, their own deeds giving no cause for exclamation—must not be retrospectively shunned on account of a sort of snobbery.

Generally speaking, snobbery of the more usual sort lies behind the neglecting of scenes of *criminous* nine days' wonders. The notion that it is not quite nice to express a fascination with celebrated crimes has resulted in some strange pretences—the strangest, it seems to me, in regard to 39 Hilldrop Crescent, an address which in the summer of 1910 became as famous as 10 Downing Street, and which still rings a bell in many people's minds. For the benefit of other people, let me explain that 39 Hilldrop Crescent, in the district of North London called Holloway, was where the American Dr. Crippen murdered his also-American wife, who was best known as Belle Elmore, her stage name as a singer, his motive probably being that he wanted to be free to marry his English mistress, Ethel Le Neve; he, with Ethel (she dressed as a boy), sought to escape to America, and, for the first time, wireless telegraphy was used in aid of catching a murderer.

In the 1960s, hearing that the house, damaged by a bomb during the Second World War, was to be replaced by a block of council flats named after Margaret Bondfield, a boring trades-union politician, I wrote to the local mayor, suggesting that Margaret Bondfield should be given her due on some other council estate, thereby allowing the block in Hilldrop Crescent to be sensibly, appropriately designated: as Crippen Court, perhaps, or Le Neve's Folly, or—best of all, I considered—Elmore's End. The mayor politely turned down my suggestion; he made it clear, carefully without saying so, that the very idea of signifying the site of a murder appalled him.

I did not pursue the matter; I did not try to make him understand that the act of murder is rarely significant toward making a murder case celebrated—that, speaking of Crippen, his apparently inaugural use of the drug hyoscine as a means of murdering certainly made him notable to connoisseurs of crime—but that the Crippen *case* caught the public imagination, and had retained it, far more because of events preceding and following the murder than because of the murder itself.

It has since occurred to me that a virtually sure way not merely of making snobs about murders cure their genteelness but also of inverting their snobbery is to mention that the British royal family considers that one murder at any rate—and that in a royal home—warrants efforts to keep it in mind. At the Palace of Holyroodhouse, in Edinburgh, men are employed to show visitors around the chambers and passages associated with the murder, in 1566, of Mary Stuart's friend, David Riccio.

Edinburgh has other criminous remembrances. In the High Street stretch of the Royal Mile to Holyroodhouse, granite blocks, embedded heart-shaped in the pavement, mark where the Tolbooth Gaol, demolished in 1817, was entered: publicists of the city declare that a custom of spitting on the heart survives, but I have seen no more spittle there than on undecorated parts of the pavement. Diagonally across the Mile, at the edge of the stretch called Lawnmarket, is a pub named after Deacon Brodie, who—a bourgeois by day, a burglar by night—gave Stevenson the idea for *Dr. Jekyll and Mr. Hyde.* And farther west in the Mile, in Grassmarket, a small garden has been made, intentionally where a scaffold stood until 1784. (Deacon Brodie, having been nocturnally successful until 1788, was hanged elsewhere, on gallows that he had overoptimistically paid the hangman to modify.)

A short distance on from the far-from-Royal end of the Mile, where the mean thoroughfares of High Riggs and West Port meet, is a pub that until 1969 was the Main Point Bar. In the summer of that year it was revamped so as to become the Burke & Hare—a name reckoned to be apt because opposite, on the side of West Port sometimes almost shadowed by the Castle, is where Tanner's Close used to be: the site is part of the site of a present office-building. In 1972, I noted that the Burke & Hare "is like a psychedelic space-capsule; there are a few naive wall-paintings, and behind the bar are modern portraits, quite pretty but hardly lifelike, of the murderers."[1] Subsequently, so I'm told, the Burke & Hare was for a while a "go-go pub" (meaning that some of the female employees—please God, only female ones—served toplessly), and more recently, perhaps still, has been a "live-music pub." Its name providers deserve, if not a better memorial, a more fitting one.

> Up the close and doun the stair,
> But and ben[2] with Burke and Hare;
> Burke's the butcher, Hare's the thief,
> Knox the boy that buys the beef.

The roles ascribed in that verse, the most abiding of many that commented on the affair in the last two months of 1828, fit the rum-ti-tum scansion better than they fit the facts that came to light in those months. Knox—who I hope you will feel sorry for, sorrow about—enters the tale, unwittingly salient to it, after its beginning. Before that beginning, there are some things you should know about Burke and Hare.

Both were called William. They were born about the same time, the early 1790s, in different parts of Ireland—quite where, whether in Catholic or Protestant places, has become a matter of dispute but is not important. In 1818, or thereabouts, they migrated to Scotland, still strangers to each other, and worked as labourers, always far apart, on the cutting of the Union Canal between Edinburgh and Falkirk, a distance of twenty-five miles, which took until 1822. Meanwhile, Burke (who may have left a wife and children in Ireland) cohabited with an

---

1. *Bloody Versicles: The Rhymes of Crime*, 1972; revised edition, Kent, Ohio, 1993.
2. The phrase means "out and in."

ugly Scotswoman, "the upper half of her face out of proportion to the lower," who called herself Helen M'Dougal; the surname was that of a man she had lived with but never married. After being paid off as a labourer, Burke, with Helen M'Dougal accompanying and assisting him, peddled secondhand goods in and around Edinburgh; eventually, having picked up the rudiments of cobbling, boots and shoes were his main stock in trade. In the late summers, six in all, the couple helped farmers with the harvest, each earning more than they would have made from peddling.

Compared with Burke, Hare prospered. As a navvy, he had toadied to the leader of his gang, himself an Irishman, who was known as Log— probably the source or a shortening of "Logue." Once the canal was ready, its owners reemployed Log, now as an overseer of "lumpers" of cargo ("stevedores" they would be called today, except by trades-unionists, who would insist on "handlers"), and Log, in turn, reemployed Hare. From what one gathers of Log, he was not of the type to give favours generously, and so he may have extorted a tribute from Hare—a once-and-for-all slice of his first pay packet or slighter acknowledgments regularly. Or perhaps, being subtle as to the remittance of returns from a favour, he persuaded Hare to rent bed space in the doss house which he and his wife Margaret kept, they themselves living there, in Tanner's Close—an alley so called because there was a tannery, its smell almost smothering residential ones, at the closed end. In any event, Hare became one of the Logs' lodgers. Since there is no reason to suppose that the house looked much different by the winter of 1828, one of the several descriptions of it printed then may be quoted here:

> The entry from the street begins with a descent of a few steps, and is dark from the superincumbent land.[3] On proceeding downward, you come to a smallish self-contained dwelling of one flat, and consisting of three apartments. One passing down the close might, with an observant eye, have seen into the front room; a ticket, "Beds to let," invited vagrants to enter. The outer apartment was large, occupied all round by these structures called beds, composed of knocked-up fir stumps, and covered with a few grey sheets and brown blankets, among which the squalid

3. In the particularly Scots sense, "land" means a group of dwellings.

wanderer sought rest, and the profligate snored out his debauch under the weight of nightmare. Another room opening from this was also comparatively large, and furnished much in the same manner. The door stood generally open, and, as we have said, the windows were overlooked by the passengers up and down; but, as the spider's web is spread open while his small keep is a secret hole, so here there was a small apartment, or rather closet, the window of which looked upon a pigsty and a dead wall.

Hare's stay at the house long outlasted that of other lodgers and would have lasted longer but for a falling out with Log, who ended the argument by ousting him. A reason will soon appear either for the rumour or for crediting the rumour that the disagreement arose from Log's suspicion that Hare was "making free" with Margaret Log. Supposing that Log was suspicious, then he must also have doubted Margaret's fidelity, for no man could have made free with her without her consent: unaccountably nicknamed "Lucky," she was built like a present-day woman shot-putter, that condition derived from her years of hard labouring as a member of her husband's gang of canal diggers.

It is reasonable to presume that Hare, as well as being ejected from the lodging house, was sacked from his job as a lumper. There are only guesses as to where he lived and how he made a living until some time in 1826, when, learning that Log had died, he thoughtfully returned to Tanner's Close to console the widow. Finding that a similarly thoughtful lodger was already consoling her, he engineered the man's departure. Even while the muscular Margaret was outwardly mournful, she and Hare took up where, according to the uncharitable view, the late Log had forced them to leave off; within months of Mrs. Log's becoming a widow, she felt entitled, under a Scots secular law that perceived living in sin as a marital state once it was engrained, to call herself Mrs. Hare. But though Hare could now make free with her to her heart's content, he could not, she insisted, live free of charge, slothful when out of her bed. And so he did odd jobs; and in the first two late summers of his undocumented marriage, left Margaret managing her main inheritance, which was still known as Log's lodging house, while he harvested out of town on a farm at Penicuik, a ten-mile walk away.

If Hare had ever met his countryman William Burke before (which is as some legends have it), neither had been much impressed by the other; but their toiling together at Penicuik, their carousing at night, and their sharing of a barn for sleep—Burke's woman, still calling herself Helen M'Dougal, ever present—established a friendship; and at the end of the harvest time, Hare, saying that he wished to prolong the friendship—perhaps thinking, too, of pleasing Margaret by bringing her custom—invited Burke, which meant Helen as well, to stay at "his" lodging house in Tanner's Close, an invitation that was accepted.

More than a year later, drawings and pen portraits of Burke and of Hare, most of the efforts intended to conform with mind-pictures of human monsters rather than to be lifelike, made both men seem protean. Of the reporters' descriptions that I have read, the following strike me as being most likely the least inaccurate:

> Burke . . . is a man rather below the middle size, and stoutly made, and of a determined, though not peculiarly sinister, expression of countenance. The contour of his face, as well as the features, is decidedly Milesian.[4] It is round, with high cheek-bones, grey eyes, a good deal sunk in the head, a short snubbish nose, and a round chin, but altogether of a small cast. His hair and whiskers, which are of a light sandy colour, comport well with the make of the head and complexion, which is nearly of the same hue. He has what is called in this country a *wauf* rather than a ferocious appearance, though there is a hardness about the features, mixed with an expression in the grey twinkling eyes, that is far from inviting.
>
> Hare's . . . eyes are watery, curiously shaped, and have certainly a peculiarity about them, which seems to hover betwixt leering and squinting; the forehead is low; combativeness is large—destructiveness middling[5]; the nose, mouth, and chin, very vulgar and commonplace; and his countenance, on the whole, though it may betray more or less of what we may call a sinister expression, indicates anything but intense ferociousness. Nothing can better describe his appearance than the common remark that "he is a poor silly-looking body"; for though Hare is certainly

4. The word means "Irish-looking," from *Milesius*, a mythical king of Spain; his sons and their followers are said to have seized Ireland.

5. Both of these assertions are according to phrenology, the so-called science of gauging a person's characteristics from bumps on his head, which was all the rage.

no beauty, everyone has seen hundreds of uglier men. He can neither read nor write, and his mind, in other respects, is just as untutored as an Esquimaux Indian's. He is five feet six inches high and weighs 10 stones.

It has lately been suggested that the invention of the wheel arose from an attempt to make earrings. Though that suggestion is probably wrong, it is probably not far wrong. Many innovations arise unintendedly, as offshoots from purposes; others can be credited to or blamed upon a pure serendipity, away from any sidetrack: hardly any bright ideas arrive already pristine, not needing the slightest refinement. Looking at Burke and Hare as trailblazing entrepreneurs, one sees not just one or two, but all three of those facts exemplified.

Their business partnership can be said to have been founded on Thursday, 29 November 1827, a couple of months after they had laboured amid the alien corn of Penicuik. That day began miserably for the Hares, with the discovery that their longest-abiding lodger, an army pensioner called Donald, his surname apparently unknown to anyone in the house, had died during the night. The Hares' misery was not from bereavement, nor even from the thought of inconveniences that Donald's dying on the premises would put them to—but from his having died just prior to when his pension was due, owing (so the story goes) four pounds. (The amount of his debt is open to question. Unless Margaret Hare had frequently lent cash to Donald, feeling secure that she would be repaid on his pension day, the debt was the accumulation of threepences—that sum being what it cost to spend a night in Log's lodging house. Four pounds of threepences—240 pennies in the pound then, remember—was the equivalent of 320 nights' lodging, and nothing that one knows of Margaret suggests that she would have allowed anyone to prolong "tick" for anywhere near as long as ten and a half months. If "four pounds" is no exaggeration, then—accepting the subsequent reckoning that there were seven dossing beds, each meant for three occupants, and assuming that the house was full most nights—it was as if the Hares had lost a fortnight's receipts.)

Hare, Margaret too, perhaps, sought condolence from Burke—from Helen M'Dougal too, perhaps. But Burke, rather than commiserating, remarked to the effect that the cloud cast by Donald's death might have a golden lining: maybe Donald's change of status, from pensioner to corpse, had increased his monetary value. Burke soon explained what he meant. I shall take longer.

Medical men had complained of a dearth of bodies for dissection since before anatomy was recognised as a medical science. The situation had been greatly improved early in the sixteenth century, while Henry VIII reigned in England, James V in Scotland, by acts that allowed surgeons and barbers to have the bodies of executed felons for, so far as Henry was concerned, "anatomies with out any further sute or labour to be made to the kynges highnes his heyres or successors for the same. And to make incision of the same deade bodies or otherwyse to order the same after their said discrecions at their pleasure for their further and better knowlage instruction in sight learnying & experience in the scyence or facultie of Surgery." Since there were, roughly speaking, 2,000 executions per annum in Henry's name (and, though no one in Scotland seems to have tried to keep tally during James's near-enough concurrent rule, surely an annual average there and then that measured up, per capita, to England's), the supply of fallen bodies fell not far short of the demand: in England, at any rate, may have come close to being sufficient during the supposed reign of Henry's juvenile son Edward, between 1547 and 1553, when the annual average of hangings at London's Tyburn alone was 560.

But over the next two and a half centuries, while the number of theoretically capital offences grew (to a neat peak of 222 in 1810), the number of offences that were in fact punished helpfully for anatomists dwindled to a couple of dozen, and they provided annually only a hundred or so "subjects" (that was the anatomists' euphemism for corpses put to scientific ends). From about the middle of the eighteenth century, matters were made worse by the mushrooming growth of private schools only or especially of anatomy, each needing almost as frequent a supply of subjects as did the long-established colleges of surgeons and the medical faculties of universities.

All sorts of proposals were put forward in parliament, in the press, and elsewhere, for reducing, even remedying, the shortfall: suicides of the discreet sort—who though they had not disfigured their bodies outwardly, were clearly careless of them—should be eligible; the remains of paupers should be dissected before being buried, still more higgledy-

piggledy than at present, in communal graves (support for that proposal: "returns obtained from 127 of the parishes situate in London,
Westminster, and Southwark, or their immediate vicinity, show that
out of 3,744 persons who died in the workhouses of these parishes
in the year 1827, 3,103 were buried at the parish expense, and that of
these about 1,108 were not attended to their graves by any relations");
all persons who came to their death by duelling, prizefighting, or any
other dangerous activity that warranted discouragement, ought to be
offered—sight unseen, lest pernickety anatomists thought to pick and
choose those tidily wounded from those that weren't; "as prostitutes
have, by their bodies during life, been engaged in corrupting mankind,
it is only right that after death those bodies should be handed over to
be dissected for the public good"; all medical men should bequeath
their own bodies. None of the notions was taken up.

And so (much as in the 1920s and early 1930s, in the United States,
the illegality of alcohol gave rise to illegality of a far worse kind, col-
loquially called bootlegging), the anatomists' insufficiency of legally
proper subjects led to the creation of a black market: at first, a market
solely in bodies from undertakers or kept absent from undertakings
that, rather like Hamlet without the Prince, had coffins without occupants, that omission superficially repaired by the inclusion of ballast to
about the right body weight. But before long, as anatomists outbid one
another for legally improper subjects and thus pushed up the recommended retail price, and as once-impeccable anatomists accepted that
as they couldn't lick their body-buying rivals, they had better join them,
the subjects suppliers, their numbers growing too, looked for ways of
ensuring an adequate stock, and, in many cases, looked downward.

Auxiliary to the petty crime of corpse selling, the crime of grave-
robbing became almost as prevalent; it was only a bit more risky in
terms of legal consequences in the event of apprehension, for, there
being no property in a dead body, a prosecution for felony could not
be brought unless some portion of the shroud or coffin could be
proved to have been stolen with the body; even if such evidence exist-
ed (which was rarely: in 1828 the magistrate of a busy court reckoned
that he had had no more than half a dozen cases of theft from burial grounds in as many years), defendants were usually cautioned or
fined—hardly ever imprisoned. Grave-robbers were far more worried
that they might be caught in or, while laden, after the act by relatives

or friends of their plunder; when that happened, the consequences were often brutally severe, sometimes fatal.[6] One precaution against undisciplined citizens' arrest was the "casing" of the site and environs of an intended dig, so as to ensure that there was no all-night sentry or regularly visiting watchman; another, which might be in addition to the casing, was the posting of a menial, sharp of both sight and hearing, to keep watch while the work was in progress; yet another, most expensive but best of all, was the bribing of employed sentries or watchmen to look the other way or to miss out the place of excavation from duty rounds—such dereliction not only paid for but agreed to on the understanding that, following the emptying of the coffin, the soil that had been dug out would be shovelled back and patted, leaving the grave looking unspoiled, giving no reason for the guard's usual employers to question his conscientiousness.

The employment of guards was but one of the initiatives aimed at repelling or resisting the grave-robbers. Most of the initiatives were intended to make the employment of guards unnecessary; few fulfilled that intention. In some burial grounds, bijou lodges, not unlike Wendy houses but more secure, were built, their purpose being to store bodies until they were too putrid to serve as subjects. (One such lodge survives in the burial ground in the village of Crail, on the coast of Fife, northeast of Edinburgh.) A report published about 1810 in a Scots paper speaks of a bereaved father whose determination to keep the body of his son safe from dissection was greater than his desire that the body should remain intact:

> Curiosity drew together a crowd of people on Monday, at Dundee, to witness the funeral of a child, which was consigned to the grave in a novel manner. The father . . . had caused a small box, inclosing some deathful apparatus, communicating by means of wires with the four corners, to be fastened on top of the coffin. Immediately before it was lowered into the earth, a large quantity of gunpowder was poured into the box, and the hidden machinery put into a state of readiness for execution. The common opinion was that if anyone attempted to raise the body he

---

6. I shall stick to calling them "grave-robbers" because each of the several nicknames for them—for instance, sack-'em-up-men, body snatchers, and, the loveliest, resurrectionists—was particular to a part, or one or several parts, of the country.

would be blown up. The sexton seemed to dread an immediate explosion, for he started back in alarm after throwing in the first shovelful of earth.

Iron-founders and blacksmiths did a brisk trade in mort-safes, cages that fitted snugly over and around tombstones (some still to be seen in Greyfriars Churchyard, Edinburgh); often more decorative than the tombstones they protected, mort-safes were not a sure protection of what lay beneath the stones: certain grave-robbers, most likely ex-miners, were able to reach their quarry, irrespective of mort-safe, simply by burrowing diagonally rather than digging vertically. Another use of iron toward keeping remains secure—one that must have required a doubling of the customary number of pallbearers—was as a material for coffins. Going by an advertisement in *Wooler's British Gazette* for 13 October 1822, a Mr. Edward Lillie Bridgman, who traded in funerary equipment from premises on Fish Street Hill, close to London Bridge, seems to have believed that iron coffins were his prerogative:

> Many hundred dead bodies will be dragged from their wooden coffins this winter, for the anatomical lectures (which have just commenced), the articulators, and for those who deal in the dead for the supply of the country practitioner and the Scotch schools. . . . Those undertakers who have IRON COFFINS must divide the profits of the funeral with EDWARD LILLIE BRIDGMAN. TEN GUINEAS reward will be paid on the conviction of any Parish Officer demanding an extra fee, whereby I shall lose the sale of a coffin. The violation of the sanctity of the grave is said to be needful, for the instruction of the medical pupil, but let each one about to inter a mother, husband, child, or friend, say: shall I devote this object of my affection to such a purpose?; if not, the only safe coffin is Bridgman's PATENT WROUGHT-IRON ONE, charged the same price as a wooden one, and is a superior substitute for lead.

One cannot make out whether the extent of grave-robbing came near what Mr. Bridgman and his competitors did their copywriting best to alarm the public into believing that it was. Facts and figures are few and, geographically, far between: nearly all of them are in regard to happenings in and around one or other of the main seats of medical learning, Edinburgh and London. Rough counts that were occasionally made in those cities were dependent upon the market researchers' sly quizzing of the anatomists' porters and students, most of whom at first gave equally sly replies, and then, when fuddled by the drink provided coaxingly by the researchers, said whatever the researchers wanted them to say. The counts, inefficient in any case, were deficient of data that had nothing to do with dissection—a skewing omission, because some graves were robbed in aid of unscientific practices, either necrophilic or, as the following cutting from the *Universal Spectator* of 20 May 1732 instances, commercial:

> John Loftas, the Grave Digger, committed to prison for robbing of dead corpses, has confess'd to the plunder of above fifty, not only of their coffins and burial cloaths, but of their fat, where bodies afforded any, which he retail'd at a high price to certain people.[7]

James Blake Bailey refers to "a statement by the police in 1828 that the number of persons who, in London, lived regularly on the profits of exhumation, did not exceed ten; there were, in addition to these, about two hundred who were occasionally employed."[8] But by no means all of the bodies dissected in Edinburgh and London, or intended to be, were of Edinburghians[9] and Londoners—a fact exemplified by an incident at Liverpool, an account of which was printed as a broadsheet:[10]

DISCOVERY OF THIRTY-THREE HUMAN BODIES, IN CASKS, ABOUT TO BE SHIPPED FROM LIVERPOOL FOR EDINBURGH, ON MONDAY LAST, OCTOBER 9, 1826.

Yesterday afternoon, a carter took down to one of our quays

---

7. The author of this clipping was suggesting candle makers, perhaps: a line of the ballad "The Surgeon's Warning" by Robert Southey (1774–1843) has the repentant eponym admitting, "I have made candles of infants' fat." Or maybe Loftas's retail was of suet or, cooked beforehand, dripping—possibilities that remind one of the domestic servant Kate Webster, who in 1879, at Richmond, Surrey, having murdered her mistress, chopped up the body, boiled scraps of it, and soon afterwards, possibly irrelevantly, touted two large pots of dripping to a fellow-frequenter of her local pub.

8. Bailey, the librarian of the Royal College of Surgeons of England, wrote this in his book *The Diary of a Resurrection* (London, 1896).

9. That term preferable, surely, to the proper "Edinburgher," which sounds like a haggis in a bun.

10. Readers familiar with broadsheets will know that it is wise to be wary of what any of them say; generally, truth is not allowed to mar a sensational tale. But most of the statements made on this broadsheet are verified by reports published subsequently in the *Liverpool Mercury*.

three casks, to be shipped on board the Carron Company's vessel, the *Latona,* addressed to "Mr G. Ironson, Edinburgh." The casks remained on the quay all night, and this morning, previous to their being put on board, a horrible stench was experienced by the mate of the *Latona* and other persons, whose duty it was to ship them. This caused some suspicion that their contents did not agree with their superscription, which was "Bitter Salts," and which the shipping note described they contained. The mate communicated his suspicions to the agent of the Carron Company, and that gentleman very promptly communicated the circumstances to the police.

Socket, a constable, was sent to the Quay, and he caused the casks to be opened, when Eleven Dead Bodies were found therein, salted and pickled.

The casks were detained, and George Leech, the cartman, readily went with the officer to the cellar whence he carted them, which was situated under the school of Dr McGowan, at the back of his house in Hope Street;[11] the cellar was padlocked, but, by the aid of a crow-bar, Boughey, a police officer, succeeded in forcing an entrance, and, on searching therein, he found four casks, all containing human bodies, salted as the others were, and three sacks, each containing a dead body. . . . In this cellar were found twenty-two dead bodies, pickled and fresh, and in the casks on the quay, eleven, making in the whole thirty-three.

The carter described the persons who employed him as of very respectable appearance, but he did not know the names of any of them.

Information of the above circumstances was speedily communicated to his Worship, the Mayor, who sent for Dr McGowan. This gentleman is a reverend divine, and teacher of languages; he attended the Mayor immediately, and, in answer to the questions put to him, we understand he said that he rented his cellar in January last to a person named Henderson, who, he understood, carried on the oil trade, and that he knew nothing about any dead bodies being there. . . .

---

11. I wish I knew *where* in Hope Street this was—because for two or three years in the late 1950s, I rented a flat in that street, handily opposite the ornate Philharmonic pub, which is diagonally across from the Philharmonic Hall. Presently, the street called Hope links the Anglican cathedral with the newer Roman Catholic one.

Mr Thomas Wm. Dawes, surgeon, of St Paul's Square, deposed that he had examined the bodies, by the direction of the Coroner. In one cask he had found the bodies of two women and one man; in another, two women and two men; in the third, three men and one woman, and in the other casks and sacks he found 22 [*sic*] bodies, viz., nine men, five boys, and three girls; the bodies were all in a perfect state. . . . There were no external marks of violence, but there was a thread tied round the toes of one of the women, which is usual for some families to do immediately after death. Witness had no reason but to believe that they had died in a natural way, and he had no doubt the bodies had all been disinterred. The Season for Lectures on Anatomy is about to commence in the capital of Scotland. . . .

The bodies, by the direction of the Coroner, were buried this morning in the parish cemetery, in casks, as they were found.

A good many of the bodies dissected in Edinburgh hailed from Dublin—for, contrary to the legend of Scots meanness, Irish grave-robbers could get better prices from the anatomists of Edinburgh, who also paid shipping costs, than from those of Dublin. Indeed, the respective prices were so far apart that some Irish middlemen, having bought bodies ostensibly for home use, made profit from them by despatching them to Edinburgh. In January 1828, Irish nationalists, irked by the discovery that a porter at the Royal College of Surgeons in Ireland was engaged in such unpatriotic export, murdered him; whether his body was donated to his employers or, to the financial good of a cause, travelled elsewhere, one cannot tell.

Enough has been said, I think, to show that, by the time that the pensioner known only as Donald died in the later Log's lodging house in Tanner's Close, a quite considerable cottage—or, usually, church-yard—industry served anatomists' purposes and that Edinburgh (which had recently become two-faced: part of the city to the north of its Castle so beautiful that its dubbing as "the Athens of the North" was a sort of flattery to Athens; part of the city to the south of its Castle ugly as sin and so kippered by smoke as to be called Auld Reekie) was the perfect place in Great Britain, indeed, in the world, for setting up a business specialising in the supply of fresh corpses.

⌣

But the firm of Burke & Hare was not considered by either of the partners to be one at its outset; the selling of Donald's body was meant
to be a one-off transaction, a means of reimbursement of his debt, no
more than that.

As several persons already knew of Donald's death (foremost among
them, presumably, the two surviving occupants of his deathbed), and
were already spreading the knowledge around West Port, it was necessary to dissemble his interment. And so an undertaker was called in, he
arriving, unconcerned about measurements, with a coffin in tow; and
the minute he had fitted the body into the coffin and hurried away to
Greyfriars churchyard, there to make a booking for space in the next
available paupers' pit, Burke used his cobbling crowbar carefully to lift
the coffin lid; then he and Hare lumbered the body into the small back
room (the window of which, you will remember, looked upon a pigsty
and a dead wall), then both men—hurrying, for fear that the undertaker might induce the Greyfriars sexton to cramp a ready-dug pit, and
return importunately—filled the coffin with an apt amount of tree rind
filched from the pile of it that the nearby tanner used toward turning
skin into leather; then Burke banged the lid back on while Hare swept
stray bits of tree rind out of sight; and then they rested.

Briefly, though. Knowing not even the basic formalities of what
they had to do next, they set off long before they should have done
to find a buyer. It was still daylight when they headed east, unloaded,
making for Surgeons' Square.[12] Reaching South Bridge (which was,
is, adjunct to the North Bridge, a viaduct spanning a deep hollow between the New and Old Town), they encountered a young man somehow or other acquainted with Burke. The encounter made the story
of them very different from how it should have turned out.

The young man was a student of medicine. Knowing that, Burke
told him that he himself and Hare were on their way to 2 Surgeons'
Square, the off-campus premises in which Alexander Monro III, professor of anatomy at Edinburgh University, dissected, usually lec-
turing the while, and explained—on the quiet, of course—what they
hoped to accomplish there.

The young man was studying anatomy under Robert Knox. He may,
just making conversation, have mentioned that Knox—known behind

12. The square was subsequently erased; it was a hundred yards or so east of South
Bridge, roughly where Infirmary Street curves into High School Yards.

his back as "Old Cyclops" because an attack of smallpox soon after his birth in 1793 had blinded one of his eyes—was reckoned, except by rivals, to be the most informed and informative anatomist in the city; that his school, which had become his alone two years before, following the death of its founder, John Barclay, who had taught and eventually employed him, was far and away the most successful of the private schools of anatomy; that there was no comparison between Knox and the third of the Alexander Monros, who was more butcher than anatomist, a professor only because his father and grandfather had each, in turn, graced the same chair—and whose lectures demonstrated his dependence on his grandfather's notes, which he parroted, with the inclusion even of such phrases as, "When I was a student in Leyden in 1719."

Getting to his point, the student advised Burke and Hare to amend their destination in Surgeons' Square from No. 2 to No. 10—Dr. Knox's Rooms for Practical Anatomy and Operative Surgery—and they said that they would do so.

And, momentously to the outcome of the story, they did so—only to be shooed by an uppity doorman to the tradesmen's entrance; and there, once their shy mutterings were comprehended, only to be told that such dealings were done after dark: they could return that night if they wished—no appointment was needed, since someone was always on duty to take delivery and to negotiate a price.

They traipsed away.

There was still a chance that Robert Knox would not be ruined; that some more expendable anatomist would be sacrificed.

However, rather than seeking a daytime buyer, they returned to Tanner's Close, and there whiled away the time until dusk—when, having thought to wrap Donald's body, they took it (Burke, the burlier, sometimes allowing Hare respite by carrying it pickaback) to 10 Surgeons' Square: a distance of about a mile, twice as far as Greyfriars, which they passed on their right.

They arrived so early in the dark as to be met not only by the head porter, David Paterson, but also by three students of such seniority and promise that Knox either waived their fees or even paid them a little something for assisting him. Their names were William Fergusson, Thomas Wharton Jones, and Alexander Miller: all three would achieve fame and fortune from surgery—especially Fergusson, who in 1866 was knighted by Queen Victoria, and in the following year became her sergeant-surgeon. The first thing that Burke and Hare were told was that it was best for all concerned if they kept their surnames to themselves; and so they were merely "John and William" when, at Paterson's bidding, they carried their load upstairs to the lecture room, deposited it on a slab which, when Knox was demonstrating, made a frame for the focus of as many as three hundred pairs of studying eyes, slid away the sacking and then the shirt, and stood aside while Fergusson, Jones, and Miller appraised—certainly noting the freshness and the absence of signs of burial, putting those twos together to make four, but, the need for subjects being what it was, keeping the joint conclusion to themselves. Words were whispered to Paterson—words that he translated in his mind into a price: £10—about the average. Nudging the clearly novice John and William further aside, away from earshot of the students, he offered £7.10 shillings. Take it or leave it, he said. And they, believing that hesitation might cause him to lower the offer, surely not to be more generous, said, as with one voice, done.

£7.10 shillings. Giving that sum meaning is hard. Government reckonings of inflation do not go so far back; even if they did, one would trust them no more than one trusts today's. It is sensible, I think, to see that sum in relation to the threepence a night that the Hares charged for lodging—that, so far as Burke was concerned, taking Helen M'Dougal into account, was sixpence. Presently, no doss house—not even one with as few mod cons as the Hares'—provides accommodation for under a couple of pounds a night. But let us say a pound. Again reminding you that there were 240 pennies in the pound until we British were decimalised, simple arithmetic—too simple, you may think—shows that as there were 80 threepences in the pound, and as one of those threepences bought a night's stay in Log's lodging house, threepence then would be worth at least a pound now; ergo, $7^1/_2$ of Burke's and Hare's pounds would amount, at least, to our £600 (close to $1,000 U.S.).

No wonder, then, that Burke and Hare were happy. Hare was so taken aback by the happiness that, without thinking of what Margaret would say, he split the proceeds fairly: £4.5s. retained (which, if the extent of Donald's debt to Margaret is believed, left Hare with a Crown), and £3.5s. for Burke (who, after all, had initiated the venture and had done the lion's share of the labour). It would be nice to say that Burke, who for the first time in his life could afford munificence, insisted upon covering the overhead expenses associated with the undertaking of the rind-filled coffin; but there is no evidence that he did.

⤸

Between one and three weeks went by. That is as accurate as it is possible to be; the Christmas of 1827 was coming. Meanwhile, one of the
Hares' lodgers began to look sickly. Whereas we know three things
about the subject matter of Burke and Hare's first transaction at 10
Surgeons' Square—that his first name was Donald, that he was a retired soldier, and that, therefore, he had reached a decent age—only
two things are known about his immediate successor: his first name,
which was Joseph, and his trade, which was corn-milling. The minute
Joseph began to look sickly, both Burke and Hare expressed concern—
though, so they subsequently insisted, for different reasons, Hare's
being that if it turned out that Joseph was suffering from typhoid,
cholera, or some other contagious disease, the lodging house would
have to be closed for a time, and Burke's being that he might catch
whatever it was that Joseph was suffering from.

Each for his own reason, they agreed upon euthanasia. Telling
Joseph of the medicinal worth of whisky, which he was only too glad
to believe, they dosed him into unconsciousness, thus making redundant Hare's spread-eagling of himself over Joseph while Burke pressed
a pillow on the latter's face. There were no undertaking expenses: if
anyone enquired as to Joseph's whereabouts, they could reply that he
had gone away—which in no time at all was a truth. Whoever accepted
the body on behalf of Robert Knox cannot have observed the merest anything suggesting that death might, just might, have resulted
from a contagious disease; he or they must have caught a whiff of the
whisky, but, perhaps, was or were so entranced by a scent quite different from the expected kind as to be uninquisitive of it. Joseph's body
being a better prospective subject than Donald's had been, David
Paterson was told to pay more for it—and did, delighting John and
William by giving them ten of the sovereigns that since 1817 had been
valued at a pound apiece.

⤸

Delighted them: encouraged them, too. From now on, in the absence
of corpses that had become so through natural causes or of lodgers
whose smothering could, with a little creative thought, be justified as
humane, Burke and Hare manufactured death. They were helped in

that trade, on a part-time, beck-and-call basis, by their women and one or two of Burke's immigrant kin.

The striking difference between their story and those of the majority of other persons known to have committed "serial killings" is that, while they were busy, no one influential had the slightest idea that a serial of killings was in progress: most of their victims, whether lured or conveniently present, had flitted about too frequently to be noticeable by their absence. A problem that taxes the ingenuity of lots of murderers, that of doing away with a body, was no problem at all for the Edinburgh partnership, whose creations were *intended* for destruction in aid of a science. Just think what an immense advantage that was to Burke and Hare—of how the depriving of it from latter-day serial killers put them to far more work after their killings than beforehand.

Perhaps to mislead any eavesdroppers on their shoptalk, Burke and Hare used jargon for some nouns of their trade: the things that were jargonised as "subjects" by the men of Surgeons' Square were, to them, "shots," and their acts of murder were "tricks." Though the jargon was subsequently translated and utilised by reporters of their activities, none of it caught on with the public (but one reporter's turning of Burke's name into a verb was accepted so widely as to earn entry into English dictionaries, the present best of which retain it—"burke, v.t. to murder, esp. by stifling: hence [fig.] to put an end to, quietly").

The exact number of persons murdered by Burke and Hare, or by one or other of them, was never established; each of them admitted, in effect, to having lost count. The minimum number, inclusive of Joseph the miller, is sixteen.

༄

A little was left of 1827 when Hare—perhaps taking an unintending stroll rather than prowling for prey—met and made conversation with an old woman, Abigail Simpson; her complaint of footsoreness was his cue to ask her to the lodging house to rest awhile. As she had done once a week for years, since her retirement from the domestic service of a rich man, she had walked from her cottage at Gilmerton, five miles southeast of Edinburgh, specially to present herself at the kitchen door of the rich man's house in the New Town and to receive from one of his present servants her pension of eighteen pence and from another a can of broth. She was on her way home when Hare met her; and so the encounter must have been on South Bridge, part of the straightest route to Gilmerton—and so, as that place was about a mile from Tanner's Close, Hare must have enveigled her by more than the promise of a nap, probably by the promise of whisky. In any event, having been ushered into the small back room, she was made more drowsy by Hare's hospitality. Burke, joining them, showed off his tenor singing voice: not ostentatiously, for people were sleeping in other rooms, but with the sincerity that always watered his eyes when he sang Irish sentimental songs, which made up his whole repertoire. A lullaby did the trick—or rather, made the "trick" opportune. The moment Abigail snored, she was smothered. Burke wiped his eyes. Alexander Leighton, a historian of the partnership and, of all its historians, the most observant of equivocations in it, would enquire in regard to Burke's musicalness on this occasion and on some similar ones:

> Could that man have had any sense of the beautiful in the sentiments of the lyrics which, it was said, he sang with feeling, if not pathos? Can it be possible that such a sense can be consistent with a demoralisation such as his? We suspect that it is. We are led to expect its impossibility by a reference to opposite, if not antagonistic, feelings: we cannot love and hate the same object. This is true, and would seem to disprove our proposition *à priori*. We can reconcile the contradiction only by having recourse to the different faculties of the imagination and the sense. The poet who has ravished his readers by a description of the beauty of female virtue and innocence has been found in a brothel. One of the most touching religious poems in the world has been sung by one who, among brawling revellers, maligned religion and its votaries. The praises of temperance have been enchantingly poured forth by a bacchanal. The oppressor of the poor has wept at a representation of affecting generosity. Anyone may fill up the list without perhaps including a hypocrite. The imagination has its emotions, and the sense its feelings, or, perhaps, no feelings. The why and the wherefore touch the ultimate, and we are lost; but the fact remains, as proved by evidence, that William Burke could, in song, be pathetic.[13]

13. *The Court of Cacus,* London, 1861.

Abigail Simpson's body, carefully made anonymous, was the first that John and William presented to Robert Knox in person; his only comment to them, framed unquestioningly, was that the body was fresh. The trick produced a gross profit of £10. ls.6d—the small change of that amount being the pension payment that the old woman had travelled so far to collect. No doubt the eighteen pennies were claimed by Hare as reimbursement for the single overhead, his spiritual means of making Abigail ready for the pillow. As was to be so for all but one of the subsequent deals, the disbursement from Knox was divided one half to Hare, two-fifths to Burke, and a tenth to Margaret—she having insisted that she was entitled to that share as proprietor of the murder scene. (Though some of the later tricks were done elsewhere, she still took her tenth—perhaps, without saying so, considering it as danger-money, for by the time of the first murder on other premises, she and the unpercentaged Helen M'Dougal had overheard their men, both drunk, mutually moaning that opportunities were scarce and discussing the possibility of producing a related subject, which in Hare's case, he having no true relatives in Edinburgh, could only have meant Margaret.)

Neither of the next victims was known by any name to those who profited from them. First, an Englishman who sold matches on street corners came to the lodging house, meaning to sleep there; so weak was he that Hare did not waste even a nightcap on him and merely stood by while Burke, not bothering with a pillow, pinched his nose with one hand and barred his mouth with the other. The body was barely away when the Hares alone, and quite as arrogantly, made another: Margaret enticed an old woman in and plied her with whisky until she was unconscious; Hare, told of the catch when he returned for supper, entered the small back room, arranged the bed ticking so as to impede the old woman's breathing, went back and ate the meal that his wife had meanwhile dished up, and later checked that, partial undressing apart, a delivery was ready for 10 Surgeons' Square.

Unlike those murders, both done with a casual efficiency, the next was about as organised as a tossed salad. I shall tell of it in collaboration with the anonymous compiler of one of the first books on the entire case, sometimes altering his tense and always indicating his contributions in quotation marks.[14]

14. *West Port Murders* (Edinburgh, 1829).

On the night of Tuesday, 8 April, a pair of prostitutes, Janet Brown and Mary Paterson, neither more than twenty, was apprehended for some offence other than prostitution, probably for being drunk and quarrelsome, and lodged in the watch-house of Canongate, the final stretch of the Royal Mile to the Palace of Holyroodhouse. It would be as well for you to get your bearings: Canongate runs east from High Street, which, at its centre, cuts across the bridges and separates them as north and south; as you know, Tanner's Close was about a mile west of the bridges—therefore, well over a mile west of Canongate.

Janet, "though a girl of the town, seems to have been possessed of a considerable intelligence." She was pretty; petite. Mary was altogether beautiful—of tresses, features, form. "Well educated, she had lost in youth the guiding care of a mother. Her beauty was a snare to her, and her perverse will, though accompanied but not modified by a kind heart, greatly tended to accomplish her downfall."

They were released from custody before daybreak on the Wednesday. Without having to walk far, they went to the house of a Mrs. Laurie, "where they had formerly lodged"—and which was certainly either a brothel or a sort of specialising temps agency. Mary, already thinking of making up for the night's work she had lost, put her hair in paper curlers. She was still wearing them when, at about 7 A.M., she and Janet left Mrs. Laurie's and sauntered back to Canongate—to an ever-open spirits shop run by a man named Swanston. "They had there a gill of whisky, and while drinking it, they observed Burke, who, in company with Swanston, was drinking rum and bitters."

Now, what Burke was doing out, and in Swanston's, at that time of the morning cannot be surely explained. Some authors have suggested—no: stated—that he was reconnoitring for prey; but other possible explanations appear more likely—among them, that he had sought sexual pleasure from Helen M'Dougal at a time of the night or month that seemed inconvenient to her, and, angry at her rebuff as well as being still keen for satisfaction, had flounced out, chiefly to emphasise his anger but also in the hope of picking up an insomniac prostitute in Swanston's, which, despite its proximity to a watch-house, was a public house of ill repute.

He entered into conversation with the girls Brown and Paterson, and affected to be much taken with them, and three gills of rum and bitters were drunk at his expense. He wished them to accom-

pany him to his lodgings, which he said were in the neighbourhood, and upon Brown expressing reluctance, was very urgent
that she should go, saying that he had a pension and could keep
her handsomely, and make her comfortable for life, and that he
would stand between them and harm from the people in the
house. This particular attention to her she supposed to be in consequence of finding her more shy and backward than Paterson,
who was always of a forward, fearless disposition. They consented
to go along with him, and he promised them breakfast when they
reached the house. He purchased, before leaving Swanston's, two
bottles of whisky, and gave one to each of the girls to carry.

As has been indicated, Burke was not the only one of his family to
have emigrated to Scotland. His brother Constantine, who was properly married and conventionally employed (as a scavenger, or street-
cleaner, by the Edinburgh council), dwelt in a house in Gibb's Close,
a dark alley off Canongate. It was to that house that Burke took the
girls—surprisingly to Constantine and his wife, Elizabeth, who were in
bed. Now acting his lie that he lodged in the house, "Burke swore and
abused the woman [Elizabeth] for her negligence at not having the fire
lighted"—and neither she nor Constantine undermined his lie.

The fire was lighted up, and breakfast, consisting of tea, bread,
eggs, and smoked haddock, prepared; but during this process,
the two bottles of whisky were produced and partly drunk by
Burke, Constantine, his wife, and the two girls. Constantine partook only of part of it, having in the meantime left the house
to do his work as a scavenger. Before the whisky was finished,
however, Burke requested Brown to leave the house along with
him. He accompanied her to a neighbouring public house [not
Swanston's], where he gave her two bottles of porter which he
also partook of, and a pie.

It appears that Constantine had delayed his scavenging or gone to it
by a roundabout route, taking in Tanner's Close, for while Burke and
Janet Brown were at the pub, a matter of fifteen minutes or so, Helen
M'Dougal turned up at Constantine's house. She seemed calm when
they returned. She had not introduced herself, or been introduced, to
Mary Paterson, who was by now showing signs that she had drunk

quite a lot of rum and whisky; and she did not introduce herself to Janet. Burke made no introductions. Embarrassed by those omissions of social etiquette, "Constantine's wife whispered to the girls that the woman lately arrived was Burke's 'wife.' Upon Helen M'Dougal's up-braiding him for his conduct, Brown apologised for being in his company, mentioning that they did not know him to be a married man, otherwise they would not have come, and proposed then to leave the house. M'Dougal replied that she did not blame them, but that it was his constant practice to desert her and spend his money upon loose women. She requested them to sit still, and seemed anxious that they should not go away." Burke must then have piped up, saying something in his defence, and Helen M'Dougal must have made a more provocative remark, thus starting a quarrel between them. "It got more violent, and she took up the eggs which had been set down for breakfast and threw them into the fire. Upon this, Burke took up a dram glass and flung it at her; it hit her forehead above the eye and cut it."

At the commencement of the uproar, Constantine's wife ran out of the house, as Brown subsequently supposed for the purpose of bringing Hare; indeed, as she saw no other person dispatched anywhere, it is difficult to account otherwise for this vampire's speedy appearance. Burke then succeeded in turning Helen M'Dougal out of the house, locking the door upon her. By this time Paterson was lying across the bed in a state nearly approaching to insensibility. Burke pressed Brown to go along with him into bed; but, as she herself subsequently observed, much as she might have been disposed to yield to his wishes, she could scarcely have done so after the brawl she had so recently witnessed, and while M'Dougal was still making a noise at the door and knocking for admittance, and she peremptorily refused. She persisted in her wish to be allowed to depart, promising to return in a quarter of an hour. Upon this promise she was suffered to depart, and Burke at her request conducted her past M'Dougal, who was still upon the stairhead apparently much enraged.

She went straight to Mrs Laurie's, and jestingly told her that she had got fine lodgings now; but after informing Mrs L. of the circumstances, she agreed to go back along with Mrs L.'s servant, and endeavour to get Paterson removed. Upon her return she did not recollect perfectly the close in which the house was situated, and applied at Swanston's for a direction to the residence of the man who had left his public house with herself and Paterson. She was told, among other things, that she would probably find him in his brother's in Gibb's Close. Even after getting into the close and the stair, she did not recognise the house, and entered that of a decent woman, enquiring if it was there she was before. She was informed that they kept company with no such people, but it would likely be in the house upstairs. They proceeded up accordingly, and found there M'Dougal and Hare and his wife. Mrs Hare ran forward to strike Brown, but was prevented. Between her leaving Burke's and returning, there was only about an interval of twenty minutes.

During those twenty minutes, Mary Paterson was smothered to death, and her body tucked out of sight, probably beneath the bed. It was extraordinarily stupid, doing a murder then and there—but that reproving comment should be viewed in the light of a general statement, which is that stupid murderers are less likely to be caught than are studious ones. Supposing that I had to choose between allying myself in a murderous way with a couple like Burke and Hare or with a pair of geniuses like Leopold and Loeb, I should choose the former alliance without thinking twice. Stupid acts are hard for sensible people to credit, difficult for them to understand. Private murders that the murderers try to *keep* private are usually suspected, detected, through logic of some sort; if those murderers are illogical, then anyone with a flow-charting mind (which is what detectives are supposed to have) is likely to be baffled by them. Had Burke and Hare and their women possessed, between them, as much intelligence as did Janet Brown, the murder of Mary Paterson would have been the final instalment of the serial.

When Janet asked where her colleague was, the Hares and Helen M'Dougal "alleged that she had gone out with Burke, and added that they expected them back soon, and invited her to take a glass of whisky with them. She did so, in the hope that Paterson might quickly return. Mrs L.'s servant then left them, and M'Dougal commenced a narration of her grievances from Burke's bad conduct, and railed at him for going away with the girl. In a short time the servant returned for Brown, Mrs L. having become alarmed at her report. No attempt was made to detain Brown; but she was invited to return, which she promised to do."

"In the afternoon she did go back, and was informed by Constantine Burke's wife that Burke and the girl had not returned." (One gathers, then, that the woman of the house had it to herself. If she had done any tidying, no more even than making up the bed and emptying the potty, she can hardly have failed to notice that her brother-in-law and his friends had left something behind. Either she had done no tidying or was a wonderfully calm liar.)

Some time before six in the evening, when it was getting dark, Burke and Hare—the former having slept his hangover away—came to collect their belonging. They did not take long to undress it of all but a chemise (ungratefully, or because Constantine's wife had outsize measurements, Burke called back in a day or so for the other garments) and to put it in a canal-boat sack that one of them had thought to bring. Though, as Closes went, Gibb's was much handier than Tanner's to Surgeons' Square, the route through back-doubles was crowded with children who had nowhere safer to play; and a group of them, eager for diversion from hopscotch, followed Burke and Hare and made them hurry by chanting, presumably in fun, "They're heaving a corpse."

Having arrived, panting, at No. 10, they were met by William Fergusson (he who would become surgeon to the Queen) and a less tutored student: "a tall lad" is the sole description of him, but he should, he really should, have made his name from the fact that, from a single glance at the dead face of Mary Paterson, he thought that it was as like that of a girl he had perused in Canongate a few nights before "as one pea is like another." And he said as much, forcing Fergusson—who also had recognised the body—to ask "John" for its provenance. Burke replied that he and William had bought the body from an old woman, a stranger to them, at the back of Canongate. No other question was asked. For a reason that can only be surmised, Fergusson told one of the suppliers to cut off the beautiful tresses, paper curlers and all, and gave him a pair of surgeon's clippers to do so. Perhaps as a tacit way of expressing his disquiet, Fergusson offered only eight pounds for the finest subject that John and William had yet provided. They did not dare to haggle.

Days later, another of Knox's students saw the body—and was more disturbed by it than either Fergusson or the tall lad had been. For he had known Mary Paterson intimately, paying for that right. That none of the three students—nor any of those that two of them gossiped with—spoke warningly to Knox is proved by what he did. Rather than dissecting the body when its turn became due, he, delighted by its beauty, had it preserved to illustrate his lectures on muscular development for the next three months; whisky, which had so greatly contributed toward Mary Paterson's death, was the agent of her corpse's salvation. Knox shared his delight with artistic friends, by arranging private viewings; and he allowed two artists to draw portraits of the submerged still life.

Meanwhile, Janet Brown pestered Constantine.

> Whenever she saw him, which she frequently did at his work early in the morning, she enquired after her friend. His answers were always very surly; on two occasions saying, "How the h—ll can I tell about you sort of people; you are here today and away tomorrow;" and on another, "I am often out upon my lawful business, and how can I answer for all that takes place in my house in my absence." It was pretended that Paterson had gone off to Glasgow with a packman; but this reply did not satisfy Brown, as she knew that Paterson was a well-educated girl, and could write sufficiently well to send an account to her friends if she had left Edinburgh. No more satisfactory intelligence, however, could be obtained.

Janet must have wondered whether Mary was dead. But if the idea of murder entered her mind, it was dispelled as far-fetched.

Before summer, when all of the anatomists reduced the prices they paid for subjects, Burke and Hare made two further sales, having killed—perhaps vice versa—an old Irishwoman named Effie, who had survived by selling oddments discarded by people in the New Town to people in the Old Town who could make use of them (bits of leather, for instance: Burke, when cobbling, had often bought them from her, and that was how she had got to know him well enough to make her enticement easy); and a woman of whom nothing is known other than that she too was old. When Burke first spotted her, in West Port, she was so drunk—and therefore ready primed for the intention that had brought him out—that she would surely have keeled over but for the flanking support of two constables, whose occupation he considered no hindrance to his now-specific intention; speaking to one of them, Andrew Williamson, with whom he was on good terms, having given him tidbits of information about local ne'er-do-wells, he offered to relieve him and his fellow-officer of their burden, thus freeing them for less onerous duties, and Williamson was much obliged.

On a day early in June, Burke found an embarrassment of opportunities. While making his way to Log's with a man whose drunkenness was almost the equal of that of the woman he had accepted from the constables, he was intercepted by yet another old woman. She was accompanied by a boy of about twelve—he was her grandchild; he was a deaf mute. Both were tired, for they had walked from Glasgow, meaning to stay with friends in Edinburgh. She told Burke the friends' address, and asked if he could direct her to it. Burke knew that the address was close by; but he hemmed and hawed while deciding between a bird in the hand and two in the bush. Then, the decision made, probably on the basis that the drunken man would be available, just as drunk, some other time, he sat him in the gutter, and, turning to the old woman from Glasgow, told her that her friends lived some distance away—but in the direction of his lodgings, where she and her grandson were welcome to bide awhile, refreshing themselves until he pointed them toward their journey's end. At Log's, she was introduced to the others; and they—Margaret, who was noticeably pregnant, especially—made a fuss of the boy, and every so often expressed sadness at his afflictions, speaking softly though he could not hear. Then Margaret, saying that the boy was safe with her, told the old woman to follow the men into the small back room. The old woman, expecting the promised refreshment, did so. Eventually, the men returned.

And some time later, the boy, frightened but unable to scream, was murdered too.

The partners may have been considering a "double event" for weeks—ever since Burke had bought a horse and cart, both decrepit, or before that transaction, he in that case thinking of it as a solution to additional haulage problems. But though they had, or thought they had, transport sufficient for concurrent deliveries, they believed that they required a single container for more than one body. A large herring barrel was acquired, into which they contorted the bodies of the Glaswegian woman and her grandson. Then they humped the barrel onto the cart. Burke had learned soon after his purchase that the ancient horse could not cope with heavy loads, so he and Hare walked beside the cart once the horse was ambling, and put their shoulders behind it on rising ground. Having laboured as far as the Meal Market, the horse took a "dour fit," refusing to go farther. Efforts to make it obedient failed—but drew a crowd. Burke, more furious than worried, engaged a porter with a "hurley-barrow," and the barrel was transferred. The porter, it was afterward nicely said, "had fewer scruples than the horse," and dragged his vehicle to Surgeons' Square. Burke followed; Hare stayed behind, to make arrangements regarding the horse and cart—which, according to the writer just quoted (and I must tell animal lovers to skip to the next paragraph), amounted to having both towed to a neighbouring tanyard, "where it was found that the poor beast had two large dried-up sores on his back, which had been stuffed with cotton, and covered over with a piece of another horse's skin."

Meanwhile, Burke, having paid off the porter, was experiencing difficulties associated with the barrel, the contents of which, pliable when inserted, had stiffened, making them hard to extract. The help of several students was required before assessment could be carried out by William Fergusson.

It would not be surprising if—despite the sixteen pounds realised from the sales—Burke, depressed by the loss of his horse and cart, and Hare, petulant at the troubles they had put him to, had a row. That would have been one of several between them at about this time. As a counterpoint to their disharmony, Margaret was using her pregnant state as the excuse for being more snappy than usual. Helen M'Dougal, made miserable by all of this, was accused by the others of casting gloom, and was sometimes smacked by Burke on that account. There is a tale that Margaret broached the idea to Burke that, as Helen was such a drag, he might be advised to take her away somewhere, murder her (whether or not with the extra motive of financial profit was up to him), send back word of her passing for the Hares to pass around, and return long enough later as to have obviated the need to buy mourning dress. Burke and Helen did go away at the end of June, to stay with relatives of hers at Maddiston, near Falkirk, but they both returned to the city at the end of July—not, however, to Log's, but to a house in an unnamed close, separated from Tanner's by the eastward Weaver's Close. They subrented a room in the house from John Broggan, whose wife was a cousin of Burke's. Some four months from the start of their tenancy, a reporter noted,

In approaching Burke's you enter a respectable looking land from the street, and proceed along a passage and then descend a stair, and turning to the right a passage leads to the [front] door, which is almost opposite to the house of Mrs Law [of whom further mention will be made shortly]; a dark passage within the door leads to Burke's room. The room is small, and of an oblong form; the miserable bed occupied nearly one end of it (that next the door). Everything presented a disgusting picture of squalid wretchedness; rags and straw, mingled with implements of shoemaking, and old shoes and boots, in such quantities as Burke's nominal profession of a cobbler could never account for. A pot full of boiled potatoes was a prominent object. The bed was a coarse wooden frame, without posts or curtains, and filled with old straw and rags. At the foot of it and near the wall was [a] heap of straw. The window looks into a small court, closed in by a wall. At the top of the stairs leading down to the room is a back entrance from a piece of waste ground. There are several outlets from it.

The breach between the partners was widened, chiefly by Burke—who at first suspected, and then established through enquiries at 10 Surgeons' Square, that Hare had done a deal while he, Burke, was at Maddiston—and partly by Hare, who at first felt cut to the quick, and then, ignoring the outcome of Burke's inquiries, took umbrage at the fact that Burke was so distrustful of him as to have made them. But eventually, each recognising that he needed the other—or that if he tried to go it alone, he would be up against fierce competition—they resolved their differences, or made out that they had. The business recovered.

August and September comprised the slack season; they were the months of vacation for all of the schools of anatomy (Knox's impending term, commencing on Monday, 6 October, was meanwhile advertised on handbills: "FEE for the First Course, £3, 5s; Second Course, £2, 4s.; Perpetual [until the end of July 1829: any of the parents or guardians who paid the undiscounted lump sum would wish that they had opted for the instalments arrangement], £5, 9s. N.B.—*An Additional Fee of Three Guineas includes Subjects*. Arrangements have been made to secure as usual an ample supply of Anatomical Subjects."). Prior to the respective reopenings, subjects were required only for lecturers' private use and for their crammings of promising students or hopeless ones who were rich enough to be able to afford bespoke tuition. Even so, Burke and Hare did four tricks—at least four—during that period.

Item. Since the death of her husband in 1826, a Mrs. Hostler had eked out a living by doing other people's washing. As she had no mangle of her own, a friend, Mrs. Janet Law, had allowed her the use of hers, and so she had become a regular visitor to the unnamed close, arriving from her home in Grassmarket with a basketful of wet and rumpled linen, cranking the load between the wooden rollers of Mrs. Law's mangle, panting out gossip (for she was a busybody) as she did so, relaxedly telling further tales while sharing her whisky flask with Mrs. Law (who was taciturn compared with her but equally fond of a dram), and then departing with a basketful of damp and folded linen. In the weeks round about the arrival of Burke and Helen M'Dougal in the house across the close, she often amended the routine of her trip by popping into that house to give prenatal counselling, founded on her own experiences long ago, to Mrs. Broggan, who may not have wanted but certainly needed it; and when the baby was born, she gate-crashed the celebration, which, almost as rowdy as a wake, was also attended by the Broggans' new tenants and two friends of theirs from Tanner's Close. One can believe Burke's subsequent recollection that Mrs. Broggan was not at the party; but his statement, made almost in the same breath, that her husband was absent too seems to have been a kindly lie—though why he should have lied (Hare was prevented from telling the truth by his insistence that he wasn't at the party either) is hard to fathom, considering that, while all but one of those who were at the party were still recovering from it, Broggan borrowed £1.10s. from Burke and the same sum from Hare, and straightway absconded. While the party was in full swing, Mrs. Hostler, who had been the life and soul of it, left the room with Burke. She was singing her favourite song, "Home, Sweet Home." It was the last that anyone heard of her. The total of three pounds that Broggan got from Burke and Hare came from the eight that the body of Mrs. Hostler fetched.

Item. During their month in the country, Burke and Helen M'Dougal had stayed with relatives of her former "husband." Before leaving, Burke had told one of them, Ann M'Dougal, who seems to have been much the same age as Helen, that he would like to repay her favours by putting her up in Edinburgh. Almost certainly, he did not then regard her prospectively, as raw material for his trade; nor when she wrote from Maddiston, accepting the invitation; nor during the first weeks of a stay that he had imagined would last a few days. But anyone who has suffered from providing indeterminable hospitality will understand his eventual cracking under a pressure made more pressing by Hare. It is not known whether Helen was openly understanding. Burke, pricked by remorse at the ending of a "distant relative," insisted that Hare had to do the actual smothering—but nonetheless expected his accustomed share of the proceeds. Though Ann had meant to stay longer, only a short time passed before her real relatives in Maddiston grew concerned at her continued absence. Some of them travelled to Edinburgh, hoping to learn what had become of her. Perhaps they did not know Burke's still-new address; if they called at Log's, they would not have been directed. They finished up at Constantine's—where, quite by chance, they found Helen. She was very drunk. When they explained the purpose of their trip, she said that they need not have troubled themselves, as Ann was murdered and sold long before. Thinking that she was joking in the worst possible taste, they smiled politely and left, returning to Maddiston without having made further inquiries.

Items. Mary Haldane, a prostitute long past her prime, was delighted when Hare, observing her on her beat in Grassmarket, indicated that she was to follow him to Tanner's Close. Her delight was short-lived. She left three daughters, they enumerated as follows: "One was married to a tinsmith named Clark, carrying on business in the High Street of Edinburgh; the second was serving a sentence of fourteen years' transportation for some offence; while the third was simply following the unfortunate example of one who should have sheltered her from evil influences." The third, whose name was Peggy, was not left for long. Becoming anxious at her mother's disappearance, she asked around, and received information from several people, all of whom had known "Mistress Mary" at least by sight, for though she had been but one of many prostitutes of the Grassmarket, she had been the one least used and so most often on display—and made still more conspicuous by the fact that her smile, intended to be enticing, had revealed that she was left with only a single central tooth. Hearing from David Rymer, a grocer in West Port, that her mother had gone with Hare, Peggy went to Tanner's Close. Margaret Hare, perhaps postnatally depressed, flew into a tantrum at the very idea that her husband had consorted with a loose woman—but instead of ordering Peggy out, invited her in. Hare,

returning, instantly slipped away to summon Burke. Shortly afterward, the bed in the small back room, still cold from the body of Mary
Haldane, accommodated her daughter's.

⤳

In the week when October began, the week in which the anatomists of
Edinburgh stocked up for their new terms, revising their rates upward,
Burke and Hare killed James Wilson—who, being mentally retarded in
relation to his age, which was eighteen, was known to many people
in the Old Town, and not just behind his back, as "Daft Jamie." After
his disappearance was explained, a pamphlet devoted to him alone
described his life, partly as follows:

His father died when he was about twelve years of age; and his
mother being a hawker, he was left, during her absence, pretty
much to his own devices. He generally wandered about the streets,
getting a meal here and a few pence there. He was one of those
wandering naturals known to everybody, and being a lad who,
while deficient in intellect, was kind at heart, he was a universal
favourite, only the very small and the very impudent boys troubling him. He was such a simpleton that he would not fight to
defend himself. Little boys, about the age of five or six, have frequently been observed by the citizens of Edinburgh going before
him holding up their fists, squaring, and saying they would fight
him; Jamie would have stood up like a knotless thread, and said,
with tears in his eyes, that he would not fight, for it was only bad
boys who fought; the boys would then give him a blow, and Jamie
would have run off, saying, "That wiz nae sair, man, ye canna
catch me." Then about a thousan' gets [brats] hardly out o' the
egg-shell, would have taken flight after him, bauling out, "Jamie,
Jamie, Daft Jamie." Sometimes he would have stopped and turned
round to them, banging his brow, squinting his eyes, shooting
out his lips (which was a sign of his being angry), saying, "What
way dae ye ca' me daft?" "Ye ir," the little gets would have bauled
out. "I'm no, though," said Jamie, "as sure's death; devil tak me,
I'm no daft at a." "Ye *ir*, ye *ir*," the gets would have bauled out. He
then would have held up his large fist, which was like a Dorby's
mell [stonemason's mallet], saying, "If ye say I'm daft, I'll knock

ye doun." He would then have whirled round on his heels and run off again, acting the race-horse.

   Robert Kirkwood, another half-wit, was familiarly known as Boby Awl. Jamie and Boby were fast friends, and no one could get them to fight, though frequent attempts were made to do so. They seemed to have a fellow-feeling for each other, and each of them firmly believed that his companion, and not himself, was "daft."

When the activities of Burke and Hare were exposed, Daft Jamie was given more words than the rest of the victims put together. So many of the words make up obvious inventions as to raise a suspicion that many of the others make up subtle ones. Therefore, one may as well be content with an account that implicitly admits poetic licence:

ATTENDANCE give, whilst I relate
How poor Daft Jamie met his fate;
'Twill make your hair stand on your head,
As I unfold the horrid deed:—

That hellish monster, William Burke,
Like Reynard sneaking on the lurk,
Coyduck'd his prey into his den,
And then the woeful work began:—

"Come, Jamie, drink a glass wi' me,
And I'll gang wi' ye in a wee,
To seek yer mither i' the town—
Come drink, man, drink, an' sit ye down."

At last he took the fatal glass,
Not dreaming what would come to pass;
When once he drank, he wanted more—
Till drunk he fell upon the floor.

Like some unguarded gem he lies—
The vulture waits to seize its prize;
Nor does he dream he's in its power,
Till it has seized him to devour.

The ruffian dogs,—the hellish pair,—
The villain Burke,—the meagre Hare,—
Impatient were the prize to win,
So to their smothering pranks begin:—

Burke cast himself on Jamie's face,
And clasp'd him in his foul embrace,
But Jamie waking in surprise,
Writhed in an agony to rise.

But help was near—for it Burke cried,
And soon his friend was at his side;
Hare tripp'd up Jamie's heels, and o'er
He fell, alas! to rise no more!

No sooner done, than in a chest
They cramm'd this lately welcom'd guest,
And bore him into Surgeons' Square—
A subject fresh—a victim rare!

And soon he's on the table laid,
Expos'd to the dissecting blade;
But where his members now may lay
Is not for me—or you—to say.

But this I'll say—some thoughts did rise:
It fill'd the Students with surprise,
That so short time should intervene
Since Jamie on the streets was seen.

But though his body is destroy'd,
His soul can never be decoy'd
From that celestial state of rest
Where he, I trust, is with the bless'd.

One to go.[15]

15. Left out are several stanzas of the "Elegiac Lines on the Tragical Murder of Poor Daft Jamie," published as a single sheet by W. Smith, of 3 Bristo Port, Edinburgh, who also made a mint of "thrip pences" from *A Laconic Narrative of the Life and Death*

Perhaps I suffer from an optical illusion, but my perception that Friday the Thirteenth appears more often than the law of averages insists that it should as the date of a murder or of a murderer's downfall makes me wonder whether the superstition of it arose from others' same perception or is a more reliable superstition than most. Burke and Hare did their last murder on a Friday that was not a thirteenth. The next best date, however: the final day of October, which is Hallowe'en.

Whereas most of the earlier victims were short of names, the last victim had so many that the legally required cataloguing of all of them whenever she was mentioned during the preliminaries of the trial must have accounted for a good five minutes of the proceedings: "Madgy or Margery or Mary M'Gonegal or Duffie or Campbell or Docherty." Ringing a further change, albeit slight, several of those employed to note the testimony verbatim preferred Dougherty to Docherty. I shall follow the subsequent majority minimisation, which left "Mary Docherty."

She was Irish. Having mislaid a grownup legitimate son in Glasgow, she had found him there, only to mislay him again; failing this time to find him in Glasgow, she had reasoned that he must be in Edinburgh and had come there in search of him. By the morning of Hallowe'en, her quest had brought her to David Rymer's shop, where spirits as well as groceries were on sale. It was there that Burke entered into conversation with her. Using the promise of a bowl of porridge as bait, he led her across West Port and through the unnamed close to his place.

It was already quite crowded, and every so often throughout the rest of the morning, it became more crowded still. Helen was invariably there; after dishing up the porridge for Mary Docherty, she poured her a dram or two—or more—sufficient, at any rate, to make her feel so at home that she took off, and washed, a red-and-white striped bedgown that she wore like a petticoat. Also ever-present were two rela-

---

of *Poor Jamie,* and of shillings from *An Authentic Narrative of the Life and Death of Robert Kirkwood*—that work given its ending by the fact that Boby Awl had recently been killed by the kick of a donkey; his body went to Alexander Monro's dissecting room. Mr. Smith's advertisement before publication of the latter booklet asserted that it would be "very entertaining to any who might read it, though they never saw the Oaf. There will be nothing inserted to offend or corrupt the morals, so that an abbess or modest damsel may peruse it without blushing." All of the "Elegiac Lines" and the *Laconic Narrative* are reproduced, with many other pieces of ephemera, in *Burke and Hare: The Resurrection Men,* edited and with an introduction by Jacques Barzun (New Jersey, 1974).

tives of Helen's—James Gray and his wife, whose name, like that of a former relative of Helen's, was Ann. The Grays were staying there while looking for permanent accommodation in or near the Grassmarket, which was James's birthplace: within a few days, he would be feted, and everyone would know something about him—at the very least that "after an attempt to learn his trade as a jeweller, he enlisted in the Elgin Fencibles, transferring afterwards to the 72nd Regiment, and recently returned with his wife to Edinburgh after an absence of seventeen years." Among those who popped in and out of the room were other tenants of the house and Mrs. Law, from across the close. Burke himself left for a while, explaining to Mary Docherty that he had to fetch drinks for a party on the true eve of All Hallows', which he hoped she would stay for. Actually, that was only one reason for his absence: while he was out, he found Hare and told him that he had "a shot for the doctors"; and he obtained a tea chest, free of charge, from Rymer's. Soon after his return, the Hares arrived and were introduced to Mary Docherty. They sized her up, comparing her with the tea chest.

What with one thing and another, the morning passed quickly, and so did the afternoon, and it was dark before the partners got round to discussing their business matter. Mary Docherty was in a state fit for their purpose; but the trouble was that the party, begun earlier than was meant, was proving so successful that it looked like going on all through the night. In considering how to curtail the revelry without causing offence, Burke suddenly realised that, even if that could be accomplished, a problem would remain: the Grays—who, as houseguests, would remain when all the party guests had gone. Forgetting his wish to be inoffensive, he shouted at the Grays above the others' din that they were making too much noise; they were to leave forthwith, he shouted—and when they asked where they could go, suggested Log's. With them out of the way, he turned his attention to the rest of the inconvenient crowd—most of whom, being slow to take offence, took their time before departing, the thickest-skinned of them not until eleven or so. Of course, he was not rude to Mary Docherty.

While Helen and Margaret waited in the passage, far less from a sense of delicacy than as a precaution in case an ejected partygoer wandered back, their men did the trick.

What Burke did shortly afterward, at about midnight, makes one wonder whether he and his partner had been *commissioned* to provide a subject promptly—and, supposing that they had, whether any

Drawings made during the trial of, clockwise from top left, William Burke, William Hare, Helen M'Dougal, and Margaret Hare (holding daughter) (from *Murder in Low Places*)

of their previous tricks were done in fulfilment of an order rather than on spec. Leaving Hare to do some tidying, he hurried from the house, up the close, and along West Port—to No. 26. That was the home of David Paterson, Dr. Knox's porter—a fact that indicates, if nothing else, that Paterson knew the identities of "John and William."

Paterson lived at 26 West Port with his mother and a teenaged sister, Elizabeth—who, answering Burke's knock, informed him that David was not yet back from work. Burke said that he would wait. Paterson arrived within a few minutes. According to his testimony at the trial, Burke told Paterson "he wanted me to go to his house."

Q. Did you go?

A. Yes.

Q. Did you find people there?

A. I found Burke and another man and two women.

Q. After you went in, what passed?

A. [Burke] told me he had procured something for the doctor, pointing to the head of the bed, where there was some straw; he said it in an under-voice. I was near him at the time.

Q. Was anything shewn to you at that time?

A. Nothing.

Q. What did you understand he meant?

A. I understood him to mean a dead body, a subject.

Q. What were his exact words?

A. His words were, "There is something for the doctor" (pointing to the straw) "which will be ready tomorrow morning."

Q. Was there sufficient straw to cover the body?

A. There was.

Q. Was that woman [Helen M'Dougal] there?

A. She was. . . .

Q. Do you know these people?

A. I know them by the name of Hare; they are the other persons that were at Burke's house that night. . . .

Q. What did you say to him when he called on you?

A. I told him if he had anything for Dr Knox, to go to himself and agree with him personally. I afterwards saw Burke and Hare in Dr Knox's rooms in Surgeons' Square, along with Dr [Thomas Wharton] Jones, one of Dr Knox's assistants. This was between twelve [midnight] and two.

Q. Did anything pass there?

A. Either Burke or Hare told Dr Knox they had a dead body for him, which they would deliver there the next night; and I had orders from Dr Knox to be in the way to receive it, or any parcel that might come.

Having quoted that testimony, I must say that I do not believe that Paterson told the whole truth. But I say that uncritically of him. The witness oath is only slightly more frightening to religious persons than to irreligious ones, whose earthly fear of it is that it will be used against them if they are caught out in a salient lie and prosecuted for perjury. Anyone in a situation similar to Paterson's would be as sparing of the truth as he was.

The morning after the night before began surprisingly early, considering that Burke and Hare cannot have got to their respective beds much before three. By 9 A.M. on that first day of November, they, their women, three of the people who had stayed until near the end of the party, and the Grays, full of apologies for the rowdiness that Burke had used as an excuse for getting rid of them, were drinking in his place. The last-mentioned five of the company were unaware that the body of Mary Docherty lay beneath the straw. Which does not mean that none of them commented on her apparent absence. When Mrs. Law enquired what had become of the "little woman," Helen M'Dougal snapped that she had "kicked the d——d b——h's backside out of the door," and, seeing that Mrs. Law expected some explanation of that action, went on to say that Mary Docherty had become "very fashous" [annoying]—"asking for warm water, then cold water, and then asking for a flannel clout and soap to wash herself with, to make her white." Perhaps thinking that that explanation sounded insufficient (or, more likely, that Mrs. Law may have been awoken by Mary's protesting at the trick), Helen added that, after the party, Burke and Hare had "begun a fighting," thereby causing Mary to "roar out murder"—which, the last straw so far as she, Helen, was concerned, had resulted in Mary's being "thrust out of the house, for an old Irish limmer [hussy]."

Ann Gray (who, incidentally, had a year-old baby; where it was all this time is as unreported, as are the whereabouts of Margaret Hare's even younger child) seems to have thought of getting back into her hosts' good books by doing some housework: not a lot—"I washed the floor and put a little sand on it." But by noon the place was messier than previously, partly because Burke had thrown whisky about, explaining that he "wanted to get quit of it to get more." Feeling peckish, he told Ann Gray to cook a pan of potatoes. However, when she went close to the pile of straw, meaning to reach under the bed for the potatoes, he shouted at her "to come out of that, as she might set the bed afire with her pipe." That being the second time he had ordered her away from the proximity of the straw, she took notice of it; and began thinking that either her memory was at fault or the pile had grown since Hallowe'en; and, long before five in the afternoon, was convinced that her memory was perfectly all right. But, until then, she was never left alone long enough to satisfy her curiosity as to how a pile of straw—which should, if anything, have slumped—had swollen. The coast at last clear, she rummaged.

The minute her husband returned from wherever he had been, she indicated her find. Picking up their few belongings (the baby too, presumably), they hurried from the room—only to meet Helen in the passage.

James Gray:

> I asked what was that she had got in the house; and she said, what was it? and I said, I suppose you know very well what it is. She fell on her knees in a supplicating attitude, imploring that I would not inform of what I had seen. She offered me some money, five or six shillings, to put me over till Monday; and there never would be a week after that but that I might be worth ten pounds a week. I said my conscience would not allow me to do it. She followed us; and when we got out to the street, we met Mrs Hare, and she enquired what we were making a noise about—and said, can't we go into the house, and decide our matters there, and not make a noise about them here.

Compromising, the Grays went with Margaret and Helen to a pub. There is little doubt that if they had gone back to the house, neither of them would have emerged alive. In the pub, while Margaret was spendthrift in buying rounds, Helen repeated the better of her offers to James and agreed wholeheartedly when Ann expressed concern at the disgrace that might fall upon their family. But after nearly an hour, James indicated to his wife that it was time to leave—and to all three women that he had decided that he must do The Right Thing.

As the Grays headed east, toward the police office next to St. Giles's Cathedral, Margaret and Helen scampered in search of their men. Burke, the first to be found, took immediate action: he too went east, hurriedly—to Allison's Close, off Cowgate, which was the home of a porter, John M'Culloch. He got M'Culloch to follow him back to the unnamed close. Hare had been found by the time they arrived. The three of them lifted the body from the straw and wedged it into the tea chest; M'Culloch, the heaviest, sat on the lid to press it down; the three tied ropes round the chest; Burke and Hare heaved it on to M'Culloch's shoulders. He set off. He did not need to be told his destination. Either the women did not want to let the partners out of their sight, or the partners felt that the women should not be left on their own to try and fool the police: whichever, all four hurried out of the close and followed the lumbering M'Culloch, catching up with him before he reached the end of West Port and crossed into Cowgate.

As that group continued on their way, just to the north of them, in the parallel High Street, a smaller group—made up of the Grays and a constable, John Findlay—set off in the direction of West Port.

The arrival of the latter group at Burke's place was observed by a young girl who helped Mrs. Law about her house. She told Constable Findlay of the recent comings and goings, mentioning in particular the final exodus, begun by a strange man carrying an obviously heavy tea chest. Findlay may have accepted the Grays' theory that the body they claimed to have seen had been removed in the chest—but still, he was perplexed as to what he should do next. In the end, he decided to do nothing other than "provide a police presence" until a superior officer turned up and told him what to do.

Meantime, the impromptu cortège reached 10 Surgeons' Square. The women waited outside while M'Culloch, at David Paterson's bidding, took his load to the basement, and Burke and Hare (no longer mere "John and William") learned from Paterson that they had a good reason to have an argument with him, and did so. The good reason was that Paterson, quite forgetting that they had made an appointment, had neglected to consider their cash-on-delivery requirement, and, its being a Saturday night, hardly ever a transacting time, was not carrying cash. M'Culloch, returning to ground level, discerned what the argument was about, heard from Burke or Hare that they could not pay him, and joined in. Paterson said, well, then, he would have to inconvenience Dr. Knox at his home.

He set off there, the three incommoded men following him, the two tut-tutting women following them: quite a journey—south from South Bridge, along Nicholson Street, along Clerk Street, and halfway down Newington to Newington Place, next to a cemetery larger than that of Greyfriars. He went into the doctor's house. Soon afterward emerging, he told the suppliers that the doctor had had, or could only spare, five pounds—which they would have to accept on account of the ten they were owed. He led the way to a local, bought drinks for himself and the retinue out of the fiver, and handed over the change—five shillings of which went to M'Culloch. The peculiar amount left must have needed complicated arithmetic so as to work out its three-way split, and, probably, the landlord's help in dividing the cash into its percentages of 50, 40, and 10—unless, of course, Margaret Hare for once forewent a share, and her husband, not wishing to display his difficulty with figure-work in so large a company, agreed to an easy 50–50.

Paterson went back to Surgeons' Square, M'Culloch left the others in Cowgate, the Hares bade adieu to Burke and Helen at the entrance to Tanner's Close, and the latter couple walked the few further steps to their home. The time, by then, was close to eight.

Shortly before, Constable Findlay had been reinforced by a superior officer, Sergeant Major John Fisher, who had only acknowledged his salute, not told him what to do, as he, the sergeant major, was intent on hearing what the Grays had to say.

He was still listening when the residents returned.

Sergeant Major Fisher:

I asked Burke what had become of his lodgers, and he said that there was one of them, pointing to James Gray, and that he had turned out him and his wife for their bad conduct. I then asked him what had become of the little woman that had been there on the Friday, the day before, and he said that she was away. And I asked, when did she leave the house, and he said, about seven o'clock in the morning. He said William Hare saw her go away. Then I asked, was there any other person saw her go away, and he said, in an insolent tone of voice, there were a number more.

I then looked to see if I could see any marks on the bed, and I saw the marks of blood on a number of things there; and I asked Helen M'Dougal how they came there, and she said that a woman had lain in there about a fortnight before, and the bed had not been washed since. She said, the little woman can be found, she lives in the Pleasance; and she said she had seen her that night in the Vennel, and that she had apologised to her for her bad conduct the night previous. I asked her then, what time the woman had left the house, and she said, seven o'clock at night.

Burke and Helen had not got their story straight enough. Burke: "seven o'clock in the morning"—Helen: "seven o'clock at night." Noting that discrepancy, the sergeant major reckoned that he had cause to take them to the police office; but he was most polite in saying so, telling them "that it was all personal spite [on the part of the Grays]—that he must take them to the office, as he had been sent down."

And so, on this evening that had already seen the making of several pedestrian groups, yet another was made, its composition representative of all of its predecessors: two policemen (the junior one of whom should have been told by the other to stay on guard, even if that had meant the impolite use of both of their sets of handcuffs), the accusing Grays, and the couple who, if only one of them during their tale-tallying had considered that seven o'clock struck twice a day, might well have fooled the senior policeman away from a decision to make the group. Burke, though, swaggered to the police office, for he was confident of the fable that a murder charge depends upon the finding of a body; and Helen, taken in by her man's panache, did her best to swagger too.

At the police office, the couple were interviewed by a superintendent. The sergeant major listened to the first few minutes of the exchange, and then strolled back to Burke's place. Before he was joined there by the superintendent and a police surgeon, Dr. Black, he talked with Mrs. Law, she having come from across the close to suggest that he should. At one point, she altered the course of their conversation, for her gaze had been caught by something on the bed that, strangely enough, no one seems to have noticed until then: a red-and-white striped bedgown. Mrs. Law was convinced that it was the little woman's. The sergeant major agreed with Mrs. Law—and, later, the superintendent agreed with the sergeant major—that if the little woman had gone of her own volition, whether at 7 A.M. or at 7 P.M., the recent continuously chilly weather would have reminded her not to leave her bedgown behind.

The official version of two important events that occurred early next morning, which was Sunday, keeps them separate and in this order:

First, a crowd of policemen entered 10 Surgeons' Square, and some of them went to the basement, unroped a tea chest, and emptied it of the body of a little woman (subsequently recognised as Mary Docherty by several people, Mrs. Law among them).

Second—at eight o'clock—fewer policemen entered Log's lodging-house, roused the Hares (who, once fully awake and informed of the reason for the call, acted astonished), got them to put on the rest of their clothes, and took them to the police office, where they were lodged in separate cells, away from the separate cells of Burke and Helen M'Dougal.

Now, I believe that the officially second event occurred before the officially first event. And I believe that there was a cause-and-effect relationship between them—that something said by one or both of the Hares led to the apparently warrantless raiding of 10 Surgeons' Square. Why else should the police have picked on that place, one among dozens of schools of anatomy? Indeed, why should the police have picked on any school of anatomy? All that they are officially said to have known prior to the raid is that a little woman had disappeared in mysterious, probably sinister, circumstances; that if she was dead, her body had probably been carried away in a tea chest; that Burke and his woman had probably made lying statements; that Hare—referred to by Burke simply as a witness to the truthfulness of the same part of each of his statements (the first to the sergeant major, the second to the superintendent), and by Helen M'Dougal similarly, though only in her statement to the superintendent—was probably guilty of *some*thing if Burke and his woman were guilty of *any*thing; that if Mrs. Law's juvenile helpmate had observed efficiently, both of the Hares, Burke, and Helen M'Dougal had left the close soon after an unknown man carrying a now-suspicious chest had set off for an unknown destination. The police had not yet identified the carrier as John M'Culloch—and so had not learned the destination from him. Mrs. Law knew nothing of the Burke & Hare business partnership—and so had not given the sergeant major any clue pointing even in an eeny-meeny-miney-mo fashion to the schools of anatomy, let alone directly to Dr. Knox's establishment.

Yet that was where the policemen chose to call. Maybe those policemen had no connection with the policemen at the St. Giles office: it has happened (most notably in recent times in England toward the downfall of the mass-murdering "Black Panther," Donald Neilson) that policemen working on one case have stumbled upon evidence vital to the solution of another case that they knew little or nothing about. Excepting such serendipity, Dr. Knox's establishment was raided because of something said by one or both of the Hares.

❧

Edinburgh, as well as being a centre of anatomical excellence, was renowned for the study and practice of other medical disciplines: pathology was one—its fairly recent offshoot, forensic pathology, another. A simple but sure way of telling whether a forensic pathologist is good or suspect lies in the fact that good forensic pathologists are sometimes unable to arrive at the firm conclusions that their employers would like. Robert Christison, professor of medical jurisprudence at Edinburgh University, who "minutely examined" the body of Mary Docherty at the St. Giles's police office, starting on the Sunday and continuing the next day, found many signs suggesting that she had been murdered—but none that permitted him to go farther than saying that murder was a "probability."

The reports of the case in Monday's papers failed to live up to their headlines. In the *Edinburgh Evening Courant*, for instance, "Extraordinary Occurence" was followed by a report so replete with innuendo that most people who read it must have read it again in the forlorn hope of fathoming what made the occurrence extraordinary.

But never mind—the public's mystification encouraged and assisted rumourmongers, and long before the day was out, people were turning up at police offices—not just in Edinburgh, though mainly there, but throughout Scotland, even south of the border—either to give accounts of their own miraculous escapes from the murderers of West Port or to explain why they were convinced of the fate of missing friends or relatives. Most of those people went away dissatisfied with their reception. There were at least two, however, whose information was seized upon.

Janet Brown, who can never have imagined that she would enter a police office of her own accord, told of the disappearance of her friend and colleague, Mary Paterson. She impressed whoever it was she told by giving the names and addresses of the women associated with her profession who could corroborate parts of her narrative. Taken first to Constantine Burke's house, the interior of which she had already described, she accused both Constantine and his wife of having provided the scene of a crime (they, like several other of the partners' occasional helpers, were arrested on suspicion); and taken second to William Burke's place, she sorted from a mess of old clothes a number of items that she said were Mary's.

The mother of Daft Jamie Wilson appears to have suggested that he was a victim after lots of persons unrelated to him had made the same suggestion: perhaps, if she had been more prompt, arriving before her son's nickname was scribbled on many police memos, no one would have paid much attention to her. Taken to Burke's place—which, by then, was awkward to reach, for West Port was clogged with sight-seers—she picked out some garments that she thought were Jamie's, and a snuff-spoon that she was sure was his.

During the first fortnight of the investigation, Burke and Helen M'Dougal each fell into the trap of agreeing to make far longer and more detailed statements than the slight ones they had made just be-fore and shortly after their arrest. There had been only one discrep-ancy between their slight statements, but the more they talked, the more the discrepancies grew. The Hares also made further statements during this period—but, for a reason that will instantly appear, what they said was never publicly divulged.

During the second fortnight, the Hares received word from the lord advocate, the law officer who had the final say as to whether or not prosecutions were to be brought, that if they agreed to "peach" against the other couple, they would be granted immunity from prosecution—would get off scot-free. (Though the "proposal" was put to Hare alone, it obviously applied to his wife as well.) I believe that the *if* was a legal fiction—that the Hares had been peaching (or, to use the present-day expression, singing) for quite some time, probably from when, if my previous belief is correct, one or both of them had said something that sent the police to 10 Surgeons' Square. Subsequently, spokesmen for the lord advocate tried to gloss his decision to let the Hares turn king's evidence by saying that he was faced with a "some-or-none" predica-ment: there was insufficient evidence against the Hares to guarantee their conviction, and without their evidence against Burke and Helen M'Dougal, both of *them* might be acquitted. One can punch so many holes into that excuse that it finishes up as watertight as a colander. Unfortunately, one cannot be astonished at the most gaping of the holes, punched with the fact that the combined weight of the Hares' guilt was greater than the combined weight of the guilt of Burke and Helen M'Dougal—for though the Hares certainly deserve to be called "The First of the 'Supergrasses,'" they were no more super than many of their present-day successors, whose "songs" are about people they hired to help with crimes that came unstuck.

༼

Whether by accident (caused by a logjam in the High Court of Justiciary's calendar) or by design (prompted by a desire to have things over and done with before the festive season, thus giving a sort of present to the populace), the trial began at 10:15 A.M. on Christmas Eve, a Wednesday, the intention being to have verdicts before the day was out. Those in charge feared that rowdies might take the law into their unskilled hands, and so, the night before, three hundred policemen were brought into Edinburgh from constabularies round about; leave was stopped for infantrymen at the Castle and cavalrymen at the barracks of Piershill; the defendants and the two protected witnesses were transported—each in a separate covered wagon, each wagon flanked by armed outriders—from Calton Gaol, at the east of the New Town, to the venue of the trial, Parliament House, behind St. Giles's Cathedral.

A reporter would write, not once with tongue in cheek, that

> it was not so much to the accounts published in the newspapers, which merely embodied and gave greater currency to the statements circulating in society, as to the extraordinary, nay, unparalleled circumstances of the case, that the strong excitement of the public mind ought to be ascribed. These were without any precedent in the records of our criminal practice, and, in fact, amounted to the realisation of a nursery tale.
>
> The recent deplorable increase of crime has made us familiar with several new atrocities. Poisoning is now, it seems, rendered subsidiary to the commission of theft: stabbings, and attempts at assassination, are matters of almost everyday occurrence: and murder has grown so familiar to us that it has almost ceased to be viewed with that instinctive and inexpressible dread which the commission of the greatest crime against the laws of God and society used to excite.[16]

16. Did that sentence appeal to Thomas De Quincey (who was then living in Edinburgh) and prompt him toward his famous comments: "If once a man indulges himself in murder, very soon he comes to think little of robbing; and from robbing he comes next to drinking and Sabbath-breaking, and from that to incivility and procrastination. Once begin upon this downward path, you never know where you are to stop. Many a man has dated his ruin from some murder or other that perhaps he thought little of at the time"? Those comments appear in the "Supplementary Paper on Murder, Considered as One of the Fine Arts," which was published in *Blackwood's Magazine* (Edinburgh) of November 1839, and which speaks nostalgically of "the sublime epoch of Burkism and Harism."

But the present was the first instance of murder alleged to have been perpetrated with the aforethought purpose and intent of selling the murdered body as a subject for dissection to anatomists: it was a new species of assassination, or murder for hire: and as such, no less than from the general horror felt by the people of this country at the process, from ministering to which the murderers expected their reward, it was certainly calculated to make a deep impression on the public mind, and to awaken feelings of strong and appalling interest in the issue of the trial.

Of the extent of the impression thus produced, and the feelings thus awakened, it was easy to judge from what was everywhere observable on Monday and Tuesday. The approaching trial formed the universal topic of conversation, and all sorts of speculations and conjectures were afloat as to the circumstances likely to be disclosed in the course of it, and the various results to which it would eventually lead. As the day drew near, the interest deepened; and it was easy to see that the common people shared strongly in the general excitement. The coming trial, they expected, was to disclose something which they had often dreamed of, or imagined, or heard recounted around an evening's fire, like a tale of horror, or a raw-head-and-bloody-bones story, but which they never, in their sober judgment, either feared or believed to be possible; and hence, they looked forward to it with corresponding but indescribable emotions. In short, all classes participated more or less in a common feeling respecting the case of this unhappy man and his associate; all expected fearful disclosures; none, we are convinced, wished for anything but justice. . . .

So early as seven o'clock in the morning of Wednesday, a considerable crowd had assembled in the Parliament Square and around the doors of the Court; and numerous applications for admission were made to the different subordinate functionaries, but in vain. The individuals connected with the press were conducted to the seats provided for them a little before eight o'clock; the members of the Faculty[17] and of the Society of Writers to the Signet[18] were admitted precisely at nine; and thus, with the jurymen impannelled, and a few individuals who had obtained the

17. "Faculty" refers to "The Faculty of Advocates in Scotland."
18. The Society of Writers to the Signet is oldest body of law practitioners in Scotland; their duties correspond to those of solicitors in England.

entrée by virtue of orders from the Judges, the Court became at once crowded in every part.

About twenty minutes before ten o'clock, the prisoners were placed at the bar. The male prisoner was dressed in a shabby blue surtout [greatcoat], buttoned close to the throat, a striped cotton waistcoat, and dark-coloured small clothes. The female prisoner was miserably dressed in a small stone-coloured silk bonnet, very much the worse for the wear, a printed cotton shawl, and a cotton gown. Both prisoners, especially Burke, entered the Court without any visible sign of perturbation, and both seemed to attend very closely to the proceedings which soon after commenced.

The Judges present were the Right Honourable the Lord Justice Clerk [Lord Boyle] and Lords Pitmilly, Meadowbank, and Mackenzie. Their Lordships having taken their seats, the Lord Justice Clerk said: William Burke and Helen M'Dougal, pay attention to the indictment that is now to be read against you.

But that was the cue for the first delay. Patrick Robertson, one of Burke's four counsel (all instructed by an agent for the poor), objected to the reading of the indictment, explaining, "It contains charges which I hope to be able to show your Lordships are incompetent, and the reading of the whole of the libel must tend materially to prejudice the prisoners at the bar." Henry Cockburn, the senior counsel of Helen M'Dougal's four (also instructed by the aforementioned agent), made a similar objection.[19] Both were turned down by Lord Meadowbank, who growled that he was "against novelties"—whereupon the clerk of court read an indictment which charged both prisoners with the murder of Mary Docherty, and Burke alone with the murders of Mary Paterson and Daft Jamie Wilson.

That over, Patrick Robertson presented defences against the indictment—a task in which he was eventually assisted by his leader, Sir

19. Cockburn was the greatest Scots lawyer of his time—some would say of all time—Cockburn was near fifty when he defended Helen M'Dougal. For the past fifteen years, he had appeared as counsel for prisoners—most of them of his own Whig persuasion—who were accused of political offences. In 1834 he was appointed, as Lord Cockburn, a judge of the court of session, and three years later he became a lord of justiciary. He contributed many articles to magazines, particularly the *Edinburgh Review*. His journals were published posthumously—as *Memorials of His Time* (Edinburgh, 1856); also *Journals of Henry Cockburn* (2 volumes; Edinburgh, 1874) and *Circuit Journeys* (Edinburgh, 1889), which is the wonderfully entertaining record of his judicial travels from the autumn of 1837 until a few days before his death in the spring of 1854.

James Moncrieff, the dean of faculty.[20] The defences were that Burke ought not to be tried on one occasion for three "unconnected" murders, and that his trial ought not to be combined with that of Helen M'Dougal, "who was not even alleged to have any concern with two of the offences of which he was accused." The second of those defences against the indictment was echoed by Henry Cockburn—his ground being that "the accumulation of panels [Scots for "defendants"] and of offences . . . exposed his client to intolerable prejudice."

The Lord Advocate, Sir William Rae—he who had authorised immunity for the Hares, and who now led three advocate-deputes for the prosecution—fought long and hard to keep the indictment intact; but the judges decided that, though the precedents he quoted were as good as those quoted on behalf of the prisoners, the prosecution should be restricted to one charge: if the jury failed to convict on that, the lord advocate could "proceed *seriatim* on the other acts that were not that day to be tried."[21] Not managing to hide his anger, Sir William said that as he was "tied down to proceed with the trial of one of the crimes," he would choose "the third case libelled" (Mary Docherty): "On that footing, there seems nothing to prevent my proceeding against the woman as well as against the man. She can suffer no prejudice in now being brought to trial for the single act on which she is charged as art and part guilty along with Burke."

The deal struck with the Hares had become a very poor one from the lord advocate's bureaucratic point of view; and, since he was supposed to be a guardian of justice as well as a tactician of the law, an even worse deal so far as the people of Scotland were concerned. In the case of the murder of Mary Docherty, there was very nearly as much evidence against William Hare as there was against his ex-partner—more evidence against William Hare than there was against Helen M'Dougal—about the same amount of evidence against Helen M'Dougal as there was against Margaret Hare. The inequities were apparent. They would be turned to the benefit of one of the defendants.

The judges' diminishing of the indictment, unaccompanied by a single understanding word as to the practical problems that raised for the lesser members of the prosecution team, must have sent those members into a frenzy of activity while a jury (the Scottish fifteen) was

---

20. Moncrieff was the president of the Faculty of Advocates in Scotland.

21. Rae, by the way, was an intimate friend of Sir Walter Scott; he is referred to as "Dear loved Rae" in the introduction to the fourth canto of *Marmion*.

being selected from among the forty-five men ordered to be available as representatives of the various areas within the judicial region—the City of Edinburgh, the Town of Leith, and the Counties of Edinburgh, Linlithgow, and Haddington. The occupations of the selected jurymen were as follows: agent, banker, builder (two such), brewer, cooper, engraver, grocer (three), ironmonger, manager of the Hercules Insurance Company, merchant (three—one of them being John M'fie, of Leith, who was chosen as chancellor: in most other English-speaking countries he would have been called the foreman of the jury).

In the expectation of three counts to the indictment, the prosecution had arranged for fifty-five witnesses to be on hand—including six associated with 10 Surgeons' Square: Robert Knox, three of his graduates who had stayed on as assistants (Thomas Wharton Jones, William Fergusson, Alexander Miller), a student (James Evans—was he the "tall lad" who recognised Mary Paterson?), and David Paterson. The winnowing of the witnesses who had become irrelevant left eighteen, of whom only one, David Paterson, was associated with 10 Surgeons' Square.

Though that drastic reduction meant a shortening of the testimonial part of the proceedings, that part had been delayed for two hours by the legal argument that had resulted in the reduction—and so the judges were concerned that if they didn't keep things moving, virtually uninterrupted by adjournments, they might still be on the bench when they were supposed to be in their pews for the Christmas morning service at St. Giles's.

With no breaks for airings of the courtroom, its atmosphere soon became stagnant—prompting the lord justice clerk to order the opening of a large window, an act that alleviated the stench at the expense of warmth; spectating advocates and Writers to the Signet wrapped their gowns round their heads—"giving to the visages that were enshrouded under them," it occurred to a reporter, "such a grim and grisly aspect as assimilated them to a college of Monks or Inquisitors, or characters imagined in tales of romance."

At four in the afternoon, no refreshments having been provided, "Burke asked when he would get dinner, and being informed it would be about six, begged that he might have a biscuit or two, as he would lose his appetite before that time. Both panels ate bread and soup heartily; and although they displayed no external marks of inward emotion, they frequently, especially the woman, took copious draughts of water"—which presumably means that some kind of latrine was discreet within the dock.

It may be that, though the panels must really have been hungry and thirsty, they exaggerated their relief with the intention of showing their contempt for the witnessing Hares and in the hope of putting them off their respective strokes. The judges' disregard of normal mealtimes—as well as of most normal meals—means that one has little help toward the assessment of when particular witnesses were called. Hare was the fifteenth witness, his wife the sixteenth. The previous witnesses were, in order of appearance, a surveyor (who proved his plans of the unnamed close), a woman with whom Mary Docherty had stayed on the night before Hallowe'en, and a man who was a lodger in the same house on the same night (both the landlady and the lodger had subsequently identified the body), David Rymer's shopboy, three residents of the unnamed close, David Paterson's sister, Paterson himself, another resident of the unnamed close, Ann and James Gray, John M'Culloch (who, lacking immunity, was carefully laconic regarding his porterage of the body), and Sergeant Major John Fisher. Going only by the fact that the number of transcript pages devoted to the evidence of those fourteen witnesses is about the same as the number of pages that report questions, answers, and legal arguments during Hare's turning of king's evidence, it seems likely that he took the stand late in the afternoon.

His entrance produced a great sensation in the Court.

LORD JUSTICE CLERK: You understand that it is only with regard to [Mary Docherty] that you are now to speak? *To this question the witness replied by asking, "T'ould woman, Sir?"*

LORD JUSTICE CLERK: Yes.

LORD ADVOCATE: You are a native of Ireland, Hare? *A.* Yes.

How long have you been in this country? *A.* Ten years.

LORD JUSTICE CLERK: Are you a Roman Catholic? *A.* Yes.

Do you wish to be sworn in any other way than that now administered by my brother? *A.* I never was sworn before, Sir, and I am no judge of that.

(The New Testament was handed to the witness.)

LORD MEADOWBANK: Now, you will observe that there is a representation of the Cross on the book of the New Testament; lay your right hand upon the Cross, and repeat the words of the oath after me.

(The witness was sworn in this manner.)

The examination-in-chief went pretty well as the lord advocate had hoped and planned. But he sat down without relief, alert to every question from Henry Cockburn, every answer from Hare. Cockburn began the cross-examination most politely, prefixing the first question "Mr. Hare." That question and the following four were to do with Hare's legitimate occupations since his arrival in Scotland. The sixth, "Have you been engaged in supplying bodies to the doctors?" was answered "Yes." The seventh, put just as politely—perhaps intentionally phrased confusingly—was, "Have you been connected in supplying the doctors with subjects upon other occasions than those you have not spoken to yet?"

According to some reports of the trial, Hare replied, "No—than what I have mentioned"; according to others, he had no chance to reply before the lord advocate, speaking as he jumped to his feet, said, "I object to this course of examination."

At Cockburn's request, the witness was withdrawn. Then Cockburn fought against the objection: "I may as well explain at once that I hold myself entitled to ask this gentleman to reveal his whole life. In particular, I mean to ask him this specific question: 'Have you ever been concerned in murders beside this one?' I am ready to admit that he is not bound to answer; but I am entitled to put that question, let him answer it or not as he pleases. It will be for the jury to judge of the credit due to him after seeing how he treats it."

For half an hour, Cockburn—with Burke's Sir James Moncrieff joining in—argued one way, the lord advocate the other. And the judges argued between themselves. The point at issue was made nicer by the fact that the judges had already agreed that Burke should not be prejudiced by being tried on one occasion for more than one murder. Cockburn won.

The witness was recalled.

COCKBURN: Hare [*no "Mr." now, or ever afterward*], you mentioned when last here that you were concerned in supplying the medical lecturers with subjects. Did you assist in taking the body of the old woman to Surgeons' Square? *A.* Yes.

Were you ever concerned in carrying any other body to any surgeon?
A. I never was concerned in furnishing none, but I saw them do it.

LORD JUSTICE CLERK: You are not bound to answer the question about to be put.

COCKBURN: Hare, I am going to put a very few questions to you, and you need not answer them unless you please. . . . Now, Hare, you told me a little ago that you had been concerned in furnishing one subject to the doctors, and you had seen them doing it. How often have you seen them doing it? (*The witness said nothing.*) Do you decline answering that question? *A.* Yes.

Now, sir, I am going to ask this question, which you need not answer unless you please—Was that of the old woman the first murder that you had been concerned in? (*The witness said nothing.*) Do you choose to answer or not to answer? *A.* Not to answer.

I am going to ask another question which you need not answer unless you like—Was there murder committed in your house in the last October? (*The witness said nothing.*) Do you choose to answer that or not? *A.* Not answer that.

You mentioned that Burke came and told you that he had got a "shot" for the doctors, and that you understood that that meant that he intended to murder that woman or somebody? *A.* That was his meaning.

How did you understand that? Was that a common phrase amongst you? *A.* Amongst him.

And so it went on. Cockburn was happier when Hare refused to answer then when he did. The silences added up to a loud admission of guilt. Reading the full transcript of the cross-examination of Hare, one is struck by a feeling of déjà vu, for it seems like a trial run for the presently familiar exhibitions given by witnesses before U.S. House Committees who have been granted only partial immunity from prosecution or who make the monotonous most of the one thing they respect about the Constitution, which is that there is a Fifth Amendment to it.

A moment after Hare was led from the court by an usher (in Scots legal parlance, a macer), another usher led his wife to the witness box. There being no creche in Parliament House, she held her baby daughter in her arms. The child had whooping cough—brought on, probably, by the dampness of Calton Gaol—and, according to Henry Cockburn, "its every paroxysm fired her [Margaret] with intenser anger and impatience"; others, however, suspected that she initiated some of the whooping, by slyly tweaking the child under cover of the swaddling clothes, either to give herself a noisy time in which to consider awkward questions or to hinder the jury's hearing of answers of hers that she was not altogether happy with. The lord advocate may occasionally have wished that he had a remote-control tweaker: for instance, when, in answer to a question he posed as to what had gone through her mind when, late on Hallowe'en, she—and Helen—returned to the room and saw no sign of Mary Docherty, she replied, "I had a supposition that the old woman had been murdered"—*and added:* "I have seen such tricks before."

Apparently it had been arranged between the two sets of defenders that Cockburn should do the whole of the cross-examination of Hare, Moncrieff the whole cross-examination of his wife. Although Moncrieff was almost up to Cockburn's standard as a speech maker, he lacked the agility of mind that went toward Cockburn's brilliance as a questioner: he had prepared a script of what Margaret Hare had to be asked, and, ignoring opportunities she gave for improvisation, stuck to it. She agreed with him that she had said, in examination-in-chief, that when she and Hare first went to Burke's place on the night of the murder, Mary Docherty was there. Then:

Was Burke not in when you went in there? *A.* I am not sure.
Did he go in a little after? *A.* I do not recollect whether he was in, or
    whether he came in or not. I have a very bad memory.

Think what Cockburn would have done with that last comment! If Moncrieff, doing the very least, raised his eyebrows at it, the movement was not noticed by any of the reporters who peered through the gloaming of the courtroom to catch something visual to write about. The only thing they noted was that Moncrieff, asking no further questions, sat down. All in all, Margaret Hare—and the lord advocate—got off far more lightly than they deserved.

Just two more witnesses, both doctors: Alexander Black, the police surgeon, and Robert Christison, the forensic pathologist. Then the statements of each of the panels, admitted by their respective counsel, were read aloud.

That ended the case for the prosecution.

You may need to be reminded that, in those days, defendants were not allowed to speak for themselves. As neither Burke nor Helen M'Dougal brought forward "exculpatory evidence," the lord advocate straightway began his closing speech. About an hour before, across the yard from Parliament House, the bellmen of St. Giles's Cathedral had rung in Christmas.

Rae devoted the centre of his speech to his decision to let the Hares turn king's evidence, saying, inter alia,

> It is naturally revolting to see such criminals escape even the punishment of human laws; but this must be borne, in order to avoid greater evils; and it may form some consolation to reflect that such an example of treachery, by a *socius criminis,* must tend to excite universal distrust among men concerned in similar crimes, if any such should hereafter exist. Fortunately for the safety of life, a crime of this nature cannot, in all its details, be accomplished without assistance; and nothing can be more calculated to deter men from its commission than the probability of the perpetrators readily betraying each other.

Rae finished soon after three in the morning.

Now it was Moncrieff's turn.

Speaking loudly, in the hope of keeping the jurymen awake, he apologised to them in advance for the length of his address. "We have been sitting here, gentlemen, about seventeen hours. . . . But when you consider that the lives of these prisoners are in your hands, I am sure I need say nothing more to entitle me to your utmost indulgence while I submit to you the observations which appear to me to be material on behalf of the prisoner Burke." Meaning to swerve their minds from the rumours they must have heard since All Hallows', he spoke to them as if confident that, by a kind of magic, their taking of the juror's oath had made them, each and as a group, more critical of conjecture than other Scotsmen and groups of Scotsmen. And he tried to persuade them that there was nothing very special about the charge:

> Gentlemen, this case may be represented as anomalous and unprecedented in some views of it; but I must beg your attention . . . to this plain view of the matter—that the thing of which this prisoner is accused is simply and singly murder. There is no

aggravation, and no other crime or offence charged; and when, therefore, it is supposed that this case is of an extraordinary and unprecedented nature, this can only refer to the motive by which it is said the prisoners were actuated in committing the murder. But what does that amount to but that the motive was a miserable gain? There is surely nothing anomalous or unprecedented in that. A vast proportion of murders of which we hear are committed from the same motive of gain—to conceal robbery, or escape in housebreaking. And what difference does it make to the crime of wilful murder, whether the motive be to rob a man of his watch or a few shillings, or to sell his body for a few pounds?

Rae had done his best to give credence to the Hares' testimony; Moncrieff had the easier task of discrediting it:

What is there to restrain them from telling the most deliberate series of falsehoods? . . . Hare is a person who tells you that, for the paltry object of a few pounds, he was leagued with another to destroy a fellow creature; and when he is asked if he had ever committed other murders, *declines to answer the question.* That is the person that comes before you this day—and he comes, not with the motive of a few shillings or pounds, but the tremendous motive of saving himself from an ignominious death, which the law would inflict upon him if he did commit these horrible crimes. . . . Just change the position of the parties, and suppose that Mr Hare was at the bar, and Burke in the witness box. I do not know what case you might get from Burke or M'Dougal; but nothing could hinder them from making as clear a case against Hare and his wife, totally transposing the facts, and exhibiting the transaction as altogether the reverse of what Hare says it is.

Moncrieff finished about five in the morning.

It would not be surprising if some members of the jury, desperate for sleep, for refreshment, for relief from the cramping and numbing, had cried out in anguish at the sight of Henry Cockburn pulling himself to his feet—at being reminded, or realising, that the two conflicting speeches they had survived were to be followed by a third, presumably not much different from the second. Maybe there were some muted wails—causing Cockburn to begin by saying, "Considering the hour, I will not hasten, but hurry over, the facts and the views upon which I feel the firmest conviction that you can pronounce no verdict, so far as the female prisoner is concerned, but one that will declare that the charge against her has not been proven."

Until now, the two sets of defenders had worked in concert, their respective spokesmen trying to avoid saying anything that they knew the others preferred to be said only by the speaking prosecutors. When Cockburn departed from the arrangement, he did so discreetly, inserting a remark that Moncrieff must have appreciated, and making it seem that he was not so much deserting Burke's defenders as welcoming the prosecutors to his side:

> In stating these facts and views, I shall assume—though in the face of the admirable address which you have just heard, I cannot admit—first, that there was a murder committed, and second, that it was committed by the prisoner Burke. Still I maintain that there is not sufficient credible evidence to convict this woman. And if you know how to interpret the pleadings of counsel as well as we do, you would have seen perfectly well that the Lord Advocate himself feels that there is a most material difference between the cases of the two panels.

After quoting authorities on what did and did not make a person accessory to a crime, Cockburn ingeniously drew conclusions from certain facts. No doubt he would have been less daringly ingenious if the jury, the judges, and the prosecutors had been more alert. Certainly, he would not have risked a particularly audacious theory, which went as follows: one of the neighbour-witnesses had spoken of hearing, late on Hallowe'en, a woman's shouts of "Murder!" and "Police!"—they intermingled with sounds like "the stifled moans of an animal suffocating"; the intermingling, said Cockburn, showed that the shouting woman was not the moaning woman—ergo, said Cockburn, the shouting woman was none other than Helen M'Dougal, she doing her utmost either to prevent a murder or to broadcast the news that murder was being done.

Cockburn exhausted was a better advocate than his closest rival just back from holiday. Anyone else, after twenty hours of thought and talk and questioning and acting, would surely have started to search for words, to stumble over them: he became stronger still—began to rage, but was always in control of the rage.

I believe, gentlemen, that if you will ransack both your notes and your memories, you will find no material circumstances, independently of those mentioned by the accomplices, against the female prisoner. Before coming to the testimony of the accomplices, I should wish you to ask yourselves whether these circumstances form *sufficient* evidence against her. I apprehend that they not only don't form sufficient evidence, but that they form absolutely no evidence at all. . . . Accordingly, the prosecutor *concurs* with us in thinking that, without the accomplices, he has no case. His Lordship has pretended, indeed, to argue otherwise. But his own conduct establishes what his real conviction is. It is always the duty of the public prosecutor to bring the guilty to trial when he can. He has no right to take culprits from the bar and place them in the box unnecessarily; and, therefore, the very fact that an accomplice has been made a witness is a proof that, in the opinion of the public accuser, he could not do without them. If the prosecutor's statement be true, these two accomplices were the property of the gibbet. Why, then, has justice been robbed of their lives? Because the Lord Advocate tells you that their being made witnesses was "a *necessary* sacrifice.". . .

Really, gentlemen, we give the prosecutor a most *un*necessary and unjust advantage when we talk of the credibility of these his *necessary* witnesses, and allow them to work up every circumstance according to their own pleasure. I cannot form the idea of any jury's being satisfied with less evidence than what the accuser thinks indispensable. Our learned friend who prosecutes here has demonstrated by his conduct that he is satisfied that you ought not to convict without the evidence of the associates; and thus we are absolutely driven to consider what credit is due to those witnesses. If you shall agree with me in thinking that it is an absolute sporting with men's lives, and converting evidence into a mockery, to give the slightest faith to anything that these persons may say, then we have the authority of the public accuser himself for holding that you must acquit. . . .

The prosecutor seemed to think that they gave their evidence in a credible manner, and that there was nothing in their appearance beyond what may be expected in that of any great criminal, to impair the probability of their story. I entirely differ from this; and I am perfectly satisfied that so do you. A couple of such witnesses, in point of mere external manner and appearance, never did my eyes behold. Hare was a squalid wretch—on whom the habits of his disgusting trade, want, and profligacy seem to have been long operating, in order to produce a monster whose will, as well as his poverty, will consent to the perpetration of the direst crimes. The Lord Advocate's back was to the woman, else he would not have professed to have seen nothing revolting in her appearance. I never saw a face in which the lines of profligacy were more distinctly marked. . . .

It is said that they are corroborated. Corroborated! These witnesses corroborated!! In the first place, I do not understand how such witnesses admit of being corroborated. If the prosecutor has a case without them, let him say so. But if he has not—if something material must depend upon these witnesses—it is in vain to talk of corroboration; because, in truth, the thing to be corroborated does not exist. You may corroborate a *doubtful* testimony—but the idea of confirming the lies of these miscreants is absurd. The only way to deal with them is to deduct their testimony altogether. It is like corroborating a dream. The fiction and the reality may possibly be both alike—but this accidental concurrence does not make the one stronger than the other.

It was close to quarter to eight when Cockburn—his throat raw by now, making his normal way of rolling the letter R more guttural—paused for a moment and then launched into the peroration of his great speech: a plea to the jury that they should be "completely deaf to the cry of the public for a victim"—

The time will come when these prejudices will die away. In that hour, you will have to recollect whether you this day yielded to them or not—a question which you cannot answer to the satisfaction of your own minds unless you can then recall, or at least are certain that you now feel, legal grounds for convicting this woman, after deducting all the evidence of the Hares and all your extrajudicial impressions.

If you have such evidence, convict her.

If you have *not,* your safest course is to find that the libel is not proven.

The lord justice clerk summed up, taking three-quarters of an hour about it, and the jury retired to consider their verdicts at half past eight, as daylight greyed the court.

Reports say that the stubbled masses of spectators in the public enclosure stayed glued to the seats that they had occupied, most of them, for more than twenty-four hours; the substances of the gluing are nowhere intimated at.

Some of the same reports say that Burke was so confident that Helen M'Dougal would be found guilty too that he gave her directions as to how she should behave when the chancellor of the jury spoke of her, and "desired her to look at and observe him" when the Lord Justice Clerk was passing sentence.

Other reports say that the crowd outside Parliament House was almost as dense as, and more unruly than, the crowd that had littered the forecourt till late on Christmas Eve.

Fifty minutes went by.

Then, at 9:20, the jury returned.

The chancellor, John M'Fie, announced the verdicts—

Burke: *Guilty.*

M'Dougal: *Not Proven.*

Applause broke out—noisy enough to be heard in the forecourt, where the crowd, though not knowing what was being applauded, joined in.

Helen burst into tears. One can be sure of that. But if the applause was as instantaneous, as thunderous, as all the courtroom reports say it was, one can only accept what the reporters claimed that Burke murmured to her by assuming that a reporter who could lipread did so and was generous enough to communicate the reading to his rivals: *"Nelly, you are out of the scrape."*

The dozen participating advocates—three quartets—were too tired to show much interest in the scene. Moncrieff shook hands with Cockburn. Rae concentrated on making his papers tidy. If he still believed that he was right to have employed the Hares, the subsequent information that the verdict against Burke was not unanimous—that two jurors had held out for Not Proven in his case—must have dented that belief. The two jurors' uncertainty could only have been raised on moral grounds.

As was the custom—ludicrous if a sentence was mandatory—the highest judge had to call upon another to propose the sentence. Lord Meadowbank having, at considerable length, proposed that Burke should be hanged and his body given for dissection, the lord justice clerk, black-capped meanwhile, told Burke that the proposal was accepted and, departing from the mandatory on behalf of poetic justice, added, "I trust that if it is ever customary to preserve skeletons, yours will be preserved in order that posterity may keep in remembrance your atrocious crimes." Yes: *crimes.* Though Burke had been found guilty of only one, Lord Boyle had no doubt that he had committed others as atrocious.

The black cap removed, his Lordship told Helen M'Dougal,

> The jury have found the libel against you Not Proven—they have not pronounced you Not Guilty of the crime of murder charged against you in this indictment. You know whether you have been in the commission of this atrocious crime. I leave it to your own conscience to draw the proper conclusion. I hope and trust that you will betake yourself to a new line of life, diametrically opposite from that which you have led for a number of years.

Less as a kindness to her than because the authorities were anxious to avoid breaches of the peace such as lynchings, she was taken with Burke to the jail. For the same precautionary reason, the Hares had been returned to the jail as soon as the lord advocate had begun his closing speech. It may have crossed some civil servant's mind that Robert Knox also was at risk; but the only precaution arranged in that regard was the stationing of two constables, one within sight of Knox's house, the other on the doorstep of 10 Surgeons' Square.

The hanging of Burke was scheduled for 28 January. Until then, the daily papers were always able to report incidents relating to the case; for some of the stories, particularly those given a "Mob Disturbance" sort of headline, the reporters were indebted to editorialists for having fomented them.

No later, apparently, than the early evening of the day after the trial, Burke handed a warder his pocket watch and the remains of his share of the half payment for the body of Mary Docherty, requesting that they be passed on to Helen M'Dougal. "Poor thing," he is reputed to have said, "It is all I have to give her. It will be of some use to her, and I will not need it." That evening, either Helen was forced to leave the jail or she insisted upon her right to leave. Brazen or because she could not think of anywhere else to go, she walked to her home, slept there until late the next day, and then, naturally thirsty, went to a pub. She was recognised by the landlord, who so loudly refused to serve her that a crowd gathered and, also recognising her, became menacing. A pair of patrolling policemen intervened, needing their truncheons to do so, and hurried her to a watch-house. The crowd had followed, growing in numbers en route; their baying at the watch-house attracted more passersby, and before long Helen's rescuers felt distinctly uneasy—so much so that they decided to bundle her out of a back window. The stealthy evacuation proved unnecessary, however, for when one of the policemen shouted through a front window that the woman was being detained as a witness against the Hares, the crowd contentedly dispersed.

Over the next couple of days, recognitions of Helen created other crowds, from whom she was rescued by other policemen; escorted out of the city, she returned; again recognised, she was rescued and escorted, not merely out of the city, but almost to her hometown. Continuing there, she received no welcome from relatives—they being relatives also of the disappeared Ann M'Dougal—and soon moved on, probably travelling south and eventually across the English border. (Forty years or so later, a newspaper noted that "It would seem that Helen M'Dougal, the paramour of Burke the murderer—and who gave origin to the word 'burking'—was living in New South Wales until the other day, when she was accidentally burnt to death at Singleton. Such was the information, at all events, conveyed by telegraph from Sydney to Melbourne on the 13th of last August. It is stated in the message that the miserable woman was sent out many years ago to the colony in which she has at length come to a tragic end."[22] The phrases "It would seem," "Such was the information" and "It is stated" suggest

---

22. Neither the title of the paper nor the issue date is known. The complete cutting is reproduced by Jacques Barzun, in *Burke and Hare*.

that the writer of the note was unconfident of it. Helen may well have been transported, either because she had again fallen foul of the law or because a guardian of the law, tired of the frequent need to rescue her, felt that she, he, and his colleagues would be better off if she were out of harm's way.)

On Sunday, 28 December, while Helen was being dashed from one crowd or another in the region of the Royal Mile, an incident occurred to the south, in Newington Place, that caused the policeman stationed there to run off for reinforcements. A band of tipsy citizens gathered outside Dr. Knox's house, shouting variations on the question "Where are the doctors?" which had been posed by certain editorialists who believed, or claimed to believe, that the deletion from the trial witness list of Knox and his medical associates indicated a cover-up. By the time the posse arrived, the band had scattered, having chucked stones through practically every window in the house.

The incident was the first of many representing the public's distrust of Knox and distaste for what he was guessed to have done. Even without such incidents, he would have had ample cause for concern: ever since he and his school had first been referred to in reports of the case, many registered students had cried off, applications for tuition had dried up—and conventional, grave-robbing suppliers of corpses had deserted him. A few friends were faithful, but efforts by some of them to restore his good name only provoked more-publicised opposition; on 14 January, Sir Walter Scott wrote in his journal, "I called on Mr Robinson and instructed him to call a meeting of the Council of the Royal Society, as Mr Knox proposed to read an essay on some dissections. A bold proposal truly from one who had so lately the boldness of trading so deep in human flesh. I will oppose the reading in the present circumstances if I should stand alone." Punsters were having a fine time, mixing the name Knox with the word "noxious"; and printers of broadsheets and chapbooks were pocketing profits from their hacks' attacks on the doctor—one example being a song, meant to be sung to the tune of "Macpherson's Farewell," which had this rousing opening verse:

In Scotland, the Slaughter-house-keeper may pay
His Journeymen Butchers, and thrive on his prey;
The victims are quickly cut up in his shop,
And he pockets the profits, secure from the drop.

Burke too, languishing in a condemned cell, nursed a grievance against Robert Knox. He felt that the doctor was morally obliged to pay the five pounds owed on the body of Mary Docherty, never mind that it had been confiscated, and that he was entitled to receive the full sum, Hare having broken their agreement in a most unbusiness-like fashion.

Speaking only of the mundane, Margaret Hare had come off worse than the other three. Hare had had little to lose when, with Log out of the way, he reprised his romantic overtures to her; Burke and Helen M'Dougal had had nothing to lose when they moved into Tanner's Close. She, on the other hand, had been a woman of substance, nicely provided for by her inheritance of the lodging house. Now the substance was gone: her premises were irreparable following their sacking by vandals and souvenir seekers. And, adding acid to the lemon, Hare had made her a mother (not for the first time, according to a rumour that sprang from the sighting of small bones, most likely animal, in the yard at the back of Log's). All things considered, it is understandable that she was so vexed with Hare that she vowed never to speak to him again.

If nearly all of the circumstances had been different, there would be a touch of East Lynne about the scene on the evening of Monday, 19 January, when Margaret, carrying her child (recovered from whooping cough?—no one seems to know), was coaxed through the small door set into the main door of Calton Gaol, and, her feet crunching in the cold, cold snow, stumbled away toward the bridges. Recognised, hooted at, and followed ominously by passersby on one or other of the bridges, she broke into a trot, was pelted with snowballs, and was rescued by constables, who took her into the nearest watch-house. That was the last that Edinburgh civilians saw of her. After a week or so, she was smuggled out of the city. On 10 February, the *Glasgow Chronicle* reported that she was in one of that city's police offices, safe from "the hands of an infuriated populace"—"She had left Edinburgh a fortnight ago with her infant child, and has since been wandering the country *incog*. She states that she has lodged in this neighbourhood four nights with her infant and 'her bit duds.' . . . She occasionally burst into tears while deploring her unhappy situation, which she ascribed to Hare's utter profligacy, and said all she wished was to get across the channel, and end her days in some remote spot in her own country in retirement and penitence." On the 12th, she sailed from nearby Greenock on the *Fingail,* bound for Belfast. Though there appears to be no report of her homecoming, there is no reason to suppose that she did not complete the voyage. And there is no reason for believing a story, put about more than thirty years later, that she and her daughter were then living, or had until recently lived, in Paris. I am intrigued by the thought that if her daughter survived long enough to have a child or children, someone reading this story may, certainly without knowing it, be descended from two of its protagonists.

Had Burke made all of the long confessions published under his byline, he would not have had the time for all of the intent bible-studying, loud lamenting, and quieter praying that the prison priest said that he did—nor would he have had the energy, considering the indisputable fact that he was given only bread and water to keep him alive until the day of his hanging.[23] The custom of offering condemned persons the opportunity of eating a last, hearty breakfast was a thing of the future: when Burke awoke, for the last time, on the Wednesday morning, he may have been given an extra-large chunk of bread, but that would have been the only culinary kindness.

The day before, he had surreptitiously been taken from Calton Gaol to the lockup house in Libberton's Wynd, which was convenient to the High Street, the place of execution. It was a shame for the High Street traders that their upstairs windows had been booked long in advance: if they had delayed the opening of their respective box offices until the Tuesday, when the city was perpetually drenched with rain, they could have been very exorbitant: as it was, none of them got more than thirty shillings per window.

The rain eased off near two o'clock on the important morning. At about the same time, the carpenters finished making the scaffold. In common with present-day royal occasions, tourists and unemployed natives, some encumbered with babies, had been camping by the cordoning ropes for hours. They were dried out by a biting wind. They

---

23. Referring to one of Burke's stories, James Hogg, the "Ettrick Shepherd" (himself the author of *Confessions of a Justified Sinner*), complained that it was "First ae drunk auld wife, and then anither drunk auld wife—and then a drunk auld or sick man or twa. The confession got unco monotonous—the Lights and Shadows o' Scottish Death want relief—though, to be sure, poor [Mary] Paterson, that Unfortunate, broke in a little on the uniformity; and sae did Daft Jamie."

sang pop songs; it would be nice to know whether one of the numbers was to the tune of "Macpherson's Farewell," but the reports give no details of the repertoire. By seven, they were forced to their feet; if they had continued to sit or lie, thereby taking up undue space, comparative latecomers—the latest only able, by standing on tiptoe, to glimpse the top of the scaffold—would have turned uglier.

While the crowd grew and was compressed, preparations went on within the lockup house, where there was another crowd. Either through a wish for ecumenicalism, rare in Scotland, or from a desire to share the Catholic glory, some Presbyterian ministers had joined the priests; Burke accepted the diverse prayers, and joined in with some of them. As he was being led to a makeshift robing room, he almost bumped into the executioner, a man named Williams. "I am not just ready for you yet," Burke remarked. He obeyed an order to put on the "dead clothes," black with the exception of a thin scarf of white linen. The jacket and trousers, cut to accommodate men of all shapes and sizes, billowed around him. Glasses of wine were distributed. Burke spoke a toast which none of the others acknowledged: "Farewell to all present and the rest of my friends." Williams appeared. He knotted a rope round Burke's wrists. Everything was ready; and everyone—including bailies (magistrates), sheriffs, the clergy, policemen. On the dot of eight o'clock, the procession emerged into the daylight—

and proceeded up Libberton's Wynd, the windows of which were also filled with spectators. When Bailies Crichton and Small, who were foremost in the procession, reached the top of the wynd, and were observed by that part of the crowd who were in a situation to see them, a loud shout was raised, which was speedily joined in by the whole mass of spectators. When the culprit himself appeared, ascending the stair toward the platform, the yells of execration were redoubled, and at the moment that he came full in view, they rose to a tremendous pitch, intermixed with maledictions, such as "the murderer! *Burke* him! choke him! hangie!" and other expressions of that sort. The miserable wretch, who looked thinner and more ghastly than at his trial, walked with a steady step to the apparatus of death, supported between his confessors, and accompanied by the [Presbyterian] Reverend Messrs. Marshall and Porteous, and seemed to be perfectly cool and self-possessed.

When he arrived on the platform of the scaffold, his composure seemed entirely to forsake him, when he heard the appalling shouts and yells of execration with which he was assailed: he cast a look of fierce and even desperate defiance as the reiterated cries were intermingled with maledictions, such as we have already described. His face suddenly assumed a deadly paleness, and his faculties appeared to fail him. Deafening cries of "hang Hare too," "where is Hare?" "hang Knox," were mingled with the denunciations against Burke.

His appearance betrayed considerable feebleness, whether from disease or emotion we cannot say. His head was uncovered, and his hair, which was of a light sandy colour approaching nearly to white, along with his dress, gave somewhat of a reverend aspect to him.

Having taken his station in front of the drop, he kneeled with his back toward the spectators, his confessor on his right hand, and the other Catholic clergymen on his left, and appeared to be repeating a form of prayer, dictated to him by one of these reverend persons; the position called forth new shouts and clamours of "stand out of the way," "turn him round."

When he arose from his kneeling posture, he was observed to lift a silk handkerchief on which he had knelt, and carefully put it into his pocket. He then cast his eyes upwards toward the gallows; and took his place on the drop, the priest supporting him, though he did not seem to require it from any bodily weakness. There was some hesitation displayed in his manner, as if loath to mount; one of the persons who assisted him to ascend, having rather roughly pushed him to a side, in order to place him exactly on the drop, he looked round at the man with a withering scowl which defies all description. While the executioner, who was behind him, was proceeding with his arrangements, some little delay took place, from the circumstance of his attempting to unloose the handkerchief at Burke's breast. Burke, perceiving the mistake, said "the knot's behind," which were the only words not devotional uttered by him on the scaffold, and the only time he spoke to anyone excepting the priests.

When the hangman succeeded in removing the neckcloth, he proceeded to fasten the rope round Burke's neck, which he pulled tightly, and after adjusting it, and affixing it to the gibbet, put a white cotton nightcap upon him, but without pulling it over his face.

While this was going on, the yells, which had been almost uninterrupted, became tremendous, accompanied by cries of "You——, you will see Daft Jamie in a minute," "give him no rope." He seemed somewhat unsteady; whether from terror or debility, we cannot say.

When the Reverend Mr. Reid retired, the executioner advanced, and offered to draw the cap over his face. He manifested some repugnance to its being done; but, with some little difficulty, this part of the fatal preparations was also completed.

The assistants withdrawn, he uttered an ejaculation to his Maker, beseeching mercy, and immediately gave the signal, throwing the handkerchief from him with an impatient jerk, as violently as his pinioned arms would permit, and was instantly launched into eternity.

The whole proceedings on the scaffold occupied only ten minutes, and precisely at a quarter past eight o'clock the drop fell. The fall was very slight. It was nearly so imperceptible that at one instant he seemed standing, and engaged in an active operation; on the next, with almost no change visible, he was hanging helplessly suspended only by the cord that was suffocating him.

Though no sympathy could be felt for such a despicable and cold-blooded monster, it is still a fearful sight to witness death snatching his victim with such circumstance. If any feeling of pity could be aroused by this, it must have been heightened by the terrific huzza raised at the moment he was thrown off, and the populace saw their enemy in the death struggle. In all the vast multitude there was not manifested one solitary expression of sympathy. No one said, "God bless him"; but each vied with another in showing their exultation by shouting, clapping of hands, and waving of hats. This universal cry of satiated vengeance for blood ascended to heaven, rang through the city, and we are assured was distinctly heard by the astonished citizens in its most remote streets. Never perhaps was such a noise of triumph and execration heard, and we may safely say never on a similar occasion.

The magistrates, clergymen, and executioners, immediately upon the drop falling, retreated from the scaffold, and left it under the charge only of about half a dozen city-officers, who walked about to keep them from the cold, and looked as if they would willingly have followed the example of their superiors.

There was nothing which could be called struggling observable on the now apparently lifeless body. It seemed as if, slight as was the jerk given by the fall, instantaneous death had been produced, although the neck could not have been dislocated, yet the body swung motionless except from the impetus given by the fall, until about five minutes after the suspension, when a slight convulsive motion of the feet and heaving of the body indicated that vitality was not entirely extinguished. Upon observing this, another cheer was raised by the crowd who were anxiously watching the body. It was repeated at intervals as the motions were renewed. This happened we think perhaps twice after the first, each time diminishing in force until the last seemed merely a slightly tremulous motion of the feet, imperceptible except to those who were gazing intently upon the body. A very gradual swinging around appeared to be produced by the action of the wind. The head also, as usual, leaned a little to one side, which added a more miserable character to the scene.

At a particular part of the crowd, a cry of "to Surgeons' Square" was now raised by some individuals, and a large body detached themselves from the mass and proceeded in that direction. We are informed that the detachment which thus broke off, though large when it left the Lawnmarket, was gradually diminished by stragglers who dropped off in its progress, until upon reaching its destination it was not able to cope with the party of policemen who were stationed there in anticipation of such an attack. At this time a baker had the hardihood to attempt a passage down the High Street with a board on his head and a few rolls on it, and, contrary to expectation, succeeded in accomplishing it. At one time his board was nearly capsized, but an escort of fellow tradesmen quickly rallied round him, and guarded him safely past the danger. A chimney-sweeper with his ladder was not so fortunate as the baker, as his brethren probably did not muster so strong, and he had to retreat without accomplishing his purpose. With such incidents the mob was amused, while the melancholy spectacle was exhibited before them, and their laughter and glee continued unabated up to their dispersion.

After hanging a considerable time, some individual from below the scaffold, the under part of which was boxed in for the reception of the body when it should be cut down, gave the body a whirl round, but no motion except what was thus given was observable. From the same place was handed up to the town-officers on the platform shavings and chips taken out of the rude coffin underneath. These were held up to the populace, and some chips thrown over among them—conduct which did not appear very decorous from the official attendants upon such a solemnity. At ten minutes to nine o'clock, Bailies Crichton and Small again came up Libberton's Wynd, still habited in their robes and with their staffs, but did not ascend the scaffold. The executioner mounted it and immediately commenced lowering the body, which was done by degrees and rather leisurely. Again the people made the welkin ring with three hearty cheers when they saw their vengeance completed.

The body was lowered precisely at five minutes before nine o'clock, having hung exactly for forty minutes. Upon its falling into the space under the scaffold, a scramble took place among the operatives for relics, consisting of pieces of the rope, shavings from the coffin, &c. &c. The body was placed in the shell and almost immediately carried on men's shoulders to the lock-up house.

The populace, upon seeing this winding up of the business, quietly dispersed. All Wednesday, however, large groups visited the scene.

During the night, the body was removed from the lockup house.

But for a chance encounter on South Bridge, exactly fourteen months before, Burke and Hare would have offered the body of Donald the pensioner to the university's anatomist, Alexander Monro III; they would probably have sold to him, or to his representatives, the bodies that they subsequently made. He, not Robert Knox, would have suffered as a result of the partnership's liquidation.

Burke's body was presented to Alexander Monro. He had the glorious task of dissecting it. Before doing so, he hosted a private reception at which the body was centrepiece. Among those who accepted the invitation were the surgeon Robert Liston (who was famed for a brute force that allowed him to amputate limbs as if they were wishbones: some of his patients recovered), the phrenologist George Combe (who, along with other deducers from cranial bumps, would draw all sorts of conclusions, none controversial, from Burke's), and the sculptor George Joseph (who sketched Burke's head and, vying with Combe, took measurements of it, with the intention of making a bust).

Reflecting upon Munro's drawing power, his lecture room within the precincts of the university was only "quite crowded" when, at one o'clock on the Thursday afternoon, he began dissecting, "having previously done everything in his power to satisfy the curiosity of those who wished to have a view of the features, by exposing them in the most favourable position." By three o'clock, when he downed tools, the room was less crowded, probably because squeamish spectators had withdrawn, distressed by the fact that "the class-room had the appearance of a butcher's slaughter-house, from blood flowing down and being trodden upon."

The anxiety to obtain a sight of the vile carcass of the murderer was exceedingly great, particularly after the dismissal of Dr Monro's class; and the Doctor, in the most obliging manner, accommodated everyone to the utmost extent the apartment would admit of. About half-past two o'clock, however, a body of young men, consisting chiefly of students, assembled in the area, and becoming clamorous for admission *en masse*, which of course was quite impractical, it was found necessary to send for a body of Police to preserve order. But this proceeding had quite an opposite effect from that intended. Indignant at the opposition they met with, conceiving themselves to have a preferable title to admission, and exasperated at the display of force in the interior of the University, where they imagined no such interference was justifiable, the young men made several attempts, in which they nearly succeeded, to overpower the Police, and broke a good deal of glass in the windows on either side of the entrance to the Anatomical Theatre. It was attempted to clear the yard with but indifferent success; indeed, the Police were overmatched, and could only stand their ground by avoiding the open area.

The disturbance lasted from half-past two until nearly four o'clock, when an end was at once put to it by the good sense of Professor [Robert] Christison, who announced to the young men that he had arranged for their admission in parties of about fifty at a time, giving his own personal guarantee for their good conduct. This was received with loud cheers, and immediately the riotous disposition they had previously manifested disappeared. We cannot think why this expedient was not thought of earlier; for if it had, there would have been no disturbances of any kind. The whole fracas, indeed, was a mere ebullition of boyish impatience, rendered more unruly by their extreme curiosity to obtain a sight of the body of the murderer. Several of the policemen were severely hurt; but, *en revanche,* we believe not a few of the young men have still reason to remember the weight of their batons, and some severe contusions were received. South Bridge Street, in front of the College, was kept in a continued uproar, and almost blocked up by the populace who were denied access to the interior, and had the approaches not been guarded, fresh accessions of rioters might have given it a more serious aspect.

On Friday, however, matters were better arranged. An order was given to admit the public generally to view the body of Burke, and of course many thousands availed themselves of the opportunity thus afforded them. Indeed, so long as daylight lasted, an unceasing stream of persons continued to flow through the College Square, who, as they arrived, were admitted by one stair to the Anatomical Theatre, passed the black marble table on which lay the body of the murderer, and made their exit by another stair.

To give a better idea of what the countenance had been, the skull cap which had been sawn off the preceding day was replaced, and the outer skin brought over it, so as to retain it in the proper situation.

The immense concourse of people whose curiosity induced them to visit this sad and humiliating spectacle of fallen and degraded man may be judged of when it is mentioned that, by actual enumeration, it was found that upwards of sixty per minute passed the corpse. This continued from ten o'clock until darkening, and when we left at nearly four o'clock the crowd was increasing; we cannot compute the number at less than twenty-five thousand persons, and counting the other days on which many saw him, though the admissions were not so indiscriminate, the amount cannot be reckoned under thirty thousand souls. A greater number of males probably than was present at the execution, and a far greater concourse perhaps than ever paid homage to the remains of any great man lying in state.

We understand, though we did not witness it, that some women whose curiosity presented a stronger impulsive motive than could in them be counteracted by the characteristic grace of a female—modesty—found their way with the mob into the room where the naked body was exposed. It is not likely, however, that their curiosity will, in such a case, again get the better of their discretion, as the males, who reserve to themselves the exclusive right of witnessing such spectacles, bestowed such tokens of their indignation upon them as will probably deter them from again visiting an exhibition of the sort; seven in all is said to be the number of females in Edinburgh so void of decency; but in justice even to them we may presume that they did not anticipate such an exposure.

Next day, Saturday, all ingress was denied, and again the front of the College presented a scene of confusion sufficiently annoying to those in the neighbourhood, and to passers-by. Long after they had ascertained that no admission was allowed, the people continued gazing at the outer walls, and when their curiosity was abundantly gratified by this, or their patience exhausted, fresh arrivals of unwearied spectators arrived.

As a discreet fulfilment of the hope expressed by Lord Boyle: after the last member of the public had seen Burke's body, the fleshy parts of it were evacuated, what remained was put aside long enough to become no more than a skeleton, and that became—and is still—an exhibit in the university's unpublic medical museum. Appropriately, some of the discarded skin was treated by a tanner; when leathery enough for the purpose of binding, it was made into the cover of a pocket-book—thus making Burke, in Professor Richard D. Altick's words, "one of the select company of murderers who were hanged, drawn, and quartoed."[24] The pocket-book has, so to speak, joined the skeleton.

24. Altick, *Victorian Studies in Scarlet: Murders and Manners in the Age of Victoria* (London, 1973). Altick, an American who has written several fine books, some dealing with aspects of life in Britain in the nineteenth century, only glances in this one at Burke and Hare; he takes more notice of William Corder, the murderer of

The people of Edinburgh were niggardly in one respect, generous in another. A subscription "set on foot for the purpose of conferring on James Gray and his wife a lasting mark of gratitude" failed to raise more than about ten pounds. But a subscription to enable Jamie Wilson's mother and sister to bring a private prosecution (still known in Scotland as a Bill of Criminal Letters) against Hare raised so much money that the organisers could afford not just one leading advocate but two, as well as supernumeraries, and were left with cash in their hands. The action, opposed by the lord advocate, went through several hearings until, on 2 February, there was stalemate; three days later, the Wilsons' lawyers announced that their clients had given in.

In the evening of that day, a Thursday, Hare was slipped out of jail by a turnkey, who accompanied him in a carriage to the place in Newington, just past Knox's house, which was the final boarding point in the city for the mail coach to Portpatrick, whence vessels sailed to Ireland. Hare would have been muffled up, leaving only his eyes and nose visible, even if the temperature had been above zero. A second-class, outside coach seat had been reserved for him. The turnkey shouted, "Goodbye, Mr. Black," as the driver whipped the horses.

Hare's alias lasted about sixty miles, half the distance to Portpatrick. It was broken by a sort of coincidence that superstitious or religious readers may think was arranged. One of the other passengers was a lawyer; he had helped in the Wilsons' action; his position on rather than in the coach suggests that his bill was outstanding. Recognising Hare, he said nothing—until an incident indicated that Hare was financially better off than he was. According to a report that appeared in the following Monday's *Edinburgh Courant*, under the heading "Riot at Dumfries!"

> After travelling a stage or two, the guard, without knowing *Black,* consented to allow him to get inside the coach, as the night was damp and cold, but he had only got up one or two of the steps at the coach door when a highly respectable legal gentleman . . . called out, "Would you put a murderer inside?" This led to the dis-

---

Maria Marten in the Red Barn at Polstead, Suffolk, who was hanged in August 1828, not quite three months before the Edinburgh case was revealed. The Moyse's Hall Museum in Bury St. Edmunds, the town which hosted that execution, has many associated items, including a copy of the record of the trial bound in Corder's skin.

covery, and the coach had not long arrived at Dumfries when the news of his infamous arrival became generally known. A crowd instantly assembled, evincing the most determinedly hostile intentions. For protection, the wretch was locked up in the tap-room of the Kings Arms Inn until the Portpatrick mail should start, which is usually about nine o'clock [on Friday morning]. Until that hour the mob, though it continued to increase, many coming no doubt to get a glimpse of such a notorious character, was tolerably quiet, under an expectation that he would take his departure by the Portpatrick mail. By nine o'clock, for half a mile on the road, the crowd became immense.

The coach drew up to the inn door, but for Hare to have ventured out would have been certain destruction, and, consequently, the coach drove off without him. It had not proceeded far when it was stopped by the populace, and a most strict search was made in case he was concealed; even the boot was examined. Being disappointed, the people became more enraged, and, in consequence, the magistrates were seriously alarmed for the peace of the town. As a russe, they caused a post-chaise to draw up at the front of the inn, into which, it was stated, Hare would proceed on his journey. They, at the same time, however, got another chaise to the bottom of the yard of the inn, whence he contrived to escape unobserved from a back window and to walk along to the vehicle, which was driven rapidly to the gaol, followed by the mob, who soon found out the trick. The gaol was then assailed with stones, most of the windows of the Court Room were broken, and one of the doors forced. The police and constables, however, succeeded, with some difficulty, in restoring order, but the crowd remained in the street till after dark. During the night, the wretch was taken out of gaol and privately conveyed on foot out of town, on the Carlisle road, under an escort of police officers.

The last sure sighting of Hare was on the Sunday morning, when he was into England, a mile or so past Carlisle. There are legends, of course; most seem to have borrowed from earlier ones, at least so far as blindness is concerned: those of the 1830s have him tripping or being thrown into a pit, stirring a flurry of quicklime, some into his eyes—and by the turn of the century, long after whenever he died, he was recollected as a blind beggar on the *north* side (a nice convincing touch, that) of Oxford Street in the West End of London. I shouldn't be surprised if he, in fact, returned to Ireland and lived there happily ever after.[25]

There was no need to make up satisfying tales about Robert Knox. The truth was good enough.

A week after Hare's release, it was announced that a committee had been formed, under the chairmanship of the Marquess of Queensberry, to evaluate the rumours against Knox; Sir Walter Scott had been invited to serve on the committee, but, not wanting the rumours to be disturbed, had refused "to lend a hand to whitewash this much to be suspected individual." Hundreds more who suspected a whitewash gathered in different parts of the city to scream and shout as much. Most of the gatherings centred upon effigies of Knox, and one of those became an unruly procession to Newington Place, where the effigy was hanged from a tree in the doctor's garden and set on fire. A subsequent effigy-following procession was more dense (advance notification of it having been published in the *Weekly Chronicle*: "The cavalcade will move in the direction of Portobello where, it is supposed, the Doctor burrows at night") and better prepared—in that a collection was taken beforehand to cover fines imposed on those arrested en route to or at the destination, a long-disused gibbet near the Portobello sea front. Very shortly afterwards, the Marquess of Queensberry, whose family motto was not "Modesty is the better part of valour," loudly resigned as chairman of the committee while being the soul of reticence as to the reason for his resignation.

The committee reported its findings in the middle of March. There were many, too many, of them, the main ones being that Knox had had no idea that he was using murdered subjects—but that if he had been at all inquisitive of the provenance of the bodies, of the men who had offered them for sale, he would have soon found out. Which

25. Thomas De Quincey, in his "Supplementary Paper on Murder," while speaking of "Quintius Burkius and Publicus Harius," has the enquiry made of members of the Society of Connoisseurs in Murder, "By the way, gentlemen, has anybody heard lately of Hare?"—and has the enquirer adding, "I understand he is comfortably settled in Ireland, considerably to the west, and does a little business now and then; but, as he observes with a sigh, only as a retailer—nothing like the fine thriving wholesale concern so carelessly blown up at Edinburgh. "You see what comes of neglecting business"—is the chief moral . . . which Hare draws from his past experience."

meant, to those who were determined to find this meaning, that Knox was guilty, at the very least, of having turned a blind eye to clear indications of mass murder. John Wilson, professor of moral philosophy at the university, hid behind the pseudonym "Christopher North" when writing, in the next issue of *Blackwood's Magazine*:

> Dr Knox stands arraigned at the bar of the public, his accuser being—human nature. . . . He is not now the victim of some wild and foolish calumny; the whole world shudders at the transactions; and none but a base, blind, brutal beast can at this moment dare to declare, "Dr Knox stands free from all suspicion of being accessory to murder."

Knox was, to use a modern expression, on a hiding to nothing: any admission of laxity would cue a chorus of demands for a confession that he had been wittingly lax—silence was golden for his enemies. He kept silent; tried to persuade his supporters to keep their support discreet. Learning that his students intended to give him "a lasting proof of their attachment," he wrote them a long letter, which ended,

> In this situation I am unwilling to receive any token of your friendship which must be associated in my own mind with the heaviest calamity of my life, and which, moreover, I am perfectly aware, cannot at present be accompanied by the sympathy of the public.
>
> Allow me therefore to say I shall consider your abandoning your design as a stronger proof of your attachment than your ever having formed it.
>
> With the warmest wishes for your happiness, believe me very gratefully,
> Yours, etc.,
> R. KNOX

But the students, feeling unable to forego "the gratification of carrying their design into effect," presented him with a gold vase; the note with it, altogether protesting too much, reached an apex of silliness at the end: "The public voice has at length exonerated you from charges of which we know you from the first moment felt the injustice." *The Scotsman* rightly described the gift as "injudicious."

The strength of Knox's self-control is indicated by the fact that there is only one anecdote of its being broached. On a summer's day, he went with another doctor to an Edinburgh park:

> They talked to a little girl who was playing there and at length Dr Knox gave her a penny and said, "Now, my dear, you and I will be friends. Would you come and live with me if you got a whole penny every day?" "No," said the child, "you would, maybe, sell me to Dr Knox." The anatomist started back with a painfully stunned expression, his features began to twitch convulsively, and tears appeared in his eyes.[26]

There is no surer dating of that incident than that it happened during a summer before the autumn of 1842. In most of the seasons until then, Knox's troubles outweighed his joys. Continuing reduction of his student roll caused him to leave Surgeons' Square; he worked for a few months at another medical school in the city, for as short a time at a school in Glasgow, and then became a freelance lecturer, accepting whatever engagements were offered. In 1837, the professor of pathology at Edinburgh University gave notice of his retirement, and Knox applied for the chair, making what appeared to be a one-horse race; but four members of the medical faculty, one of them Robert Christison, tried to have the race called off by proposing the abolition of the chair, saying that they were willing to take turns at giving free lectures on general pathology; the city council, keen to keep the chair but worried by the opposition to Knox's occupancy of it, got the professor of pathology to withdraw his notice. Knox then applied for the post of lecturer in anatomy to the art students of the Scottish Academy; he didn't get a single vote. Four years later, he applied for the chair of physiology; he was not surprised that it went to the son of the unretired professor of pathology. In that year, 1841, his wife died from puerperal fever; early in the next, one of his sons died from scarlet fever. In the autumn he moved from Edinburgh to London. None of the victory celebrations was reported in the Edinburgh papers.

He was poor. Unable to obtain a position in a London school of medicine, he gave talks on racial differences and later turned his notes

---

26. This anecdote is quoted in Isabel Rae's good biography *Knox the Anatomist* (Edinburgh, 1964).

into a book, *Races of Men* (which contains prophesies on black and brown militancy that have come true). He wrote other books, some on anatomy, and may have made a decent amount from *Fish and Fishing in the Lone Glens of Scotland,* which was published in New York as well as in London, where its price was a shilling; he also contributed scores of articles, some on anatomy, to medical and veterinary journals.

In May 1847, one of the medical journals, *The Lancet,* published a letter from a lay person, expressing surprise at the fact that a young man of Nottinghamshire who had studied medicine for only nine months had won the College of Surgeons' diploma. The letter sparked off others, *The Lancet*'s lead writer joined in, and before long there was proof positive that the young man had forged several student-attendance certificates—one certifying that he had studied under Dr. Knox in the winter of 1839. The forger was permitted to keep his diploma—and, of course, to continue practising in more ways than one. With a single exception, none of those whom he had claimed to be his teachers was penalised for having "evaded the faithful enforcement" of regulations. The exception was Knox. The Royal College of Surgeons of Edinburgh cancelled his licence to lecture and notified the twenty-two other licensing boards of the decision, demanding that they follow suit. (Isobel Rae [see note 26] remarks that "one of the more extraordinary things about this extraordinary case is that today not one of those [boards] still in existence can produce the correspondence. So Knox's letters in his own defence are for ever lost.")

In 1854, his sixty-first year, Knox applied to be sent to the Crimea as a physician or staff surgeon and asked William Fergusson to support his application. Fergusson wrote to him: "You seem to me as full of energy as ever, and I need hardly say that your intellectual powers seem equal to any of those former efforts which in early days made you dux of the High School of Edinburgh, and the first teacher of anatomy in Europe." Knox was turned down by the Army Medical Department.

Two years later, he at last got a job—as pathological anatomist to the Cancer Hospital (Free) in London. He worked there until a fortnight before his death, from heart disease, in December 1862. The corpse of the only survived victim of the West Port murderers was buried in the nonconformist part of a graveyard, eventually beneath a flat stone which, bearing no inscription; it might have borne this one, which is the final stanza of Southey's "The Surgeon's Warning":

So they carried the sack pick-a-back,
   And He carved him bone from bone,
But what became of the surgeon's soul
   Was never to mortal known.

A Postscript on an Italian
(or Lincolnshire) Subject

The fact that the murders in Edinburgh, at least sixteen of them, had no parliamentary consequence, whereas a single similarly motivated murder in London two years after the last of them *did,* may be seen by Scottish Nationalists as a further reason for patriotic paranoia.

The rarity of old books is governed in the main by whether they were published between boards or as paperbacks. Though titles published only in the latter format were almost always comparatively mass-produced, they were less likely to be kept, let alone treasured, by the owners of them new—less likely to be handed on or down—and still less likely to get to dealers in secondhand books who could be bothered to sort them into their subjects rather than shove them, any-old-how, in trays outside their shops, never minding raindrops and indiscriminate kleptomaniacs. I have one of the few remaining copies of a paperback that must have sold in thousands around the Christmas of 1831 and was probably sold out before the New Year came in. It is, so parts of the crowded title page say,

THE TRIAL

of

BISHOP, WILLIAMS, AND MAY,

at the

OLD BAILEY, DEC. 2, 1831,

for the

MURDER OF THE ITALIAN BOY,

CARLO FERRIER

Corrected and Revised by W. Harding, Short-Hand Writer.

LONDON:

PUBLISHED BY W. HARDING,

3, PATERNOSTER-ROW

Led along by three of the lawyers representing the Crown, of whom a Mr. Adolphus[27] was most in evidence, the prosecution witnesses told the following story:

> Just before noon on Saturday, 5 November [Guy Fawkes Day], the bell of the dissecting room at King's College, London, was rung.[28] The porter, William Hill, admitted John Bishop and James May, who were about the same age, in their early thirties.
>
> He had known both of them before. May asked him if he wanted anything, and he said, "Not particularly," but asked him what he had got. May said a male subject. Hill asked him what size? He said a boy about fourteen, and he demanded twelve guineas. Hill said that they could not give that price, for they did not particularly want it; but if he would wait, he would acquaint Mr [Richard] Partridge, the demonstrator of anatomy, with the matter. He accordingly went to Mr Partridge, who said he would see them. Hill then went back to them, and told them to go round to the place appropriated for them.
>
> There, Mr Partridge joined them. They could not agree as to the price. Mr Partridge said that he would not give twelve guineas for the subject. May then told him that he should have it for ten guineas. Mr Partridge left them, and went into the dissecting room. Hill followed Mr Partridge, and in consequence of what Mr Partridge said to him, he returned to Bishop and May, and told them that Mr Partridge would only give nine guineas for the subject. May said that he would be d——d if it should come in for less than ten guineas. May was tipsy at the time. On his going

27. I believe that this was the German-parented *John* Adolphus, who, astonishingly to mere mortals, wrote tomes on the history of Britain and its Empire while pursuing an extremely busy law career. In 1820, when he was fifty-two, he unsuccessfully defended Arthur Thistlewood and other Cato Street Conspirators who had intended to murder members of the Cabinet; during the next twenty years, he appeared in several celebrated murder trials (e.g., of James Greenacre, whom he successfully prosecuted). In 1840 he led the successful prosecution of the Swiss valet François Courvoisier for the murder of his master, Lord William Russell; though during the trial Courvoisier admitted to his counsel, Charles Phillips, that he was guilty, Phillips, in his closing speech, not only pledged his word to the jury that Courvoisier was innocent but tried to fasten the crime on another. Adolphus stood aside from the furore when those deceits were found out, saying that he was absent for most of Phillips's speech, attending to business in another court.

28. In 1840, Dr. Knox's best student, William Fergusson, was appointed professor of surgery there; the surgeoncy to King's College Hospital went with the job. He resigned the professorship of surgery in 1870 but until his death seven years later was clinical professor of surgery and senior surgeon to the hospital.

out to the door, Bishop, taking Hill aside, said to him, "Never mind May, he is drunk; it shall come in for the nine guineas in the course of half an hour." They then went away.

About a quarter past two o'clock on the same afternoon, they returned in company with Thomas Williams and a man named Shields.[29] They had a hamper with them: Shields seemed to be employed as the porter for carrying it. May and Bishop carried the hamper into another room, while Williams and Shields remained where they were. On opening the hamper, a sack containing a body was found in it. May and Bishop remarked that it was "a good one," to which observation Hill assented. May being tipsy, they turned the body very carelessly out of the sack. Hill perceived that the body was particularly fresh, and that there was no sawdust about the hair of it. He asked the men what the subject had died of. They said that they did not know, and that that was no business either of his or of theirs. Hill replied that it certainly was not. In consequence of the opinion which he formed from the appearance of the body, he went to Mr Partridge, and detailed to him what he had seen, and what he thought about the matter.

Mr Partridge accordingly returned to the room where the body was lying, to see it. May and Bishop had been removed from that room to the room into which they were originally introduced, and where the other two men were also. Mr Partridge, without seeing them, after seeing the body, went to the secretary's office. In the meantime, several of the gentlemen connected with the College saw the body, and their suspicions were also excited.

Mr Partridge having returned to the place where the men were, showed them a £50 note, and told them that he must get that changed, and that then he would pay them. Mr Partridge having pulled out his purse while speaking to them, and there being some gold in it, Bishop said, "Give me what money you have, and I shall call on Monday for the remainder." May proposed that Mr Partridge should give him the £50 note, and he would go out and get it changed. Mr Partridge, smiling, said, "Oh, no," and then left them.

---

29. Shields was an alias; his real name, John Head, was tattooed on his left forearm, surrounded with "rudely done flower-pots, etc." It appears that he was about the same age as Bishop and May.

In about a quarter of an hour Mr Mayo, the professor of anatomy at the College, came down with Mr Rogers, a police inspector, and a body of police, and the men were all taken into custody. Before that took place, Bishop said to Hill, "Pay me only eight guineas in the presence of May; give me the other guinea, and I will give you half-a-crown."

The body was delivered to the police station in Covent Garden, together with the hamper and sack.

Joseph Sadler Thomas, superintendent of F Division of the Metropolitan Police (which, as it had been in existence for only two years, was usually referred to as the New Police):

The body was placed in the back room in the station-house, with the hamper. Bishop, May, Williams and Shields were put in the outer room. I asked May what he had to say, for he was charged with having come into the possession of the subject in an improper manner. He replied, "I have nothing at all to do with it; the subject is that gentleman's" (pointing to Bishop). "I merely accompanied him to get the money for it." I then asked Bishop whose it was, and he said that it was his, and that he was merely removing it from Guy's Hospital to King's College. I then asked Williams what he knew about it. He replied that he knew nothing about it, and that he had gone with them to King's College to see the building. I asked Bishop in the first instance what he was, and his answer was, "I am a b——y body-snatcher." I think that all the prisoners at the time, Bishop and May especially, were labouring under the effects of liquor. May was carried into the station-house on all fours, and with his smock-frock over his head.

That night, a postmortem examination was carried out by Richard Partridge, with the assistance of four other medical men. It is understandable why one of the assistants, Mr. Mayo, the professor of anatomy at King's College, was not called to give evidence—for, according to another of the assistants, talking out of court, Mr. Mayo, as well as being quaint of both stance and speech, was apt to jump from one conclusion to another, no matter how far apart conclusions were: "Mr Mayo, who had a peculiar way of standing very upright with his hands in his breeches' pockets, said with a kind of lisp he had, 'By Jove! the boy died a nathral death.' It was then found that one or more of the upper cervical vertebrae were fractured. 'By Jove!' said Mr Mayo, 'thith boy wath murthered.'"

Over the next few days, several people identified the body as that of an Italian boy, Carlo Ferrier, who had been brought to England two years before by an Italian who seems to have been a sort of one-man band, playing the pandean pipes as accompaniment to a street organ, but who had been deserted by him after six weeks; from then until All Hallows' Day, when the boy was last seen alive, he had begged a living with the aid of what one of the witnesses described as "a cage—like a squirrel-cage—with two white mice in it, which was suspended by a string round his neck." The usual site of his begging was on Oxford Street, near where it crossed Regent Street. (There is nothing to stop anyone who believes that William Hare became a blind beggar on the north side of Oxford Street from believing that he arrived there soon enough to be a competitor of Carlo Ferrier and his mice.)

A dozen witnesses spoke of happenings on Friday, 4 November. The first of the dozen was Thomas Mills:

> I live at 39 Bridgehouse Place, Newington Causeway, Elephant & Castle, and am a dentist. Between nine and ten o'clock that morning, James May called and offered a set of teeth for sale; they were twelve human teeth, six for each jaw. He offered the set for a guinea. It was then that I observed that one of them was chipped; that lessened their value. I said that I would give twelve shillings for them, and I remarked that they did not belong to one set. He said, "Upon my soul to God, they all belonged to one head not long since, and the body has never been buried." I gave him the twelve shillings.

The evidence of some others of the dozen fitted together to make a pub crawl. Henry Lock said,

> I was in November a waiter at the Fortune of War, Giltspur Street, in the City. I saw Bishop, Williams and May there at eleven o'clock in the morning. They had some drink, and went away about twelve o'clock. There was a strange man with them. About three o'clock in the afternoon they came in again, and remained until about five. About eight o'clock the same evening they all

returned with another man, who appeared to be a coachman. About nine o'clock May went to the bar, with something in a handkerchief, which proved to be teeth. I observed to him that they appeared to be young ones, and were worth two shillings. May said they were worth two pounds to him. He and his companions shortly afterwards left.

Thomas Wigley:

I am a porter at coach-houses. On 4 November, early in the evening, I was in the Fortune of War, when Bishop came in, and was followed in a few minutes by May. In a few minutes Williams came in, and Bishop observed, "Here he comes, I knew he was a game one." Bishop said to May before they went away, "You stick to me, and I will stick to you."

James Seagrave:

About six o'clock that evening I was with my cabriolet [a two-wheeled, one-horse vehicle] on the stand in Old Bailey [at the southern end of Giltspur Street]. Having put the nose-bag on my horse, I went into the King of Denmark watering-house to take my tea. I was called out, and saw May and Bishop. May asked me if I wanted a job, and said he had a "long job." He took me to one side and said he wanted me to fetch a "stiff un," which I understood to mean a dead body. I told him I did not know, but asked him what he would stand; he said that he would stand a guinea. I said that I had not finished my tea and that my horse had not done his corn. I went into the public house, followed by May and Bishop. They took their seats, and called for tea for two. Some person in the room jogged me by the elbow and hinted that the men were "snatchers," and I determined not to go with them. I afterwards saw them outside, making a bargain with another coachman.

Edward Chandler:

I was on 4 November porter of the King of Denmark. May and Bishop came in with Seagrave, a cabriolet-driver, and they had some tea and a pint of gin together. May put some gin into Bishop's tea, and Bishop asked him, "Are you going to hocus me, or burke me?" I do not know what *hocus* means.[30]

George Gissing:

I am twelve years old. I go to school and church. My father keeps the Birdcage public house, Bethnal Green [just over a mile northeast of Old Bailey]. On the evening of 4 November, about half past six o'clock, I saw a yellow hackney-chariot draw up opposite my father's house, which is very near Nova Scotia Gardens. I know Bishop's cottage in Nova Scotia Gardens. Williams and his wife live with Bishop. I saw Williams standing on the forewheel of the chariot, talking to the driver. Then I saw a strange man carrying a sack in his arms, and Bishop holding up one end of it. They put it in the chariot. Williams helped it in. The sack appeared to be heavy, as if something heavy was in it. Bishop and the other man got into the chariot with Williams, and they drove up Crabtree Road and towards Shoreditch Church, on the road to the City. The strange man was not May. Bishop is Williams's brother-in-law, and they kept the wedding at my father's house.

The present-day scarcity of porters—or rather, of porters who can be bribed to carry anything—makes one envious of the seeming ubiquity of them in London in 1831. Of course, the fact that such a lot of the evidence so far mentioned related to happenings in pubs helps to explain why a lot of porters have also been mentioned: porters' thirstiness for a kind of stout was so voracious that the drink itself had become known as porter. Two more porters helped the prosecution: their names were Thomas Davis and James Weeks, and they were both employed to carry things to, from, and within the dissecting room at Guy's Hospital, on the south side of London Bridge. They were on duty at seven o'clock in the evening of 4 November. Thomas Davis:

Bishop and May came to the hospital, May carrying a sack. I knew them before. They asked me if I wanted to purchase a

30. According to Pierce Egan (*Boxiana* [London, 1821]), "To hocus a man is to put something into his drink, on the sly, of a sleepy, stupifying quality, that renders him unfit for action."

subject. I declined, and they asked if I would allow them to leave it in the hospital until the following morning. I acceded to their request, and locked the body up in a room. I only saw a foot out of the sack, and I believed that it was either that of a boy or a female; it was not large enough for that of a man.

Half an hour later, Bishop and May turned up at Grainger's Anatomical Theatre, in Webb Street, close to Guy's, and offered a subject to the curator, James Appleton:

I knew them; Williams, too. They had not the body with them. Bishop said that it was a fresh subject, a boy of about fourteen years of age. I declined to purchase it, and they went away.

How they, and Williams (who, presumably, had loitered outside both Guy's and Grainger's), spent the rest of the night is not stated in the trial transcript. May's tipsiness next morning would be excellent circumstantial evidence that he, at least, did not get to bed early were it not for the direct evidence of the aforementioned Henry Lock that, at eight o'clock that morning, May, Bishop, and Williams were in the vicinity of the Fortune of War. They were accompanied by the porter named Shields. (As you know, later in the day he carried a hamper on their behalf. It seems likely that Shields was the "strange man" observed by young George Gissing. Shields, who should have been a star witness at the trial, did not give evidence—which surely means that he had already given the police information, on the understanding that he would neither be charged as an accessory nor be called as a witness.) Henry Lock:

Bishop, addressing Williams, asked, "What shall we do for a hamper?" Williams made no answer. Bishop requested Shields to go over to St Bartholomew's Hospital [in West Smithfield, a short stroll from the Fortune of War] to get a hamper, but he refused to go. Bishop then went himself for it, and soon returned with a hamper. They then all left together.

Their destination was Guy's. They arrived in the dissecting room there shortly after eleven. Thomas Davis and James Weeks were still, or back, on duty. Weeks unlocked the anteroom, the sacked body that had been stored in it was put in the hamper, that was hoisted on to Shields's shoulders, and he and the three unburdened members of the party exeunted.

You will have noticed some time ago that, whereas in Edinburgh toutings and deliveries of bodies were restricted to hours of darkness, either no such restriction was put upon the three Londoners or they ignored such a restriction and were not told off about it. It seems safe to say that, whether they were unrestricted or undisciplined, they would hardly have undertaken their subsequent journey at such a busy hour of daylight if they had been quite sober. The party probably proceeded across London Bridge to the Monument, turned left into Cannon Street, passed St. Paul's, and carried on down Ludgate Hill (where they, Shields especially, would have been tempted to pop into the King of Denmark in Old Bailey), along Fleet Street, and on to the Strand, which was then the sole location of the King's College that has since been distributed about London. Williams either departed from the others somewhere along the route or (as it appears he had done both at Guy's and at Grainger's) stayed close but out of sight, on this occasion with the hampered Shields as company, while Bishop and May opened negotiations with William Hill, the porter to the college's anatomists. You know what happened in and adjacent to the dissecting room.

Within the fortnight following Guy Fawkes Day, as the result of interviewing, rummaging, and digging by many members of the New Police, the case against the three prisoners was clinched. It is unnecessary to mention, let alone to quote the evidence of, all of the trial witnesses who had helped during that fortnight. Two of the witnesses, both residing near Nova Scotia Gardens, swore that they had seen "*an* Italian boy" in their neighbourhood on Thursday, 3 November. More telling than their evidence was that of Edward Ward, who was aged six ("and a half," he insisted) :

> Previously to being sworn, he was examined as to the nature of an oath. The child, with infantile simplicity, said that he knew it to be a very bad thing to tell a lie; that it was a great sin; and that he who would swear falsely would go to h——l, to be burnt with brimstone and sulphur. He was then sworn.
>
> He stated that he lived with his father near to the Nova Scotia cottages; that a few days before Guy Fawkes Day, his mother hav-

ing given him a half-holiday, he went to Bishop's cottage to play with Bishop's children, three in number, a boy older than himself, a little girl, and a boy about his own age. As a toy, Bishop's children produced a cage, which went round and round and which contained two white mice. He never before saw either a cage or mice with Bishop's children.

The evidence of Constable Joseph Higgins, more than being telling, made the case just about conclusive:

He went to the cottage, 3 Nova Scotia Gardens, tenanted by Bishop, accompanied by another policeman. They minutely searched the premises and, with an iron-rod, probed the garden in several places. The rod met with resistance in one part of the garden, and on digging they discovered a cap, a jacket, a pair of trousers, and a small shirt. In another part they dug up a blue coat, a drab striped waistcoat (altered from man's size so as to fit a boy), and a pair of trousers with the braces attached to them. The waistcoat had stains of blood on the collar and shoulders. They were buried about 12 inches under the surface, and were covered with cinders and ashes. (The coat and one of the pairs of trousers were sworn to by those who had identified the body of Carlo Ferrier as having been his.)

He—Constable Higgins—went to May's lodgings, near the New Kent Road [the eastern end of which was only a few hundred yards from Webb Street, in which Grainger's Anatomical Theatre was situated], and found some awls. On one of the awls he discovered drops of blood apparently fresh. (Thomas Mills, the dentist, was here recalled for the purpose of stating that the awl was such as would serve to extract teeth in the coarse manner in which those sold to him had been extracted.)

Mr. Adolphus having closed the case for the prosecution, the prisoners' written defences were read aloud by an officer of the court. *Bishop* stated that during the past five years he had "occasionally obtained a livelihood by supplying surgeons with subjects" but that he had "never disposed of any body that had not died a natural death—he had been in the habit of obtaining bodies from workhouses, with their clothes on." He generously declared that neither Williams nor May knew how he had come by the body said to be that of the Italian boy. Unless the transcription of his written defence omits the most important part of it, he gave no indication as to where that body had come from. *Williams,* in his defence, stated that he had "never engaged in the calling of resurrectionist"—it was "by accident" that he had joined Bishop and May in the dissecting room at King's in the early afternoon of 5 November. *May,* though admitting that he had been a resurrectionist for six years, claimed that he had met Bishop quite by chance in the Fortune of War on 4 November, and had subsequently accompanied him for want of something better to do.

Bishop's counsel called one witness—a dealer in old clothes who remembered selling Bishop's wife a cloth cap in 1829 (as the cap dug up from the back yard of 3 Nova Scotia Gardens, and identified as that of the Italian boy, was "of brown hair, with green-leather front," the dealer's evidence was peculiarly unhelpful to Bishop)—and May's counsel called three, all women, "who admitted themselves to be in the habit of seeing gentlemen": one said that May was with her, nonstop, from the early afternoon of 4 November until noon next day, and both of the others said that any blood on May's clothes "was wholly owing to an accident which happened to a jackdaw"—an animal that deserves to have become as proverbial of moot serological evidence as has a trout in the milk of the undoubtable circumstantial kind.

The jury was sent out at 8 P.M. on the only day of the trial, and returned half an hour later.

Every eye was now fixed upon the prisoners.

Bishop advanced to the bar with a heavy step. There was something of heaviness in his aspect, but altogether his countenance was mild. His face had that pallid bluish appearance which so often betokens mental suffering.

Williams came forward with a short quick step. When he came in front and laid his hand on the bar, the rapid movements of his fingers on the board—the frequent shifting of the hand, sometimes letting it hang down for an instant by his side, then replacing it on the board, and then resting his side against the front of the dock—showed the perturbed state of his feelings. Williams had that kind of aspect with which men associate the idea of sharpness and cunning, and something of mischief, but nothing of the villain.

May came forward with a more firm step than either of his fellow-prisoners. He was the best-looking of the three; he had a countenance which most persons would consider open and manly. There was an air of firmness and determination about him, but neither in him nor in his companions was there the slightest physiognomical trait of a murderer, according to the common notions on the subject. They were that kind of vulgar men in appearance of which one sees hundreds every day, without being struck with any indication in them of good or evil disposition.

The jury returned the verdict of Guilty against all three defendants, and the judge, Lord Chief Justice Tindal, passed the sentence of death upon them.

They heard the sentence as they had heard the verdict, without any visible alteration in their manner. They stood at the bar as if they expected that something more would be added. When ordered to be removed, May raised his voice, and, in a firm tone, said, "I am a murdered man, gentlemen, and that man" (pointing to Bishop) "knows it." Williams said, "We are all murdered men." He then addressed himself to one or two of the witnesses at the side bar, and said that before three months they would suffer for the false evidence they had given against him. Bishop made no observation, but retired from the bar even more absorbed by his awful situation than he had appeared before. In a short time after, the crowd outside the court dispersed—

perhaps before the crowd inside the court did, because the Duke of Sussex, who had sat through the trial, stood up as soon as it was over and made a lengthy speech praising everyone (well, nearly everyone: he omitted reference to the tea-lady at Covent Garden police station) who had "helped towards redressing an injury inflicted upon a pauper child, wandering friendless and unknown in a foreign land." Some of his unprepared audience said "Hear, hear" to his conclusion: "I am indeed proud of being an Englishman, and prouder still to be a prince in such a country and of such a people."

The Duke may still have been some way from that conclusion when, next door, in Newgate Gaol, Bishop and Williams, ignoring a chaplain's advice that they should compose their minds after the "agitation" of the trial and partake of some refreshment after standing almost snackless for eleven hours, insisted upon confessing to the murder of "the lad described in the evidence"—who, they said (and it is hard to see why they should have lied in this regard), was not an Italian boy but a Lincolnshire one who had come up with cattle to Smithfield meat market. They confessed also to the murder of a woman named Fanny Pigburn, a boy perhaps named Cunningham, and a Negro who was quite anonymous to them, adding that those victims, all sold as subjects, had, like the "Lincolnshire boy," been "hocussed by administering laudanum to render them insensible and then suffocated by throwing them headforemost into the well in the garden of 3 Nova Scotia Gardens." And they "entirely exculpated May from all participation in the murders."

The trial was on a Friday.

The hangings were scheduled for the following Monday.

On the morning of the Saturday between, May wrote poetry:

James May is doomed to die,
And is condemned most innocently.
The God above, He knows the same,
And will send a mitigation for his pain.

But on the Saturday afternoon, God learned, before May did, that *His* mitigation was not needed: the Sheriffs decided that May's sentence should be mitigated to transportation for life. When he was told that he was being sent to Australia,

the poor wretch fell to the earth as if struck by lightning. His arms worked with the most frightful contortions, and four of the officers could with difficulty hold him; his countenance assumed a livid paleness—the blood forsook his lips—his eyes appeared set, and pulsation at the heart could not be distinguished. It was nearly a quarter of an hour before May was restored to the use of his faculties. Until then, all persons present thought that he could not possibly survive—it was believed, indeed, that the warrant of mercy had proved his death-blow.

(In a different way, it *was*. Soon afterward, he was put on board a prison-hulk, the *Grampus,* bound for Botany Bay; but he did not complete the voyage. A careful report of his death at sea ascribes it to "the annoyance he received from the other convicts.")

On Monday, 5 December, as arranged, the brothers-in-law Bishop and Williams were hanged concurrently outside the Debtor's Door of Newgate, across the road from the King of Denmark watering house.[31] There was a tremendous turnout. By half past six in the morning, the crowd was packed so tight in Old Bailey that a two-hundred-strong contingent of policemen, ordered to form a cordon around the gallows, was unable to get through; an emergency arrangement was made for the policemen to file through the court building, into the adjoining jail, and out through the Debtor's Door. The crowd stretched west along Holborn as far as Hatton Garden, east along Newgate Street to St. Martin's le Grand, and north along Giltspur Street, past the Fortune of War, to Smithfield. At eight o'clock, when Bishop and Williams were led on to the scaffold, the crowd in Giltspur Street, suddenly become a mob, pressed forward with such force that a heavy barrier toppled—

and a number of persons of both sexes fell with it. The screams of the females, and the confusion that ensued, was truly alarming. One female, of very respectable appearance, with her husband, was most dreadfully injured, the barrier having fallen upon their chests, and a number of others pressing upon them. A city constable was also under the barrier, and his cries were most deplorable. In this dreadful situation did the sufferers remain for some minutes. A cry of "Stand back; for God's sake, stand back!" was raised, but all to no avail, and people in all directions were trampling upon one another. At length, a space of ground was obtained, and the individuals were rescued from their perilous situation, and carried to St Bartholomew's Hospital. Before

31. No doubt actual brothers were executed in tandem before adequate records of capital punishment were kept, but what appears to be the first such event in fairly modern times took place on 23 May 1905, the brothers on that occasion being Alfred and Albert Stratton, the murderers of Thomas and Ann Farrow in the "colour and oil store" in Deptford High Street, Southeast London, that Thomas Farrow had managed for a quarter of a century; the Strattons were the first persons found guilty of murder chiefly on the basis of fingerprint evidence. Their execution was performed by the brothers John and William Billington.

nine o'clock every bed in Colston Ward was occupied by persons who had been injured, many of them seriously so, and a number of others who had been brought in much hurt had, after being bled, been enabled to proceed to their homes.

Bishop and Williams were dead by then, their bodies being cut down. Past nightfall, Bishop's body was delivered to King's College, and Williams's to the Tuson Theatre of Anatomy in Little Windmill Street, each to be dissected in compliance with the law.[32] The work on and in Bishop's body was done by the lisping Mr. Mayo, a running commentary being provided by the college professor of forensic medicine, a Dr. Watson. George Guthrie, the surgeon at Tuson's, had been premature with an announcement that he had been allotted the body of May. On Sunday, 4 December, hearing a rumour that that body would not be available, he had written to the secretary of the College of Surgeons of England: "If May is not executed, pray do me the favour to beg Mr Clift [who appears to have been the clerk in charge of the despatch department at the surgeons' headquarters in Lincoln's Inn Fields] to send to Little Windmill the best of the two remaining." Supposing that Mr. Clift was of an obliging nature, it would be interesting to know the criteria he applied in choosing Williams's body as the better.

The porter Shields. What of him? Soon after the trial, the news broke that he worked part-time as watchman and gravedigger at the cemetery of the Roman Catholic Chapel in Moor-fields. Sacked from there, without notice, the minute the report was published, he applied to be a porter in Covent Garden fruit market. He was recognised by some marketers, who, downing their baskets and shouting "Burker!" and other less apt epithets, chased him off the premises and along Russell Street, the fleetest of them almost catching up with him before he reached the sanctuary of the police station, where he was well-known. There is no further report of Shields's movements, whether fast or at his working pace.

On 15 December, Henry Warburton, a radical member of Parliament (for Bridport, Devon), who had tried before to get changes made to the law governing the dissection of human bodies, tried again—and

32. This is the southern bit of Windmill Street that, speaking of the present topography of the area near Piccadilly Circus, makes a shortcut—east of the London Pavilion and West of the Trocadero—from Shaftesbury Avenue to Coventry Street, which leads toward Leicester Square.

this time, with the invaluable posthumous aid of the Italian or Lincolnshire Boy, succeeded. The clauses that concern us in his "Bill for Regulating Schools of Anatomy" gave permission for bodies to be given up, no fewer than forty-eight hours after death, by executors "or other persons having lawful possession" (those including functionaries in charge of hospitals or workhouses), so long as (*a*), at least twenty-four hours before a giving-up, the person occupying the specially created post of inspector of anatomy had been told, (*b*) a death certificate had been signed by someone with a suitable medical qualification; the bodies of executed criminals were not to be dissected but were either to be "hung in Chains or buried within the Precincts of the Prison." The Bill passed through both Houses, Commons and Lords, and received the Royal Assent on the first day of August 1832.

Politicians have been, and are, indirectly responsible for many murders. But some of them, by being sufficient for the passing of the Anatomy Act, the "Surgeons' Charter," made the multifarious motives for murder one fewer.

Index